STUDIES IN FINANCIAL OPTIMIZATION AND RISK MANAGEMENT

COMPUTATIONAL DATA ANALYSIS TECHNIQUES IN ECONOMICS AND FINANCE

STUDIES IN FINANCIAL OPTIMIZATION AND RISK MANAGEMENT

STUDIES IN FINANCIAL OPTIMIZATION AND RISK MANAGEMENT

COMPUTATIONAL DATA ANALYSIS TECHNIQUES IN ECONOMICS AND FINANCE

MICHAEL DOUMPOS
CONSTANTIN ZOPOUNIDIS
AND
CHRYSOVALANTIS GAGANIS
EDITORS

nova publishers
New York

Library of Congress Cataloging-in-Publication Data

ISBN: 978-1-63463-957-6

Published by Nova Science Publishers, Inc. † New York

CONTENTS

PREFACE

The vast volume of financial data and the globalization of financial markets, create new challenges for researchers and practitioners in economics and finance. Computational data analysis techniques can contribute significantly in this context, by providing a rigorous analytic framework for decision making and support, in areas such as financial times series analysis and forecasting, risk assessment, trading, asset management, and pricing.

The aim of this edited volume is to present, in a unified context, some recent advances in this field, covering the theory, the methodologies, and the applications of computational data analysis methods in economics and finance. The volume consists of papers published in the fifth volume of the Journal of Computational Optimization in Economics and Finance (published by Nova Publishers), which aims towards the publication of high quality researchers articles in this field.

The contents of this volume cover a wide range of topics, including among others stock market applications, corporate finance, corporate performance, as well as macroeconomic issues.

Sincere thanks must be expressed to all authors whose contributions have been essential in creating this book. I also owe a great debt to those who worked long and hard to review all the submitted articles and contributed to the achievement of a high standard of this edited volume.

In: Computational Data Analysis Techniques ISBN: 978-1-63463-957-6
Editors: M. Doumpos, C. Zopounidis and Ch. Gaganis

Chapter 1

OPTIMUM CURRENCY AREAS WITHIN THE US AND CANADA: A DATA ANALYSIS APPROACH

Efthimia Chrysanthidou, Periklis Gogas and Theophilos Papadimitriou*
Democritus University of Thrace, Greece

ABSTRACT

Over the last few decades Robert Mundell's theory (1963) of Optimum Currency Areas (OCA) has attracted significant attention between researchers and policy makers especially after the formation of the European Monetary Union and the debate over whether the eurozone countries actually consist an OCA. In this paper, we take this debate to the area that was originally the subject of Mundell's motivation: the US and Canada. We employ the methodology of Correspondence Analysis and Hierarchical Cluster Analysis, in a sample of macroeconomic data from the fifty US states and the ten Canadian provinces for 2009 in an effort to investigate whether the current currency split between north (Canada) and south (the US) is an OCA or possibly another split may be more appropriate.

Our results show that three OCAs are identified within US states and Canadian provinces: one that includes regions of eastern US and Canada, one that includes regions of central-eastern and eastern US and Canada and finally one with regions of western US and Canada.

Keywords: Optimum Currency areas; Correspondence Analysis; Hierarchical Cluster Analysis

* Corresponding Author: Theophilos Papadimitriou, Democritus University of Thrace, Int. Economic Relations and Development Dept, Komotini Campus, 69100, Greece, Phone: +306976409712, fax: +302531039830, email: papadimi@ierd.duth.gr web: http://www.ierd.duth.gr/en/index.php?cid=65andst=1

1. INTRODUCTION

During the last decades there have been several attempts from different groups of countries to adopt a common currency. The reason for this is that a monetary integration would eliminate currency risk resulting in favorable conditions for trade and business within the monetary union. This will result in increased efficiency by reducing hedging and uncertainty costs and optimum factor allocation.

Generally when the conditions among two or more regions are suitable for creating a monetary union, then these areas are called Optimal Currency Areas (OCA). Robert Mundell developed a theory for OCA in 1963, for which he was awarded the Nobel Prize in economics for 1999. Not only did Mundell set the background of OCA, but he also proceeded on an empirical study of U.S. and Canadian regions.

According to Mundell's study, these two countries should not be monetarily separated in the way they are today, between the northern and the southern part that use the Canadian and U.S. dollar respectively.

Instead he argued that the two regions should be divided into two groups one in the East and one in the West. In other words, one group would include the regions of eastern U.S. and eastern Canada and the other would include the regions of western U.S. and western Canada. Many studies investigated the effectiveness of different groups of countries as monetary unions under Mundell's approach on OCAs. Eichengreen (1991) argued that the E.U is a less effective OCA than a North American union, by studying the real exchange rates of both regions. Sideris (2010) used real exchange rates as well in order to investigate whether the six latest countries-members of the Eurozone are suitable to adopt the euro. Frankel and Rose (1996) studied the business cycles of twenty industrialized countries using data spanning thirty years to discover if they can establish a monetary union. They concluded that the countries with closer trade relations tend to have more correlated business cycles and therefore they fulfill the criteria of creating an OCA.

Eichler and Karmann (2011) examined seven different emerging market regions in order to test which of them form an OCA. Four of them are convenient to form an OCA (Central and Eastern Europe, the Commonwealth of Independent States, East and Southeast Asia, and South Asia), while the other three (Africa, Latin America, and the Middle East) do not. Kouparitsas (2001) investigated the OCA theory in the U.S. on a coarse level: using a VAR analysis he shows that the eight U.S. Bureau of Economic Analysis regions deviate significantly from Mundell's notion of an OCA. Crowley (2001) finds evidence of two OCA's in the USA, using a clustering technique based on the EM algorithm. Beine and Coulombe (2005), investigate the evolution of the OCA properties within U.S. and Canada. by studying the evolution of the share of intra-industry trade between Canadian provinces and the U.S.

They conclude that real and monetary integration is needed for long-run gains from a monetary union between the two countries. In this paper we use two data analysis methodologies (Correspondence Analysis and Hierarchical Cluster Analysis), in an attempt to group together the U.S. and Canadian states and provinces that may form an OCA with respect to their macroeconomic performance. Our goal is to explore at the state/province level whether the U.S. and Canada as a whole can be an OCA or more than one OCAs may be appropriate.

To our knowledge, it is the first time that these methods are used for such an empirical investigation of the U.S. and Canada.

This paper is structured as follows. Section 2 outlines the data set applied and describes the methodology. The empirical estimation is presented in Section 3. Section 4 concludes.

2. METHODOLOGY

2.1. Correspondence Analysis

Correspondence Analysis (CA) is a method of exploratory data analysis[1] designed to analyze two-way (or multi-way in the case of Multiple Correspondence Analysis - MCA) contingency tables. In a way similar to Principal Component Analysis (PCA), CA aims at representing a data matrix in a single two-dimensional (or even three-dimensional) plot. However, as opposed to PCA, CA a) must be applied to categorical data variables (PCA can be applied to continuous variables), b) is equipped with the X^2 metric (instead of the Euclidean metric in PCA) and c) both rows and columns can be represented in the same plot (it is impossible to do so in PCA).

The X^2 distances between each row category and each column category[2] (or each row individual and the row categories in the case of MCA) are used to form the initial plot. The data structures and the category relations are maximized by applying axis rotation to the Cartesian system. After this procedure, the first axis is the one describing the maximum information of the dataset, the second one is the next in line, etc.

MCA can be applied to an indicator matrix[3] or a Burt table. Consider the dataset describing the attributes of N individuals to m discrete variables (w.l.o.g. we can assume that every variable has k categories). An indicator matrix of the described dataset is a matrix with N rows and $m \times k$ columns (one column for every category), where each row corresponds to an individual and every column is a binary (dummy) variable representing one category of a variable. The value in every cell describes the absence (with a 0) or presence (with a 1) of the selected category for an individual. The Burt table is the symmetric cross-tabulation matrix between all the categories.

2.2. Hierarchical Cluster Analysis

In Clustering, we aim at grouping a set of data points in groups based on a similarity measure. Hierarchical Cluster Analysis performs the task repetitively, by merging, in each iteration, the two closest points based on the X^2 distance: the pair of the closest points is removed from the dataset, and in their place we put the center of the cluster (i.e. the weighted mean of all points within a class). The procedure is performed until all datapoints are grouped in the same class. The visual output of the method is an hierarchical tree plot showing all the

[1] Exploratory data analysis is a branch of Statistics exploiting the relations on the dataset without a priori assumptions.

[2] The total X^2 distance between rows and columns in a two-way contingency calculates the distance of the two variables from statistical independence.

[3] Often called "0-1" matrix in Data Analysis jargon.

clustering steps as nodes. It is up to the researcher, to set a threshold in the plot that will define the final groups: all the datapoints of a "branch" below the threshold are grouped together in a class.

2.3. Data

We collected 8 macroeconomic variables for the 50 U.S. states and the 10 Canadian provinces for the year 2009: GDP, per capita income, government deficit, unemployment rate, inflation, GDP growth, imports, and exports. The initial datamatrix has 60 rows, and 8 columns. All the variables have been separated into three classes except of GDP growth (which has been separated into 2 classes because it represents only the growth or the recession). For the purposes of this chapter we applied the MCA to the indicator matrix. The data of the 50 states of America were obtained from the Bureau of Labor Statistics and Census Bureau, while the data of the provinces of Canada were obtained from the Statistics of Canada.

3. EMPIRICAL ESTIMATION

3.1. Applying Correspondence Analysis

Applying the Correspondence Analysis to the data from the U.S. and Canada we get the symmetric plot depicted in Figure 2. We can observe that two groups emerge from the graphical representation, each group sharing the same features. The group created on the left side of the symmetric plot of Figure 1 consists of 30 regions. These regions are mostly from western and eastern U.S. and Canada. The variables that characterize the group are mostly variables of low level e.g. low per capita income, low GDP, etc. This means that this group consists mainly of low-income regions. On the contrary, the group of regions that is formed on the right side of Figure 1 consists mainly of high-income areas. These U.S. states and Canadian provinces show a high GDP, high per capita income, and high imports and exports.

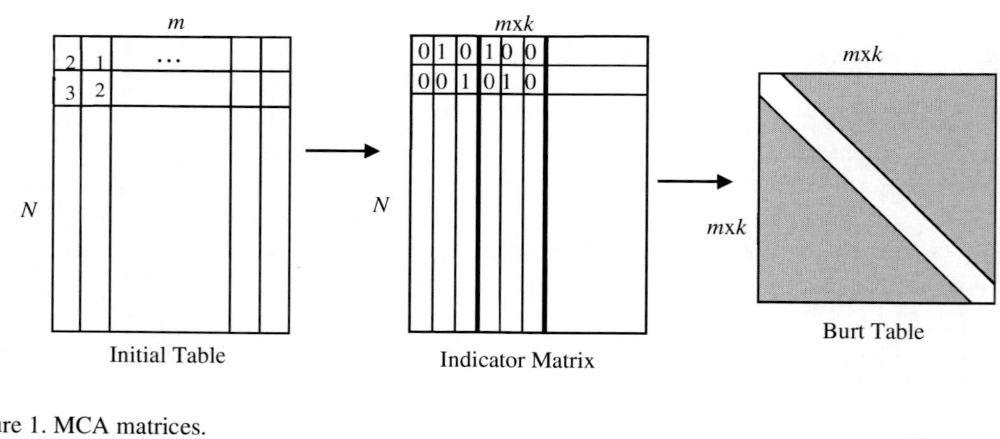

Figure 1. MCA matrices.

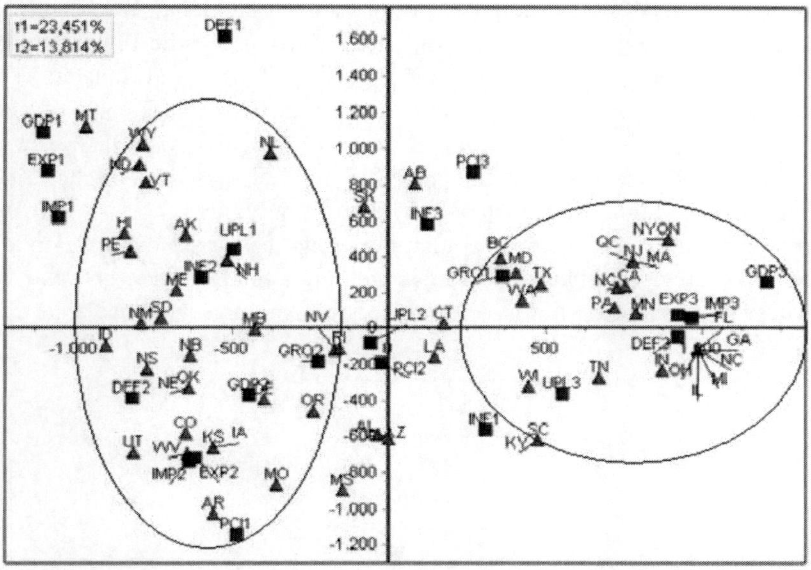

Figure 2. Symmetric Plot of the separation of the states and provinces.

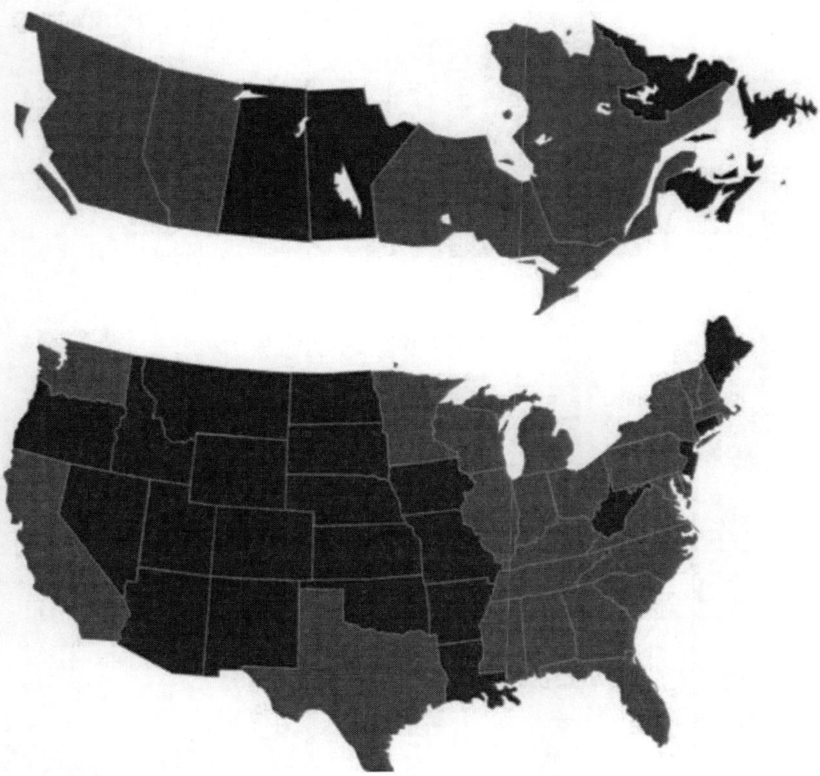

Figure 3. Colored map of the separation of the regions of USA and Canada.

The resulting groups of states and provinces of Figure 2 are depicted in Figure 3. There is a certain pattern in the division of the regions in two groups: a) the first group consists of states and provinces that belong to the east and west side of USA and Canada; b) the second one consists mainly of regions of the central part of both the U.S. and Canada.

One of Correspondence Analysis's tools is the COR indicator which helps the researcher reduce the number of data points in the plot to just the ones with higher fidelity. The symmetric plot with the higher COR datapoints is shown in Figure 4.

In the new symmetric plot we observe that the group that was previously on the left side now can be further divided in two new groups, yielding a total of three groups of states and provinces. These groups along with the relevant variables are presented in Table 1.

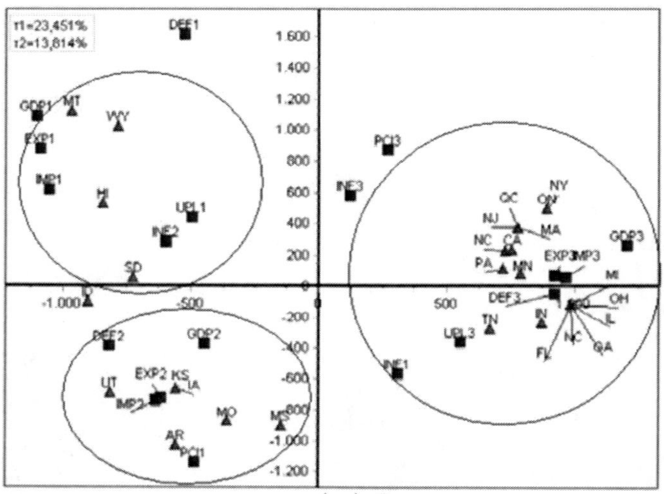

Figure 4. Symmetric plot of the separation of states and provinces with cor.

Table 1. Separated groups of regions

	Group 1	Group 2	Group 3
States/Provinces	Montana, Wyoming, Hawaii, South Dakota, Idaho	Utah, Iowa, Kansas, Mississippi, Missouri, Arkansas.	New York, Ontario, Massachusetts, Quebec, New Jersey, North Carolina, Pennsylvania, Minnesota, Ohio, Michigan, Illinois, Georgia, Indiana, Florida, California, Tennessee
Variables	Low GDP, low imports and low exports, low deficit and low unemployment	Medium levels of exports, GDP and deficit and low per capita income.	High GDP, high deficit, high imports, high exports, high per capita income

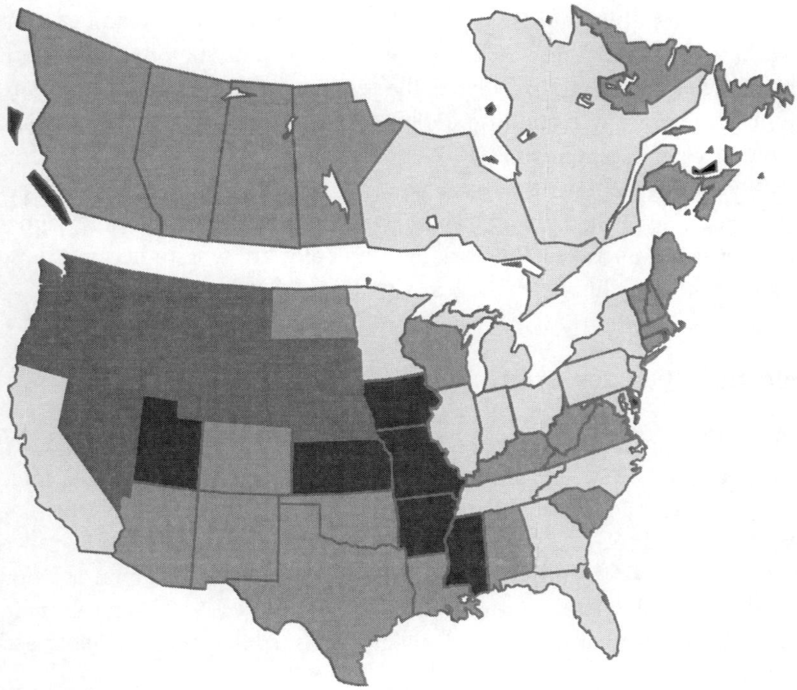

Figure 5. Colored map that show the separation of the regions of USA and Canada when we use indicator cor.

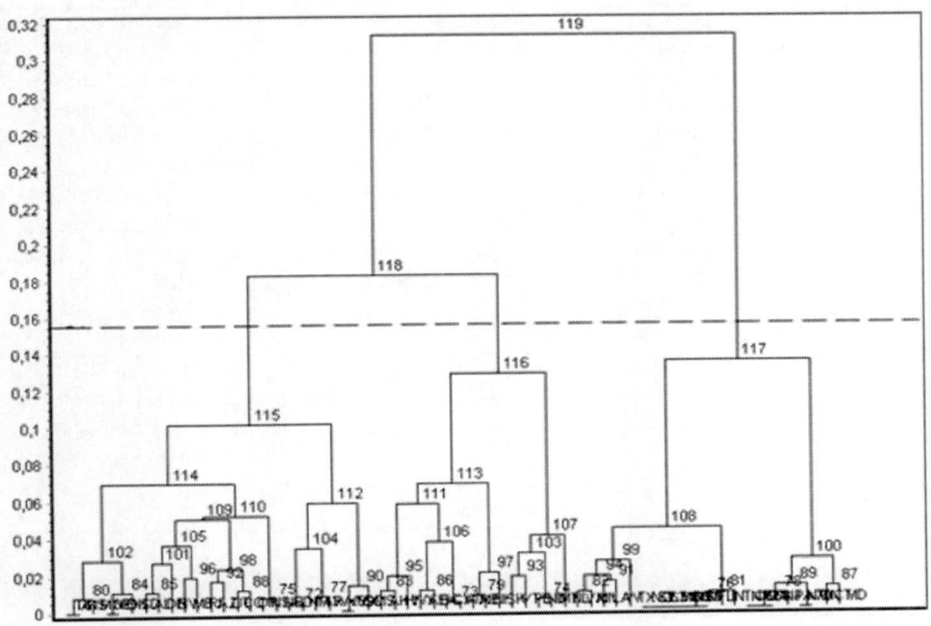

Figure 6. Hierarchical Tree of the Regions of US and Canada.

The Groups that are created in this case are three and they are also depicted in Figure 5. The first one, marked in blue in Figure 4 consists of regions in the central and western part of the U.S. with low income, low GDP, low imports and exports, low deficit and low unemployment. The second group includes the regions marked with red in Figure 5 and these regions are characterized by medium middle economic class, middle levels of exports, GDP and deficit and low per capita income.

Finally the third group marked with yellow, includes the rich and prosperous regions located on the east side of the US and Canada with high GDP, high deficit, high imports, high exports, high per capita income. The areas in gray color are not studied in this section due to the COR indicator which eliminates the less significant data.

3.2. Hierarchical Cluster Analysis

The Hierarchical Cluster Analysis, as stated above, is applied with the help of a hierarchical tree plot. The researcher selects the nodes of greatest interest for the interpretation of data and control which variables characterize them. The tree plot for the U.S. and Canada is the Figure 6.

The nodes that are taken under consideration in the above tree plot are nodes 115, 116 and 117. Therefore the data are separated into three groups, each of which contains the data of these nodes. The groups that are created under the ascending hierarchical classification are those shown in the table 2.

Table 2. Separated regions of US and Canada with Hierarchical Cluster Analysis

	Group 1	Group 2	Group 3
States/ Provinces	Virginia, Minnesota, Louisiana, Wisconsin, Texas, North Carolina, Illinois, Michigan, Ohio, GA, Florida, Indiana, Tennessee, Quebec, Massachusetts, New Jersey, Pennsylvania, New York, Ontario, Connecticut, Maryland.	Alaska, Hawaii, Wyoming, Alberta, British Columbia, California, Washington, Manitoba, New Hampshire, Saskatchewan, Vermont, Prince Edward Island, North Dakota, Montana, Newfoundland and Labrador	Idaho, New Mexico, Arkansas, West Virginia, Kentucky, South Carolina, Mississippi, Iowa, Kansas, Missouri, Nebraska, Oklahoma, South Dakota, Alabama, Delaware, Nevada, Maine, Rhode Island, Arizona, Utah, Colorado, Oregon, Nova Scotia, New Brunswick
Variables	High GDP high imports high exports high deficit	Low GDP, exports and deficit, high levels of per capita income.	Absence of high GDP and high per capita income, presence of medium-level and low level of exports per capita income.

As we can see at the table above, US and Canada are divided into three groups similar to those created earlier by factor analysis.

The first group marked with red color includes mainly the eastern U.S. states which belong to a high economic level with high GDP, high imports, high exports but also high deficit. The second group, marked with yellow color, includes (mainly) areas of the West that are characterized by low GDP, exports and deficit, high levels of per capita income. Finally the third one, marked with green color, includes western and central regions that are characterized by absence of high GDP and high per capita income, and presence of medium-level and low level of exports per capita income. These results are shown schematically on the Figure 7.

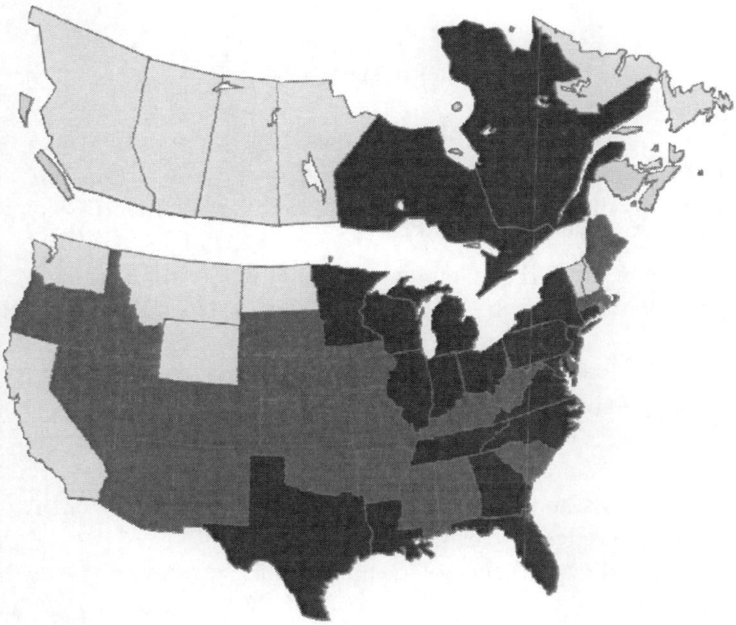

Figure 7. Separated regions of USA and Canada with Hierarchical Cluster Analysis.

CONCLUSION

With the application of Correspondence Analysis and Ascending Hierarchical Classification, we can draw some very important conclusions with respect to regional U.S. and Canada grouping. We use macroeconomic variables that according to the theory are important determinants of an optimum currency areas. We conclude that the U.S. and Canada with respect to forming an OCA can actually be divided into three parts. The first one includes regions mainly from the East that are industrialized, and characterized by high levels of economic activity as this is measured by the macroeconomic variables used in our analysis. The second part includes regions mainly from western US and Canada with diverse levels of economic activity and prosperity. Finally, a third group of regions can be identified.

This group includes a geographically diverse set of regions as it spans from east to west. The common factor though that links these regions is the relatively low level of economic prosperity as it is measured in our study in terms of income, growth, imports, exports, etc. It is important to note, that our study is based on a temporal "tomography" of the economy of the North American regions, and it is not a time-series analysis.

The significance of the conclusions above is major because it shows that the existing national borders may not be the optimum; it can be easily observed, from the results of our survey, that there is a differentiation in the separation of the areas under consideration. That means that the states and provinces should focus on their fiscal policy and on the conditions that should exist in order to meet the requirements of an OCA. Moreover, this differentiation should be an additional incentive for the creation of a regulatory framework that includes incentives for labor and capital mobility among the regions.

REFERENCES

Beine, M., and Coulombe, S. (2005). One Market, One Money: Evidence from Canada–United States Economic Integration. *The World Economy*, *28*(7), 985-1003.

Crowley, P.M. (2001) Is the US and OCA?, presented at the Southern Economic meetings in Tampa Florida, USA.

Eichler, S., and Karmann, A. (2011). Optimum Currency Areas in Emerging Market Regions: Evidence Based on the Symmetry of Economic Shocks. Open Economies Review, 22(5), 935-954.

Eichengreen, B. (1991). Is Europe an optimum currency area, National Bureau of Economic Research, Working Paper Series, no. 3579.

Frankel, J. A., and Rose, A. K. (1996). The endogeneity of the optimum currency area criteria (No. w5700). National Bureau of Economic Research.

Kouparitsas, M. (2001). Is the United States an optimum currency area? An empirical analysis of regional business cycles, FRBC, WP 2001-22.

Mundell, Robert A. (1961) “A Theory of Optimum Currency Areas”, *American Economic Review*, 51, pp. 509-17.

Mundell, Robert A. (1973), “Uncommon Arguments for Common Currencies”, in H.G. Johnson and A.K. Swoboda, The Economics of Common Currencies, pp.114-32, London: Allen and Unwin.

Sideris, D. (2010). Optimum currency areas, structural changes and the endogeneity of the OCA criteria: evidence from six new EU member states, *Applied Financial Economics,* 21 (4), 195-206.

In: Computational Data Analysis Techniques ISBN: 978-1-63463-957-6
Editors: M. Doumpos, C. Zopounidis and Ch. Gaganis

Chapter 2

DIRECTIONAL FORECASTING IN FINANCIAL TIME SERIES USING SUPPORT VECTOR MACHINES: THE USD/EURO EXCHANGE RATE

V. Plakandaras[1], T. Papadimitriou[2] and P. Gogas

[1]Department of Economics, Democritus University of Thrace, Greece

[2]Democritus University of Thrace, Greece

ABSTRACT

In this paper, we present a novel machine learning based forecasting system of the EUR/USD exchange rate directional changes. Specifically, we feed an over complete variable set to a Support Vector Machines (SVM) model and refine it through a Sensitivity Analysis process. The dataset spans from 1/1/1999 to 30/11/2011; the data of the last 7 months are reserved for out-of-sample testing. Results show that the proposed scheme outperforms various other machine learning methods treating similar scenarios.

1. INTRODUCTION

With more than $4 trillion dollars traded daily in the foreign exchange market[1], exchange rate forecasting is of great importance to both traders and policy makers. Soon after the breakdown of the Bretton Woods system, the need to model and forecast the new highly volatile and complex phenomenon of floating currency rates (Trafalis et al., 2006), led to the introduction of several empirical techniques.

The first attempts to model the exchange rate market employed structural econometric models based on economic theory fundamentals. The goal was to predict future rates through the identification of the factors that determine exchange rates. These attempts suffered from mediocre forecasting abilities (B. Balassa, 1964; R. Dornbuch, 1976; J. Frankel, 1979; Meese & Rogoff, 1983) and in response, many participants of the foreign exchange market claim

[1] Bank of International Settlements, 2011.

that the high volatility of the exchange rate market is a result of psychological trends discounting the predictive power of fundamentals (Fama, 1984).

Advances in statistical methods lead to the introduction of Autoregressive Integrated Moving Average (ARIMA) models proposed by Box and Jenkins (1973) that had better forecasting ability than structural models. The main drawback of this method is that it assumes a linear relationship between the variables involved in the estimation. A further development was the introduction of Structural Econometric Models Time Series Analysis (SEMTSA) by Arnold Zellner (1979) who combined both approaches. Nevertheless, the method suffered from high complexity and the results did not have straightforward economic interpretation. To overcome these drawbacks, C. Sims (1980) introduced the Vector Autoregressive (VAR) models adopting a more convenient interpretation of variable correlations, with the simplicity of a theory-free estimation framework.

Later, with the introduction of the Autoregressive Conditional Heteroskedasticity (ARCH) models by Engle (1982) and the generalization of this methodology by Bollerslev (1986) with the generalized ARCH (GARCH), a whole new group of empirical studies was introduced to model the conditional variance (K. Mitchell,2007; Chen S. et al., 2010; Hossein & Nasser, 2011).

The complexity and volatility of exchange rates intrigued researchers employing chaos theory as well. A number of studies focused on testing for deterministic behavior in various currencies, providing significant evidence in favor of a chaotic generating process in the exchange rates mechanism (B.Mandelbrot, 1963; De Grauwe & Grimaldi,2006; Gogas & Serletis, 1997; Bask, 2002; Das& Das,2007). Nonetheless, detection of a chaotic generating mechanism is only the first step towards forecasting. It needs to be followed by exact identification of the mechanism and necessarily produce only very short-term forecasts.

During the last decade, non-parametric models such as Artificial Neural Networks (ANN) and Support Vector Machines have been used extensively. Due to their ability of dealing with non-linear systems through data mapping, machine learning has become a popular choice among researchers in various forecasting scenarios. In particular, models based on Neural Networks (Wang, 2004; Chang et al., 2009; Huang et al., 2004) and Support Vector Machines (Huang, 2010; Kamruzzaman et al., 2003; Trafalis, 2006; Brandl et al., 2009; Zhao et al., 2009) achieved accuracy at least at par with predictions from both structural econometric and naive models. In contrast to ANN estimation, the SVM solution derives from convex optimization making the optimal solution both global and unique.

There are only a few studies that deal with exchange rate directional forecasting using pure SVM classification techniques. Ullrich et al. (2007) implemented 6 kernels on 2439 daily observations yielding a structural model with out of sample forecasting accuracy of 56% on the exchange rate EUR/USD for next day's directional forecast, on a test data set of 350 observations. Zhang and Zhao (2009) studied various technical indicators over the EUR/USD exchange rate and achieve a 60% hit-rate in weekly directional forecast, with 56 observations used for the test sample. Brandl and Leopold-Wildburger (2009) introduced a structural SVM classification model with constraints imposed on the prediction results through Genetic Algorithms. The constraints provide a stable framework from classic economic theory, in a way that domain knowledge is introduced to the forecast model. The hit-rate for monthly forecast is 73%.

In this paper we aim at constructing a structural SVM model that can optimally classify input data in an attempt to forecast the directional change of the day-to-day EUR/USD exchange rate.

The selection of a directional forecast and not of the actual rate is due to the fact that the information about the future direction of the exchange rate can lead to a clear decision in a trading strategy. Under this machine learning framework, we construct a binary forecasting model with the use of an SVM classifier into two states: future rise or fall.

2. SUPPORT VECTOR MACHINES

The Support Vector Machines model is a supervised machine learning method used for two-class data classification. Roughly, the basic concept of an SVM is to select a small number of data points from our dataset, called Support Vectors (SV) that can define a hyperplane separating the two classes' data points. When the problem is not linearly-separable, then SVM is coupled with a non-linear Kernel mapping procedure, projecting the data points to a higher dimensional space, called feature space, where the classes are linearly separable.

The procedure has two steps: the training step and the testing step. In the training step, the largest part of the dataset is used for the estimation of the separating hyperplane; in the testing step, the generalization ability of the model is evaluated by investigating the model's performance in the small subset that was left aside in the first step. Typically, 80%-95% of the dataset is used for the training step and the rest 20%-5% for testing.

In the following we describe briefly the mathematical derivations of the SVM theory.

2.1. Linear Separable Case

We consider a dataset (vectors) $\mathbf{x}_i \in R^2$ $(i = 1,2,\dots,n)$ belonging to two classes (output targets[2]) $y_i \in \{-1,+1\}$. If the two classes are linearly separable, then we define a separator

$$\mathrm{f}(\mathbf{x}_i) = \mathbf{w}^{\mathrm{T}}\mathbf{x}_i - b = 0 \tag{1}$$

in such that $\mathrm{y}_i\mathrm{f}(\mathbf{x}_i) > 0\ \forall i$

where **w** is the weight vector and *b* is the bias.

The optimal hyper plane is selected as the decision boundary that classifies each data vector to the correct class and has the maximum distance from both class. This distance is often called "margin". In Figure 1, the SV's are represented with the pronounced contour, the margin lines (defining the distance of the hyperplane with each class) are represented with the continuous lines and the hyper plane is represented with the dotted line.

The solution to the problem of finding the hyper plane can be dealt through the Lagrange relaxation procedure on the following equation:

$$\min_{\mathbf{w},b} \max_{\alpha} \left\{\frac{1}{2}\|\mathbf{w}\|^2 - \sum_{i=1}^{N} a_i \left[y_i(\mathbf{w}^{\mathrm{T}}\mathbf{x}_i - b) - 1\right]\right\} \tag{2}$$

[2]In the SVM jargon.

where $\boldsymbol{\alpha} = [a_1, \dots, a_n]$ are the non-negative Lagrange multipliers. Equation (2) is never used to estimate the solution. Instead we always solve the dual problem, defined as:

$$\max_{\alpha}\left\{\sum_{i=1}^{N} a_i - \sum_{j=1}^{N}\sum_{k=1}^{N} a_j a_k y_j y_k \mathbf{x}_j^{\mathrm{T}}\mathbf{x}_k\right\} \quad (3)$$

Subject to $\sum_{i=1}^{N} a_i y_i = 0$ and $0 \leq a_i, \forall\, i$

The solution of (3) gives the location of the hyper plane defined by:

$$\widehat{\mathbf{w}} = \sum_{i=1}^{N} a_i y_i \mathbf{x}_i \quad (4)$$

$$\hat{b} = \widehat{\mathbf{w}}^{\mathrm{T}}\mathbf{x}_i - y_i, i \in V \quad (5)$$

where $V = \{i: 0 < y_i\}$ is the set of the support vector indices.

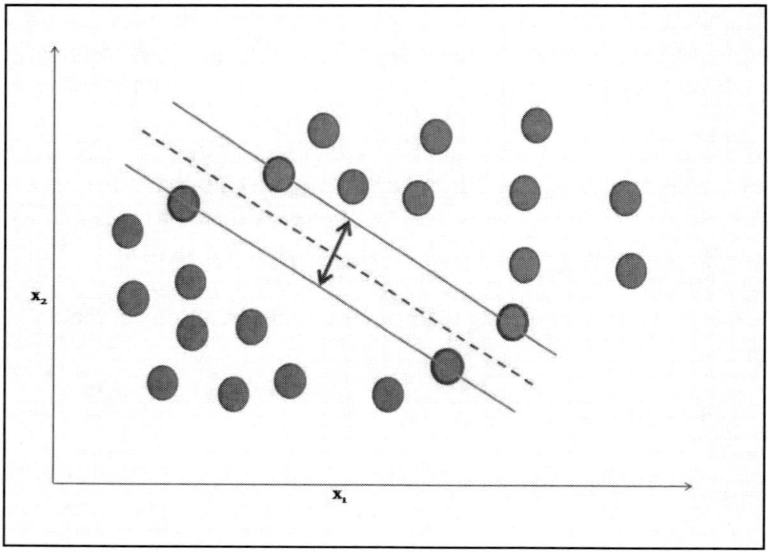

Figure 1. Hyper plane selection and support vectors. The SV's are represented with the pronounced red contour, the margin lines are represented with the continuous lines and the hyper plane is represented with the dotted line.

2.2. Error Tolerant SVM

In order to allow a predefined level of error tolerance in the training procedure Cortes and Vapnik (1995) introduced non-negative slack variables $\xi_i \geq 0, \forall\, i$ and a parameter C describing the desired tolerance to classification errors. Equation (2) is now defined as:

$$\min_{\mathbf{w},b,\xi} \max_{\alpha}\left\{\frac{1}{2}\|\mathbf{w}\|^2 + C\sum_{i=1}^{N}\xi_i - \sum_{j=1}^{N} a_j\left[y_j\left(\mathbf{w}^{\mathrm{T}}\mathbf{x}_j - b\right) - 1 + \xi_j\right] - \sum_{k=1}^{N}\mu_k\xi_k\right\} \quad (4)$$

where ξ_i measures the distance of vector $\mathbf{x}_i$ from the hyper plane when classified erroneously.

The hyper plane is defined as:

$$\hat{\mathbf{w}} = \sum_{i=1}^{N} a_i y_i \mathbf{x}_i \quad (5)$$

$$\hat{b} = \hat{\mathbf{w}}^{\mathrm{T}} \mathbf{x}_i - y_i, i \in V \quad (6)$$

where $V = \{i: 0 < y_i < C\}$ is the set of the support vector indices.

2.3. Kernel Methods

When the two class dataset cannot be separated by a linear separator (Figure 2), then the SVM classification is paired with kernel methods.

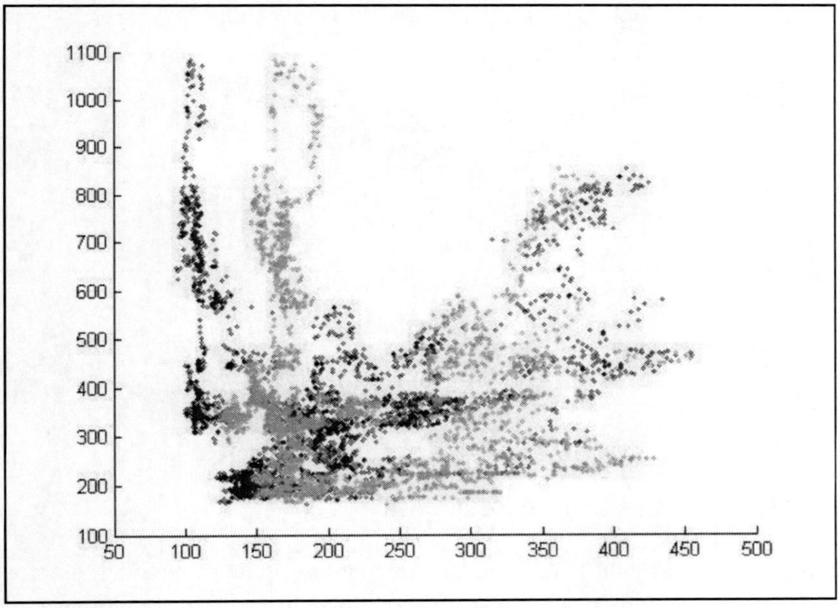

Figure 2.The Data Space. The non-separable two class scenario.

The concept is quite simple: the dataset is projected though a kernel function into a richer space of higher dimensionality (called feature space) where the dataset is linearly separable (Figure 3).

The solution to the dual problem with projection of eq. (4) now transforms to:

$$\max_{\boldsymbol{\alpha}} = \sum_{i=1}^{N} a_i - \frac{1}{2} \sum_{j=1}^{N} \sum_{k=1}^{N} a_j a_k y_j y_k \, \mathrm{K}(\mathbf{x}_j, \mathbf{x}_k) \quad (7)$$

Under the constraints $\sum_{i=1}^{N} a_i y_i = 0$ and $0 \leq a_i \leq C, \forall\, i$ where $\mathrm{K}(\mathbf{x}_j, \mathbf{x}_k)$ is the kernel function.

As the SVM theory uses the structural risk minimization rule for the selection of the hyper parameters, it always seeks for a globally optimized solution avoiding model over-fitting.

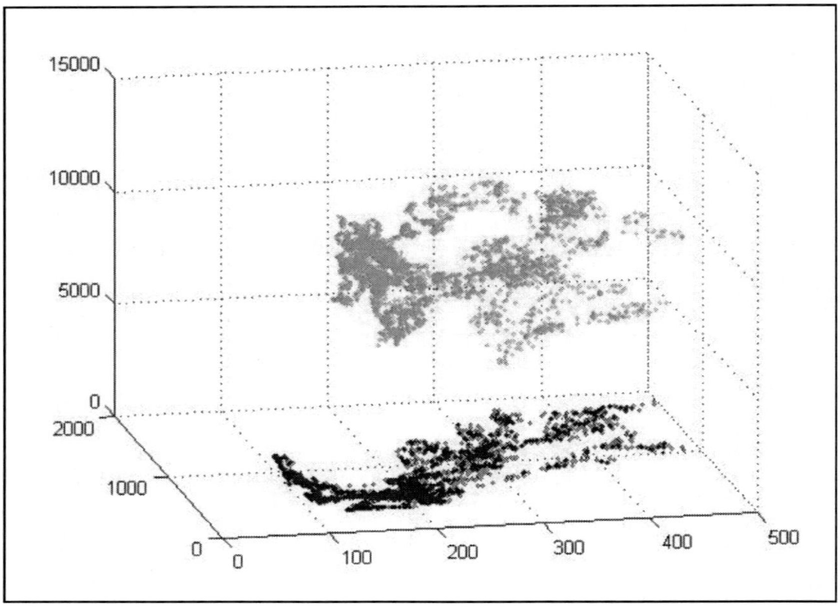

Figure 3. The Feature Space. The two classes are linearly separable.

3. Data Analysis

3.1. Data Collection and Kernel Selection

As already stated, our goal is to construct a structural prediction model. One of the most important steps in constructing our forecasting model is the correct model specification. In order to include the maximum input information, we gathered the majority of the input variables used in exchange rate theory and through sensitivity analysis we kept gradually just the variables that lead to an increase in prediction performance.

Based on economic theory and previous empirical studies, we selected 74 input variables (see the Appendix). These include macroeconomic variables for the USA, the EU, Japan and the UK, daily prices of commodities traded at the Chicago Mercantile Exchange, daily closing spot prices of precious and non-precious metals as traded at the London Metal Exchange, daily spot exchange rates for the EUR/USD and their cross rates with GBP and JPY, various stock market indices. We also introduce the Moving Averages (MA) of 3,5,10 and 30 days for the EUR/USD exchange rate, the interest rate on Treasury bonds with 6 months and 10 years maturity, the 1 week and 1 month Euribor rates and the Eonia overnight rate. In addition to that, we constructed a variable that counts the number of positive returns over the last 5 trading days for the exchange rate under investigation. Overall, the input data set contains all of the variables suggested by theory and empirical studies in the field of exchange rate forecasting. All the data series are collected from 1/1/1999 to 30/10/2011 yielding a set of 3280 observations.

The kernel used is the Gaussian Radial Basis Function (RBF) as it is considered superior in exchange rate forecasting (Kamruzzaman et al., 2003). The mathematical expression of the kernel is:

$$K(\mathbf{x}_i, \mathbf{x}_j) = e^{-\gamma \|\mathbf{x}_i - \mathbf{x}_j\|^2}, \gamma > 0 \tag{8}$$

where γ is the width-length basis parameter of the Gaussian curves.

Before performing the tests, all numerical data where scaled to [-1, 1], in order to impose the same range on all variables. Finally, all the data set was randomly permutated in order to eliminate linearity from the data.

3.2. Sensitivity Analysis

The data set is separated as follows: 19/20 for training and 1/20 for test evaluation of the predicted results (163 observations). The hyper plane parameters C and γ were selected through a ten-fold cross-validation rule and grid search on the training set (Chang & Lin, 2003). On a first step we explored the autoregressive models, using as many as 31 time lags in our tests. Results showed that the 11-lags autoregressive model outperformed the rest on the test sample, as presented on Figure 4.

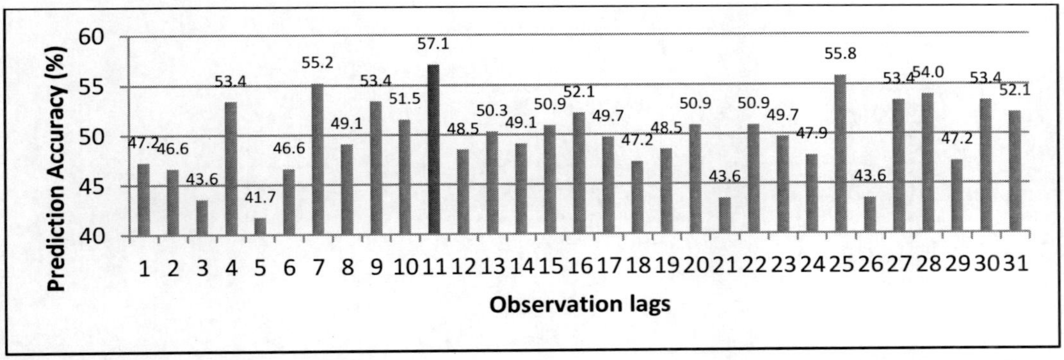

Figure 4. Results of the autoregressive model. With the red bar we mark the results of the most accurate 11-lags autoregressive model.

In Figure 5, we demonstrate the accuracy levels of the training sample for various combinations of parameters C,γ.

On a second step, we introduced the rest of the input variables through a forward selection procedure. One by one every variable was added in the best autoregressive model and the optimum setting of the hyperplane parameters is selected. Then the new model is trained with the best combination of C, γ and the accuracy of the model in out of sample forecasting is measured using the test sample. The overview of the proposed scheme is depicted in Figure 6.

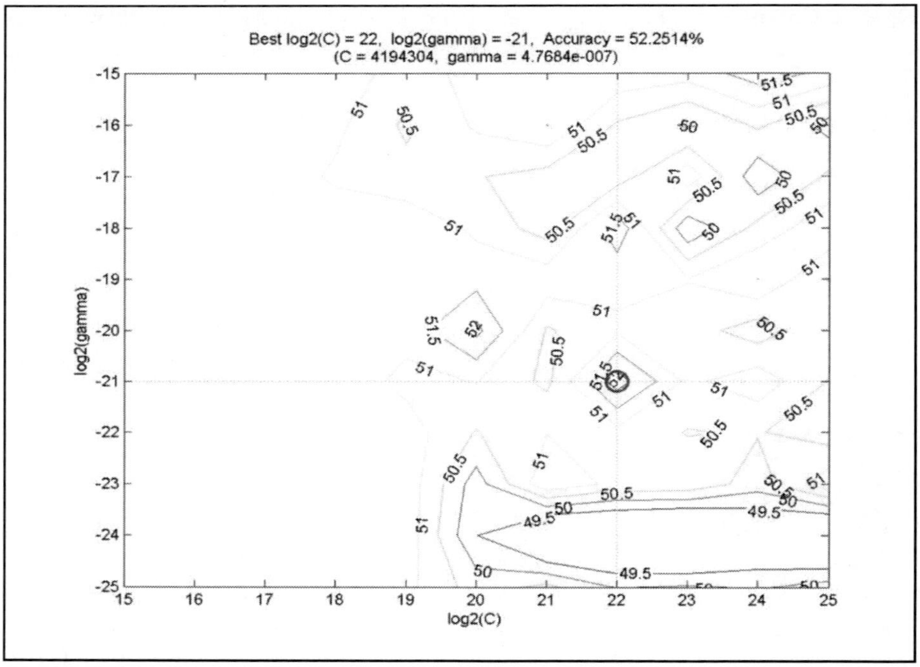

Figure 5. Best autoregressive model. The various contour colors represent different prediction accuracy levels for the various combinations of C, γ while the most accurate setting for the hyper plane parameters is marked with a green circle. The overall accuracy on the train sample is depicted on the headline of the graph.

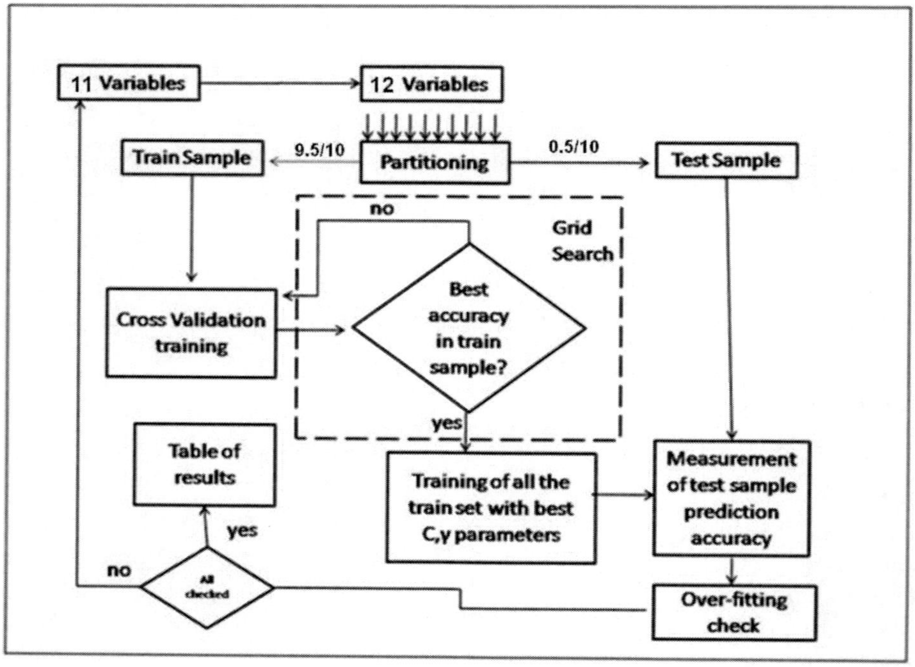

Figure 6. Sensitivity analysis with forward introduction of parameters.

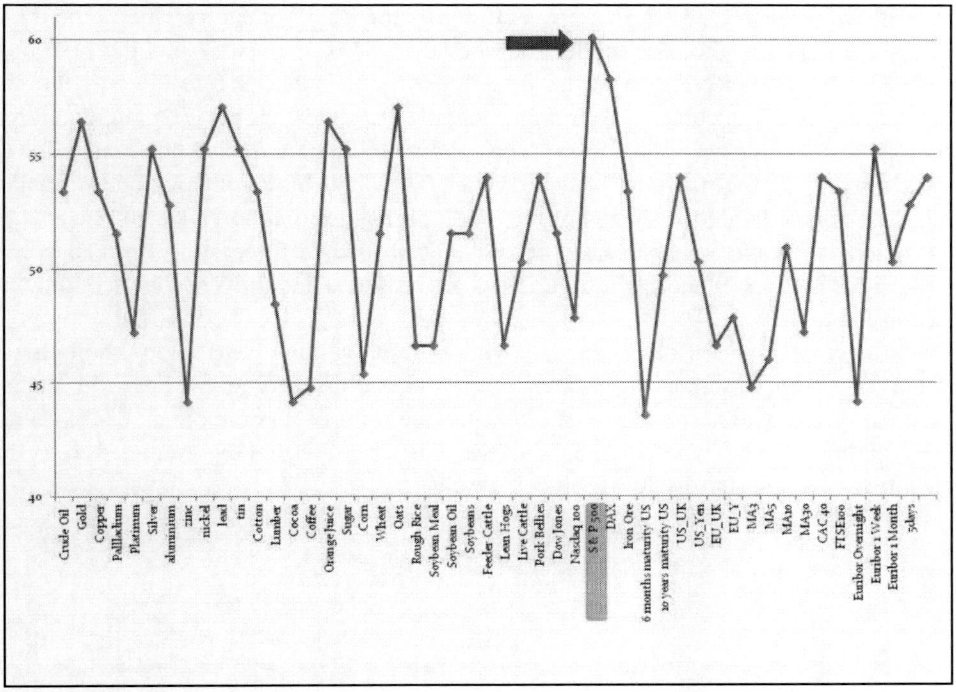

Figure7. First loop results.

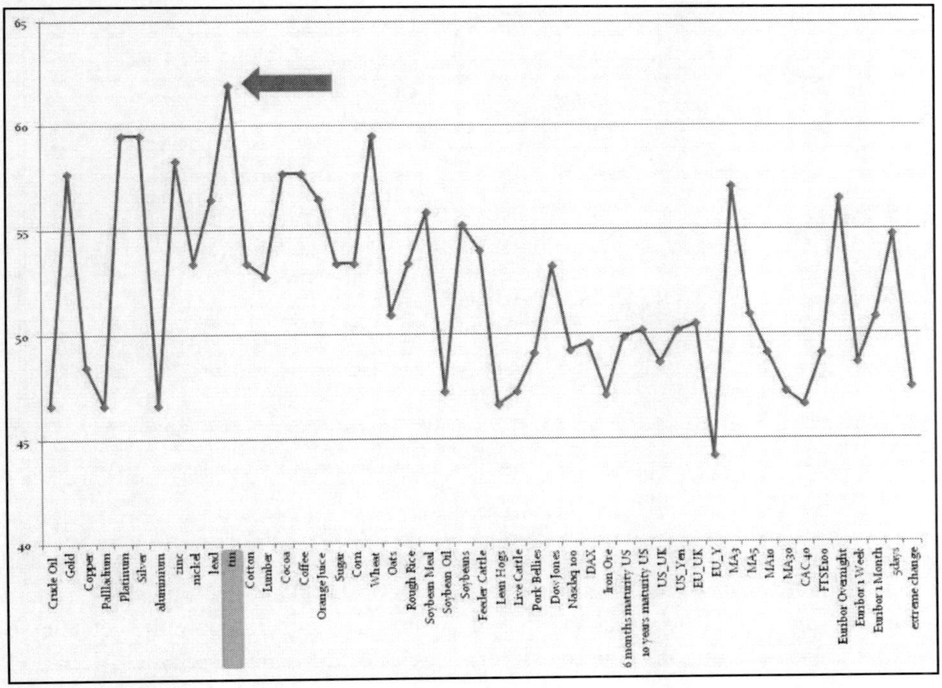

Figure 8. Second loop results.

Overall, we constructed 73 models each consisting of 12 input variables; the 11-lags autoregressive model as the base model and one at a time of the rest. When the first loop of 73 variables was completed, the variable with the best forecasting result was the index S&P500. The overall accuracy for training sample remained at 51.57% but the forecast accuracy on test sample set rose to 60%. The following diagram depicts the results for each variable. Moving one step forward, we constructed 72 models by introducing one variable at a time to a 12 variable model consisting of the S & P 500 index and the 11-lags of the exchange rate. In other words the variable with the best out of sample forecasting result becomes a constant part of the model and the rest variables are reused. The results of the second loop are depicted in Figure 8.

From the comparison of the 72 models with 13 input variables, the one with the best out of sample forecasting accuracy performance was the one incorporating 11-lags of exchange rate observations, the price of index S & P 500 and the price of tin on moment t. The accuracy for the training sample was 52.12% and the hit-rate of correctly predicted directional movements for the test set rose to 61.34% (Figure 9).

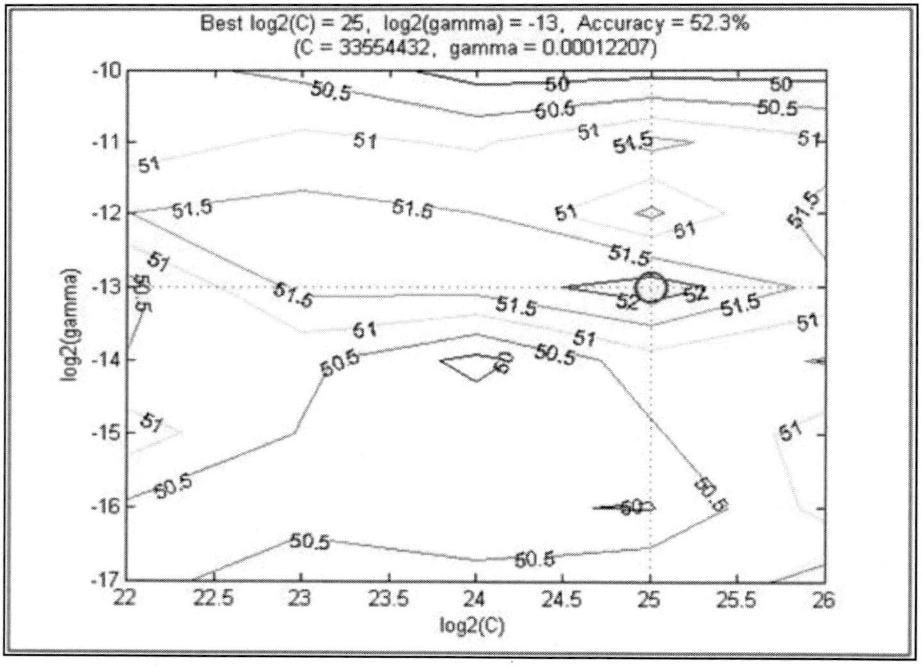

Figure 9. Best predictive model with 13 input variables consisting of 11-lags of the exchange rate observations, index S & P 500 and the daily price of tin.

Resuming the procedure, we constructed 71 models of 14 input variables consisting of the 11-lags of the exchange rate observations, index S & P 500 and the tin price on moment t and one by one the rest of the variables. In other words we try to measure the accuracy of the model with the best prediction accuracy so far, if we add to it a new variable. As in previous steps, all the variables are added one by one and the out of sample forecasting accuracy is measured. The outcome was models of lower predicting power in comparison to the best 13-variable model (less than 61.34% forecasting accuracy), as depicted in Figure 10.

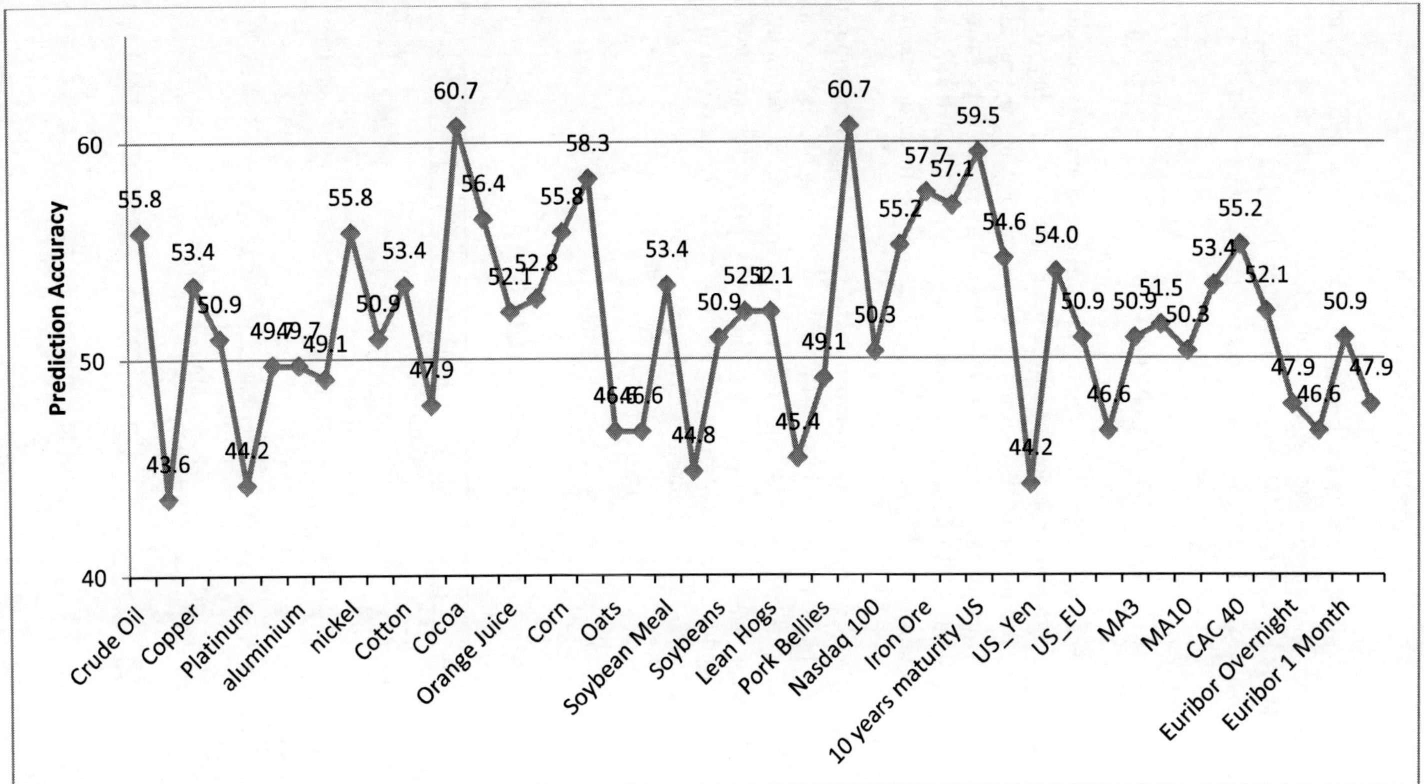

Figure 10. Third loop results.

ACKNOWLEDGMENT

The research has been co-financed by the European Union (European Social Fund (ESF)) and Greek national funds through the Operational Program 'Education and Lifelong Learning' of the National Strategic Reference Framework (NSRF) – Research Funding Program: THALES. Investing in knowledge society through the European Social Fund.

CONCLUSION

The construction of a structural SVM model with a forward input variable selection process, demonstrates considerable predictive power. Our approach produced predictions about next day's directional movement with a higher out-of-sample forecasting accuracy in comparison to previous efforts in the field of EUR/USD exchange rate forecasting with the need to collect data for only 3 variables. Moreover, it deals with daily forecasts which demonstrate wider fluctuations and thus have greater economic interest than weekly or monthly predictions.

Overall, structural SVM models seem promising and there is plenty of room for future research. Nevertheless, the main disadvantage of forward approaches is that they don't examine the models that can be produced with various combinations of the input variables, but are constrained in adding variables that improve the predicting performance of the initial model in an iterative procedure. To overcome this drawback, further research can focus on the implementation of different kernels and training techniques.

APPENDIX

Table 1. Input Variables

No	Variable Name	Observation frequency	Unit
1	CrudeOil	Daily	$/barrel
2	Gold	Daily	$/ounce
3	Copper	Daily	$/ounce
4	Pallladium	Daily	$/ounce
5	Platinum	Daily	$/ounce
6	Silver	Daily	$/ounce
7	Aluminium	Daily	$/ton
8	Zinc	Daily	$/ton
9	Nickel	Daily	$/ton
10	Lead	Daily	$/ton
11	Tin	Daily	$/ton
12	Cotton	Daily	$/ton
13	Lumber	Daily	$/ton
14	Cocoa	Daily	$/ton
15	Coffee	Daily	$/ton

Appendix. (Continued)

No	Variable Name	Observation frequency	Unit
16	OrangeJuice	Daily	$/ton
17	Sugar	Daily	$/ton
18	Corn	Daily	$/ton
19	Wheat	Daily	$/ton
20	Oats	Daily	$/ton
21	Rough Rice	Daily	$/ton
22	Soybean Meal	Daily	$/ton
23	Soybean Oil	Daily	$/ton
24	Soybeans	Daily	$/ton
25	Feeder Cattle	Daily	$/ton
26	Lean Hogs	Daily	$/ton
27	Live Cattle	Daily	$/ton
28	Pork Bellies	Daily	$/ton
29	DowJones	Daily	$/ton
30	Nasdaq 100	Daily	$/ton
31	S & P 500	Daily	index
32	DAX	Daily	index
33	Iron Ore	Daily	$/ton
34	6 months maturity T-Bond	Daily	% interest
35	10 years maturity T-Bond	Daily	% interest
36	CPI US	Monthly	% percent
37	US Debt	Annually	Million $
38	FED rate	Monthly	% interest
39	GDP US	Monthly	Million $
40	M3 US	Monthly	Million $
41	Trade Balance US	Annually	Million $
42	US Deficit or Surplus	Annually	Million $
43	US/UK	Daily	$
44	US/Yen	Daily	$
45	CPI EU	Monthly	Index (2005 base)
46	Currenta ccounts EU	Annually	Billions €
47	Debt EU	Annually	Billions €
48	Deficit EU	Annually	Billions €
49	GBP/EUR	Daily	€
50	USD/EUR	Daily	€
51	JPN/EUR	Daily	€
52	GDP EU	Annually	Billions €
53	Interest rate ECB	Monthly	% interest
54	M3 EU	Monthly	Billions €
55	MA3	Daily	€
56	MA5	Daily	€
57	MA10	Daily	€
58	MA30	Daily	€
59	Productivity EU	Monthly	Index (2000 base
60	Productivity US	Monthly	Index (2005 base)

No	Variable Name	Observation frequency	Unit
61	Unemployment EU	Monthly	% percent
62	Unemployment US	Monthly	% percent
63	UK current account	Annually	Million £
64	Japan current account	Annually	Million ¥
65	CAC 40	Daily	Index
66	FTSE100	Daily	Index
67	CPI Japan	Monthly	% percent
68	CPI UK	Monthly	% percent
69	GDP Japan	Annually	Billion ¥
70	GDP UK	Annually	Billion £
71	Euribor Overnight	Daily	% interest
72	Euribor 1 Week	Daily	% interest
73	Euribor 1 Month	Daily	% interest
74	5 days change	Daily	0-5

REFERENCES

Balassa, B. (1964), *The purchasing power parity doctrine: a reappraisal*, Journal of Political Economy, Vol. 72, pp. 584-96.

Bask Mikael (1996) *Dimensions and Lyapunov exponents from exchange rate series*. Chaos, Solitons & Fractals 7, no. 12 (December): 2199-2214.

Belkin, M., Niyogi, P., & Sindhwani, V. (2006).*Manifold regularization: A geometric framework for learning from examples*. Journal of Machine Learning Research, vol. 7, pp.2399–2434.

BollerslevT.P. (1986), "*Generalized Autoregressive Conditional Heteroskedasticity*", Journal of Econometrics, vol. 31, pp. 307-327.

Box G.E.P. and Jenkins G.M. (1976) "*Time Series Analysis: Forecasting and Control*", Holden-Day, San Francisco.

Brandl, B., & Leopold-Wildburger, U. (2009, *Increasing the Fitness of Fundamental,* Organizational Behavior Teaching Journal, 4(16), 779 - 798.

Chang Chih-Chung and Lin Chih-Jen (2011), *LIBSVM :a library for support vector machines.* ACM Transactions on Intelligent Systems and Technology, 2:27:1--27:27, 2011.

Chang, J-F, C-W Chang, and Wen-Yan Tzeng (2009) *Forecasting Exchange Rates Using Integration of Particle Swarm Optimization and Neural Networks*. Fourth International Conference on Innovative Computing, Information and Control (ICICIC) (December): 660-663.

Chen, S., Härdle, W. K., &Jeong, K. (2010). *Forecasting Volatility with Support Vector Machine-Based GARCH Model*. Journal of Forecasting, vol.433,pp. 406-433.

Cortes, C. & Vapnik, V. (1995): *Support Vector Network. Machine Learning*, vol. 20, 273–297.

Das, a, and P Das (2007) *Chaotic analysis of the foreign exchange rates*. Applied Mathematics and Computation 185, no. 1 (February): 388-396.

Degrauwe, P, and M Grimaldi (2006) *Exchange rate puzzles: A tale of switching attractors*. European Economic Review 50, no. 1 (January): 1-33.

Dornbusch R.(1976) *Expectations and exchange rate dynamic*, Journal of Political Economy, 84(6), pp.1161–1176.

Engle R.F. (1982) "*Autoregressive Conditional Heteroskedasticity with estimates of the variance of U.K. inflation*", Econometrica, vol. 50, pp. 987-1008.

Fama, E., (1984), *Forward and spot exchange rates*. Journal of Monetary Economics vol. 14, pp. 319–338.

Frankel J.A.(1979) *On the mark: A theory of floating exchange rates based on real interest differentials,* American Economic Review, 69(4),pp.610–622.

Hossain, A., & Nasser, M. (2011).*Comparison of the finite mixture of ARMA-GARCH, back propagation neural networks and support-vector machines in forecasting financial returns*. Journal of Applied Statistics, 38(3), pp. 533-551.

Huang Shian-Chang, Chuang Pei-Ju, Wu Cheng-Feng, and Lai Hiuen-Jiun,(2010) "*Chaos-based support vector regressions for exchange rate forecasting,*" Expert Systems with Applications, vol. 37 , pp. 8590-8598.

Huang W., Lai K.K., Nakamori Y. and Wang Shouyang (2004) "*Forecasting Foreign Exchange Rates with Artificial Neural Networks: A Review*", International Journal of Information Technology & Decision Making Vol. 3, No. 1 pp. 145–165.

Kamruzzaman, SarkerR.a., and Ahmad I., (2003) "*SVM based models for predicting foreign currency exchange rates,*" Third IEEE International Conference on Data Mining, IEEE Comput. Soc, 557-560.

Kilian L. & M.P. Taylor (2003), *Why is it so difficult to beat random walk forecast of exchange rates?*, Journal of International Economics 60, pp.85–107.

Macdonald, Ronald, and Jun Nagayasu (1998) *On the Japanese Yen – U .S. Dollar Exchange Rate: A Structural Econometric Model Based on Real Interest Differentials.* Journal of Economic Literature, Vol. 102, pp. 75-102.

Mandelbrot Benoit (1963), "*The Variation of Certain Speculative Prices*", The Journal of Business, vol. 36, no. 4, pp. 394-419.

Meese, Richard & Kenneth Rogoff, 1983, *Empirical exchange rate models of the seventies: Do they tit out of sample?*, Journal of International Economics, pp. 3-24.

Mitchell, K., & Pearce, D. (2007).*Professional forecasts of interest rates and exchange rates: Evidence from the Wall Street Journal's panel of economists*. Journal of Macroeconomics, 29(4), 840-854. doi

Serletis Apostolos & Gogas Periklis (1997) *Chaos in East European black market exchange rates*. Research in Economics 51, no. 4 (December): 359-385.

Sims C.A. (2002) "*The role of models and probabilities in the monetary policy process* ", Brookings Panel on economic activity , Fall 2002.

T.B. Trafalis (1999), *Artificial neural networks applied to financial forecasting*, in: C.J.C. Dagli, Buczak, Ghosh, Embrechts, Ersoy (Eds.), Smart Engineering System Design: Neural Net- works, Fuzzy Logic, Evolutionary Programming, Data Mining and Complex Systems, ASME Press, pp. 1049–1054.

Taylor, L. (2004). *Exchange rate indeterminacy in portfolio balance, Mundell-Fleming and uncovered interest rate parity models*. Cambridge Journal of Economics, 28(2), 205-227.

Trafalis, T. &Ince, H., (2006).*A hybrid model for exchange rate prediction*. Decision Support Systems, 42(2), 1054-1062.

Ullrich C., Seese D. &Chalup S. (2007) *Foreign Exchange Trading with Support Vector Machines,* Advances in Data Analysis, part 8, pp. 539-546.

Wang T., Huang H., Tian S. &Xu J. (2010), *Feature selection for SVM via optimization of kernel polarization with Gaussian ARD kernels*, Expert Systems with Applications, vol. 37, pp. 6663–6668

Zellner A. (1979), *Statistical Analysis of Econometric Models*, Journal of the American Statistical Assosiation, vol. 74, No. 367, pp.628.

Zhang, Z., & Zhao, Q. (2009).*The Application of SVMs Method on Exchange Rates Fluctuation.* Discrete Dynamics in Nature and Society, 2009, 1-8.

In: Computational Data Analysis Techniques ISBN: 978-1-63463-957-6
Editors: M. Doumpos, C. Zopounidis and Ch. Gaganis

Chapter 3

INFLATION FORECASTING IN GREECE USING A NEURO-FUZZY SYSTEM

George Atsalakis[1*] ***and Ioanna Atsalaki***[2#]
[1]Technical University of Crete, Greece
[2]Western University of Greece

ABSTRACT

This paper analyses the inflation forecasting power of a hybrid intelligent system called the Adaptive Neuro-Fuzzy Inference System (ANFIS) for forecasting the quarterly inflation rate in Greece. Recent studies have addressed the problem of inflation rate forecasting by using different methods including artificial neural networks and model-based approaches. The ANFIS combines both the learning capabilities of a neural network and reasoning capabilities of fuzzy logic in order to give enhanced forecasting capabilities, as compared to using a single methodology alone. Quarterly data that concern the rate of growth of production, imports prices, the consumer index, the rate of labor cost and the rate of growth of the Athens Stock Exchange General Index have been used as inputs to the model. Various models have been trained by leaving half the data out. Then the models have been evaluated by the data that are left out. The forecasting accuracy of the alternative ANFIS models is compared in terms of the Root Mean Square Error (RMSE) and other common error measures. The results have shown that ANFIS provides a prudent way to capture uncertainty in relationships among input variables and output variables.

Keywords: Inflation rate forecasting, neuro-fuzzy forecasting, ANFIS forecasting, fuzzy forecasting

---

* E-mail: atsalak@otenet.gr.
# Email: joanna_atsa@hotmail.com

1. Introduction

Inflation forecast is used as a guide in the formulation of monetary policy by money policy makers worldwide. Monetary policy decisions are based on inflation forecasts extracted from information from different models and other indicators, which influence the macroeconomic conditions of the economy. There is an obvious need for adequate inflation forecasts and for this reason, economic research still faces a hard task to trace back its driving forces and provide agents with optimal forecast results.

There are many indicators which are related to inflation, such as money supply, interest rates, exchange rates and the labor market conditions. Changes in the money supply lead, eventually, to proportional changes in the price level, or alternatively, long-run rates of money growth are linked to inflation. According to the Quantity Theory tradition of economics, the money stock will determine the general level of prices, at least in the long term, and according to the monetarists it will influence real activity in the short run. This relationship has traditionally played an important role in the macroeconomic policy as governments try to control inflation. It is important to distinguish that only an increase in the aggregate price level is defined as inflation, whereas a rise in the relative prices of goods reflects the allocationary characteristics of market systems (Cassel D., 1995). Moreover, due to the process character of inflation, any analysis has to be conducted within a dynamic framework allowing for inflation to be modelled beyond transitional effects when moving from one static equilibrium to another, as well as allowing the incorporation of the interaction of multiple causes of inflation, (Branson W.H., 1981). As claimed, forecasting macro-variables with non-linear forecasting models is as good as forecasting with linear models. Traditionally, linear statistical forecasting methods have been widely used in many real-world situations. Linear models are easy to develop and implement. They are also simple to understand and interpret. There exists a vast literature on comparing time-series forecasts from neural network and linear models. Zhang, Patuwo, and Hu (1998) provide a recent survey. Linear models, however, do have the limitation in that many real-world problems are non-linear. Using linear models to approximate complex non-linear problems is often not satisfactory, particularly when the forecasting horizon is relatively long. Marcellino (2002), for example, reported that non-linear models outperform linear and time-varying parameter models for forecasting inflation, industrial production and unemployment in the euro area. Forecasting inflation is of course, very important for monetary policy, which has as a main goal monetary stability. However, it is also important to forecast specifically the country level inflation, because, country level inflation forecasting contributes to a better understanding of the different transmission mechanisms in each country. Furthermore, Marcellino, Stock and Watson (2003) found evidence that forecasting inflation at the country level and then aggregating the forecasts increases accuracy against forecasting at the aggregate level. Recently, artificial neural networks have been proposed as a promising alternative approach to time-series forecasting. Neural networks in hardware form are constructions made up of many relatively simple processors which are interconnected. Some elements (neurons) receive inputs from outside the system and all elements produce outputs. For data modeling purposes, neural networks are normally created by a computer program and used to store model parameters in the form of the architecture of the network. Weights are applied to values passed from one neuron to another and functions are employed to transfer inputs to outputs at individual neurons. The weights are adjusted each time to minimise the error between the desired output and the network output. A large number of successful applications have shown that neural networks can be a very useful tool for time-series modelling and forecasting. In many financial applications of neural networks a large number of candidate inputs are typically available. One is faced with the problem of choosing a set of inputs that are effective for the particular application and for the particular neural-network model employed. Neural networks are also relatively robust to noise in data compared to traditional statistical techniques. It seems, however, that the potential of techniques such as the neural network, which are non-traditional in econometric investigations, has not been fully exploited in the area of monetary economics. For example, Swanson and White (1997) find that artificial neural network models provide, at best, marginal improvements in the forecasts of macroeconomic variables. Neural networks have been shown to successfully learn to estimate a pricing formula for options, with good out-of-sample performance. Moreover, Stock and Watson (1998) compare the forecasting ability of univariate linear and non-linear models for several macroeconomics series and find that artificial neural networks perform quite poorly relative to the linear models.

As it seems from the above proposed methods of inflation forecasting, macro-variables are very important for the economy of any country. It is highly related with ability, where markets have to produce wealth and development. For this reason, countries which cannot control their inflation at a low level have many problems with their public economy and they are not attractive for large investments.

In this paper, a novel approach is proposed. It uses a hybrid alternative formulation of the NN methodology. The neural networks have been accused, by the researchers, of having limited application due to the 'black boxes' and not being able to indicate the degree to which an input can influence the output of the model (Shapiro, 2002; Pao, 1989). Fuzzy logic is an effective rule-based modeling in soft computing, that not only tolerates imprecise information, but also builds a framework of approximate reasoning. The disadvantage of fuzzy logic is the lack of self-learning capability. The combination of fuzzy logic and neural network can overcome the disadvantages of the above approaches. In this paper the use of a hybrid intelligent system called Adaptive Neuro-Fuzzy Inference System (ANFIS) is suggested, for forecasting the inflation rate in Greece. In ANFIS, both the learning capabilities of a neural network and the reasoning capabilities of fuzzy logic are incorporated in order to provide enhanced prediction capabilities, as compared to using a single methodology alone. ANFIS has been used by many researchers to forecast various financial problems (Jang et al., 1997; Atsalakis, 2007; Atsalakis et al., 2007, 2008; Atsalakis & Minoudaki, 2007; Atsalakis & Ucenic, 2006; Atsalakis, 2005, 2008; Ucenic & Atsalakis, 2006, 2008; Ucenic & Atsalakis, 2009; Atsalakis, & Valavanis, 2009; Atsalakis et al., 2011; Atsalakis et al., 2012).

1.1. Related Research

Over the last few decades, there has been much research directed at inflation forecasting. Gatik and Karacuka (2012) have used a neural network model to prove that inflation in Turkey has a time-varying pattern and linear models fail to track underlying levels of inflation.

Haider and Hanif (2009) have developed a neural network model that outperforms the conventional models to forecast the inflation rate in Pakistan.

Nakamura (2004) proved the importance of neural networks for inflation forecasting. He has used recent US data (1978–2002). Neural networks outperform univariate autoregressive models on average for short horizons of one and two quarters. The data have been divided into a training set and a validation set. Next, the training algorithm runs on the training set until the MSE starts to increase on the validation set. The training algorithm was the Levenberg–Marquardt algorithm, a standard training algorithm from the NN literature.

Binne (2006) compared the out-of-sample inflation forecasting performance of two non-linear models; a neural network and a Markov switching autoregressive (MS-AR) model, employing a recurrent neural network (RNN) model that distinguishes itself from standard feed-forward network models, in that activations were allowed to feed back to units within the same or preceding layers. The data cover the period 1960-1961 to 2001-2003.

Duarte and Rua (2007) have tried to assess inflation forecast accuracy over the short-term horizon, using Consumer Price Index (CPI) disaggregated data, through a bottom-up approach. They suggested the use of a new strand of models, the Factor-Augmented SARIMA models. The monthly data set referred to Portuguese CPI and covered the period from January 1988 to December 2004, comprising 204 observations, for the aggregate CPI, with partition in five components (unprocessed food, processed food, non-energy industrial goods, energy and services).

Chen (2001) examined semi-parametric non-linear autoregressive models with exogenous variables (NLARX) via three classes of artificial neural networks: the first one has used smooth sigmoid activation functions; the second one radial basis activation functions; and the third one ridge let activation functions. In an empirical application, it has examined linear and semi-parametric NLARX forecasting models of US inflation. It has found that all three of the ANN semi-parametric models which have been considered outperform a benchmark linear model in terms of both forecast mean squared error and forecast mean absolute deviation error.

Stock (2003) made an empirical assessment of the practical value of asset prices for short- to medium-term economic forecasting. He used quarterly data on as many as 43 variables from each of seven developed economies (Canada, France, Germany, Italy, Japan, the United Kingdom, and the United States) over 1959–99 (some series are available only for a shorter period).

Aron (2000) presented multi-step models for inflation and output, four quarters ahead. The inflation model has an equilibrium correction form, which clarifies medium- or longer-run influences on inflation, including opening the economy to foreign imports. The model confirmed the importance of the output gap and the exchange rate for forecasting inflation. The output model used a stochastic trend to measure long-run changes in the capacity to produce. The data concerned the period 1970-1998.

McNelis (2004) applied linear and neural network-based “thick” models for forecasting inflation based on Phillips–curve formulations. Thick models represented “trimmed mean” forecasts from several neural network models. They outperformed the best performing linear models for “real time” and “bootstrap” forecasts for service indices for the euro area.

2. Model Presentation

2.1. ANFIS Architecture

With the ANFIS approach, implementation of the model design differs in form from the more traditional NN in that it is not fully connected, and not all the weights or nodal parameters are modifiable. Essentially, the fuzzy rule base is encoded in a parallel fashion so that all the rules are activated simultaneously, so as to allow network training algorithms to be applied. As in Jang's (2007) original work, here a back-propagation algorithm is used to optimize the fuzzy sets of the premises in the ANFIS architecture, and a least-squares procedure is applied to the linear coefficients in the consequent terms.

Let X be a space of objects and x be a generic element of X. A classical set $A \subseteq X$ is defined as a collection of elements or objects $x \in X$ such that each x can either belong or not belong to the set A. By defining a characteristic function for each element x in X, a classical set A by a set of ordered pairs $(x, 0)$ or $(x, 1)$ can be represented, which indicates $x \in A$ or $x \notin A$, respectively. On the other hand, a fuzzy set expresses the degree to which an element belongs to a set. Hence the characteristic function of a fuzzy set is allowed to have values between 0 and 1, which denotes the degree of membership of an element in a given set. So a fuzzy set A in X is defined as a set of ordered pairs:

$$A = \{(x, \mu_A(x)) \mid x \in X\} \quad (1)$$

Here $\mu_A(x)$ is called the membership function (MF) for the fuzzy set A.

The MF maps each element of X to a membership grade (or a value) between 0 and 1. Usually X is referred to as the universe of discourse or simply the universe. The most widely used MF is the generalized bell MF (or the bell MF), which is specified by three parameters $\{a_i, b_i, c_i\}$ and defined as in Loukas (2001) and Jang and Chuen-Tsai (1995):

$$\mu_{A_i}(x) = \frac{1}{1 + \left[\left(\frac{x - c_i}{a_i}\right)^2\right]^{b_i}} \quad (2)$$

Parameter b is usually positive. A desired bell MF can be obtained by a proper selection of the parameter set $\{a_i, b_i, c_i\}$. During the learning phase of ANFIS, these parameters are changing continuously in order to minimize the error function between the target output values and the calculated ones (Lee 1990a, 1990b).

The proposed neuro-fuzzy model of ANFIS is a multilayer neural network-based fuzzy system. Its topology is shown in Figure 1, and the system has a total of five layers. In this connected structure, the input and output nodes represent the training values and the predicted values, respectively, and in the hidden layers, there are nodes functioning as membership functions (MFs) and rules. This architecture has the benefit that it eliminates the disadvantage of a normal feed-forward multilayer network, where it is difficult for an observer to understand or modify the network. For simplicity, it is assumed that the examined fuzzy inference system has two inputs x and y, and one output. For a first-order Sugeno fuzzy model (Jang, 1997), a common rule set with two fuzzy if–then rules is defined as:

Rule 1: If x is A_1 and y is B_1 then $f_1 = p_1 \cdot x + q_1 \cdot y + r_1$ (3)

Rule 2: If x is A_2 and y is B_2 then $f_2 = p_2 \cdot x + q_2 \cdot y + r_2$ (4)

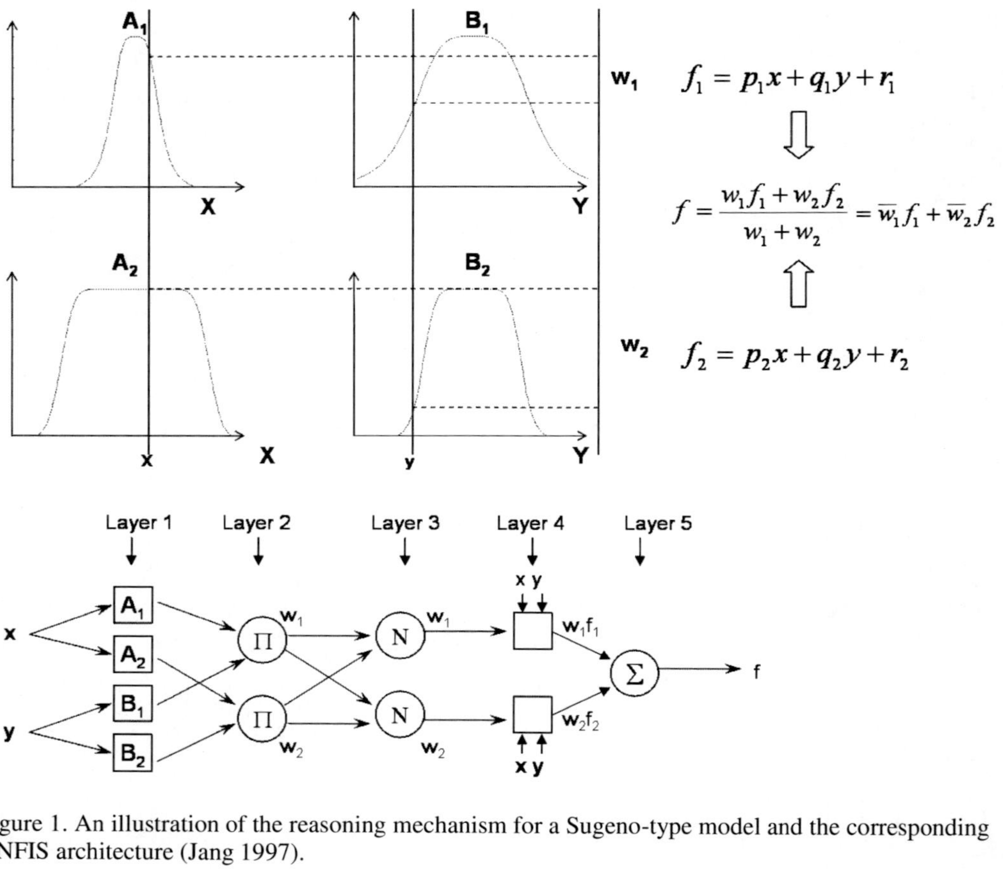

Figure 1. An illustration of the reasoning mechanism for a Sugeno-type model and the corresponding ANFIS architecture (Jang 1997).

As seen from Figure 1, different layers of ANFIS have different nodes. Each node in a layer is either fixed or adaptive (Jang 1993). Different layers with their associated nodes are described below:

Layer 1: Every node i in this layer is a square node with a node function.

$$O_{1,i} = \mu_{A_i}(x) \quad for\ i = 1, 2, or$$

$$O_{1,i} = \mu_{B_{i-2}}(y) \ \ for \ i = 3,4, \tag{5}$$

where x is the input to node i and A_i is the linguistic label (small, large, etc.) associated with this node. In other words, $O_{1,i}$ is the membership function of a fuzzy set A_i and it specifies the degree to which the given input x satisfies the quantifier A_i. Usually $\mu_{A_i}(x)$ is chosen to bell-shaped, with a maximum equal to 1 and a minimum equal to 0, such as the generalized bell function:

$$\mu_{A_i}(x) = \frac{1}{1+\left[\left(\frac{x-c_i}{a_i}\right)^2\right]^{b_i}} \tag{6}$$

where a_i, b_i, c_i is the parameter set. As the values of these parameters change, the bell-shaped functions vary accordingly, thus exhibiting various forms of membership function on the linguistic label A_i. Parameters in this layer are referred to as premise parameters.

Layer 2: Every node in this layer is a circle node labelled $\prod$, which multiplies the incoming signal and sends the product out.

$$O_{2,i} = w_i = \mu_{Ai}(x) * \mu_{Bi}(y), \ \ i = 1,2. \tag{7}$$

Layer 3: Every node in this layer is a circle-fixed node labelled N. The i-th node calculates the ratio of the i-th rule's firing strength to the sum of all rules' firing strengths:

$$O_{3,i} = \overline{w}_i = \frac{w_i}{w_1 + w_2}, \ \ i = 1, \ 2. \tag{8}$$

For convenience, outputs of this layer are called normalized firing strengths.

Layer 4: Every node i in this layer is an adaptive square node with a node function:

$$O_{4,i} = \overline{w}_i \cdot f_i = \overline{w}_i (p_1 \cdot x + q_i \cdot y + r_i) \tag{9}$$

where $\overline{w}_i$ is a normalized firing strength from Layer 3 and $\{p_i, q_i, r_i\}$ is the parameter set in this layer. Parameters in this layer are referred to as consequent parameters.

Layer 5: The single node in this layer is a circle fixed node labelled $\sum$ that computes the overall output as the summation of all incoming signals:

$$overall\ output = O_{5,i} = \sum_i \overline{w}_i \cdot f_i = \frac{\sum_i w_i \cdot f_i}{\sum_i w_i} \tag{10}$$

This architecture develops an adaptive network that is functionally equivalent to a two-input fist-order Sugeno fuzzy model with four rules, where each input has two membership functions. The main advantage of this model is its transparency and efficiency.

2.2. Learning Algorithm of ANFIS

The learning algorithm of ANFIS is a hybrid algorithm, which is a combination of gradient descent and the least-squares method. More specifically, in the forward pass of the hybrid learning algorithm, node outputs go forward until Layer 4 and the consequent parameters are identified by the least-squares method (Jang, 1993). In the backward pass, the error signals propagate backwards and the premise parameters are updated by gradient descent. Table 1 summarizes the activities in each pass.

Table 1. Errors for one-step-ahead forecasting results

	Forward pass	**Backward pass**
Premise parameters	Fixed	Gradient descent
Consequent parameters	Least-squares estimator	Fixed
Signals	Node outputs	Error signals

The consequent parameters are optimized under the condition that the premise parameters are fixed. The main benefit of the hybrid approach is that it converges much faster since it reduces the search space dimensions of the original pure back-propagation method used in neural networks. The overall output can be expressed as a linear combination of the consequent parameters. The error measure to train the above-mentioned ANFIS is defined as (Jang, 1997):

$$E = \sum_{k=1}^{n} (y_k - \hat{y}_k)^2 \tag{11}$$

where y_k and $\hat{y}_k$ are the kth desired and estimated output, respectively, and n is the total number of pairs (inputs–outputs) of data in the training set.

2.3. Data and Model Parameters

The MATLAB fuzzy logic toolbox was used to train and evaluate the defined ANFIS models. The data set concerns quarterly time series of five Greek economic variables from March 2001 to December 2007 (in total 27 data pairs): the rate of growth of production (RP), imports prices (RIP), consumer index (RCI), rate of labor cost (RLC) and growth of the Athens Stock Exchange General Index (RASE). Figure 2 depicts a graphical representation of the five input variables. Fourteen data pairs have been used for training the models and the remaining 13 have been used to evaluate the out-of-sample performance of the resulting models. It must be mentioned that no processing of the data set has taken place.

After many trials it was decided that four of the inputs have two generalized gauss2 MFs and one input has three gauss2 MFs. Figure 3 depicts the initial shape of the gauss2 MFs before the training and the final MFs after the training (fine-tuning). Linguistically expressed, the MFs values are "low" and "high" in the case of the input variables with two MFs, and "low", "medium" and "high" in the case of the input variable with three MFs. The linguistic values are represented by the gauss2 MF type. These inference rules are as follows:

R1: If RP is low and RIP is low and RCI is low and RLC is medium and RASE is high, then ...

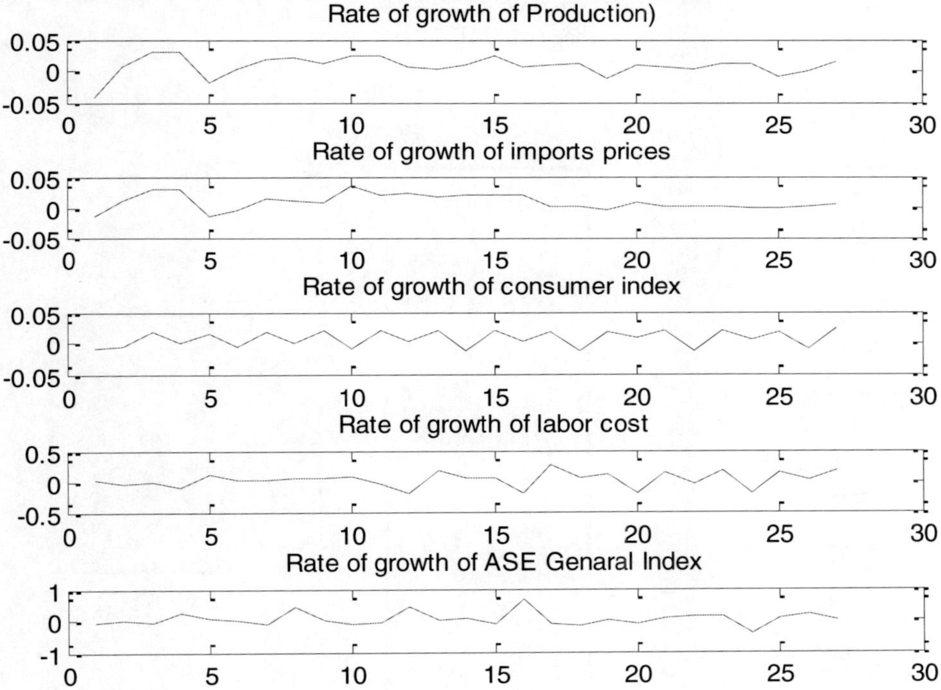

Figure 2. Graphical representation of the five input variables.

The structure of ANFIS is composed of five inputs and one output which means that the forecasting system is used to forecast the next quarter inflation rate based on the input values of the previous quarter variables. Figure 4 depicts the structure of the neuro-fuzzy model. The five input variables are fed to a Sugeno fuzzy inference model. The relevant rule activation takes place, which produces the forecasting values.

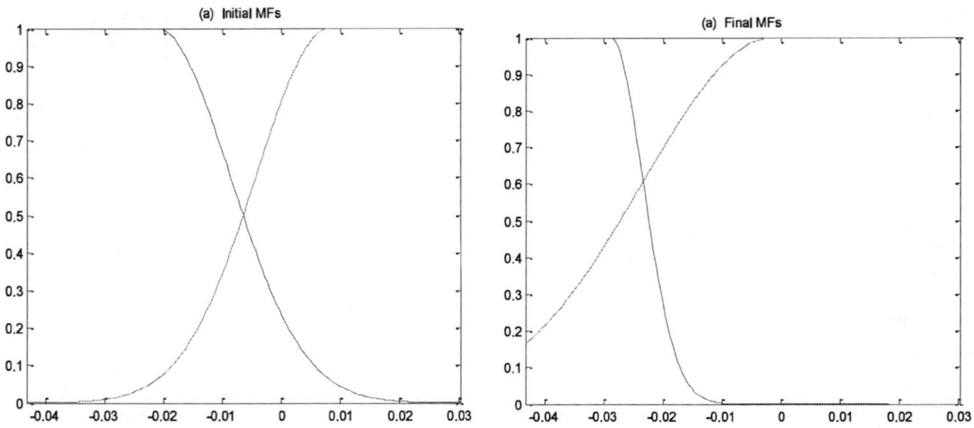

Figure 3. Initial shape and after-training shape of a MF.

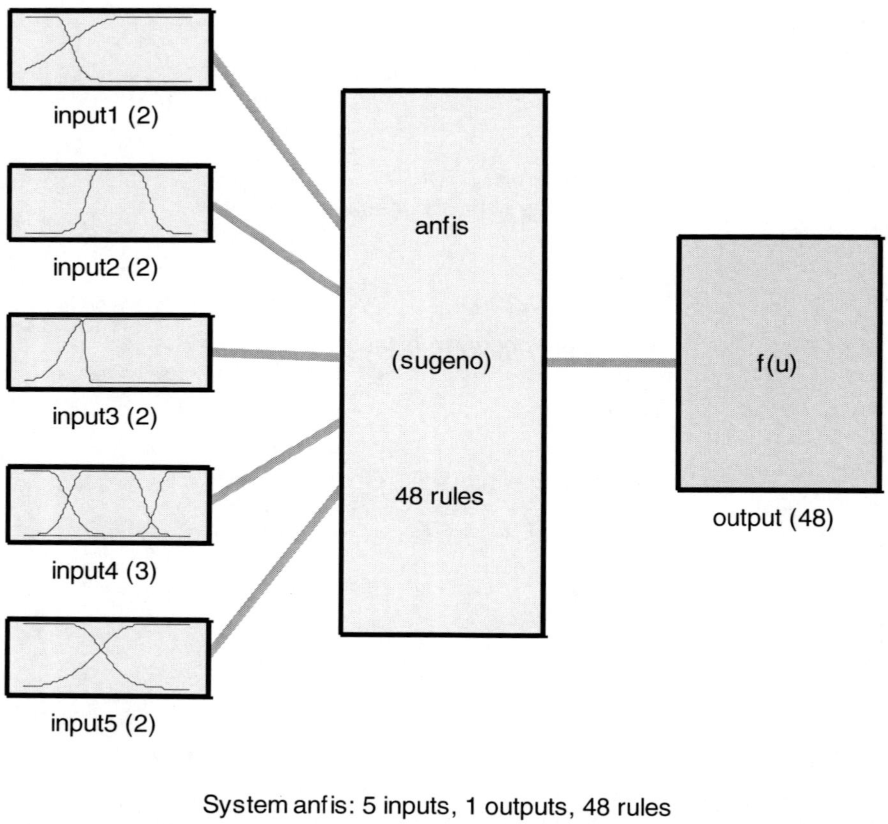

Figure 4. The structure of the suggested ANFIS model.

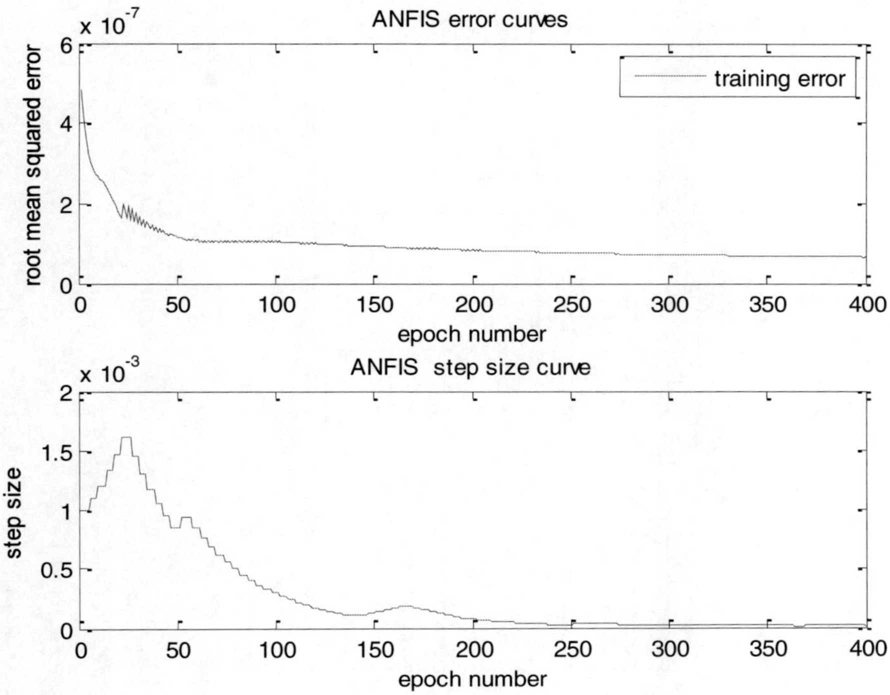

Figure 5. Error curve and step size of the suggested ANFIS model.

Table 2 describes the type and the values of the ANFIS parameters.

Table 2. ANFIS parameter types and their values used for training

ANFIS parameter type	Value
MF type	Gauus2 function
Number of MFs per input	[2 2 2 3 2]
Output MF	Linear
Number of nodes	126
Number of linear parameters	288
Number of non-linear parameters	44
Total number of parameters	332
Number of training data pairs	14
Number of evaluating data pairs	13
Number of fuzzy rules	48

The training process has been repeated until the root mean square error between the actual output and the desired output, has reached the goal of 1%. The maximum number of epochs, has been set to 400. The system has been trained for 400 epochs to converge to the optimal fuzzy inference with 48 rules. Figure 6 depicts the function of some of the rules.

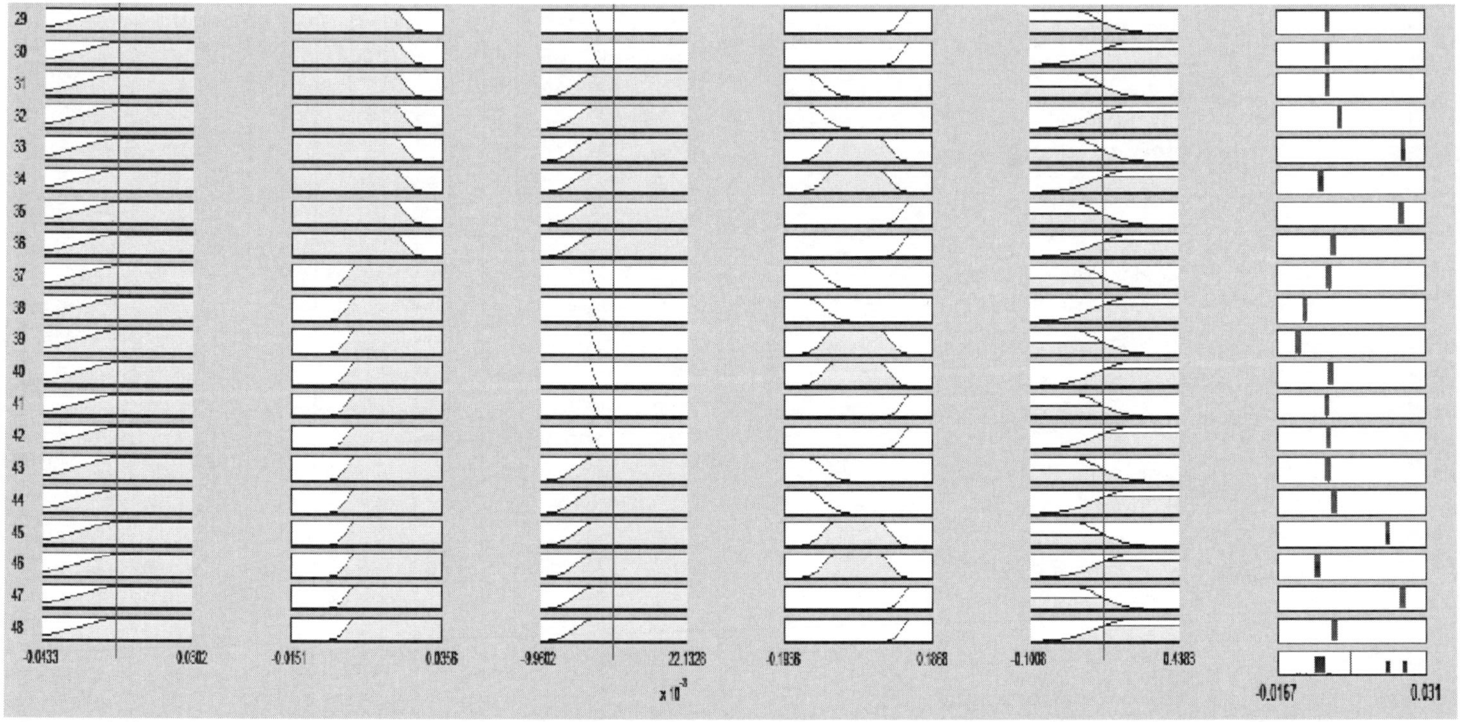

Figure 6. Some of the rules: A sample depicting the forecasting of strength by Layer 2 of the model for given inputs.

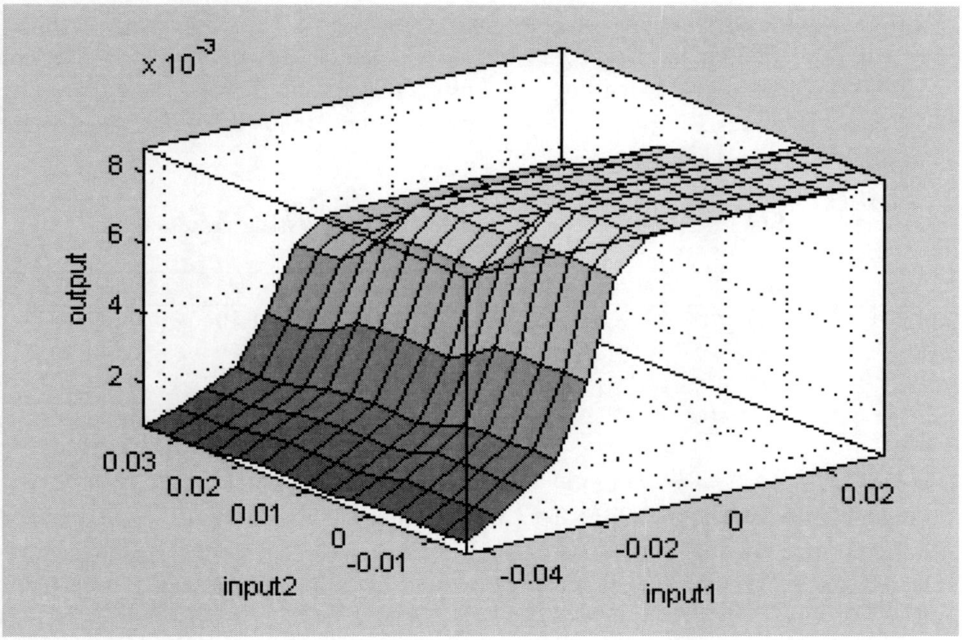

Figure 7. Fuzzy surface as depicted by the model representing an approximate relationship among two input variables.

Figure 7 illustrates a 3D representation of the control fuzzy surface as depicted by the model, representing an approximate relationship among the two of the input variables and the output of the model. The smooth distribution of the surface reconfirms the satisfactory performance results of the model.

4. Model Performance Evaluations

To evaluate the performance of the models, error analysis took place according to some well-known statistical errors: Mean square error (MSE), Root Mean Square Error (RMSE), Mean Absolute Error (MAE) and Mean Absolute Percentage Error (MAPE) (Makridakis, 1983). The observed 13 quarterly data sets, starting from December 2004 to December 2007, have been used for the out-of-sample evaluation phase.

Several simulations with all possible types of membership functions have been performed in order to select the MF type that has the lowest errors. Initially 5 models were created by using different membership function types (bell, triangular, trapezoid, gauss and gauss2 shape). The models have shown significant variations in the errors of the performance evaluation given in Table 3, with the lowest RMSE presented in bold. From all of these simulations the model with the lowest RMSE 6,63E+03 is the model that uses the gauss2 MFs. This model has been selected and used for further processing.

More simulations have been carried out in order to define the best combination of the number of the membership functions for each input variable. Keeping the gauss2 MF stable, nineteen models have been produced by using a different number of MFs per input. Table 4 presents the errors of models by combining various MFs per input. For example: in the second column, in the first line of Table 4a, the combination 2 3 3 3 3 means that the input rate of growth of production has 2 type gauss2 MFs, the rate of growth of imports prices has 3 type gauss2 MFs, the rate of growth of the consumer index has 3 gauss2 MFs, the rate of labor cost has 3 gauss2 MFs and the rate of growth of the Athens Stock Exchange General Index has 3 gauss2 MFs.

Table 3. Errors for one-month-ahead forecasting results

	Bell	Gauss2	Trap	trim	Gauss
RMSE	8,63E+03	**6,63E+03**	1,35E+04	1,21E+04	7,55E+03
MAE	7,60E+03	5,85E+03	1,11E+04	1,00E+04	6,73E+03
MAPE	5,24E+07	5,15E+07	1,06E+08	7,07E+07	5,88E+07
MSE	7,45E+01	4,39E+01	1,82E+02	1,47E+02	5,69E+01

The best model is the one with the lowest value of RMSE, which is 5728,184 E-03 (the ANFIS model with 2 2 2 3 2 MFs per input). Also MAE (4540,719 E-03) and MSE (32,81209 E-05) are low too, in contrast to MAPE which isn't. This model had presented the best generalizing ability, with a compact structure, a fast training process and a lower memory consumed.

The results of the ANFIS model have been compared to actual observations. Figure 8 shows the scatter diagram of the out-of-sample estimated values by the ANFIS model and the actual values.

Table 4a. Errors for one-quarter-ahead forecasting results

No of MFs	2 3 3 3 3	2 2 2 2 2	2 3 2 2 2	2 2 3 2 2	2 2 2 3 2	2 2 2 2 3
RMSE(E-03)	12140,14	11174,12	8459,059	6252,925	5728,184	10963,82
MAE (E-03)	10023,73	7760,503	6992,744	4634,267	4540,719	9224,659
MAPE (E+01)	70728170	129289000	60128610	48187960	52075210	79902440
MSE (E-05)	147,383	124,8609	71,55568	39,09907	32,81209	120,2054

Table 4b.

No of MFs	3 3 3 3 3	3 2 3 3 3	3 3 2 3 3	3 3 3 2 3	3 3 3 3 2	2 2 3 3 3	3 2 2 3 3
RMSE(E-03)	11787,94	14491,9	11786,7	11990,34	11591,08	12133,39	14446,12
MAE (E-03)	10131,12	10291,19	10130,62	10623,18	7243,162	10388,73	10235,42
MAPE(E+01)	80338010	73821390	80383180	82475470	49445530	81822670	73567510
MSE(E-05)	138,9556	210,0151	138,9264	143,7683	134,3531	147,2192	208,6903

Table 4c.

No of MFs	3 3 2 2 3	3 3 3 2 2	2 3 2 3 3	2 3 2 3 2	3 2 3 2 2	3 2 3 2 3
RMSE(E-03)	12031,88	7409,087	12077,26	8257,605	5864,856	7472,656
MAE (E-03)	10781,23	5932,436	9945,818	6930,124	4684,417	6266,289
MAPE (E+01)	87347740	47346550	68574900	48810490	44819060	61525980
MSE (E-05)	144,7661	54,89458	145,8602	68,18803	34,39653	55,84058

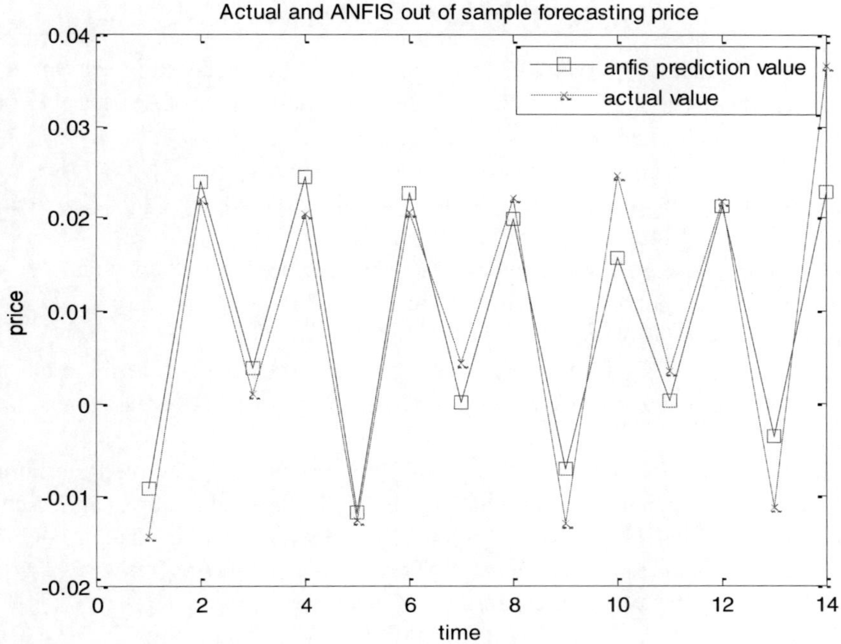

Figure 8. Out-of-sample actual and ANFIS forecasted quarterly inflation rate.

The square signs in the blue line depict the forecasting quarterly inflation rate and the asterisk in the red line depicts the actual inflation rate. The forecasting performance of ANFIS to the considered problem is satisfactory, something which clearly implies that the proposed model is working well and has an acceptable accuracy.

CONCLUSION

The stability of the prices at low levels is one of the main objectives of the monetary policies. Today inflation is used worldwide as a policy tool for maintaining price stability. For an efficiency price stability strategy an inflation rate forecasting model is considered a crucial tool to be placed in monetary policy decisions. In this paper a novel approach by an ANFIS model is addressed in order to contribute to the inflation rate forecasting problem. The results of the developed ANFIS model proved its accuracy. The data available in the form of input-output pairs can be used in ANFIS with relative ease. The proposed model, due to the generalizing ability, the compact structure, the fast training process and the lower memory consumption, can be easily used by monetary policy makers and other interested parties.

Without having solved the entire problem of inflation forecasting, the findings of this study have important managerial and practical implications.

Further improvements are still possible if more information could be inserted in the learning algorithm. Also future research could be used for normalization of the data set. In additional comparisons with other conventional or soft computing models should be carried out.

REFERENCES

Aron, Janine, Muellbauer, John, (2000), Inflation and Output Forecasting for South Africa: Monetary Transmission Implications. Centre for the Study of African Economies, Institute of Economics and Statistics, working paper.

Atsalakis, G. Makridou, G, Zopounidis, C., (2012), Forecasting Gold's price using an adaptive neuro-fuzzy inference system. *International Journal of Economics and Management,* 4, 1, 31-43.

Atsalakis, G., Dimitrakakis, E., Zopounidis, C., (2011), Elliot wave theory and neuro-fuzzy systems, in stock market prediction. The W.A.S.P. system. *Expert System with Application,* 38, 8, 9196-9206.

Atsalakis, G., Valavanis, K., (2009), Forecasting stock Market short-term trends using a neuro-fuzzy based methodology. *Journal of Expert Systems with Applications*, 36, 10696-10707.

Atsalakis, G., Belonias, L., Zopounidis, C., (2008), Federal Funds Effective Rate Forecasting by a Neuro-Fuzzy Model. Submitted in the 7th Hellenic Finnance and Accounting Association, December 12-13, 2008, Technical University of Crete, Chania.

Atsalakis G., (2007), W*ind Energy Production Forecasting by Neural Networks and Genetic Algorithms,* European Computer conference, Athens.

Atsalakis, G., Skiadas, C., Braimis, I., (2007), Probability of Trend Prediction of Exchange Rate by Neuro-Fuzzy Techniques. *Recent Advances in Stochastic Modeling and Data Analysis*. London, World Scientific Publishing Co. Pte. Ltd, 414-422.

Atsalakis, G., Minudaki, C., (2007), Prediction of Daily Irrigation Water Demand using Adaptive Neuro-Fuzzy Inference System (ANFIS), International Conference on Energy, Environment, Ecosystems and Sustainable Development. *Water Economics, Statistics and Finance,* 368-373, Ag. Nikolaos, Greece.

Atsalakis, G., Ucenic, C., (2006), Forecasting the Production Level for Wind Energy Using a Neuro- Fuzzy Model, *Journal of WSEAS Transactions on Environment and Development*, 2, 6, 823-828.

Atsalakis, G., (2005), Exchange Rate Forecasting by Neuro-Fuzzy Techniques, *Journal of Financial Decision Making,* I, 2, 15-26.

Binner, Jane, C., Elger, Thomas, C., Nilsson, Birger, Tepper, Jonathan, A., (2006), Predictable non-linearities in U.S. inflation. *Economics Letters* 93, 323–328.

Branson, W.H. & Litvack, J.M., (1981), "Macroeconomics", 2nd edition, Cambridge.

Cassel, D., (1995), "Inflation", in: *Vahlens Kompendium der Wirtschaftstheorie und Wirtschaftspolitik"*, München, 265 -323.

Chen, Xiaohong, Racine, Jeffrey, Swanson, Norman, R., (2001), Semiparametric ARX Neural-Network Models with an Application to Forecasting Inflation. *IEEE Transactions on Neural Networks,* 12, 4.

Duarte, Cláudia, Rua, António, (2007), Forecasting inflation through a bottom-up approach: How bottom is bottom? *Economic Modelling* 24, 941–953.

Gatik, N., & Karacuka, M., (2012), A comparative analysis of alternative univariate time series models in forecasting Turkish inflation. *Journal of Business Economics and Management,* 13:2, 275-293.

Granger CWJ, Terasvirta T., (1993), *Modelling nonlinear economic relationships*. Oxford: Oxford University Press, 1993.

Haider, A., Hanif, M.N., (2009), Inflation Forecasting in Pakistan using artificial neural networks. *Pakistan Economic and Social Review*, 47, 1, 123-138.

Jang, J-S.R., C-T.E. Sun and Mizutani, E., (1997), *Neuro-fuzzy and Soft Computing: a Computational Approach to Learning and Machine Intelligence*, Prentice Hall.

McNelis, Paul, McAdam, Peter, (2004), *Forecasting Inflation with Thick Models and neural networks.* Working paper series, European central bank.

Marcellino, M., (2002), "Instability and Non-Linearity in the EMU", *Working Paper* 211, Bocconi University, IGIER.

Marcellino, M., Stock, J.H., Watson, M.W., (2003), Macroeconomic forecasting in the Euro area: country specific versus area-wide information. *European Economic Review* 47, 1–18.

Nakamura, E., (2005) Inflation forecasting using a neural network. *Economics Letters*, 86, 373–378.

Pao, Y.H., (1989), *Adaptive Pattern Recognition and Neural Networks*, Addison Wesley, New York.

Shapiro, A.F., (2002), The Merging of Neural Networks, Fuzzy Logic, and Genetic Algorithms, *Insurance: Mathematics and Economics*, 31, 115-131.

Swanson, N. R., White, H., (1997), A model selection approach to real-time macroeconomic forecasting using linear models and artificial neural networks. *The Review of Economics and Statistics,* 79, 540–550.

Stock, J. H., & Watson, M. W., (1998), A comparison of linear and nonlinear univariate models for forecasting macroeconomic time series, NBER, Cambridge, MA, Working Paper.

Stock, James, H., Watson, Mark, W., (2003), Forecasting Output and Inflation: The Role of Asset Prices *Journal of Economic Literature,* XLI, 788–829.

Ucenic, C., Atsalakis, G., (2006), Forecasting the Electricity Demand Using a Neuro- Fuzzy Approach versus Traditional Methods, Journal of WSEAS Transactions on Business and Economics, 1, 3, 9-17.

Ucenic, C., Atsalakis, G., (2008), Soft Computing Methods Applied in Forecasting of Economic Indices, Case Study: Forecasting of Greek Unemployment Rate using an Artificial Neural Network with Fuzzy Inference System. *Proceedings of the 10th WSEAS International Conference on Mathematical and Computation Methods in Science and Engineering (MACMESE'08),* Bucurest.

Ucenic, C., Atsalakis, G., (2008), Soft Computing Methods Applied in Forecasting of Economic Indices, Case Study: Forecasting of Greek Unemployment Rate using an Artificial Neural Network with Fuzzy Inference System. *Proceedings of the 10th WSEAS International Conference on Mathematical and Computation Methods in Science and Engineering (MACMESE'08),* Bucurest.

Ucenic, C., & Atsalakis, G., (2009), Forecasting CPI using a neural network with fuzzy inference system. 13th *International Conference on Applied Stochastic Models and Data Analysis.* Vilnius Lithuania

Ucenic, C., Atsalakis, G., (2006), Forecasting the Electricity Demand Using a Neuro- Fuzzy Approach versus Traditional Methods, *Journal of WSEAS Transactions on Business and Economics*, 1, 3, 9-17.

Zhang G, Patuwo BE, Hu MY, (1998), Forecasting with artificial neural networks: The state of the art. *International Journal of Forecasting*, 14, 35-62.

Zhang, G., Patuwo, B. E., & Hu, M. Y., (1998), Forecasting with artificial neural networks: The state of the art. *International Journal of Forecasting*, 14, 35–62.

In: Computational Data Analysis Techniques ISBN: 978-1-63463-957-6
Editors: M. Doumpos, C. Zopounidis and Ch. Gaganis

Chapter 4

THE VALUE OF IPRS AND COMPETITIVENESS REGARDING FDI: LINEAR AND NON-LINEAR ANALYSIS

Georgios I. Zekos
Democritus University of Thrace, Greek

ABSTRACT

FDI is above all significant because it is both a source of capital and a provider of knowledge about production techniques. IPRs, granted by patents, copyrights, trademarks, etc., perform a significant role in promoting innovation and sustaining economic growth. There is a complementarity of IPRs and Competitiveness regarding FDI. *IPRs* (*zekipr2*) (Zekos 2012) seems to be a valuable variable for a price higher than Competitiveness (*GCI*) regarding FDI stocks & FDI inflows on merchandise & services. Besides, *zekipr2* is a valuable variable for a high price concerning FDI on tertiary sector.

1. INTRODUCTION

Foreign direct investment (FDI) embodying capital and technology or some intangible advantage is the act of establishing or acquiring a foreign subsidiary over which the investing company has extensive management control. There are modes of FDI such as mergers and acquisitions, joint venture and new plant with its own distinctive characteristics, advantages, and disadvantages. In order to survive competition in a foreign market, a company must possess some ownership-specific assets such as proprietary knowledge, technology, organizational structure, management or marketing skills. In this regard FDI is above all significant because it is both a source of capital and a provider of knowledge about production techniques.

The spreading recognition of the importance of competition has been supplemented by a persistent process of globalization and a clear raise in the elimination of obstacles to the flows of trade and global investment (A. Fiebig 2000). National competition laws have their bounds and limits hence they are powerless to tackle successfully international restraints. Moreover, national competition laws can converge towards some common points and standards and as a consequence there is an effort for competition law enforcement to become extra-territorial over the years because there is need to internationalize competition law. It is argued that bilateral cooperation, introduction of International competition code and harmonization and convergence of national competition systems could lead into an International system of competition law (R. Weintraub (1999)).

Productive efficiency suggests that costs of creating goods are diminished. Allocative efficiency purports that market prices for goods are close to the incremental production costs. Dynamic efficiency indicates that the suitable amount of innovation takes place for both creating new products and falling costs of existing ones. To that extent, competition is a mechanism which has the only mission of bringing about allocative effectiveness. Competition in a market economy generates, preserves, and augments all three types of efficiency. Antitrust/competition law maintains the business environment as a result that this competition can thrive. Departure from competition means a loss of allocative and perhaps productive efficiency.

Additionally, competition law should facilitate welfare concerning static and dynamic efficiency. Innovation and diffusion of new products and technologies is a key result effective competition should bring about named as 'dynamic efficiency'. The trademark of competition law is the protection of those principles and practices which facilitate the efficient functioning of markets. The majority of the world's systems of competition law share many common features including prohibitions on certain horizontal agreements such as cartels, specified vertical restraints and abuses of market power by companies. Moreover, sloppy competition law enforcement by countries produces ambiguity generating incentives for companies to consider these countries as 'competition law havens' leading to distortions of competition in the countries involved and beyond.

Intellectual property rights (IPRs), granted by patents, copyrights, trademarks, etc., perform a significant role in promoting innovation and sustaining economic growth and so allowing their holders to keep out, for a limited amount of time, other parties from the remuneration arising from new knowledge and from the commercial use of innovative products and developments based on that new knowledge providing the motivation for parties to allot financial and human resources in research and development (R & D) to reach new discoveries, innovative products and production methods.

What does intellectual property mean to companies? In the post-industrialized epoch, physical goods and assets play minor roles in company's growth. It could be argued that the earnings of utilizing knowledge assets could be expanded by increasing returns, integration with information technology and new perspective to intellectual property rights. Increasing returns, integration with information technology and new perspective to intellectual property rights build up firm basis for companies' growth and innovation and so intellectual property rights can't assist companies entirely flourishing alone without bringing other two factors into consideration.

In a knowledge-driven economy, the successful protection of IPR is emerging as a crucial ingredient of commercial triumph. With escalating levels of international trade, the quantity of trade concerning IPR increases, triggering noteworthy assets to be devoted to efficient protection. The digital revolution and other technological breakthroughs of the past several decades have brought intellectual property to the front position of economic, social, and political interest.

Positive law and economics utilizes economic analysis to predict the consequence of various legal rules and in general states that common law is effective, while normative law and economics makes policy suggestions based on the economic consequences of a mixture of policies and in general states that the law should be resourceful. It can be said that positive analysis illustrates, explains and predicts, while normative analysis compares alternatives and proposes solutions.

Aim of the article is the legal and economic examination & proof of the complementarity of IPRs and competition regarding FDI. Firstly, FDI, Competition and IPRs backgrounds will be presented. Secondly, the interrelation of competition and IPR from a legal point of view will be investigated. Thirdly, the outcome of the legal investigation will be valued independently and in combination by way of correlation between our IPR index (Zekos 2012) and GCI (the Global Competitiveness Index 2010–2011). Finally, an economic assessment of the impact of competition and IPR upon FDI by a way of linear and non-linear regression's analysis will be illustrated.

2. FDI Background

FDI assumes importance as it can generate shifts in consumption, production and technology. While the crucial participants in FDI activity include the capital-importing host country as well as the investing company, the capital-exporting home country too has an imperative role to play. FDI supposed to flow from capital-rich economies to capital-poor economies with somewhat higher rates of return to capital. Moreover, FDI is far from monolithic but covers many different types of investment activities (IMF, 2010).

A majority of FDI can be categorized into one of three forms of production - resource-seeking, efficiency-seeking, and market-seeking (Caves 2007; Cohen 2007). Efficiency-seeking FDI entails locating a part of the production process abroad to reduce overall costs and increase competitiveness. Market-seeking FDI is as a rule a horizontal production structure. There is a range of studies concerning the determinants of FDI but even though the Duninng's OLI paradigm (1977) provides some guidance it does not offer a fixed list of probable variables to test. It has to be taken into consideration the comparative importance of different determinants for various types of FDI (Blonigen, 2005) but many heterogeneous determinants may be categorized under three headings: institutional factors (the security of property rights, effectiveness of the legal system), market related factors and technological factors. Which is the interrelation and impact of IPRs and competitiveness upon FDI?

3. Competition Background

Freedom of competition covers the freedom of companies to choose their action parameters besides market power might impede both freedom of choice between different suppliers and freedom to decide on companies' action parameters in competition with other companies. Competition law has to take into account the effects of restrictive agreements, mergers, and business behavior on consumer welfare and also on a set of protected rights of competitors which might undergo losses through the infringements of these rights.

There is competition in the market versus competition for the market and competition in innovative industries is best pictured as a sequence of races to develop new technologies. Technological opportunity and winner-take-all or winner-take-most outcomes suggest that the form of competition that matters most from a welfare point of view is not that which takes place *in* a product market as is the case for mature industries. It is competition *for* the product market which means a race to be the first to bring a new product to market or to produce by means of a new technology. In contrast to mature industries where new participants gradually acquire market share, successful entry in innovative industries often results in a rapid replacement of the dominant incumbent. An increase of competition in a leveled industry lowers each company's profit ("level effect") (Boone, 2001). An escalation of competition in an un-leveled industry shrinks the profit of the least competent company but it improves the profit of the most competent company provided competition is intense "variance effect". As the technological gap between the most competent company and the least competent company enhances, stronger competitive force lowers the amount of active companies in the market.

The EU Commission has stipulated that the consumer welfare standard should be the only normative standard. In the DG Competition discussion paper it is argued that the aim of the application of Art. 82 is the 'protection of competition on the market as a means of enhancing consumer welfare and of ensuring an efficient allocation of resources. [...] That means, it is competition and not competitors as such that it is to be protected.' The existence of Articles 81 (*Article 101* TFEU) and 82 (*Article 102* TFEU) in the EU Treaty provides frameworks to protect against concerted practices as well as exclusionary conduct by dominant companies. Moreover, the core objectives of the competition policy within EU are market integration, equity, and effectiveness persuading companies to carry on and modify themselves to the technical advancement as well as rationalizing their manufacture and supply (Kent, 2008).

The key purpose of competition law, on the one hand, is to regulate company behavior that might impair the competitive process. Competition policy (or "antitrust policy" in American terminology) is, accordingly, of central substance for the effective functioning of market economies (Vickers 2005). Competition policy allows that in some conditions, society would be better off by permitting for limited market restrictions, monopolistic profits and short-term allocative inefficiencies, when these can be confirmed to advance dynamic efficiency and long-term economic growth. Etro (2007) verified that high market concentration is in fact a result of tough both price and non-price competition rather than an indicator of market power and lack of competitive forces when environment of free entry prevail but the existence of a market leader can further boost the competitive force and the roughness of price competition.

4. IPR Background

Intellectual property is a legal means by which the inventor can rule entry and rule out users from intangible assets. Each mode of intellectual property protection has discrete characteristics and limitations. Managing intellectual property is no more a legal department's affair because it involves from legal documents to strategic assets. Above all, companies are used to delineating intellectual assets in the perspective of firm legal definitions of intellectual property focusing on restricting the use, sale, and transfer of intellectual capital in forms such as patents and copyrights. On the contrary, leveraging intellectual capital entails that managers carefully advance rather than restrict its use, reflecting an expansionist attitude rather than a reductionist one seeking out opportunities. Thus, development and exploitation of intellectual property assets should concentrate on worth extraction and maximization, rather than mere legal documentation or cost minimization. Intellectual capital has emerged as the foremost unique competitive advantage of companies and so intellectual capital commercialization doesn't occur from licensing, payoff through litigation only, but takes place from appropriately merging physical assets, business strategy, and intellectual assets to obtain profit and growth. The strength of IPRs affects not only the location choices of MNEs but also the quality of technological knowledge they decide to transfer (Javorcik, 2004).

IPRs are not based on the same economic rationale as competition rules. Frequently, IP law is articulated in a non-economic term. IP rules has as one of its aims to stimulate dynamic efficiency, which is more expected to be in an economic sense (Drexl, 2008). Moreover, knowledge, when produced, is an IPR that gives the right to employ it in a way which gives prospective innovators economic motivation to innovate (Drexl, 2008). The grant of a patent swaps a decline in allocative and maybe productive static efficiency for expand in innovative activity having satisfactory incentives to innovate despite the rights granted to an early innovator. Consequently, the extent of monopoly awarded by a patent has to be limited so as not to intervene with the incentive to innovate of succeeding innovators. Patents may grant legal monopoly rights in more than one antitrust market but the ownership of a patent does not burden the patent owner with a presupposition that it possesses monopoly power in any specific market (*Tool Works Inc* case (2006)).

The significance of IPRs varies to a large extent by variables such as the technological nature of the activity and the nature of the economy. Antitrust studies business conduct based on existing property rights. Any property right, rooted in real or intellectual property, can be abused in business conduct resulting in an antitrust violation (*Microsoft Corp.* case 2001). It is very difficult to predict a conflict between the granting of patents and antitrust rules at the time of the grant due to the time separating the patent examination and the prospective antitrust violation, and numerous other factors involved how the patent holder develops products and accomplishes market power. Patent examiners do not think about prospective antitrust violations prior to granting a patent.

The key objective of intellectual property law is the backing of new and improved works—whether technological or expressive. The other rationale of intellectual property law deals with a distinctive economic problem—ensuring the integrity of the marketplace. Moreover, the rationale of intellectual property law is to advance innovation and productive knowledge creation. The legal exceptionality established by intellectual property rights cuts down transaction costs, promotes dissemination of knowledge and inspires investment in valuable ideas consistent with the underlying principles of market economies (Scotchmer (2004)).

A vital target of intellectual property law is to reward innovation and creation throughout the granting of exclusive rights to utilize a new invention, new information or a cultural good. The return deriving from IPRs is directly correlated to the duration as well as the scope of those rights. In fact, competition policy has a role in limiting monopolistic abuses linked to the exercise of IPRs.

In competitive economies the granting of most patents, copyrights, and trademarks amounts to a thin piece of market power that is doubtful to damage consumers. In contrast, IPR can augment dynamic competition by stirring up investments in new methods and differentiated products. Emmanuelle Auriol and Sara Biancini (2009) *say that* «increasing the level of protection in the less developed one does not always increase global welfare. We show that an incomplete protection regime in which the emerging country does not protect innovation can be preferred and this regime does not need to decrease innovation." Even though technological opportunity turns up to have increased extensively in areas such as software and biotechnology/nanotechnology, leading to more innovation, and so more patenting, patenting motion may also have increased separately of the underlying rate of innovation (Reitzig, Henkel and Schneider (2010)). Is antitrust and the protection of intellectual property complementary or conflicting? How do the antitrust laws associate with the intellectual property (IP) laws?

5. Competition Policy and the Exercise of Intellectual Property Rights

Intellectual property is at the centre of the "new economy." New economy products are characterized by declining average costs over a range of output, high rates of innovation, and network effects (Richard A. Posner,(2001)).. Intellectual property rights holders have expanded the boundaries of their claims, bringing those rights into ever-greater conflict with the primary principles (Reza Dibadj, 2003) and assumptions of the antitrust laws. Companies in "old economy" network industries (*MCI Commc'ns Corp. v. ATandT,* 708 F.2d 1081 (7th Cir. 1983)) such as telecommunications companies, and integrated electric power companies used their control over network links to exclude competitors.

At a high level of abstraction, the two bodies of laws seem complementary. Both pursue a welfare objective. IP laws do so by creating and defending the right of innovators to prohibit others from using their ideas or forms of materialization providing economic agents with the motivation to engage in efforts engendering technological innovations and new variety of artistic expression. Moreover, the US has recognized the complementary purposes of the intellectual property and antitrust laws. Antitrust laws protect forceful competition in the marketplace, while intellectual property laws protect the capability to receive a return on the investments needed to innovate. Both impel competition among competitors to be the first to enter the marketplace with a needed technology, product, or service. While IP law purposely subjects intellectual assets to the sole control of right owners, competition law seeks to preclude market barriers benefiting consumers by advancing competition among a multiplicity of suppliers of goods, services and technologies (Kovacic, 2005). According to Dolmans, O'Donoghue & Loewenthal (2007) the objectives of EU competition law and IP law are in actual fact the same promoting the progress of innovation and investment to the advantage of consumers and so dynamic efficiency is a shared objective for competition law and IP law.

IPRs, by granting legal exclusivity, may award to their holders the capacity to exercise market power which allows upholding prices above competitive levels for a considerable time and profit from such rise in prices leading to allocative inefficiencies and so owners of exclusive rights will expected to restrict output levels compared to more competitive situations, in the markets for the goods and services incorporating those rights in order to maximize their profits.

Only when alternative technologies are not accessible, IPRs can be said to confer to their holders' monopolistic positions in related markets appropriately defined. If IPRs brings monopolization then there is the actual prospect that the legal protection accorded through IPRs is too strong and the emergence of anti-competitive outcome could jeopardize social welfare. The course of innovation is constantly related to the expected appropriation of interim monopoly rents produced by the implementation of the innovation (J. A. Schumpeter (1934, 1939, 1943)). If IPRs generate additional barriers to entry for competitors then IPRs can notably change the incentives to put into operation innovative process. Cooper Feldman (1999) says that if innovation is not driven by IPRs then the legal protection plays merely the role of inhibiting entry in related markets as leveraging strategies.

There can be circumstances where IPR will grant market power, as when a patented invention controls a relevant market, acceptable under American IPR and antitrust law, key incentive to engage in innovative activities, and the IPR laws utilize that incentive to advance innovation. A violation of U.S. antitrust law involve anti-competitive conduct, conduct that is neither competition on the merits nor efficiency-enhancing excluding competitors or prospective competitors from the market enabling the IPR holder to generate, preserve, or extend its market power (Einer Elhauge and Damien Geradin, 2007, Sean P. Gates, 2006).

Competition law draws a line between allowed business strategies and abuse of IPRs, a line which is often distorted by horizontal agreements, exclusionary licensing restrictions, tie-in agreements, disproportionate utilization of IPRs and other selling practices. Moreover, there is a probable abuse of monopoly pricing, in particular in developing countries where operative substitutes to IPR-protected products may not be straight away available (L. Peeperkorn. 2003). The limited monopolies established by IPRs are not per se anti-competitive or very exploitative but they only turn into anti-competitive when the IPR holder broadens those rights further than their intended and proper scope.

The interface between IPRs and competition law has developed a number of types of restraints on competition making very complex the relation between IPR and competition (L. Peeperkorn, (2003)), The Supreme Court recognized that the antitrust and patent laws could co-exist (*United States v. Line Material Co.,* (1948)). The EU policy has evolved from a liberal approach in earlier years to more economics-centric approach echoed in the block exemption for technology transfer agreements of 2004, accompanied by the relevant Technology Transfer Guidelines, which explicitly cover patents. In *Nungesser* [1983], the ECJ concluded that exclusivity provisions did not automatically infringe Article 81. Transactions involving IPR agreements often generate abuse of dominant position under Article 82. As was made clear in *Microsoft* once again (*Microsoft,* [2007]), the simple ownership of an IPR does not constitute adequate objective justification to refuse a licence, provided other specific circumstances would point in the direction of a compulsory licence.

The exercise of exclusive IPRs which give monopolistic power leading to allocative inefficiencies is against the core objective of competition policy which is the protection of the competitive process making certain an effective allocation of resources, lower prices and greater consumer choice. The legal analysis shows that competition policy and IPR interrelate in many significant dimensions and there is a conflict between competition and IPR requiring a delicate treatment of their complimentary role in an economy which has to be affirmed by an economic investigation.

6. Data and Methodology

A large sample of 79 countries has been assembled for our research (Zekos 2013). The sample of countries is diverse representing several income groups and institutional environments Data for the independent variables, such as *GDP, Trade and Inflation,* are downloaded from the World Bank Indicators (1990-2010). The key independent variables of interest are the strength of IPRs and GCI. Using the Global Competitiveness Index 2010–2011 (GCI), the zekipr1, zekipr1a and zekipr2 we examine the linear and non-linear influence of IPRs and competitiveness upon attracting FDI. The analysis is focused on FDI stocks and FDI inflows on merchandise & services, and FDI on tertiary sector. The core of the research idea & the scope of the study are to prove in economic terms the role of IPRs and competitiveness separately and in combination for attracting FDI in an economy. This economic analysis will or will not prove the essence/ core of the legal theory regarding IPRs and Competition law in an economy. In other words the necessity and effectiveness of the current law of IPRs & competition will be verified / proved by the quantitative analysis.

Our IPR Indexes are formed after the examination of the laws in force of the investigated countries regarding IPRs till the end of 2010 by the combination of the following parts:

1. ZEKIPR= Membership in International Treaties + index of patent rights + index of copyright+ index of trade-mark rights + LR1 Legal System & Property Rights Rating (Rank) of countries (*Economic Freedom of the World: 2010 Annual Report,* Area Economic Freedom Ratings (Ranks), 2008)
2. ZEKIPR1= Index of Membership in IPR International Treaties + index of patent rights + index of copyright+ index of trade-mark rights + lr2 Legal System & Property Rights Rating (Rank) of countries (*Economic Freedom of the World: 2011 Annual Report* , Area Economic Freedom Ratings (Ranks), 2009)
3. ZEKIPR1a= Membership in International Treaties + index of patent rights + index of copyright+ index of trade-mark rights + LR3 Legal System & Property Rights Rating (Rank) of countries (Economic Freedom of the World: 2012 Annual Report, Area Economic Freedom Ratings (Rankings) for 2010)
4. ZEKIPR2= Membership in International Treaties + index of patent rights + index of copyright+ index of trade-mark rights

It is worth mentioning here that changes in IPRs' national laws of the examined jurisdictions & rating of the examined legal systems will bring changes in the index (ZEKIPR) and so it is feasible to have at any time an updated ZEKIPR index (table 1).

A linear model is in the form

$$Y_i = \beta_0 + \sum_{j=1}^{p} \beta_j X_{i,j} + \varepsilon_i,$$

where, for the *i*th case, Y_i is the response variable, $X_{i,1}, \ldots, X_{i,p}$ are *p* regressors, and ε_i is a mean zero error term. The quantities $\beta_0, \ldots, \beta_p$ are unknown coefficients, whose values are determined by least squares.

In detail, the following are the econometric models which are used in our investigation in order to find the impact of IPRs and GCI upon attracting FDI. The incorporation of both variables of IPRs (zekipr2) &: competition (GCI) will verify in economic terms their interrelation and co-impact upon FDI in an economy:

$$FDI_{it}= b_0 + b_1 GCI_{it} + b_2 GDP_{it}+ b_3 Trade_{it}+b_4 Inflation_{it} + u_{it} \quad (1)$$

$$FDI_{it}= b_0 + b_1 GCI_{it} +b_2 zekipr2_{it}+ b_3 GDP_{it}+ b_4 Trade_{it}+b_5 Inflation_{it} + u_{it} \quad (2)$$

$$FDI_{it}= b_0 + b_1 zekipr1_{it} + b_2 GDP_{it}+ b_3 Trade_{it}+b_4 Inflation_{it} + u_{it} \quad (3)$$

$$FDI_{it}= b_0 + b_1 zekipr1a_{it} + b_2 GDP_{it}+ b_3 Trade_{it}+b_4 Inflation_{it} + u_{it} \quad (4)$$

The first thing to notice is the two subscripts: i to denote the *i*th individual country and t to denote the *t*th time period. *FDI* represents: FDI Stocks, FDI inflows on merchandise & services, and FDI on tertiary sector respectively. b_0 is the intercept and *Zekipr1, zekipr1a, Zekipr2, GCI, GDP, Trade and Inflation* are the explanatory variables.

Gross domestic product (GDP) refers to the market value of all final goods and services produced within a country in a given period. Inflation (macro stability) is known to be negatively associated with FDI in the *pull* factors literature (Lin and Ye, 2009). The governments of nations demand the central bank to preserve a low, positive rate of inflation (Miller, R.L.; Benjamin, D.K 2004).

Predictions about the relationship between FDI and trade critically depend on whether FDI is vertical or horizontal. Whereas trade connected with cross-border vertical integration may enhance the outflow of FDI by providing incentives of cost reduction, intra industry trade may inhibit FDI that is seeking economies of scale (Goldar and Banga, 2005).

7. Empirical Results

The following table shows the correlation among the variables:

	zekipr1	zekipr2	zekipr1a	gci	trade1~v	inf10yav	l~p10yav
zekipr1	1.0000						
zekipr2	0.9171	1.0000					
Zekipr1a	0.9980	0.9156	1.0000				
gci	0.7311	0.4660	0.7282	1.0000			
trade10yav	-0.0427	0.0034	-0.0337	-0.0977	1.0000		
inf10yav	-0.4756	-0.2687	-0.4777	-0.6652	0.1342	1.0000	
loggdp10yav	0.4091	0.3455	0.3958	0.6208	-0.2068	-0.3046	1.0000

The correlation between the Global Competitiveness Index 2010–2011 and zekipr1/zekipr1a is 0.7311/ 0.7282 and so there is a high collinearity which does not allow as a regression with both variables. Besides, the correlation between GCI and zekipr2 is 0.4660 and so there is not high collinearity allowing us to utilize a regression with both variables.

7.1. Linear Results

The linear effects of IPRs and GCI upon FDI are complimentary. While the significance of GCI regarding FDI stocks utilizing model 1(Coef. 1.03***, 0.84***, 0.81***, 0.88***, 0.85***) is similar to the one of IPRs based on our index zekipr1 utilizing model 3 (Coef. 1.30***, 1.31***, 1.29***, 1.46***, 1.42***). We keep on our investigation with model 4 using OLS standardized coefficients or beta coefficients and the results indicate that ZEKIPR1a is a very significant variable regarding FDI stocks (Coef. 1.27***, 1.28***, 1.26***, 1.44***, 1.39***) concerning 10, 5, 3, 2 years average & 2010 reference. The significance of GCI is less important regarding FDI on merchandise & services (Coef. 0.98***, 0.68*)/ tertiary sector (Coef. 0.83*, 0.84*) showing that IPRs are more significant for the specific FDI on merchandise & services/ tertiary sector rather than the less considerable role of competitiveness. The regressions are based upon data of ten years average, five years average , three years average and the 2010 regarding FDI stocks and ten years average, five years average concerning FDI on merchandise & services/ tertiary sector (*** $p<0.001$, ** $p<0.01$, * $p<0.05$).

We carry on our investigation with model 2 using OLS standardized coefficients or beta coefficients and the results show that IPRs, expressed by our zekipr2 index, are less significant (Coef. 0.74*, 0.96**, 0.95**, 1.06**, 0.98**) than GCI (Coef. 0.91***, 0.72***, 0.70***, 0.79***, 0.77***) in FDI stocks and more significant than GCI for FDI on merchandise & services/ tertiary sector (table 2) proving the importance of IPRs for the specific type of FDI based mainly on the award of IPRs.

7.2. Non-Linear Results

The following table shows the value of the GCI:

	Percentiles	Smallest		
1%	3.03	3.03		
5%	3.48	3.32		
10%	3.55	3.38	Obs	79
25% .	3.96	3.48	Sum of Wgt	79
50%	4.33		Mean	4.392658
		Largest	Std. Dev.	.6230873
75%	4.91	5.43		
90%	5.33	5.48	Variance	.3882377
95%	5.43	5.56	Skewness	.1334164
99%	5.63	5.63	Kurtosis	2.216257

Firstly, we start our investigation with the non-linear price of GCI and model 1.

1) FDI stocks Model 1 GCI 25%, 50%, 75% beta coefficients

We continue our investigation with model 1 using OLS standardized coefficients or beta coefficients and the results show that GCI is significant for a value of GCI >25% (Coef. 0.82***, 0.66**) and not significant for value of GCI<25% (Coef. 0.96, 0.94) regarding FDI stocks. GCI is the second more significant variable after GDP. In addition, the results show that GCI is significant for a value of GCI < 50% (Coef. 1.35***, 1.23**) and not significant for value of GCI > 50% (Coef. 0.66, 0.62) regarding FDI stocks. Moreover, the results show that GCI is significant for a value of GCI < 75% (Coef. 1.06***, 0.82**) and not significant for value of GCI > 75% (Coef. 2.37*, 1.85) regarding FDI stocks but it seems that the significance of GCI for value >75% & < 75% remains for the long term of 10 years reference. The regressions are based upon data of ten years average & five years average (*** $p<0.001$, ** $p<0.01$, * $p<0.05$). GCI is significant for a price not very low but not a very high as well

2) FDI on merchandise & services/ tertiary sector Model 1 GCI 25%, 50%, 75% beta coefficients

On the one hand, our investigation with model 1 using OLS standardized coefficients or beta coefficients concerning FDI on merchandise & services shows that GCI is significant for a value of GCI 25% (>25% Coef., 0.73**, 0.74**, for < 25% Coef. 2.01, 1.75), a value of GCI 50% (> 50 % Coef. 0.62, 0.68, for < 50% Coef. 1.65**, 1.60*), and a value of GCI 75% (>75% Coef. 2.24, 1.62, for < 75% Coef. 1.11***, 0.89*) which is similar regarding FDI stocks.

On the other hand, we continue our investigation with model 1 using OLS standardized coefficients or beta coefficients and the results (table 3) show that GCI is significant for a value of GCI <25% and not significant for value of GCI>25% regarding FDI on tertiary sector. GCI is the first variable in significance even higher than GDP which means that a low value of GCI is significant for FDI on tertiary sector where IPRs is the basis for FDI on tertiary sector. In addition, the results (table 4) show that GCI is significant for a value of GCI <50% and not significant for value of GCI>50% regarding FDI on tertiary sector. GCI is becoming the second in significance variable after GDP but close in the importance for a higher value of GCI. Moreover, the results (table 5) show that GCI is not significant for a value of GCI <75% & > 75% regarding FDI on tertiary sector which indicates that a high level of competitiveness is not valuable in attracting FDI on tertiary sector.

Secondly, we continue our analysis with the non- linear price of zekipr2 and model 2.

The following table shows the value of zekipr2:

Percentiles	Smallest			
1%	2.76264	2.76264		
5%	2.86264	2.79945		
10%	2.94011	2.85879	Obs 79	
25%	3.04286	2.86264	Sum of Wgt. 79	
50%	3.31319		Mean	3.278342

	Largest		Std. Dev. .2418581
75%	3.49121	3.64451	
90%	3.57857	3.65714	Variance .0584953
95%	3.64451	3.69451	Skewness -.1919101
99%	3.7489	3.7489	Kurtosis 2.04742

3) FDI stocks Model 2 zekipr2 25%, 50%, 75% beta coefficients

We persist our investigation with model 2 & independent variables *zekipr2/ 25%* using OLS standardized coefficients or beta coefficients regarding FDI stocks and the results show a negative importance of *zekipr2* for a price <25 (Coef. -3.37, -2.9, -2.63, -2.50) and a significance for *GCI* (Coef. 1.79**, 1.32*, 1.30*, 1.82*) but the significance of *zekipr2* rises for a price>25% (Coef. 0.99*, 1.27**, 1.27**, 1.30*) remaining behind a more significant *GCI (Coef. 0.80***, 0.70**, 0.66**, 0.70**)*. GCI is valuable for a price of zekipr2< 25% or >25% in contrast to *zekipr2* where the significance of the variable is only for a price of >25%.

We keep on our investigation with model 2 & independent variables *zekipr2/ 50%* using OLS standardized coefficients or beta coefficients regarding FDI stocks and the results show that *zekipr2* is negative in importance for a price of <50% (Coef. -0.10, -0.03, 0.13, -0.01) with a rising importance for a price of >50% (Coef. 1.53, 1.92, 1.94, 1.78) remaining after *GCI* in importance but *GCI* is more significant for a price <50% (Coef. 1.17***, 0.99***, 0.96***, 1.10***) and a less importance for a price of >50% (Coef. 0.80*, 0.65, 0.62, 0.63). GCI is valuable for a price of zekipr2< 50% and not so valuable for a price of zekipr2 >50% in contrast to *zekipr2* where the significance of the variable is not valuable for a price of >50% and even negative for a price of <50%..

We carry on our investigation with model 2 & independent variables *zekipr2/ 75%* using OLS standardized coefficients or beta coefficients regarding FDI stocks and the results show that *zekipr2* is not significant for a price of <75% & >75% (Coef. -0.04, 0.47,-0.01, 0.68, 0.01, 1.04, 0.01, 1.21) and *GCI* is very significant for a price of <75% (Coef. 1.10***, 0.95***, 0.92***, 1.04***) and a less one for a price of >75% (Coef. . 0.54, 0.46, 0.48, 0.50). GCI is valuable for a price of zekipr2< 75% and not so valuable for a price of zekipr2 >75% in contrast to zekipr2 where the significance of the variable is not valuable for a price of >75% & <75%.

4) FDI on merchandise & services Model 2 zekipr2 25%, 50%, 75% beta coefficients

We continue our investigation with model 2 & independent variables *zekipr2/ 25%* using OLS standardized coefficients or beta coefficients regarding FDI inflows on merchandise & services and the results show a negative importance of *zekipr2* for a price <25% (Coef. -2.44, -0.49) and a non-significance for *GCI* (Coef. 1.00, -0.39) but the significance of *zekipr2* rises for a price>25% (Coef. 1.23*, 1.32*) remaining behind a more significant *GCI (Coef. 0.79**, 0.89***)*. GCI is more valuable than zekipr2 for a price of zekipr2> 25% and not so valuable for a price of zekipr2<25% like *zekipr2* regarding FDI on merchandise & services.

We persist in our investigation with model 2 & independent variables *zekipr2/ 50%* using OLS standardized coefficients or beta coefficients regarding FDI inflows on merchandise & services and the results show that *zekipr2* is less important for a price of <50% (Coef. 0.78, 1.17) with a rising importance for a price of >50% (Coef. 1.58, 1.58) remaining after *GCI* in importance but *GCI* is more significant for a price <50% (Coef. 0.92*, 0.51/ p value 0.016, 0.289) and less important for a price of>50% (Coef. 0.72*, 0.68/ p value 0.028 , 0.060) .

GCI is important for a price of *zekipr2* >50% & <50% and the long term reference of ten years.

We maintain our investigation with model 2 & independent variables *zekipr2/ 75%* using OLS standardized coefficients or beta coefficients regarding FDI inflows on merchandise & services and the results show that zekipr2 is less important for a price of <75% (Coef. 1.54, 2.30) and a rising importance for a price of >75% (Coef. 0.70, 0.79) remaining after GCI in importance regarding FDI inflows on merchandise & services but GCI is more significant for a price >75% (Coef. 0.88**, 0.56) and a less importance for a price of<75% (Coef. 0.53, 0.56). GCI is important for a price of zekipr2 <75% and only for the long term reference of ten years.

5) FDI on tertiary sector Model 2 zekipr2 25%, 50%, 75% beta coefficients

We carry on our investigation with model 2 & independent variables *zekipr2/ 25%* using OLS standardized coefficients or beta coefficients regarding FDI inflows on tertiary sector and the results show that *zekipr2* is significant for a price of >25% (Coef. 2.68**, 2.84**) and a negative one for a price of <25% (Coef. -4.64, -2.66) and *GCI* is less significant for a price of >25% (Coef. 0.75*, 0.76*) (<25% Coef. 0.70, 0.73) than *zekipr2* on the tertiary sector which is the one with the vast majority of IPRs. Hence, the development of the tertiary sector is not possible with a low level of IPRs protection and GCI is significant of a price of zekipr2 >25%. GCI is less significant for a price of zekipr2 <25% regarding FDI on tertiary sector.

We maintain our investigation with model 2 & independent variables *zekipr2/ 50%* using OLS standardized coefficients or beta coefficients regarding FDI inflows on tertiary sector and the results show that *zekipr2* is significant for a price of >50% (Coef. 2.04*, 2.59**/ p value 0.038, 0.009,) and a negative one for a price of <50% (Coef -0.17, -0.97). While *GCI* is less significant for price >50% (Coef. 0.65, 1.16, 0.53, 0.59*/ p value 0.050) than *zekipr2, GCI* is not in a negative scale than the *zekipr2* for a price of <50%. The variable *zekipr2* is important for a price of >50% regarding FDI on tertiary sector.

We go on our investigation with model 2 & independent variables *zekipr2/ 75%* using OLS standardized coefficients or beta coefficients regarding FDI inflows on tertiary sector and the results (table 6) show that *zekipr2* is less significant for a price of >75% & <75% than the significance of *GCI* regarding FDI on tertiary sector. Both variables are not significant for a price of *zekipr2*>75% & <75% regarding FDI inflows on tertiary sector.

Thus, low level of IPR's protection leads not only to insignificance of IPRs in attracting FDI but also to a negative impact upon attracting FDI. On the other hand, a higher level of IPR's protection reverses the importance of IPRs in exerting a pull on FDI. The above regressions show that competitiveness is more important than IPR in a low level of IPR protection but IPR becomes more important in a higher level of IPR protection.

Thirdly, we maintain our examination with non- linear price of GCI and model 2

6) FDI on stocks Model 2 GCI 25%, 50%, 75% beta coefficients

We persist our investigation with model 2 & independent variables GCI/ *25%* using OLS standardized coefficients or beta coefficients regarding FDI stocks and the results show non importance of *zekipr2* for a price <25 (Coef. 0.22, 0.67, 0.83, 0.83) and non-significance for *GCI* (Coef. 0.76, 0.34, 0.39, 0.65) but the significance of *zekipr2* rises for a price>25% (Coef. 0.93*, 1.01*,0.92*, 0.87/ p value 0.020, 0.011, 0.020, 0.067) remaining behind a more significant *GCI (Coef.0.74**, 0.62**, 0.57*,0.64**/ p value 0.002 ,0.010, 0.014, 0.007)*. GCI is second in importance variable after GDP and Zekipr2 is third one after GCI. GCI is more significant than zekipr2 for a price of *GCI>25%*.

We keep on our investigation with model 2 & independent variables GCI/ *50%* using OLS standardized coefficients or beta coefficients regarding FDI stocks and the results show that *zekipr2* is important for a price of <50% (Coef. 0.80, 1.24**, 1.27**,1.20*/ p value 0.009, 0.007, 0.012) with a less importance for a price of >50% (Coef. 0.50, 0.48, 0.39, 0.42) but *GCI* is less significant for a price <50% & >50% (Coef. 0.90, 0.59, 0.59, 0.77, 0.65 ,0.62, 0.62, 0.73). GCI is not valuable for a price <50% & >50% while zekipr2 is important for a price of GCI <50%.

We retain our investigation with model 2 & independent variables GCI/ *75%* using OLS standardized coefficients or beta coefficients regarding FDI stocks and the results show that *zekipr2* is not significant for a price of >75% (Coef. 1.14, 1.32, 0.96, 1.00) and significant for a price of <75% (Coef. 0.78*, 1.00**, 1.00**, 1.04**/ p value 0.016, 0.002, 0.002, 0.003) and *GCI* is significant for a price of <75% (Coef. 0.86**, 0.65*, 0.61*, 0.66*/ p value 0.013, 0.017, 0.015) and not significant for a price of >75% (Coef. .2.20, 1.65, 1.52, 1.98). There is an interrelation of significance between zekipr2 and GCI showing the complementary of the two variables. GCI is valuable like zekipr2 for a price of GCI < 75%.

7) FDI on merchandise & services/ tertiary sector Model 1 GCI 25%, 50%, 75% beta coefficients

We keep on our investigation with model 2 & independent variables GCI/ *25%* using OLS standardized coefficients or beta coefficients regarding FDI inflows on merchandise & services and the results show a non-importance of *zekipr2* for a price <25% (Coef.1.21, 1.49) and a non-significance for *GCI* (Coef. 0.91, 0.42) but the significance of *zekipr2* rises for a price>25% (Coef.1.04*,0.90*/ p value 0.020, 0.045) remaining behind a more significant *GCI (Coef.0.64*,0.70*/ p value 0.012, 0.010)*. There is significance of both variables for a price GCI>25% with a slight superiority of GCI concerning FDI inflows on merchandise & services.

We maintain our investigation with model 2 & independent variables GCI/ *50%* using OLS standardized coefficients or beta coefficients regarding FDI inflows on merchandise & services and the results show importance of *zekipr2* for a price <50% and only for ten years reference (Coef. 1.17*, 1.34/ p value 0.046) , a non-significance for *GCI* (Coef. 0.99, 0.90) and non-significance of *zekipr2* for a price>50% (Coef. 0.75, 0.67) similarly to a non-significant *GCI (Coef. 0.62,0.68)*. GCI is not valuable like *zekipr2* for a price of <50% />50%.

We continue our investigation with model 2 & independent variables GCI/ *75%* using OLS standardized coefficients or beta coefficients regarding FDI inflows on merchandise & services and the results show importance of *zekipr2* for a price <75% higher for the long term reference (Coef. 1.20**, 1.24*/ p value 0.002, 0.015) , a less significance for *GCI* (Coef.0.81**, 0.66/ p value 0.009) and non-significance of *zekipr2* for a price>75% (Coef. 1.34,1.30) similarly to a non-significant *GCI (Coef. 2.03, 1.42)*. GCI is less valuable than *zekipr2* for a price of <75%.

8) FDI on tertiary sector Model 1 GCI 25%, 50%, 75% beta coefficients

We carry on our investigation with model 2 & independent variables GCI/ *25%* using OLS standardized coefficients or beta coefficients regarding FDI inflows on tertiary sector and the results (table 7) show that *zekipr2* is significant for a price of >25% (Coef.2.59***, 1.90**/ p value0.001, 0.007) and a negative one for a price of <25% (Coef. -1.36, -1.33). *GCI* is non-significant for a price of >25% (Coef.0.50, 0.60) but GCI is significant for a price of <25% (Coef. 5.51**, 5.28*/ p value 0.003, 0.036). *zekipr2's* significance seems to be higher than GCI on the tertiary sector which is the one with the vast majority of IPRs. Hence, the development of the tertiary sector is not possible with a low level of IPRs protection. GCI is significant for a price of GCI <25% but zekipr2 is significant for a price of GCI >25%.

We continue our investigation with model 2 & independent variables GCI/ *50%* using OLS standardized coefficients or beta coefficients regarding FDI inflows on tertiary sector and the results (table 8) show that *zekipr2* is significant for a price of >50% only for ten years reference (Coef. 2.45*, 1.85/ p value 0.016) and non-significant for a price of <50% (Coef. 1.19, 1.41) and *GCI* is non-significant for a price of >50% (Coef.0.42, 0.56) & a price of <50% (Coef. 1.48, 1.35). GCI is not valuable like *zekipr2* for a price of <50% />50%.

We uphold our investigation with model 2 & independent variables GCI/ *75%* using OLS standardized coefficients or beta coefficients regarding FDI inflows on tertiary sector and the results (table 9) show that *zekipr2* is significant for a price of <75% (Coef. 2.11**,1.83** / p value0.004, 0.010) and non-significant for a price of >75% (Coef. 2.73, 2.46) and *GCI* is non-significant for a price of >75% (Coef. 1.98, 1.83) & a price of <75% (Coef.0.28, 0.65). GCI is not valuable for a price of GCI >75% /<75% while *zekipr2* is a valuable for a price of GCI <75%.

Legal and economic investigation shows that competition law and intellectual property protection are complementary. It has to be taken into consideration that the exact degree of their complimentary role depends not only on the level of competition and IPR but also on the way and accuracy of the evaluation of the index referring either to competition or to IPR.

CONCLUSION

Intellectual property, by its very nature and role, is competition dependent working appropriately only as a means of competition in competitively structured markets. Competition laws do not prevent potentially beneficial conduct. Intellectual property has a crucial task in furthering economic progress and the welfare of the world's people.

Intellectual property law and competition law should be placed on the same level none of them herald the other with the intention that potential conflicts must be solved by way of concession which takes into account the legitimate interests of both. It could be argued that an IPR system is appropriate as long as a balance is maintained between competition and IPRs. Competition rules are not intended to restrain the functioning of the intellectual property system, but rather to preserve its proper functioning.

The economic analysis utilizing our zekipr1 index shows a complementarity of IPRs and Competitiveness regarding FDI. GCI seems to be a valuable variable for lower price of *zekipr2* than a very high one concerning FDI inflows & *FDI on* merchandise & services. On the other hand, GCI is a valuable variable for a low price of *zekipr2* regarding FDI on tertiary sector. GCI seems to be a valuable variable for a lower price of GCI rather than a high one concerning FDI stocks & FDI inflows on merchandise & services. *Zekipr2* seems to be a valuable variable for a price higher than GCI regarding FDI stocks & FDI inflows on merchandise & services. On the other hand, *zekipr2* is a valuable variable for a high price concerning FDI on tertiary sector. Thus, the theoretical view of the complementarity of Intellectual property rights and competition regarding FDI and their degree of complementarity is evidenced in our economic investigation. Regarding policy implications, this research shows the significance of a high protection of IPRs in comparison to competitiveness in concern of attracting FDI inflows on the tertiary sector of products & services. A low level of competitiveness seems to be significant for attracting FDI inflows on the tertiary sector of goods & services. Besides, a high level of competitiveness seems not to be significant in attracting FDI inflows on the tertiary sector. The competitiveness of an economy seems to be more significant than IPRs in accumulating FDI stocks not only in the long but also on a sort term. The above complimentary results concerning IPRs and Competitiveness should be taken into account accordingly by the jurisdictions in their plans to attract the relevant FDI inflows.

APPENDICES

Table 1. Outcome of Estimations of the *ZEKIPR* Index

Country	zekipr2	zekipr1	zekipr1a	zekipr
Albania	3.313186813	3.858186813	3.849186813	3.84319
Algeria	2.991758242	3.449758242	3.435758242	3.43776
Argentina	3.113736264	3.558736264	3.544736264	3.55874
Armenia	3.385714286	3.932714286	3.941714286	3.93471
Australia	3.394505495	4.216505495	4.203505495	4.22551
Austria	3.465934066	4.294934066	4.273934066	4.30693
Azerbaijan	3.342857143	3.938857143	3.939857143	3.98286
Belgium	3.365934066	4.048934066	4.073934066	4.05793
Brazil	3.170879121	3.696879121	3.686879121	3.69588
Bulgaria	3.614285714	4.127285714	4.113285714	4.13529
Canada	3.101648352	3.916648352	3.917648352	3.92965
Chile	3.028571429	3.748571429	3.745571429	3.73857
China	3.285714286	3.920714286	3.910714286	3.92371
Croatia	3.578571429	4.133571429	4.154571429	4.14357
Cyprus	3.262637363	3.945637363	3.950637363	3.94664
Czech Republic	3.392857143	4.031857143	4.008857143	4.03586
Denmark	3.507692308	4.357692308	4.374692308	4.38169
Ecuador	3.085164835	3.480164835	3.482164835	3.48916
Egypt	3.257142857	3.806142857	3.781142857	3.80114
Estonia	3.550549451	4.267549451	4.279549451	4.27155

Country	zekipr2	zekipr1	zekipr1a	zekipr
Finland	3.401648352	4.268648352	4.286648352	4.26765
France	3.694505495	4.439505495	4.437505495	4.42551
Georgia	3.228021978	3.741021978	3.799021978	3.73502
Germany	3.587362637	4.403362637	4.384362637	4.40436
Ghana	2.997802198	3.546802198	3.555802198	3.5388
Greece	3.371978022	3.933978022	3.922978022	3.98598
Guyana	2.762637363	3.240637363	3.206637363	3.22864
Country	zekipr2	zekipr1	zekipr1a	zekipr
Hungary	3.514285714	4.162285714	4.148285714	4.14229
Iceland	3.2	4.031	4.033	4.043
India	3.014835165	3.586835165	3.569835165	3.60784
Indonesia	3	3.44	3.448	3.444
Ireland	3.328571429	4.113571429	4.107571429	4.12057
Israel	3.250549451	3.847549451	3.866549451	3.84055
Italy	3.657142857	4.233142857	4.252142857	4.22414
Japan	3.443406593	4.190406593	4.195406593	4.19241
Jordan	3.028571429	3.659571429	3.675571429	3.68457
Kenya	3.040659341	3.497659341	3.496659341	3.49766
Latvia	3.5	4.142	4.14	4.159
Lithuania	3.314285714	3.962285714	3.959285714	3.97229
Luxembourg	3.328571429	4.155571429	4.157571429	4.16357
Malaysia	3.036263736	3.690263736	3.722263736	3.66026
Malta	3.057142857	3.806142857	3.809142857	3.81214
Mexico	3.442857143	3.948857143	3.899857143	3.98486
Mozambique	3.013736264	3.424736264	3.436736264	3.41574
Netherlands	3.514835165	4.327835165	4.324835165	4.33684
New Zealand	3.043956044	3.923956044	3.912956044	3.94196
Nicaragua	3.235714286	3.671714286	3.688714286	3.67771
Nigeria	2.94010989	3.33210989	3.33510989	3.36011
Norway	3.337362637	4.216362637	4.202362637	4.21736
Pakistan	2.858791209	3.262791209	3.285791209	3.26279
Panama	3.028021978	3.539021978	3.534021978	3.56702
Paraguay	3	3.364	3.363	3.353
Peru	3.214285714	3.757285714	3.724285714	3.76329
Philippines	3.042857143	3.499857143	3.479857143	3.50686
Poland	3.413736264	4.038736264	4.046736264	4.00774
Portugal	3.491208791	4.159208791	4.160208791	4.17221
Republic of Korea	3.379120879	4.040120879	4.029120879	4.05512

Table 1. (Continued)

Country	zekipr2	zekipr1	zekipr1a	zekipr
Romania	3.571428571	4.158428571	4.143428571	4.15743
Russian Federation	3.573076923	4.146076923	4.100076923	4.14608
Serbia	3.571428571	4.039428571	4.063428571	4.04543
Singapore	3.271978022	4.101978022	4.109978022	4.10998
Slovakia	3.492857143	4.088857143	4.070857143	4.11686
Slovenia	3.578571429	4.199571429	4.198571429	4.18057
South Africa	3.136263736	3.752263736	3.706263736	3.76926
Spain	3.748901099	4.393901099	4.424901099	4.4049
Sweden	3.465934066	4.310934066	4.303934066	4.31293
Switzerland	3.644505495	4.488505495	4.499505495	4.48851
Thailand	2.892857143	3.466857143	3.427857143	3.48686
Trinidad and Tobago	3.278571429	3.797571429	3.734571429	3.79757
Tunisia	3.25	3.928	3.895	3.914
Turkey	3.421428571	3.980428571	3.946428571	3.98243
Uganda	2.799450549	3.284450549	3.304450549	3.26745
Ukraine	3.58021978	4.05421978	4.05921978	4.08022
United Kingdom	3.494505495	4.314505495	4.291505495	4.30551
United States of America	3.401648352	4.131648352	4.115648352	4.15165
Uruguay	3.221428571	3.787428571	3.810428571	3.78043
Venezuela	2.907142857	3.171142857	3.155142857	3.19814
Zambia	2.862637363	3.450637363	3.432637363	3.45064
Zimbabwe	2.9	3.251	3.29	3.272

Table 2. OLS model 2 FDI on merchandise & services/ tertiary sector beta coefficients

	(1)	(2)	(3)	(4)
VARIABLES	logfdiinmers10yav	logfdiinmers5yav	logfdiinter10yav	logfdiinter5yav
gci	0.77**	0.53	0.55	0.65
	(0.226)	(0.286)	(0.342)	(0.327)
zekipr2	1.17**	1.22*	2.09***	1.82**
	(0.374)	(0.469)	(0.589)	(0.586)
loggdp10yav	0.56***		0.51***	
	(0.054)		(0.083)	
trade10yav	0.00		-0.00	
	(0.001)		(0.003)	
inf10yav	0.03		-0.01	
	(0.023)		(0.037)	
loggdp5yav		0.53***		0.50***
		(0.069)		(0.079)
trade5yav		0.00		-0.00
		(0.002)		(0.003)

	(1)	(2)	(3)	(4)
VARIABLES	logfdiinmers10yav	logfdiinmers5yav	logfdiinter10yav	logfdiinter5yav
inf5yav		-0.03		-0.00
		(0.035)		(0.041)
Constant	-13.25***	-11.22***	-14.17***	-13.61***
	(1.426)	(1.918)	(2.348)	(2.368)
Observations	78	76	67	64
R-squared	0.83	0.75	0.72	0.74
Adj. R-squared	0.82	0.74	0.70	0.72

Standard errors in parentheses.

*** p<0.001, ** p<0.01, * p<0.05.

Source: G Zekos PhD thesis at Economics Department University of Peloponnese.

Table 3. OLS model 1 GCI 25% FDI on tertiary sector beta coefficients

	(1)	(2)	(3)	(4)
VARIABLES	logfdiinter10yav	logfdiinter10yav	logfdiinter5yav	logfdiinter5yav
gci	4.43**	0.72	4.49*	0.71
	(1.134)	(0.442)	(1.601)	(0.410)
loggdp10yav	0.24	0.57***		
	(0.120)	(0.109)		
trade10yav	0.01	-0.00		
	(0.007)	(0.003)		
inf10yav	0.04	-0.01		
	(0.040)	(0.057)		
loggdp5yav			0.22	0.56***
			(0.183)	(0.097)
trade5yav			0.01	-0.00
			(0.008)	(0.003)
inf5yav			0.05	0.01
			(0.059)	(0.071)
Constant	-17.37**	-9.54**	-16.81*	-9.25**
	(4.481)	(2.727)	(6.204)	(2.674)
Observations	14	53	13	51
R-squared	0.77	0.57	0.64	0.60
Adj. R-squared	0.66	0.53	0.45	0.57

Standard errors in parentheses.

*** p<0.001, ** p<0.01, * p<0.05.

Table 4. OLS model 1 GCI 50% FDI on tertiary sector beta coefficients

	(1)	(2)	(3)	(4)
VARIABLES	logfdiinter10yav	logfdiinter10yav	logfdiinter5yav	logfdiinter5yav
gci	2.28**	0.47	2.23*	0.61
	(0.743)	(0.619)	(0.870)	(0.534)
loggdp10yav	0.42**	0.48***		
	(0.127)	(0.128)		
trade10yav	0.00	-0.00		
	(0.005)	(0.004)		

Table 4. (Continued)

	(1)	(2)	(3)	(4)
VARIABLES	logfdiinter10yav	logfdiinter10yav	logfdiinter5yav	logfdiinter5yav
inf10yav	0.03	-0.35*		
	(0.042)	(0.148)		
loggdp5yav			0.43**	0.57***
			(0.141)	(0.128)
trade5yav			0.00	-0.00
			(0.006)	(0.003)
inf5yav			0.00	0.06
			(0.054)	(0.149)
Constant	-12.80***	-4.99	-12.27***	-9.23*
	(2.776)	(3.711)	(3.112)	(3.673)
Observations	33	34	31	33
R-squared	0.65	0.63	0.64	0.61
Adj. R-squared	0.60	0.58	0.59	0.55

Standard errors in parentheses. *** p<0.001, ** p<0.01, * p<0.05.

Table 5. OLS model 1 GCI 75% FDI on tertiary sector beta coefficients

	(1)	(2)	(3)	(4)
VARIABLES	logfdiinter10yav	logfdiinter10yav	logfdiinter5yav	logfdiinter5yav
gci	0.63	2.03	0.90	1.90
	(0.576)	(1.402)	(0.551)	(1.274)
loggdp10yav	0.54***	0.51**		
	(0.111)	(0.163)		
trade10yav	-0.00	-0.01		
	(0.004)	(0.007)		
inf10yav	-0.03	0.30		
	(0.046)	(0.371)		
loggdp5yav			0.55***	0.50**
			(0.103)	(0.160)
trade5yav			0.00	-0.00
			(0.003)	(0.006)
inf5yav			-0.03	0.46
			(0.050)	(0.314)
Constant	-8.36**	-15.12	-9.62***	-14.75
	(2.813)	(8.920)	(2.692)	(8.179)
Observations	50	17	47	17
R-squared	0.48	0.52	0.58	0.51
Adj. R-squared	0.44	0.36	0.54	0.35

Standard errors in parentheses.
*** p<0.001, ** p<0.01, * p<0.05.

Table 6. FDI on tertiary sector zekipr2/ 75% OLS Model 2 beta coefficients

	(1)	(2)	(3)	(4)
VARIABLES	logfdiinter10yav	logfdiinter10yav	logfdiinter5yav	logfdiinter5yav
zekipr2	1.65	1.55	0.80	2.70
	(1.059)	(2.088)	(1.024)	(1.596)
gci	0.53	0.77	0.81	0.69*
	(0.470)	(0.396)	(0.449)	(0.297)
loggdp10yav	0.51***	0.48**		
	(0.109)	(0.125)		
trade10yav	-0.00	-0.01		
	(0.003)	(0.006)		
inf10yav	-0.01	-0.02		
	(0.047)	(0.048)		
loggdp5yav			0.50***	0.39**
			(0.101)	(0.096)
trade5yav			0.00	-0.01*
			(0.003)	(0.004)
inf5yav			-0.00	0.02
			(0.051)	(0.055)
Constant	-12.72***	-11.98	-11.15**	-12.86*
	(3.549)	(6.853)	(3.459)	(5.384)
Observations	49	18	47	17
R-squared	0.64	0.89	0.70	0.92
Adj. R-squared	0.60	0.84	0.66	0.88

Standard errors in parentheses.
*** p<0.001, ** p<0.01, * p<0.05.

Table 7. OLS model 2 GCI 25% FDI on tertiary sector beta coefficients

	(1)	(2)	(3)	(4)
VARIABLES	logfdiinter10yav	logfdiinter10yav	logfdiinter5yav	logfdiinter5yav
zekipr2	-1.36	2.59***	-1.33	1.90**
	(0.998)	(0.715)	(2.013)	(0.671)
gci	5.51**	0.50	5.28*	0.60
	(1.341)	(0.400)	(2.040)	(0.384)
loggdp10yav	0.19	0.53***		
	(0.119)	(0.098)		
trade10yav	0.01	-0.00		
	(0.006)	(0.003)		
inf10yav	0.04	-0.02		
	(0.038)	(0.051)		

Table 7. (Continued)

	(1)	(2)	(3)	(4)
VARIABLES	logfdiinter10yav	logfdiinter10yav	logfdiinter5yav	logfdiinter5yav
loggdp5yav			0.16	0.53***
			(0.210)	(0.091)
trade5yav			0.01	-0.00
			(0.008)	(0.003)
inf5yav			0.05	0.01
			(0.061)	(0.067)
Constant	-15.93**	-16.17***	-14.06	-14.30***
	(4.412)	(3.050)	(7.651)	(3.063)
Observations	14	53	13	51
R-squared	0.81	0.66	0.66	0.66
Adj. R-squared	0.69	0.62	0.41	0.63

Standard errors in parentheses.
*** p<0.001, ** p<0.01, * p<0.05.

Table 8. OLS model 2 GCI 50% FDI on tertiary sector beta coefficients

	(1)	(2)	(3)	(4)
VARIABLES	logfdiinter10yav	logfdiinter10yav	logfdiinter5yav	logfdiinter5yav
zekipr2	1.19	2.45*	1.41	1.85
	(0.866)	(0.960)	(1.000)	(0.907)
gci	1.48	0.42	1.35	0.56
	(0.932)	(0.568)	(1.057)	(0.507)
loggdp10yav	0.47**	0.40**		
	(0.132)	(0.121)		
trade10yav	0.00	-0.00		
	(0.005)	(0.003)		
inf10yav	0.02	-0.28		
	(0.042)	(0.138)		
loggdp5yav			0.50**	0.51***
			(0.146)	(0.125)
trade5yav			0.00	-0.00
			(0.006)	(0.003)
inf5yav			0.00	0.08
			(0.053)	(0.141)
Constant	-14.78***	-11.34*	-14.93***	-13.55**
	(3.089)	(4.212)	(3.593)	(4.075)
Observations	33	34	31	33
R-squared	0.68	0.70	0.67	0.66
Adj. R-squared	0.62	0.65	0.60	0.60

Standard errors in parentheses.
*** p<0.001, ** p<0.01, * p<0.05.

Table 9. OLS model 2 GCI 75% FDI on tertiary sector beta coefficients

	(1)	(2)	(3)	(4)
VARIABLES	logfdiinter10yav	logfdiinter10yav	logfdiinter5yav	logfdiinter5yav
zekipr2	2.11**	2.73	1.83**	2.46
	(0.683)	(1.386)	(0.674)	(1.366)
gci	0.28	1.98	0.65	1.83
	(0.540)	(1.259)	(0.522)	(1.170)
loggdp10yav	0.52***	0.48**		
	(0.102)	(0.147)		
trade10yav	-0.00	-0.00		
	(0.003)	(0.006)		
inf10yav	-0.02	0.43		
	(0.042)	(0.339)		
loggdp5yav			0.53***	0.49**
			(0.096)	(0.147)
trade5yav			0.00	-0.00
			(0.003)	(0.006)
inf5yav			-0.01	0.62
			(0.047)	(0.300)
Constant	-13.46***	-23.68*	-14.29***	-22.84*
	(3.064)	(9.108)	(3.042)	(8.746)
Observations	50	17	47	17
R-squared	0.58	0.64	0.64	0.62
Adj. R-squared	0.53	0.48	0.60	0.45

Standard errors in parentheses.
*** p<0.001, ** p<0.01, * p<0.05.

References

BS(Econ) Aristotle University, JD Democritus University, LLM, PhD(Law) University of Hull, PhD(Econ) University of Peloponnese , Legal Adviser, Advocate and Economist zekosg@yahoo.com , zekosg@uop.gr

Blonigen, B. A. (2005). A review of the empirical literature on FDI determinants. Atlantic Economic Journal, 33 (4):383-403.

BOONE, J. (2001), "Intensity of competition and the incentive to innovate", *International Journal of Industrial Organization*, 19, 5, 705-726.

Caves, Richard. 2007. *Multinational Enterprise and Economic Analysis*, 3rd edition. Cambridge: Cambridge University Press.

Cohen, Stephen. 2007. Multinational Corporations and Foreign Direct Investment. Oxford: Oxford University Press.

Cooper Feldman, R. (1999) Defensive leveraging in antitrust, *Georgetown Law Journal,* 87(6), pp. 2079–2115.

Dolmans, M., O'Donoghue, R., & Loewenthal, P.-J. (2007). *Are Article 82 EC and Intellectual Property Interoperable? The State of the Law Pending the Judgment in Microsoft v. Commission*, Competition Policy International, Vol. 3, No. 1.

Drexl, J. (1999). *"Trade-Related Restraints of Competition – The Competition Policy Approach" in Towards WTO Competition Rules: Key Issues and Comments on the WTO Report (1998) on Trade and Competition.* Zäch, R. (Ed.)

Drexl, J. (2008). *Research handbook on Intellectual property and Competition law*, Cheltenham: Edward Elgar Publishing.

Dunning, J. H. (1977). Trade, Location of Economic Activity and the Multinational Enterprise: a search for an eclectic approach, pages 395{418. in B. Ohlin, P.O. Hesselborn and P.M. Wijkmon (eds.) "The International Location of Economic Activity", Macmillan: London.

Einer Elhauge and Damien Geradin; "*Global Competition Law and Economics*" Hart Publishing, 2007.

Emmanuelle Auriol, Sara Biancini, Intellectual Property Rights Adoption in Developing Countries October 2, 2009 WP 09-094 Toulouse school of economics P7

Etro, F. (2004). *Innovation by leaders*, Economic journal, Vol. 114, No. 495, p. 281-303.

Etro, F., 2007. Competition, Innovation and Antitrust: a Theory of Market Leaders and its Policy Implications. Springer Verlag, Berlin & New York.

European Commission, *DG Competition Discussion Paper on the Application of Article 82 of the Treaty to Exclusionary Abuses, Brussels*, December 2005

Evans, D. S. (2003): *Some Empirical Aspects of Multi-sided Platform Industries*, Review of Network Economics, Vol. 3 (2), pp. 191-209.

Fiebig, A"A Role for the WTO in International Merger Control", *Nw. J. Int'l L. & Bus* 20 (2000), p. 233

G. Zekos, IPR's protection and their impact upon FDI, 2013 PhD Thesis in Economics University of Peloponnese, Hellas.

G. Zekos, 'Constructing a New IPRs index' [2012] 4 Web JCLI http://webjcli.ncl.ac.uk/2012/issue4/zekos4.html

G Zekos, Economics and Law on Competition in US and EU, 2008 Nova Science Publications New York USA www.novapublishers.com

G Zekos, Economics, Finance and Law on MNEs, 2007 Nova Publishers, New York www.novapublishers.com

Goldar, B.N and R. Banga (2005). "Impact of trade liberalization on foreign direct investment in Indian industries", *ARTNeT Working Paper Series, No. 36*, June.

Ingo Fiedler, Antitrust in two-sided markets: Is competition always desirable? The case of a satellite broadcasting network with monopoly power, Berkeley Program in Law and Economics, Working Paper Series 10-25-2010

IMF, 2010, *Regional Economic Outlook: Sub-Saharan Africa,* Washington: International Monetary Fund.

Javorcik, B. (2004). Does foreign direct investment increase the productivity of domestic firms? In search of spillover through backward linkages. American Economic Review, 94(3):605-27.

Kovacic, W. (2005). "Competition Policy and Intellectual Property: Redefining the Role of Competition Agencies" in *Antitrust, Patents and Copyrignt, EU and US Perspectives.* Lévêque, F. and Shelanski, H. (Eds).

L. Peeperkorn, IP Licenses and Competition Rules: Striking the Right Balance, 26 WORLD COMPETITION (2003).

Lin, S., Ye, H., 2009. Does inflation targeting make a difference in developing countries? Journal of Development Economics, 89(1), 118–123.

Miller, R.L.; Benjamin, D.K.; *The Economics of Macro Issues*; Boston, MA; Pearson - Addison Wesley, 2004.

R.Weintraub, "Globalization Effect on Antitrust Law", *New Eng. L. Rev.* 34 (1999), p. 27.

Reitzig, M., Henkel, J., and Schneider, F. (2010), "Collateral damage for R&D manufacturers: how patent sharks operate in markets for technology", *Industrial and Corporate Change,* 19(3), pages 947-967.

Reza Dibadj, Saving Antitrust, 75 U. Colo. L. Rev. 745, 779-80 (2003).

Richard A. Posner, Antitrust in the New Economy, 68 Antitrust L.J. 925, 926 (2001).

Richard A. Posner, Antitrust Law at 242–44 (2d ed. 2001) (arguing that unconditioned refusals to deal by dominant firms should never be violations of section 2 of the Sherman Act).

Richard A. Posner, Antitrust Law: An Economic Perspective (1976).

Scherer, F.M. (2005) *Patents. Economics, Policy and Measurement* (Cheltenham, UK and Northampton, MA, USA: Edward Elgar).

Schumpeter, J. (1934) *The Theory of Economics Development* (Cambridge, MA: Harvard University Press).

Schumpeter, J. (1939) *Business Cycles: A Theoretical, Historical and Statistical Analysis of Capitalist Process* (New York: McGraw-Hill).

Schumpeter, J. (1943) *Capitalism, Socialism and Democracy* (London: Unwin University).

Scotchmer, S. (1999), "Cumulative innovation in theory and practice",. University of California, Berkeley.

Scotchmer, Suzanne.2004. *Innovation and Incentives*. Cambridge MA: MIT Press.

Sean P. Gates, Federal Trade Commission; *Intellectual Property and Antitrust*; Antitrust Basics Lesson III: Intellectual Property; November 8, 2006.

U.S. Department of Justice and Federal Trade Commission (2007), Antitrust enforcement and intellectual property: promoting innovation and competition, Washington DC.

Vickers, John. 2005. Abuse of Market Power. *Economic Journal* 115(504): F244–F261.*Volume 6 Issue 1 pp 117-137 December.*

World Bank, 2001 'Intellectual property: balancing incentives with competitive access', in *Global Economic Prospects*, 129-150, Washington, DC. Available at: http://www.worldbank.org/prospects/gep2002/chapt5.pdf.

Cases

Ill. Tool Works Inc. v. Indep. Ink, Inc., 126 S. Ct. 1281, 1284 (2006) ("[T]he mere fact that a tying product is patented does not support [a market power]).

MCI Commc'ns Corp. v. ATandT, 708 F.2d 1081 (7th Cir. 1983).

Nungesser v. EC Commission [1983] 1 CMLR 278.

Standard Oil Co. vs. United States, 283 U.S. 163 (1931).

United States v. Microsoft Corp., 253 F.3d 34, 63 (D.C. Cir. 2001) (antitrust defendant's claim that it had ''an absolute and unfettered right to use its intellectual property as it wishes'' was held to be ''no more correct than the proposition that use of one's personal property, such as a baseball bat, cannot give rise to tort liability'').

Verizon Commc'ns Inc. v. Law Offices of Curtis V. Trinko, LLP, 540 U.S. 398, 407 (2004).

Xerox Corp. v. Media Scis. Int'l, Inc., 511 F. Supp. 2d 372, 389 (S.D.N.Y. 2007).

In: Computational Data Analysis Techniques ISBN: 978-1-63463-957-6
Editors: M. Doumpos, C. Zopounidis and Ch. Gaganis

Chapter 5

THE MODELLING OF MAINTENANCE COST: THE CASE OF CONTAINER-SHIPS IN DRY-DOCK

***Apostolidis Agamemnon**[*1], Merikas Andreas*[2] *and Merika Anna*[3]
[1]Technical Division, Enterprises Shipping and Trading SA, Athens, Greece
[2]Department of Maritime Studies, The University of Piraeus
[3]Deree College, The American College of Greece

ABSTRACT

During the last decades, a number of academic maritime papers were focused on the container-ships. However, no research can be found so far, to deal with the maintenance cost of these vessels and in particular with their dry-docking cost. This is the first time in the literature that the determinants of dry-docking cost are unveiled. We prove that dry-docking cost is a significant element of the ship's maintenance cost and is always presented as a six figure amount.

Authors have personally collected and analysed 71 cases of container-ship repairs from one of the biggest Middle East shipyards, over a time span of four years.

Making use of this primary database they develop a simultaneous equations model and express dry-docking cost as a function of ship size, period of repairing, age, charter market's upswings or downswings and the shipping company's capacity as an effective negotiator.

The method of estimation is Generalized Method of Moments (GMM) augmented by the significant advance made by Lewbell (1997) and our results shade light on an issue, which has never before been effectively dealt with, given its immense practical significance for the decision maker.

Keywords: Shipping, maintenance cost, container-ships, econometric model, GMM

[*] E-mail: agamemnon.apostolidis@gmail.com

1. INTRODUCTION

It is widely accepted that the trading environment for ship-managers has been extremely difficult, given that major economies stagger to get back on their feet and emerging economies try hard to adapt. Decade of cost management lies ahead, says Clarksons' director Martin Stopford (2011). Operating costs have therefore taken on a greater significance in the pursuit of business survival, with repair and maintenance, personnel and administration – the softer targets - taking centre stage. So it is imperative for ship-managers to have all the necessary information about maintenance which will allow them better planning and monitoring in order to enhance their performance. A part of maintenance cost which has never been taken up by analysts, academics and professionals alike, even though its importance is generally accepted is the dry docking cost. There is an extensive literature on ships operating costs, identifying the characteristics and determinants of costs in different vessel types. This paper adds to the existing literature in two ways. First, it is the first study to investigate the relationship between dry docking cost and its determinants using hand collected ship yard information. Second, it develops the dry docking cost-profitability relationship of a ship yard treating dry docking as an endogenous variable.

We study 71 invoices of real ship repair invoices over a period of four years (2007 to 2010) and we explore potential determinants of ship repair and dry docking costs. Our finding that ship size, age, and number of stay days in the yard, constitute the main determinants of dry docking cost is consistent with the literature on operating costs as far as it concerns the ship size, Cullinane (1999); Ryder (1979); Glen and Reid (2010). Subsequently, we develop a simultaneous equation model where dry docking cost, measured by the payable amount of each invoice is treated as an endogenous variable and employ the Generalized Method of Moments (GMM) to estimate the interaction between dry docking cost and its determinants. We discover a statistically significant positive relationship between dry docking cost degree and ship size, age and number of days staying in the yard. In addition, we find a strong and negative impact of the bargaining power of the ship company on dry docking cost, a fact always suspected but never actually empirically substantiated before.

Moreover, our results largely explain why shipping firms are keen on employing as insiders negotiators for dry docking purposes. They also have significant policy implications for vessel operators, as they suggest that lower dry docking cost is not a mere effect of sound financial performance, but also, and perhaps more importantly, a requirement for it.

A literature review is conducted in section Two. Hypotheses are laid out in the successive section Three. Our sample data and methodology are presented in section Four. Section Five presents and discusses our empirical findings. The sixth section concludes the paper and provides suggestions for future research.

2. LITERATURE REVIEW

2.1. Prior Research on Operating and Maintenance Costs

No academic paper or study has been found to be devoted particularly to the dry-docking cost; the reason seems to be the scarcity of such commercial information. However, dry-docking cost constitutes a major element of the ship operating cost. Therefore authors focused on past studies and papers on ship operating costs.

Ship operating cost is investigated and approached with respective mathematical models by a number of authors. Glen and Reid (2010) are presenting a model for all elements of tanker cost (capital, operating and voyage) elasticities. They are revisiting the elasticity model of tanker costs – capital, operating and voyage costs, and finding that such model principals are still valid. They are comparing tanker data drawn during 2007-2008 with past studies, even 30-40 years ago. Ryder and Chappell (1979) assessed the costs for ships ranging in size from 80 to 480 TEU. Jansson and Shneerson (1982) did similar calculations for containerships ranging from 240 to 3200 TEU. Cullinane and Khanna (1999) studied ships size economies of containerships ranging from 1000 to 8000 TEU and tested comparable models. Veldman (2011) studied economies of ship size for container ships ranging 8,000 to 14,000 TEU.

Cullinane (1999) in his paper examined two ways to calculate containerships' operating cost. In the first, he associated the elasticity of cost to the size of the ship. Results were derived from an empirical analysis of ZIM containerships' operating costs, conducted before by Jansson (1982). Similar approaches were adopted by other researchers as well, like Heaver (1968) and Goss and Mann (1974). Later, Cullinave proposed a calculation of the operating cost as a function of ship's capital cost and particularly he assumed

operating cost = 3.5% of the initial capital cost

Same method was followed by Ryder and Chappel (1979), Gilman (1980) and Pearson (1980). Such methods have the disadvantage that they are applicable only close to the date of publication of the study. The reason is that, operating and maintenance costs are subject to inflation. On the other hand, the initial capital cost has a commodity behavior, fluctuating strongly between good shipping market times and bad times.

All above studies and models seem to give a fair approach to the estimation of ship operating costs at the time of their publication. However, the volatile environment of shipping, i.e. inflation in different countries, fluctuation of currency rate of exchange, rise and fall of steel, oil prices and energy domestic demand, waive any advantage in long term estimation.

In the future, it will be worthy to correlate ship maintenance costs with historical values of parameters such as inflation, rate of exchange versus US dollar and gross domestic product (GDP) of ship repair countries since the list of such countries is limited to China, South Asia (Singapore, Indonesia, Philippines), UAE, Turkey, Poland only to mention the most active ones. Same goes for steel and oil prices which determine the material and energy costs of a ship repair. All above can assist the future researcher to achieve a diachronic estimating model.

2.2. Containerships and Their Costs

Containerships count only six decades of existence and the container box itself was an innovation to the transportation of goods in mid fifties. It is common to make reference to container boxes by the term TEU (twenty equivalent unit). Such unit has standard dimensions

19'4'' x 7'8'' x 7'10'' with an internal cubic capacity of 33.2 m^3. We often refer to containerships by their volume capacity expressed in TEU, the number that empty reference units can be transported. During the last five years mega-carriers like Maersk and MSC pour the industry with – never before built – containerships of 12,000 and 15,000 TEU. Nowadays, shipyards and naval architects are working on designs of 18,000 TEU.

However, the fever of mega-containerships escapes the interest of the present paper, but it is worthy to mention that maintenance cost of such containerships will tremendously change what we know until now.

Expenses of a containership fall under three categories of costs:

- Capital costs: the acquisition cost and the cost of capital (interest paid)
- Voyage costs: costs occurred due to ship's sailing from one port to another such as bunker cost, canal and port fees, certificates and charts in order to comply with local requirements.
- Operating costs: Costs occurred to maintain a ship operational and seaworthy such as manning cost, lubricants, provisions, insurance, administration, spares and maintenance costs.

Both ship's flag registry and classification society – in order to renew a ship's certificates – require that a ship has conducted two dry-docking surveys within a five year period. Such two dry-docking surveys have to be equally distributed over the time of five years.

Dry-docking cost is an element of the maintenance cost of a vessel.

Moore Stephens Consultants publish, once per year, a well-reputed review on ship operating costs.

It comprises data from almost 2,000 ships. According to Moore Stephens (2008) annual publication for the year 2007 benchmark maintenance versus operating costs for containerships were recorded in the following table, where RandM stands for Repair and Maintenance:

Table 1. Maintenance Cost vs. Operating Cost (year 2007; in USD)

Container Size (TEU)	Spares	RandM	Total Maintenance Cost		Total Operating Cost
< 1,000	113,595	104,030	217,625	15%	1,488,006
1,000 – 2,000	172,691	152,174	324,865	18%	1,823,683
> 2,000	248,872	229,786	478,658	18%	2,731,041

Similarly, according to the same source (2010), maintenance and operating cost for the year 2009 can be shown as follows:

Table 2. Maintenance Cost vs. Operating Cost (year 2009; in USD)

Container Size (TEU)	Spares	RandM	Total Maintenance Cost		Total Operating Cost
< 1,000	90,057	106,566	196,623	13%	1,563,729
1,000 – 2,000	125,763	137,715	263,478	14%	1,847,985
> 2,000	228,223	241,503	469,726	17%	2,727,697

As we can see from both the above tables, the maintenance cost for all sizes of containerships it is estimated from 13% to 18% of the annual operating cost.

In the same annual report, some data are provided for annual dry-docking costs. We present those for the year 2007 and 2009 in the following Table 3. Additionally, we estimate the participation of the two dry-docking in a 5 year operating cost summary. We can notice that dry-docking cost represents a 12-13% of the operating cost, as significant as the regular repair and maintenance cost per year. Therefore, we prove that for each dollar a ship-owner is spending for maintenance he has to save one dollar for the forthcoming dry-docking as well.

Table 3. Dry-docking vs. Operating Cost (USD per year)

Container Size (TEU)	Dry-docking Cost 2007	Dry-docking Cost 2009	Share in 5 year Operating Cost
< 1,000	504,673	515,170	13%
1,000 – 2,000	469,930	587,010	12%
> 2,000	982,484	644,639	12%

Concluding, the significance of the dry-docking cost, is the main reason that motivated the authors to explore the cost's nature and determinants.

3. Hypotheses

3.1. Age

The age of a ship is counted from the delivery date, in other words, from the date the ship is delivered by the building shipyard to her owners. All insurance documents, flag and class certificates are issued for first time at that date. Drawing on these issues, we formulate our first hypothesis: Older ships – like older humans – experience higher wear. Additionally, flag and class have higher criteria for surveys of older ships. As a result, older ships demand more extensive repairs and maintenance than younger ships.

H1: Ceteris paribus, the age of the ship is positively associated with the extent of dry-docking cost.

3.2. Size

In the present study the size of containerships is taken from their deadweight (dwt) capacity which can be openly translated into 'the carrying capacity'. It is provided in weight metric tons (dwt).

$$Deadweight = cargo + bunkers + stores + provisions + crew$$

Other ship segments like tankers or bulk-carriers are classified depending on their deadweight capacity to Handymax (around 30,000 tons), Panamax (around 70,000 tons) or Capesizes (around 160,000 tons). However, container-ships are classified depending upon their container box (TEU) capacity. Cullinane (1999) correlates deadweight capacity with TEU capacity as

1 TEU = 14 tons deadweight

H2: Ceteris paribus, the size of the ship is positively associated with the extent of dry-docking cost.

3.3. Stay Days

Stay days are calculated from the ship's arrival date at the yard until the departure date. Few days are spending in the dry-dock (normally five to seven days) whereas during the remaining days the vessel is berthed alongside to complete her repair and maintenance jobs. Dry-dock facilities and berths are limited for every shipyard and constitute yard's most valuable assets. Volume of repair work is proportional to the stay days. Drawing on this argument, we formulate our hypothesis that longer stay days contribute to the increase of the dry-docking bill.

H3: Ceteris paribus, the number of stay days in the shipyard is positively associated with the extent of dry-docking cost.

3.4. Market Conditions

This is a binary variable, an indication whether the shipping market is at high levels or not. When freight rates are increased, owners silently accept to pay a repair premium to shipyards. In 2007, the Hamburg Index - Hamburg Index can be easily found at Hamburg Shipbrokers' Association website www.vhss.de - was at 12.79$/14t TEU and thus, a 2,000 TEUs container-ship was gaining a daily charter hire of 25,580$. At that time, her owners were keen to pay any additional expenses, such as repair overtime, first class airfreight for spare parts, attendance of technical specialists and so forth, in order their ship to stay as short as possible in the shipyard. According to the Lloyd's List (Wingrove, 2008), in the first half 2008 repair shipyards were urging owners to book yard slots one year in advance. Worthy to mention that, one year later, the above charter hire dropped to 6,160$/day.

H4: Ceteris paribus, the market conditions is positively associated with profitability of the shipyard.

3.5. Owners' Negotiating Capacity

This is the second binary variable in our model. Whereas, the preceding variable is reflecting the shipyards' ability to capitalise the 'good' shipping market, the new variable herewith is expressing the owners' ability to achieve better terms and conditions. For that reason they have to highlight their fleet size, financial credibility, preference frequency in a specific yard and to be better prepared regarding the dry-docking requirements.

H5: Ceteris paribus, the bargaining power of the owner is negatively associated with the extent of dry-docking cost.

4. Data and Methodology

4.1. Data Collected

Hundreds of actual dry-docking invoices have been manually collected, in order to develop the cost and profit function of dry-docking and test our above hypotheses. They spanned over a four year period (2007-2010) from one of the biggest ship repair yards which is strategically located in the Persian Gulf.

Data were collected for all types of ships, however in our present econometric model, we selected the data concerned container-ships only, in order to be consistent with the literature reviewed. On the other hand, such restriction increased the uniformity of the analyzed data and the confidence of the extracted conclusions.

We chose to collect and analyze data from only one major shipyard in order to eliminate geographical effects such as different labor cost (which varies between Europe, Middle East or Far East), exchange rate fluctuations (which was highly volatile during 2007-10) and different transportation and purchase cost of materials and spares (when yards do not have the same access to factories and manufacturers).

Invoices were classified and sorted according to the ship type, age, repair period and reason (regular dry-docking or extraordinary repair due to damage or an accident).

Briefly, a recapitulation of the data collected and elaborated on can be given in the following table:

Table 4. Collected and elaborated data (2007-2010)

Ship Size	Capacity in TEUs	Records	Average age	Average dry-docking cost
Container feeder max	< 1,000	12	18.0	511,853 $
Container ship	1,000 – 2,000	29	16.3	457,503 $
Container main liner	> 2,000	30	17.4	557,259 $
Total		71	17.0	508,839 $

As it can be shown the average dry-docking cost is within range comparing with Moore Stephens (2008; 2010) data given for the same period (see Table 3). However, for the biggest size that of bigger than 2,000 TEUs capacity the average dry-docking cost in the Persian Gulf shipyard is much lower than that of the global figure.

4.2. Methodology

In order to map the causal interdependence between dry-docking cost and its determinants, we set up a linear model of simultaneous equations:

PROF = g (LINV, AGE, DAYS, MARKET, MODE, LS)

LINV = f (AGE, DAYS, MARKET, MODE, LS)

where:

LINV=Dry-docking cost in logarithmic terms. This is the net payable amount in US dollars that a ship owner pays to the yard

AGE=Age of the ship. The age of a ship is counted from the delivery date, in other words, from the date the ship is delivered by the building shipyard to her owners.

LS = Size in logarithmic terms. In the present study the size of container-ships is taken from their deadweight (dwt) capacity which can be openly translated into 'the carrying weight capacity'.

DAYS = Stay days. Stay days are calculated from the arrival date at the yard until the departure date.

PROF=Profitability. Shipyard has an index to assess the profitability of each repair project. This index is always positive; however a certain value corresponds to the breakeven point of the shipyard's operation cost.

MARKET = dummy variable assuming the value of 1 if on arrival the market is booming and 0 if the market is in recession. Since our data spans over the years 2007-2010, we witness within this period the market enjoyed unprecedented growth rates in freights and ship values as well as a deep dive during 2009 and 2010.

MODE = bargaining power of the ship-manager measured as a dummy. More specifically, the shipyard gave discounts between 5-20% on the dry docking cost depending on the following criteria (i) if the company was a regular customer, (ii) if there was a capable mediator to bargain the price and (iii) if the company was well known and of considerable size. For all these cases the variable was assigned the value 1 and zero otherwise. At this point it must be mentioned that this is inside information emphasizing the uniqueness of the data set used. Thus, its estimated coefficient would show the impact of bargaining power on the dry docking cost.

Two of our variables, LINV and LS are expressed in logarithmic terms. There are three reasons mentioned in the literature why we should be doing that. First, to linearise a non-linear function. Second, to have individual estimated parameters expressing elasticities and third, to scale out differences in the magnitudes of the data series. This third reason is adopted in our case. The proper methods of estimation are the well-known 2SLS and 3SLS. The drawback of 3SLS is that it depends heavily on the parametric modelling of all the endogenous variables (that is LINV and PROF jointly with LS, DAYS, and the *complete* set of variables that are jointly determined in this context). Therefore, 2SLS is preferable but it is not flexible in terms of delivering robust standard errors, so we can resort to Generalized Method of Moments (GMM).

We choose the GMM over 2SLS because one of our dependent variable, i.e. LINV is endogenous. Therefore, in the presence of heteroskedasticity GMM is more efficient than a simple Instrumental Variable (IV) estimator method – like the 2SLS - but even in the absence of heteroskedasticity is no worse asymptotically than the IV estimator method.

The general idea of GMM can be explained as follows. Suppose we have an equation of the form: $Y_t = \beta_1 X_{t1} + ... + \beta_k X_{tk} + u_t$. Some or all of the explanatory variables may be endogenous and correlated with the error term, u. In that case, suppose there are variables $Z_1, ..., Z_m$ correlated with the Xs but not with the error term. Then we could use the Zs as instruments and solve the orthogonality conditions:

$$n^{-1}\sum_{t=1}^{T} Z_{jt}\left(Y_t - \beta_1 X_{t1} - ... - \beta_k X_{tk}\right) = 0, \; j = 1, ..., m \text{, in terms of } \beta.$$

Of course when $m > k$ (more instruments than explanatory variables) this has to be done in the least squares or some other sense. Indeed, the modern literature of GMM has provided many such criteria, some of which can even be used to deliver heteroskedasticity-robust or autocorrelation-robust standard errors, depending on the problem. For an accessible treatment of modern GMM, see Hansen (2002) and Wooldridge (2001).

The problem with GMM is how to proceed when we are not really certain that a given variable is an instrument or not. A proper instrument is a variable correlated with the regressors but uncorrelated with the error term. Such variables may be hard to find and this is indeed so, in most empirical applications.

Assume our set of instruments is X= [AGE, DAYS, LS, MODE] where none of them appears explicitly on the left hand side of our equations. To provide more orthogonality conditions we use not only X but also X⊗X that are squares and cross-products of the variables in X. In our case this would mean twenty instruments (k=20) in total. Initial results though were rather disappointing, so we proceeded with re-estimation of the model making use of Lewbel (1997) contribution to GMM estimation.

A significant advance in 2SLS and GMM has been provided by Lewbel (1997). Suppose we have the equation Y=f(W,Z) where W are predetermined variables and Z are endogenous variables. Suppose G=G(W) is any function of W, for example G(W)=W. Let lower letters denote deviations from the means. Lewbel (1997) showed that valid instruments for this equation are: g*z, g*y and y*z. Moreover, under symmetry of the error terms, valid instruments are also z^2 and y^2. Now if no genuine predetermined variables are available (that is, there are no variables in G and thus in g) then under broad conditions, y*z, z^2 and y^2 can be always considered as instruments always satisfying at least the order condition for (local) identification.

$$PROF_i = g\,(LINV_i, AGE_i, DAYS_i, LS_i, MARKET_i, MODE_i) + u_{i1}$$
$$LINV_i = f\,(AGE_i, DAYS_i, LS_i, MARKET_i, MODE_i) + u_{i2}$$

The error terms can be correlated and exhibit arbitrary patterns of heteroskedasticity, since we use cross-sectional data. Heteroskedasticity occurs when $var(u_t) \neq 0$, which makes hypothesis testing invalid. In our case we use GMM as a more efficient estimator compared to 2SLS to deal with arbitrary heteroskedasticity error terms. Best reference for it we consider Wooldridge (2001).

The orthogonality conditions have as follows:

$$n^{-1}\sum_{i=1}^{n}(PROF_i - f(LINV_i, DAYS_i, AGE_i, MARKET_i, MODE_i, LS_i,;\theta))X_{ik} = 0$$

$$n^{-1}\sum_{i=1}^{n}(LINV_i - z(DAYS_i, AGE_i, MARKET_i, MODE_i, LS_i,;\theta))X_{ik} = 0$$

θ is the vector of parameters in the linear models *f, and z* . This provides a total of 2k (thirty in our case) equations for the fifteen parameters (including constant terms) and provides the fundamental basis for GMM. Thus, we run GMM estimations for two models.

An important issue in GMM estimation is the issue of weak instruments. If instruments are weak, Two Stage Least Squares method (2SLS) and GMM can lead to biases even in large samples, and the distributions can be far from normality. This issue is dealt with in Stock and Yogo (2002). As noted in Stock and Watson (2003, p.350) a simple guide is the calculated F-statistic in the first stage (reduced form) regression. If F is greater than 10, we need not worry, but this number of course depends on the number of instruments used. About the weak instrument problem Wooldridge (2001) demonstrates that in certain instances the problem of weak instruments can result in the (biased) Ordinary Least Squares (OLS) estimator being preferred.

	R^2	F-Statistic
PROF	0.93	43.8
LINV	0.88	37.4

Critical value at 0.05 level is 11.51(Table I, page 39, Stock and Yogo (2002)).

In the present paper the F-statistic values in the first stage of regression are well above the critical value.

5. Discussion of Results

Running our model under the estimation method of GMM we are reaching finally the following equation for dry-docking cost:

LINV = 6.68 + 0.043 x DAYS - 0.014 x AGE + 0.465 x MARKET – 0.148 x MODE + 0.563 x LS

whereas, profitability is deriving as:

PROF = 21.86 - 5.9 x LINV + 0.307 x DAYS - 0.205 x AGE + 3.88 x MARKET – 11.74 x MODE+ 7.71 x LS

The following table recapitulates the GMM estimation of our model:

Our findings support our hypotheses and are consistent with the literature. In our model all variables have the expected signs and the impact of ship size, age and stay days in the yard have a positive and highly significant impact on dry-docking cost. Furthermore, it appears that lower dry docking bill, goes hand to hand with better profit performance, and as such it evolves as an important item in the investor's decision making process.

Table 5. Modelling Results

Estimation Method: Generalized Method of Moments		
	Dep.Variable:LINV	Dep.Variable:PROF
	Coefficient	Coefficient
Const.	6.683025	21.86395
	(6.683025)***	(1.133245)
Linv		-5.909560
		(-2.548308)***
Days	0.043122	0.307987
	(0.043122)***	(2.916380)***
Age	-0.014733	-0.205566
	(-0.014733)**	(-2.726386)***
Market	0.465602	3.886806
	(0.465602)***	(2.099862)**
Mode	-0.148304	-11.74985
	(-0.148304)	(-6.670488)***
Ls	0.563254	7.715084
	(0.563254)***	(4.601187)***
J-statistic	0.141343	

It is worthy to mention that results of the current study offer a comprehensive tool to both sides of the dry-docking bill: the shipyard operator-investor as well as the customer-ship manager. Focusing on our model, which passes comfortably the weak instruments test, it appears that lower dry-docking bill contributes significantly towards greater profitability. Additionally, it is shown that the larger the ship is and the longer the number of days she stays, the higher the dry-docking cost will be.

Moreover, from the above dry-docking cost equations we can observe a significant and negative impact of the bargaining power of the shipping company on the formation of the dry docking cost. This result which is reported for the first time in the literature renders support to the view that professional customers are treated in a preferential way. Furthermore, it appears from our results that market conditions in shipping affects positively and strongly yard profitability, a finding which allies with the results reported for the shipping industry as a whole. Finally, the value of the J-statistic confirms the validity of our model.

Conclusion

This research contributes to the existing literature on container-ship maintenance costs by conducting an investigation of the relationship between dry-docking cost and its most significant determinants for a major ship repair yard. It extends previous research, which largely deals with other types of operating costs, by arguing that the dry docking cost is an essential item of a ship's maintenance cost and as such it needs to be carefully studied and taken into account together with its determinants by the investor, in his quest for enhanced profitability.

On the basis of information derived from the study of 71 bills of real ship repair projects over a period of four years, we constructed a fundamental relationship and employed a GMM model to explore potential determinants of dry docking cost. We strengthen the literature that depicts size, age, number of stay days, as the main determining factors behind maintenance cost.

Our results provide justification for the apparent keenness of shipping firms in making more and more to put their maintenance cost under close monitoring for sound financial performance. Thus, the main policy implication of our study for ship management is that performance could be substantially propped up by being aware of the precise structure of the dry docking cost.

The pace for bigger container-ships is based on the principle of economy of scale. In the future, when dry-docking or maintenance cost figures are available for such mega-size vessels - those of more than 15,000 TEUs - it will be interesting for researchers to investigate any diseconomy of scale. The shipping industry has never experienced before such big container-ships and it is a question whether economy of scale is applicable to all cost elements.

Additionally, a study on dry-docking cost geography could be welcome, comparing similar dry-docking projects in different regions as well as a comparison of dry-docking elements for same size/age but different type of ships, e.g. tanker versus container-ship.

References

Baylson, B. (2008), "Dry-dock accounting on the move", *Fairplay Magazine*, 14 August 2008, pp 26-27.

Cullinane, K. and Khanna, M. (1999), "Economies of Scale in Large Container Ships", *Journal of Transport Economics and Policy,* Vol.33, Part 2, pp 185-208.

Gilman, S. (1980). "Ship Choice in the Container Age". Liverpool: Liverpool Marine Transport Centre.

Glen, D. and Reid, S. (2010). "Tanker Cost Elasticities Revisited", *Maritime Policy And Management*, 37 (6), pp 585-600.

Goss, R.O. and Mann, M.C. (1974). "Cost of ship time", London: Government Economic Service Occasional Papers.

Hansen, L.P. (1982), "Large Sample Properties of Generalized Method of Moments Estimators", *Econometrica,* Vol.50, pp 1029-1054.

Hansen, L.P. (2002), "Method of Moments in International Encyclopaedia of the Social and Behaviour Sciences", N.J.Smelser and P.B.Bates (editors), Pergamon: Oxford.

Hausman, J. Stock, J.H. and Yogo, M. (2005), "Asymptotic properties of the Hahn–Hausman test for weak-instruments", Economics Letters, Vol.89 (3), December 2005, pp 333–342.

Heaver, T.D. (1968). "*The Economics of Vessel Size*", Ottawa: National Harbour Board.

Jansson, J.O. and Shneerson, D. (1982), "The optimal ship size, *Journal of transport economics and policy*", Sept.1982.

Lewbell, A. (1997), "Constructing Instruments for Regressions With Measurement Error When No Additional Data are Available, With an Application and RandD", *Econometrica*, Vol.65(5), pp 1201-1213.

Moore Stephens (2008), "OpCost 2008: *Benchmarking Vessel Running Costs ",* London.

Moore Stephens (2010), "OpCost 2010: *Benchmarking Vessel Running Costs*", London.

Pearson, R. (1980). "Container ships and Shipping", London: Fairplay Publications.

Ryder, S.C. and Chappell, D. (1979), "The Optimal Speed and Ship Size for Liner Trades", Liverpool Marine Transport Centre.

Stock, J. and Watson, M. (2003). "Forecasting Output and Inflation: the Role of Asset Prices", Department of Economics, Princeton University.

Stock, J.H., Wright, J.H. and Yogo, M. (2002), "A survey of weak instruments and weak identification in Generalized Method of Moments", *Journal of Business and Economic Statistics*, Vol.20 (4), pp 518 – 529.

Stopford, M. (2011), Lloyd's List, October 20th, 2011.

Veldman, S. Glansdor, P. and Kok R. (2011), "Economies of size of large containerships based on internal and external costs", European Conference on Shipping, Intermodalism and Ports, Chios, Greece, June 2011.

Wingrove, M. (2008), "Owners face repairs crisis", *Lloyd's List*, 23 July 2008.

Wooldridge, J.M. (2001), "Applications of Generalized Methods of Moments Estimation", *Journal of Economic Perspectives,* Vol.15 (4), pp 87-100.

In: Computational Data Analysis Techniques ISBN: 978-1-63463-957-6
Editors: M. Doumpos, C. Zopounidis and Ch. Gaganis

Chapter 6

DISCOUNTED CASH FLOWS THROUGH EXPERTONS IN BUSINESS VALUATION PROCESS

***Anna M. Gil-Lafuente*[1] *and C. Castillo-López*[1,*]**

[1]Department of Business Administration, University of Barcelona, Barcelona, Spain

ABSTRACT

The aim of this paper is to contribute to the analysis on how to measure the value of a company through different techniques which have been used in the literature. We propose a methodology based on the expertons and fuzzy logic. We have investigated different applications of fuzzy methodology, with the aim of deciphering what could work best to determinate the value of a company in the process of valuation. Following the theory of the expertons, we have used the discounted cash flow method to assess organizations.

The conclusion in the paper will allow future academic researchers one step forward in the eradication of uncertainty on traditional methods of business valuation, through the application of the fuzzy logic algorithms presented in this article, allowing us to move one step beyond in the valuation of companies.

Keywords: Valuation of companies, Uncertainty Estimation, Subjective variables, probabilistic sets

1. INTRODUCTION

The literature in the field of valuation of companies, it is not clear in which method is the best one to be used for that purpose. Analysts most used methods, do not collected in its entirety the uncertainty found during the process of valuation of a company. Through previous studies and accomplished bibliometric analysis, we have detected a gap in terms of application of fuzzy methodology on existing models for business valuation. We believe that

* Corresponding author: Tel +34 616248080 E-mail: cclopez@economistes.com

if we apply certain techniques from fuzzy logic, we can improve the valuation of a company, because we will be dealing with uncertainty in a correct way. We have found in studied papers that the most widely used method for business valuation during the last ten years is the discounted cash flows method. For that reason we will focus our study on this method. We show why is necessary to apply fuzzy methodology when using the discounted cash flow method. We discuss the necessity of applying fuzzy methodologies to address the uncertainty that exist in the different variables involved in the value calculation for this method.

The theory of the expertons is considered, according to the studied literature, an extension of the concept of probabilistic set for uncertain environments, which cannot be measured with exact numbers, but could be measured with numeric intervals.

The main problem identified in the literature on business valuations, lies with the subjective factors involved in the determination of the value of the company. It could deepen to try to explain not only the financial data involved in the final value, but also experimental evidence produced by speculative risks (Barberis, N., et al., 2001). Since the beginning of the discipline it has been great effort to differentiate the concepts of price and value. The price is the result of the quantity agreed between the buyer and the seller. It is obvious that the price contains valuable information for calculating the value, but is not the best indicator of the intrinsic value (Bhojraj, S., et al., 2002). The value is the estimation of the price that could have a company depending on multiple factors. This value depends on the expectations of the buyer or seller. At the same time, different buyers will have different expectations, so the valuation made will be also different for each other.

This paper presents a review of the academic literature referred to valuation of companies and fuzzy methodology, trying to find those aspects common to both fields. Following by fuzzy logic applications, with special emphasis to the theories related with the uncertainty. We discuss basic concepts in the universe of the fuzzy methodology such as: confidence intervals, fuzzy numbers, triangular fuzzy numbers, fuzzy subsets and random fuzzy subsets, to finally reach to expertons.

2. Preliminaries

2.1. Literature Review in Business Valuation

Although there is a vast academic literature on methods and models used in business valuation, the majority of the studies rest on a common scientific basis: the value of the company will be determined by the present value of cash flows that are expected in the future (Gonzalez Jimenez, L., & Blanco Pascual, L., 2010). Nevertheless, some studies provide evidence that DCF are far from the market value of 10% approximately. There are also studies demonstrating that models based on the benefit for action (BPA), adjust the proper value better than discounted cash flows (DCF).

In practice the DCF model has become the most popular, as it may seem that it is the most consistent with the objective of creating value, and encompasses the majority of factors that can influence the value of a company. It shows a more appropriate vision of the company value than methods based on the balance sheet (Copeland, T., et al., 2000).

There are studies (Yao, J., et al., 2005) that show with numerical examples that the inclusion of the fuzzy philosophy in the DCF model gets a more accurate value and help investors to better measure their assets. Real options become the preferred methodology to minimize the effects of the uncertainty on academic literature, over traditional methods of valuation (Ucal, I., & Kahraman, C. 2009) or probabilistic approaches (Carlsson, C., & Fuller, R. 2003). Subtle Sets are used to measure the value of goodwill, leaving behind the accounting methods, which do not correctly treat uncertainty, and thus determine a more adjusted the company's value (Ionita, I., & Stoica, M. 2009).

Summarizing, the main limitations found in business valuation methods are that they are based on calculations between quantitative variables, but there are an infinite number of qualitative factors that influence the present value, which are not included in the valuation methods used (Gil-Lafuente, A.M., 2012). Fuzzy mathematics would allow us to include these qualitative variables in calculations to determine a tighter than its actual value of the company.

2.2. Fuzzy Methodology in Business Valuation

Research in the field of uncertainty has been an issue that for many decades has attracted increased interest since it is a fundamental and common in science concept. In 1965 was the first publication of Lofti. A. Zadeh "Fuzzy sets" on fuzzy sets (Zadeh, L. A. 1965). The initial idea that offered was a new logic allowing the binary logic (which can only take value 0 or 1), the multivalent logic (in which variables can take any score between 0 and 1 of the function characteristic of permanence).

Against the Aristotelian principle of third except, prevailing in the processes of modeling for more than 2000 years, the so-called "principle of simultaneity Gradual" (Gil Aluja, J. 1996), according to which a proposition can be both, true or false condition of assigning a value to the truth and falsehood value was imposed in 1996. In this way, it got a much more complete math that would make it possible to represent the information in a way most suited to the complex reality in which we live.

From a business context and support the concept of (Gil-Lafuente, A. M. 2005) confidence interval, is possible because represents the inaccurate information in a more general way considering all the possible scenarios, from the position more optimistic to the most pessimistic in each of the variables considered. This has been useful, particularly to manage forecasts, especially ex-ante estimates, since usually the events are conditioned by subjective and uncertain elements.

3. Fuzzy Methodology for Uncertainty

To understand theories relating to uncertainty, we analyze basic concepts in the fuzzy methodology universe such as: confidence intervals, fuzzy numbers, triangular fuzzy numbers, fuzzy subset and probabilistic set, to finally reach to expertons (Kaufmann, A, & Gil Aluja, J. 1987).

3.1. Confidence Intervals

We will say that segment A is a confidence interval if we assume that the only information available in relation to a magnitude is greater or equal to a_1, and less than or equal to a_2.

$$A = [a_1, a_2], a_1 \leq a_2, a_1, a_2 \in R \tag{1}$$

3.2. Fuzzy Numbers

When we have a finite or infinite sequence of confidence intervals, which comply with the following properties:

1. Each confidence interval value will be á∈ [0, 1], and won't be the same á value for any other. The resulting value is called presumption level.
2. the á level confidence interval $A_\alpha = [a_1{}^{(\alpha)}, a_2{}^{(\alpha)}]$ must comply:

$$(\alpha' < \alpha) \Rightarrow (A_\alpha \supset A_{\alpha'}), \alpha, \alpha' \in [0, 1] \tag{2}$$

I.e., confidence intervals should fit strictly or not, with the other.

3. There is only one interval that can be reduced to a unique real.

In this case, the finite or infinite sequence of confidence intervals will be what we call by fuzzy number, which we represent by a capital letter, with the symbol~ below, $\underset{\sim}{A}$.At the same time, the confidence level á interval will be appointed by $A_á$ and we'll call it also "α-cut of$\underset{\sim}{A}$". We will say $A_\alpha$is a functional application ofα.

3.3. Triangular Fuzzy Numbers

The triangular fuzzy number (TFN), is represented by 3 numbers $a^{(1)}$, $a^{(2)}$ y $a^{(3)}$), as follows:

$$\underset{\sim}{A} = (a^{(1)}, a^{(2)}, a^{(3)}); \text{ where} a^{(1)}, a^{(2)}, a^{(3)} \in R y a^{(1)} \leq a^{(2)} \leq a^{(3)} \tag{3}$$

The essential feature of the TFN is that their functions are lineal:

$$\forall \propto \in [0, 1]:$$
$$A_\alpha = [(a^{(2)} - a^{(1)})\alpha + a^{(1)}, -(a^{(3)} - a^{(2)})\alpha + a^{(3)}] \tag{4}$$

3.4. Fuzzy Subsets

The theory of fuzzy subsets was defined by (L.A. Zadeh, 1965). Since then fuzzy subsets have become an ideal instrument to treat problems with the uncertainty data. To define the concept of fuzzy subset, we consider a set or referential E and a regular subset A (Kaufmann, A., 1975). We say that for every point or element x of A it comply:

$$\mu_A(x) = 1\ six \in A \mu_A(x) = 0\ six \notin A \quad (5)$$

Where μ is the characteristic function of A, called "membership function".

The fuzzy subset is constructed when the elements of A, instead of taking only the value of 1 if x ∈ A, could also take a value a ∈ $[0,1]$, including zero.

$$\mu_{\underset{\sim}{A}}\ (x) = a \in [0,1] \quad (6)$$

A generalization of the concept of fuzzy set would be the probabilistic set.

3.5. Expertons

The concept of experton lies in two elements, the probabilistic set, and the confidence interval. The merging of the two of them, originate the appearance of the experton, i.e., a probabilistic set, created through the merger of experts, but with opinions that have been expressed with intervals (Kaufmann, A. 1988; Kaufmann, A. y Gil Aluja, J. 1993).

Any experton has no strict horizontal growing monotony (i.e., the bottom left is less than or equal to the upper right). Any experton has no strict vertical growing monotony (i.e., every number at level α' is larger or equal to every number at level α, if α < α'). Level 0 is always 1. Under mathematical formulation would be:

$$\begin{gathered} \forall \alpha \in [0,1]: a_1(\alpha) \leq a_2(\alpha) en[a_1(\alpha), a_2(\alpha)] \\ \forall \alpha, \alpha' \in [0,1]: (\alpha' > \alpha) \rightarrow \big(a_1(\alpha) \leq a_1(\alpha'), a_2(\alpha) \leq a_2(\alpha')\big) \\ (\alpha = 0) \rightarrow (a_1(\alpha) = 1, a_2(\alpha) = 1) \end{gathered} \quad (7)$$

4. Application on Business Valuation

When faced with business valuation, the financial information in the annual accounts is essential vital. It will form the basis of the creation of value for shareholders and will reflect the ability of the Organization to meet the goal which was created. However, there is other information that is not included in the financial statements even more important, such as the expectations. Financial information is very important, but do not complete all the necessary information when analyzing the business valuation. We want to show, in addition to the information which is not contained in the mandatory documents, within what we believe known financial information and voluntary information, there may be subjectivity. Uncertainty may affect the assessment of such information, since we are dealing with expected data which is not a certain reality.

Only the information in financial statements is certain. The information derivate from them (auditory reports) and any other information from the company website, reports, presentations, etc., it's not included on the business valuation methods (Gil-Lafuente, A.M., & Barcellos, 2010; Audretsch, D & Link, A., 2012; Imam, S., et al., 2008).

What we want to demonstrate is the lack of information on business valuation methods most widely used according to what we have found in the academic literature, the DCF method. We will discuss variables involved and that these variables may not be correct without taking into account the fuzzy logic introduced in the algorithms on this work.

5. Discounted Cash Flows

We will now focus on methods based on DCF. As we have found in the literature reviewed (Gonzalez Jimenez, L., & Blanco Pascual, L., 2010; Hrvol'ova, B., et al., 2011), the main methods used in valuing companies are based on discounting cash flows.

The basic formula for calculating the present value of these cash flows is based on the following expression:

$$Company\,Value = \sum_{i=1}^{n} \frac{CF_i}{(1+k)^i} + \frac{V_n}{(1+k)^n} \quad (8)$$

CF are the expected cash flows; k discount rate applied; V_n is the residual value of the company at the end of the study period, and n is the number of years over which is expected to be generated income in the future.

Therefore, those will be the factors that can affect business valuation according to the DCF method (Fernández, P., 2005).

Some researchers (Knight, R., Bertoneche, M. 2001) have found that under the DCF method the value could be overestimated. First for being too optimistic with the cash flows that will be generated in the future, this may cause an increase in the value. And the second would be to underestimate the cost of capital (discount rate). If we combine the two effects, the gap could be higher.

If we also add that neither is true the number of year over which is expected to be generating cash flows, the uncertainty of estimation is maximum.

Another point for the uncertainty is that this calculated period expected by the company, does not have to coincide with the actual period of value creation that will take the Organization in the market.

I would be remiss to these three variables add a fourth that would be the residual value of the company at the time n.

Below is a small study of in that the values of the four factors may vary if we don't apply any methodology that would reflect the subjectivity of each of the parameters.

5.1. n- Number of Years

As number of years in businesses valuation, we understand the time we consider to generate cash flows in the organization. The question is to quantify for how long the company will forecast future cash flows.

The time horizon of the projection, therefore, will depend on many factors, among which may be considered: stability expected in the economy, the industry and the company in particular, the variability of the macroeconomic variables, such as inflation, interest rate, exchange, taxation rates.

The perception and experience of the financial analyst who develops the assessment also affect the given number of years.

The type of organization and business is carried out, are also critical when evaluating the estimate of the exact number of periods will be taken into consideration (Garicano, T. 2004).

5.2. CF- Cash Flow

To calculate cash flow, we use the information collected through the financial statements and adjusted to Free Cash Flows (FCF) (Knight, R., Bertoneche, M. 2001).

If we have to calculate these amounts for future periods, we will be working with a level of increasing uncertainty, considering that these are cash flows that are considered in the DCF formula.

5.3. k- Discount Rate

As a discount rate we should take the weighted average cost of capital (WACC). The formula is as follows:

$$WACC = \frac{D}{V} k_d (1 - t) + \frac{E}{V} k_e \quad (9)$$

The first part is the percentage of debt times the cost of debt considering the taxes. The second part of the formula is the percentage of equity times the cost of equity.

The percentage of debt and equity, are not constant throughout the life of the organization. If there is a change in the percentages, the value of the WACC will change, and affect the calculated value of the company.

The cost of debt (k_d) will not generate excessive problems, because it could be a known value and certain. The cost of equity (k_e) could be more difficult to calculate. The most common method for calculating the cost of capital is through the CAPM model (Capital Asset Pricing Model).

5.4. V_n- Residual Value

In some cases the residual value of a company could mean more than fifty percent of the total value, so it also constitutes as a fundamental variable in the analysis. Of the various theories about how to determine the residual value, the most used ones are (Martínez Conesa, I. y García Meca, E. 2005): book value of the company, liquidation value, future value of cash flow in perpetuity and future value of profits in perpetuity.

For its calculation we need to know the certain value of the previous variables, because we need the present value of this residual value.

RESULT AND CONCLUSION

Once we have analyzed the four variables, now already we can express with more security the consequences on the reliability of the valuation if it will be done through the opinions expressed by the experts. The uncertainty detected in each of the variables would have been treated properly using fuzzy logic. This is why we believe that the inclusion of the fuzzy logic will enable future lines of research and development of traditional methods, providing them with a greater adaptability to business realities and the changing circumstances of the environment.

REFERENCES

Audretsch, D., & Link, A. (2012). Valuing an entrepreneurial enterprise. *Small Business Economics,* 38(2), 139-145.

Barberis, N., Huang, M., & Santos, T. (2001). Prospect theory and asset prices. *The Quarterly Journal of Economics,* 116.

Bhojraj, S., & Lee, C. (2002). Who is my peer? A valuation-based approach to the selection of comparable firms. *Journal of Accounting Research*, 40(2).

Carlsson, C., & Fuller, R. (2003). A fuzzy approach to real option valuation. *Fuzzy Sets and Systems,* 139(2), 297-312.

Copeland, T., Koller, T., & Murrin, J. (2000). *In Makinsey and Company (Ed.), Valuation: Measuring and managing the value of companies* (2nd ed.). United States of America: Makinsey and Company.

Fernández, P. (2005). In Management 2000 (Ed.), *Companies evaluation. How to measure and manage value creation* (Third Edition ed.). Spain: Managment 2000.

Garicano, T. (2004). The discount cash flows and multiples valuation. *Harvard-Deusto Finance and Accounting* (59), 12-21.

Gil Aluja, J. (1996). Lances and misadventures of the new paradigm of decision theory. In *Proceedings of the III Congress of SIGEF, Volume I.*

Gil-Lafuente, A. M. (Ed.). (2005). *Fuzzy logic in financial analysis*. Springer.

Gil-Lafuente, A. M. (2012). A paradigm shift in business valuation process using fuzzy logic. *Studies in Fuzziness and Soft Computing*, 287

Gil-Lafuente, A. M., & Barcellos. (2010). The expertons method applied in the dialogue with stakeholders. *The 2nd International Conference on Computer Supported Education* (CSEDU). Valencia-Spain, 7-April-2010.

Gonzalez Jimenez, L., & Blanco Pascual, L. (2010). Enterprise valuation with track-record ratios and rates of change. *European Journal of Finance*, 16(1), 57-78.

Hrvol'ova, B., Markova, J., & Nincak, L. (2011). Modern methods of valuation of shares. *Ekonomický časopis*, 59(2), 148-162.

Imam, S., Barker, R., & Clubb, C. (2008). The use of valuation models by UK investment analysts. *European Accounting Review*, 17(3), 503-535.

Ionita, I., & Stoica, M. (2009). A new approach method of company valuation. *Romanian Journal of Economic Forecasting*, 10(1), 115-122.

Kaufmann, A. (1975). In Academic Press (Ed.), *Introduction to the theory of fuzzy subsets* (D. L. Swanson Trans.). New York: Academic Press.

Kaufmann, A., and Gil Aluja, J. (1987). *Operational management techniques for the treatment of uncertainty.* Barcelona: Editorial Hispano Europea.

Kaufmann, A. (1988). Theory of expertons and fuzzy logic. *Fuzzy Sets and Systems*, 28(3), 295-304.

Kaufmann, A. and Gil Aluja, J. (1993). In Editorial Milladoiro (Ed.). *Special techniques for managing experts*. España, 1993.

Knight, R., Bertoneche, M. (2001). *Financial performance*. England: Reed Educational and Professional Publishing Ltd (Reed Elsevier plc group), 2001.

Martínez Conesa, I. and García Meca, E. (2005*). In Spanish Association of Accounting and Business Administration* (Ed.). Assessment of listed companies. Main methods, the role of intangibles and cases study. Spain: AECA.

Ucal, I., & Kahraman, C. (2009*). Fuzzy real options valuation for oil investments.* Ūkio Technologinis Ir Ekonominis Vystymas, 15(4), 646-669.

Yao, J., Chen, M., & Lin, H. (2005). Valuation by using a fuzzy discounted cash flow model. *Expert Systems with Applications*, 28(2), 209-222.

Zadeh, L. (1965). *Fuzzy sets. Information and Control*, 8, 338-353.

In: Computational Data Analysis Techniques ISBN: 978-1-63463-957-6
Editors: M. Doumpos, C. Zopounidis and Ch. Gaganis

Chapter 7

LEVERAGE PREMIUM IN A SOUTHERN EUROPEAN FRAME

Panayiotis G. Artikis*[*] and Georgia Nifora
Department of Business Administration
University of Piraeus
Greece

ABSTRACT

This paper aims to investigate the impact of leverage on stock returns in four southern European countries, members of the Euro zone, Greece, Italy, Portugal and Spain. These countries are in the eye of the ongoing European dept crisis cyclone. Debt is a theoretical source of financial risk, thus a positive leverage effect is expected. The sample used consisted of Greek, Italian, Portuguese and Spanish listed, no financial, companies over the past decade (2000-2010). Following Fama and French (1993), we perform a portfolio level, regression analysis to test if leverage is a priced risk factor. The present work enhances the few and contradictory empirical evidence in the area, by focusing on a totally different, bank-oriented- environment.

The empirical findings, on the full sample, show that leverage does explain stock returns. The leverage risk factor presents a negative relationship with stock returns, at the low leverage deciles, and a positive one, at the medium and high leverage deciles, in all countries. At the industry level analysis, a significant positive leverage effect is isolated only at few industries. Therefore, the negative impact of leverage on firm's value holds for the observed four countries at the observed period.

Keywords: Asset pricing; Fama-French; Leverage; Industry; Beta; Price Earnings ratio; Book-to-market ratio; Size; Momentum; Market Risk Premium

JEL: Classification Codes: G11, G12, G32

---

[*] Correspondent author: Department of Business Administration, University of Piraeus, 80 Karaoli and Dimitriou Str., 18534 Piraeus, Greece, Tel: 0030-210 4142200. E-mail: partikis@unipi.gr

1. INTRODUCTION

This paper aims to shed light on the impact of a firm's capital structure on its value. This issue has been placed in the centre of corporate finance field, since the pioneer work of Modigliani and Miller (1958, 1963: hereafter MM). In 1963, MM empirically proved that returns increase in leverage. Undoubtedly, debt is one of the principle sources of financial risk. Rational, risk-averse investors should demand a leverage premium, indicating an expected positive relationship between firm's leverage and stock returns.

The vast majority of the studies in the area of capital structure investigate either the determinants of leverage or the existence of an optimal capital structure. Also, there are a few studies that examine the relationship between leverage and stock returns, with contradictory results, mainly in the USA and UK market oriented economies.

The objective of the present research is to provide additional empirical evidence in the relationship between leverage and stock returns, which up to now has attracted limited attention in the literature. In doing so, we treat leverage as an independent factor, in line with previous work (Hamada, 1969; Bhandari, 1988; Korteweg, 2004; Dimitrov and Jain, 2006; George and Hwang, 2010), and examine whether leverage is an asset pricing factor that can explain stock return variability. Furthermore, we perform our analysis both on a full sample basis and on an industry basis in order to investigate if the impact of leverage on stock returns varies as to the firm's industry classification, since, industry class is generally considered as an important risk factor.

By using leverage as an independent factor the results of the present study can be converted to a practical tool, that is to say a successful investment (leverage) strategy. It is an aspect where limited work has been undertaken, and to the best of our knowledge, it is the first to be undertaken in the Continental European, bank-oriented environment. The completely different politico-economical, legal, and institutional framework (the arm's length system of USA and UK vs. the control-based system of Continental Europe, Drobetz and Pensa 2007) the few previous studies have been carried out, justify the necessity of further exploration of the above relationship. Thus, the main objective of the present paper will be achieved through the analysis of a dataset from Greece, Italy, Portugal and Spain, i.e. four countries from Continental Europe that has a bank oriented economy, contributing by this way the necessary accumulation of non-US and non-UK research.

The importance of country specific characteristics on the capital structure theme has been emphasized in the literature (Rajan and Zingales, 1995; Psillaki and Daskalakis, 2009; Oztekin, 2009; Brounen et al., 2006; Andritzky, 2003; Alves and Ferreira, 2011). Specifically, Antoniou et al. (2008) examined firms operating in capital market oriented economies and bank oriented economies and concluded that the capital structure decision of a firm is not only the product of it's own characteristics, but also the result of the environment and traditions in which it operates. Jong et al. (2008) give evidence that creditor right protection, bond market development and GDP growth rate have a significant influence on capital structure issues, highlighting the importance of country–specific factors in the corporate finance field. Moreover, literature on the corporate governance issues suggest that there may be strong differences in corporate objectives between the "Anglo-American' and the Continental European Financial systems-the maximization of shareholders vs. the maximization of all stakeholders objective", Bancel and Mittoo (2004).

Furthermore, the impact of financial choice on stock returns will be examined in a different stock exchange environment, as the aforementioned capital markets have differentiating characteristics from other countries of the Euro zone. Specifically, the above mentioned countries, while members of the Euro zone, have a medium stock market compared to other European stock exchanges in terms of market capitalization, number of firms listed and turnover volume.

Besides, the Greek, Italian, Portuguese and Spanish legal system is different from that of the Anglo-Saxon countries. For instance, the American-British legal system is based on common law. The Greek, Italian, Portuguese and Spanish legal system (like the French and German) is based on code law traditions (Antoniou et al., 2008; Alves and Ferreira, 2011). Furthermore, Greece, Italy, Portugal, Spain and Ireland constitute a group of European countries which are in the middle of a debt crisis cyclone that threatens the European solidarity, the euro-monetary unity, the stability of the foreign exchange rate of the euro and last but not least the cleavage of the global economy. These economies have attracted international investors' attention and fear. The above-described institutional, economic, and legal environment in the Southern European Region contains many idiosyncrasies that are not observable in other developed markets, thus makes the investigation of the relationship between leverage and stock price performance very interesting.

In summary, the main contributions of this study are: a) We enhance the capital structure studies by broadening the limited work that has been accomplished on the base of leverage as an explanatory variable of returns, b) we use the leverage-mimicking factor, that has been applied before by Sivaprasad and Muradoglu (2010), in four countries of southern Europe with many idiosyncrasies and a debt crisis evolving, c) we provide evidence on the impact of industry classification on the relationship between leverage and stock returns and d) by focusing on the role of leverage as a strategic investment instrument or a separate risk factor, we cast light on a notion that has been ignored by the vast majority of European CEOs[1]. If a return premium can be extracted from this research, a strategic instrument can be arisen.

The rest of the paper is organised as follows: Section 2 presents the literature review; section 3 describes the data collection and sample selection; section 4 details the methodology of the study; Section 5 presents the empirical results. Finally, Section 6 presents the conclusions.

2. Literature Review

MM argued that financing decisions do not matter, in perfect capital markets, as the total value of a firm is the same irrespective of the debt equity ratio. Actually, MM set the foundation for defining the coordinates where the capital structure is relevant to the value of the company: the real financial world. In the modern business economy, capital structure choice is one of the key corporate decisions that affect the performance of firms, so investment decisions can not be independent from financial ones. However, limited studies that examine the relationship between leverage and returns have been undertaken with contradictory results.

[1] Bancel et al. (2004, pp.13) "There is little evidence that debt is used for strategy or tactical reasons. For example, the support for issuing short term debt to capture higher returns for shareholders or for reducing the chance that firm will undertake risky projects is almost negligible"

Masulis (1983) showed that change in leverage is positively related to change in stock returns. He studied daily stock returns of all companies that have gone through pure capital structure changes, in the market of United States of America (USA) during 1963-1978. Bhandari (1988) provided evidence that leverage has a significant positive effect on expected common stock returns in the USA over the period 1948-1979. His returns were adjusted for inflation. He controlled for idiosyncratic risk through size and beta.

Fama and French (1992, 1996) found that leverage based on book values is associated with lower average returns. Their sample concerns the USA market and covers the period 1963-1991. George and Hwang (2010), who examined a sample of USA firms over the period 1965-2003, proved a negative effect of leverage on returns.

Korteweg (2004) found a negative relationship between leverage and returns at the USA market. His work was also based on pure capital structure changes, during the period 1979-2001. Dimitrov and Jain (2008) revealed a negative effect of leverage changes on stock returns at the USA market as well as on earnings-based measures of performance. Their sample covers the period 1973-2001. Nissim and Penman (2003) also spotted a negative effect of leverage on profitability. They found that the portfolios with the lowest financial leverage perform better than portfolios with high financial leverage. They also found a negative effect of total leverage on future returns. Penman et al. (2007) found that returns are inversely related to leverage. Their sample regards the USA market over the period 1962-2001. They break-down the book-to price effect into two components, which represent the operating and financial risk respectively.

Sivaprasad and Muradoglu (2010) examined the United Kingdom market during the period 1980-2004 and proved that capital structure is value relevant for equity investors, though the effect doesn't always move towards the same direction. They found different effects of leverage on returns at different levels of analysis. Muradoglu and Sivaprasad (2009) also proved an inverse relationship between book leverage and portfolio returns (over risk free). Gomes and Schmid (2010) investigated the USA market over the period 1963-2006 and found a negative impact of leverage (based on book values) on stock returns. They argued that the link between leverage and returns is more complex. It usually depends on the investment opportunities available to the firm. In the presence of financial market imperfections, leverage and investment are generally correlated so that high levered firms are also mature firms with relative more (safe) book assets and fewer (risky) growth opportunities. They concluded that investment and financing strategies must be examined jointly under the presence of financial frictions in the real markets world.

Garlappi and Yan (2011) examined USA market during the period 1969-2003 and unveiled a hump-shaped relationship between default probabilities and expected returns and a momentum profits concentration among high credit-risk firms with significant expected shareholder recovery upon financial distress. They consider that the presence of potential shareholder recovery upon financial distress alters the risk structure of equity (non-linear dependence of equity beta) and causes the expected return to be hump-shaped in default probabilities. This non-monotonic relationship between risk and default probability in turn leads to hump-shaped value premia with respect to default probability.

George and Hwang (2010) argued that the negative relation between leverage and returns, found by the most researchers, (the so called distress risk puzzle) is not a market mispricing. They stated that the idea that equity risk is increasing in leverage relies on the frictionless markets assumption that makes investment and financing decisions separable, i.e.

firms' capital structure choices are unrelated to asset risk. It is possible that market friction leads low leverage firms to have greater exposure to systematic risk, which dominates the amplification effect of leverage on equity risk. In this case, expected returns to low leverage firms will indeed be exposed to greater systematic risk than high leverage firms.

3. Data Collection and Sample Derivation

The sample used in the empirical tests consists of all non-financial companies listed on the Athens Stock Exchange (ASE), Borsa Italiana S.p.A (Milan Stock Exchange, MSE), NYSE Euronext Lisbon and Bolsa de Madrid (Madrid Stock Exchange) from 1998/12-2009/3 for Greece and 2000/12 to 2010/3 for the other three countries. Stock prices, index market prices, market capitalization, accounting data of the sample firms and risk-free rates of return are sourced from the Bloomberg Professional Database. The number of sample firms ranges from 163 in 1999 (139, 49, 83 in 2000)[2] to 224 in 2009 (227, 59, 107 in 2010), resulting in 28,524 (20,340, 5,712, 10,404) monthly observations. All non-financial companies listed in the final year of the research are included in the initial sample. Also, firms de-listed each year are identified and consequently added to the initial sample. Companies that have changed name under the selected period are identified and treated as a single unit. Moreover, companies that either merged or are acquired over the study period are treated as a new unit following the event[3]. By this way, a selection bias towards historically successful firms is limited to a great extent. Listed companies, which have been under suspension for more than 50% of year t, are excluded from the final sample. Moreover, firms with no available financial information for book, market equity or leverage for at least twelve months in a row are not included in the sample either. Financial data is necessary for the construction of fundamental variables for the various portfolios of each year of the research period. Following Fama and French (1992), we also exclude companies with negative BE/ME ratios at 12/31 of year t–1. Last but not least, stock prices are adjusted for dividends and stock splits.

4. Methodology

The present paper involves the performance of a step–wise regression analysis of the excess returns (ER_{it}) of the sample stocks against the returns of five risk factors, i.e. market risk premium (MRP), size (SMB), value (HML), momentum (WML) and leverage (HLMLL). The step–wise regression analysis approach will help us to observe the change in the explanatory power of the independent variables (i.e. statistical significance and numerical value of the parameters). Specifically, the following models will be tested: i) a univariate model involving the leverage risk factor, ii) a two factor model with the market risk premium added to the leverage risk factor, iii) the Fama and French Three Factor Model with the

[2] In parenthesis the Italian, Portuguese and Spanish data are recorded respectively.

[3] The number of firms that are de-listed, renamed, merged etc. each year is negligible (below ten). These firms are not used into the calculation of the HLMLL (leverage) factor, and since our analysis is not a panel one but a time series approach, we consider that there is no impact on the results arising from the different number of sample firms we have each year.

leverage factor, and iv) a five factor model involving leverage, Fama and French (1993) and Carhart (1997) momentum factors:

$$ER_{it} = \alpha_i + l\ HLMLL + e_{i,t} \tag{1}$$

$$ER_{it} = \alpha + b\ MRP + l\ HLMLL + e_{i,t} \tag{2}$$

$$ER_{it} = \alpha + b\ MRP + s\ SMB + h_i\ HML + l\ HLMLL + e_{i,t} \tag{3}$$

$$ER_{it} = \alpha + b\ MRP + s\ SMB + h\ HML + w\ WML + l\ HLMLL + e_{i,t} \tag{4}$$

where, ER_{it} is the monthly stock returns in excess of risk free rate for portfolio i, in month t, α stands for constant, HLMLL is returns on equal-weihte, factor mimicking portfolio for leverage, MRP is the excess returns on the market porfolio, SMB mimics the risk factor in returns related to size, HML is meant to mimic the risk factor in returns related to book-to-market ratio, WML mimics the risk factor in returns related to momentum, b, s, h, l are the regression coefficients of the above explanatory variables and ε_{it} is the error term.

The analysis is applied on: a) a full sample level and b) an industry level. The full sample level analysis involves the estimation of all 4 regression models for both: a) one portfolio consisting of all stocks and b) four portfolios where leverage is used as the criterion to allocate stocks[4]. At the industry level analysis the sample stocks are first allocated into 9 industries (Technology, Oil and Gas, Basic Material, Consumer Goods, Consumer Services, Health Care, Industrials, Telecommunications, Utilities) based on the Bloomberg Industry Classification (ICB) and then the analysis involves the estimation of all 4 regression models for each industry separately.

4.1. Dependent Variable

In order to construct the four levered portfolios, for both the full sample level and the industry level analysis, all stocks at the end of December of each year t from 1999 to 2009 (2000 to 2010) are ranked on leverage and divided into four leverage groups (portfolio L1 consists of the low levered firms, while portfolio L4 consists of the high levered firms). A broad definition of Leverage is used (Total Debt to Total Assets), in order to capture the substitutability between the various forms of debt (Schwartz, 1959). Having formed the four leverage portfolios we calculate their monthly returns as logarithmic difference between successive closing prices of the shares [ln (p_{t-1}/p_t)] and then we subtract the return of the 12 month (Greek, Italian, Portuguese and Spanish) Government Treasury Bill adjusted on a monthly basis, in order to arrive at their excess returns from April of year t to March of year t+1. The excess returns on the four portfolios from April 1999 (2001) to March 2009 (2010) are the dependent variables in the time–series regressions. We use the excess return of the

[4] All statistical tests were also performed with eight leverage portfolios in order to check if our results are dependent on the number of portfolios. The findings for the eight levered portfolios are not different from those of the four portfolio analysis and are not presented here due to space considerations. The results can, however, be requested from the authors.

levered portfolio, in order to find out whether the mimicking portfolios capture common risk factor in returns associated with debt levels.

The monthly returns on the four portfolios are equal–weighted, as proposed by Lakonishok et al. (1994) and Sivaprasad and Muradoglu (2010). We choose to use equal weight portfolios[5] due to the idiosyncrasies of the investigated stock markets, which are dominated, in terms of market capitalization, by a few very large companies as compared to the majority of the medium to small sized companies, providing more unbiased results. The calculation of monthly equal weighted excess returns for each portfolio starts at the end of April of year t in order to make sure that the financial statements of fiscal year t-1 are available to investors and thus avoid look–ahead bias. Moreover, the four portfolios are rebalanced each year of the selected period allowing for companies to move freely across portfolios depending on the ranking of their leverage.

4.2. Independent Variables

The market risk premium was calculated as the monthly logarithmic return of a market portfolio in excess of the risk–free rate for the period from April 1999 (2001) to March 2009 (2010). The market return is approximated by the Athens Stock Exchange (ASE) General Index for Greece, the FTSE MIB Index for Italy, the PSI20 index for Portugal and the IBEX Index for Spain.[6] As a risk–free asset the return of the 12–month (Greek, Italian, Portuguese and Spanish) government Treasury bill was used.

In order to calculate the returns of the SMB, HML, HLMLL and WML risk factors all stocks, at the end of March of each year t from 1999 to 2008 (2001 to 2009) were ranked: a) on size (capitalization) and allocated into two size groups (small and large), b) on their book equity to market equity ratio (BE_{t-1}/ME_{t-1}) at 31/12 of year t-1 and divided into three BE/ME groups (30% of stocks are allocated to the low BE/ME portfolio, 40% to the medium BE/ME portfolio and 30% to the high BE/ME portfolio), c) on their average monthly return of the previous year, from the highest to the lowest, and allocated into three momentum portfolios ("winner" portfolio is defined as the top 30% stocks with the highest last year average return, "loser" portfolio is defined as the bottom 30% stocks and the "medium" portfolio is defined as the middle 40% stocks), and d) on their leverage ratio at 31/12 of year t-1 and allocated into two leverage portfolios (Low and High). As a result, we form thirty six stock portfolios at the intersection of the two size, three BE/ME, three momentum and two leverage deciles.

The SMB factor is a portfolio that is long on small sized stocks and short on big sized stocks and is neutral on the momentum, value and leverage effect. The HML factor is a portfolio that is long on high BE/ME stocks and short on low BE/ME stocks and is neutral on the momentum, size and leverage effect. The WML factor is a portfolio that is long on winner stocks and short on loser stocks and is neutral on the size, value and leverage effect. The HLMLL factor is a portfolio that is long on high leverage stocks and short on low leverage stocks and is neutral on the size, momentum and value effect.

It must be noted that the portfolio construction procedure for the calculation of the risk factors returns was performed with annually rebalancing frequencies and the stocks within the

[5] Value weighted analysis is also performed, and yields approximately to the same results.

[6] Detailed description of the indexes and eligibility criteria can be found at www.ase.gr, www.borsaitaliana.it , www.euronext.com and www.bolsamadrid.es.

portfolios were equally weighted. The annual rebalancing was adopted because the book value and the leverage of the sample firms is available once a year, at the end of each calendar year, thus, making the HML and HLMLL factors inconsistent if intra-annual balancing was followed.

Finally, all the necessary tests (Breusch-Godfrey Serial Correlation LM, Durbin-Watson, Ramsey reset, omitted variable, sample selection, heteroskedasticity, multicollinearity) that ensure that the OLS procedure yields to best linear unbiased (BLUE) estimators have been applied. Furthermore, our econometric models lacks of Endogeneity as indicated by the Hausman test.[7]

5. Empirical Results

The descriptive statistics of the explanatory variables (Table 1) show that all risk factors except the market risk premium have a mean and median value that marginally deviates from zero. Furthermore, the Augmented Dickey –Fuller test for unit root results indicate that our variables are stationary (Io).

Table 1. Descriptive Statistics of Explanatory Variables

Panel A: ITALY	HLMLL	HML	MRP	SMB	WML
Mean	-0.000001	-0.000430*	-0.034103**	-0.000510	0.000850*
Median	0.0000	-0.0005	-0.0243	-0.0014	0.0012
Maximum	0.0082	0.0112	0.1567	0.0156	0.0070
Minimum	-0.0087	-0.0072	-0.2146	-0.0102	-0.0069
Std. Dev.	0.0033	0.0025	0.0629	0.0043	0.0025
Skewness	-0.2859	1.0940	-0.4537	1.0094	-0.2589
Kurtosis	3.3282	7.8349	3.9673	5.3157	3.5102
Jarque-Bera	1.9557	126.7362	7.9163	42.4713	2.3781
Probability	0.3761	0.000	0.0191	0.000	0.3045
Observations	108	108	108	108	108
Panel B: GREECE					
Mean	-0.000427	-0.000778*	-0.008982	-0.000000	-0.007939
Median	-0.000779	-0.000625	0.000485	-0.001141	0.000373
Maximum	0.022702	0.009627	0.173545	0.026147	0.038187
Minimum	-0.012407	-0.014841	-0.330641	-0.024924	-1.000000
Std.Dev.	0.004425	0.004219	0.079103	0.008265	0.091846
Skewness	1.282966	-0.876531	-0.820570	0.770211	-10.63348
Kurtosis	9.086487	4.960525	4.682594	4.747383	115.3499
Jarque-Bera	218.1466	34.58441	27.62230	27.13124	65373.96
Probability	0.000000	0.000000	0.000001	0.000001	0.000000
Observations	120	120	120	120	120

[7] The results of the statistical tests are not reported due to space considerations, however, they can be requested from the authors.

Panel C: PORTUGAL					
Mean	-0.000503	-0.000431	-0.032771**	-0.000320	0.000726
Median	-0.000204	-0.000296	-0.026263	-0.000698	0.000454
Maximum	0.021910	0.018578	0.076320	0.039745	0.022414
Minimum	-0.046504	-0.015261	-0.282191	-0.024057	-0.009090
Std. Dev.	0.008258	0.006334	0.061276	0.011042	0.004643
Skewness	-1.302908	0.015386	-1.206808	0.503830	1.059963
Kurtosis	11.00632	3.501361	5.725679	4.484081	6.756975
Jarque-Bera	319.0115	1.135392	59.64690	14.48043	83.74024
Probability	0.000000	0.566830	0.000000	0.000717	0.000000
Observations	108	108	108	108	108
Panel D: SPAIN					
Mean	-0.000591	-0.000683*	-0.02620**	0.000282	0.000316
Median	-0.000693	-0.000537	-0.018869	0.000444	0.000238
Maximum	0.033751	0.005378	0.134893	0.009248	0.010075
Minimum	-0.024134	-0.022732	-0.211727	-0.009442	-0.013754
Std. Dev.	0.005128	0.002903	0.060995	0.003516	0.003158
Skewness	1.980821	-3.932075	-0.628614	-0.066109	-0.696390
Kurtosis	23.65105	32.07743	3.996632	3.033904	6.759248
Jarque-Bera	1989.721	4083.039	11.58254	0.083840	72.32303
Probability	0.000000	0.000000	0.003054	0.958946	0.000000
Observations	108	108	108	108	108

The table reports the monthly summary statistics for all explanatory factors of the research model. HLMLL is the realized return on a portfolio that is long on high levered stocks and short on low levered stocks. MRP is the market risk premium. SMB is the realized return on a portfolio that is long on small sized firms and short on big sized firms. HML is the realized return on the portfolio that is long on high BE/ME stocks and short on low BE/ME equity stocks. WML is the realized return on the portfolio that is long on winner stocks and short on loser stocks. **, *** used for the mean test, denote, respectively, significance at the 10% and 5%, significance level.

5.1. Full Sample Level

5.1.1. One Factor Model

The empirical results of the one factor model (Table 2), involving the leverage risk factor, are approximately the same for Greece and Italy and uncover a positive relationship (almost in all cases) between stock returns and leverage, both on the levered portfolio and the all stocks basis. However, (except for portfolio's L4 coefficient, which appears to be high, positive and significant in Italy) both the regression model and the rest coefficients are not significant, limiting the importance of the findings in the above countries. The very low coefficient of determination indicates that leverage cannot explain, by itself, the cross-section of stock returns in Greece and Italy. In Portugal, returns increase in leverage only at the high debt levels. At the low debt levels, returns decrease in leverage. This non monotonic relationship is statistical and economic significant almost in all cases, in this country. The coefficient of determination ranges across deciles, from 6% to 18%.

Table 2. One Factor Model on a Full Sample Basis

$ER_{im} = a_i + l_i\ HLMLL_m + e_i$				
Portfolio	a_i	l_i	R^2 adj.	DW
Panel A: Italy				
(1)	-0.0379 (-5.68)***	-0.6221 (-0.30)	-0.0085	1.50
(2)	-0.0372 (-5.72)***	0.6346 (0.32)	-0.0084	1.40
(3)	-0.0369 (-5.62)***	3.2181 (1.59)	0.0140	1.44
(4)	-0.0373 (-5.74)***	4.8395 (2.42)**	0.0433	1.48
ALL	-0.0373 (-5.78)***	2.0175 (1.01)	0.0003	1.43
Panel B: Greece				
(1)	-0.0137 (-1.01)	1.3876 (0.42)	-0.0056	1.59
(2)	-0.1375 (-1.28)	2.4730 (0.84)	-0.0000	1.78
(3)	-0.0160 (-1.39)	5.5198 (1.49)	0.0273	1.59
(4)	-0.0150 (-1.33)	5.2707 (1.41)	0.0258	1.70
ALL	-0.0146 (-1.35)	3.6628 (1.13)	0.0090	1.63
Panel C: Portugal				
(1)	-0.0357 (-5.72)***	-2.0945 (-2.75)***	0.0058	1.52
(2)	-0.0322 (-5.73)***	0.4745 (0.69)	-0.0048	1.31
(3)	-0.0285 (-3.31)***	2.9186 (2.05)***	0.1300	1.16
(4)	-0.0366 (-6.16)***	3.5787 (4.95)***	0.1800	1.59
ALL	-0.0333 (-4.35)***	1.2193 (1.18)	0.0250	1.16
Panel D: Spain				
(1)	-0.02288 (-4.86)***	1.7316 (1.9)*	0.0240	1.3
(2)	-0.02134 (-3.81)***	0.9582 (0.88)	-0.0020	1.27
(3)	-0.02018 (-3.82)***	6.8117 (6.62)***	0.2900	1.33
(4)	-0.02509 (-4.34)***	5.1621 (4.59)***	0.1600	1.28
ALL	-0.02235 (-4.39)***	3.6655 (3.7)***	0.1100	1.23

Table 3. Two Factor Model on a Full Sample Basis

$ER_{im} = a_i + b_i\,MRP + l_i\,HLMLL + e_i$					
P/F	a_i	b_i	l_i	R^2 adj.	DW
Panel A: Italy					
(1)	-0.0055 (-1.45)	0.9538 (17.70)***	-2.1289 (-2.05)**	0.75	1.83
(2)	-0.0046 (-1.39)	0.9582 (20.20)***	-0.8789 (-0.96)	0.80	1.98
(3)	-0.0036 (-1.14)	0.9802 (21.51)***	1.6697 (1.90)*	0.82	1.98
(4)	-0.0055 (-1.53)	0.9355 (13.94)***	3.3617 (3.41)***	0.77	2.12
ALL	-0.0048 (-1.50)	0.9569 (20.93)***	0.5059 (0.57)	0.80	1.98
Panel B: Greece					
(1)	-0.0040 (-0.59)	1.1294 (13.12)***	0.2626 (0.17)	0.59	1.57
(2)	-0.0035 (-0.51)	1.1961 (13.96)***	1.2816 (0.83)	0.62	1.76
(3)	-0.0054 (-0.72)	1.2369 (12.97)***	4.2878 (2.51)***	0.60	1.66
(4)	-0.0045 (-0.63)	1.2237 (13.37)***	4.0518 (2.48)***	0.61	1.69
ALL	-0.0044 (-0.63)	1.1965 (13.7)***	2.4709 (1.58)	0.61	1.65
Panel C: Portugal					
(1)	-0.0123 (-2.32)***	0.7420 (9.22)***	-3.816 (-6.39)***	0.47	2.15
(2)	-0.0051 (-1.56)	0.8569 (17.20)***	-1.5143 (-4.1)***	0.73	2.4
(3)	-0.0009 (-0.24)	0.8743 (15.4)***	0.8890 (2.11)***	0.73	2.04
(4)	-0.0166 (-3.051)***	0.6337 (7.69)***	2.1076 (3.45)***	0.47	2.13
ALL	-0.0087 (-2.78)***	0.7770 (16.32)***	-0.5837 (-1.65)	0.72	2.14
Panel D: Spain					
(1)	-0.0073 (-2.3)**	0.6477 (12.62)***	-0.8506 (-1.39)	0.61	1.93
(2)	-0.0028 (-0.74)	0.7755 (12.55)***	-2.1318 (-2.9)***	0.60	1.71
(3)	-0.0045 (-1.1)	0.6551 (9.87)***	4.2012 (5.32)***	0.63	1.71
(4)	-0.0048 (-1.35)	0.8504 (14.85)***	1.7736 (2.6)***	0.73	2.1
ALL	-0.0048 (-1.48)	0.7322 (13.85)***	0.7480 (1.19)	0.68	1.82

In Spain a very significant positive leverage effect is spotted, almost in all deciles, as well as at the full sample. For example, in L3 decile (medium to high levered firms), 29% of the variation of returns can be explained by leverage factor. Furthermore, the economical and statistical significance is high, since 1% per cent increase in leverage is associated with 6.8% increase in excess returns.

The table reports the results of the one factor model regression. ER_{im} is the realized monthly return in excess of the risk free rate of the 4 levered and the all stocks portfolios, calculated from April 1st of the year following the announcement of the leverage ratios. HLMLLm is the realized monthly return on a portfolio that is long on high leveraged stocks and short on low levered stocks. Total number of observations are 120 for Greece and 108 for Italy and Portugal respectively. *, ** and *** denote statistical significance at the 10%, 5% and 1% level, respectively and t-statistics are in parentheses.

The table reports the results of the MRP plus the leverage factor model regression. ER_{im} is the realized monthly return in excess of the risk free rate of the 4 levered and the all stocks portfolios, calculated from April 1st of the year following the announcement of the leverage ratios. MRP is the realized monthly return of the market and leverage risk premium. $HLMLL_m$ is the realized monthly return on a portfolio that is long on high leveraged stocks and short on low levered stocks. Total number of observations are 120 for Greece and 108 for Italy and Portugal respectively. *, ** and *** denote statistical significance at the 10%, 5% and 1% level, respectively and t-statistics are in parentheses.

The table reports the results of the FandF plus the leverage factor model regression. ER_{im} is the realized monthly return in excess of the risk free rate of the 4 levered and the all stocks portfolios, calculated from April 1st of the year following the announcement of the leverage ratios. MRP is the realized monthly return of the market and leverage risk premium. SMB_m is the realized monthly return on a portfolio that is long on small sized stocks and short on high sized stocks. HML_m is the realized monthly return on a portfolio that is long on high BE/ME stocks and short on low BE/ME stocks. $HLMLL_m$ is the realized monthly return on a portfolio that is long on high leveraged stocks and short on low levered stocks. Total number of observations are 120 for Greece and 108 for Italy and Portugal respectively. *, ** and *** denote statistical significance at the 10%, 5% and 1% level, respectively and t-statistics are in parentheses.

5.1.2. Two Factor model

The empirical results of the two - factor model (Table 3), involving the leverage risk factor and the market risk premium, show an increased explanatory power of the model as indicated by the adjusted coefficient of determination. Furthermore, HLMLL turns out to be a significant risk factor in the last two high leverage deciles in Greece and Italy, which appears a positive and big in magnitude coefficient. However, the coefficient is negative in the two Italian low levered portfolios (L1 and L2) but significant only in the first of them. Portugal's and Spain's results are approximately the same as those of the previous model.

5.1.3. Fama and French Three Factor Plus Leverage Model

The next model involves the regression of the three factors of the Fama and French model plus the HLMLL leverage factor model against the excess returns of the sample stocks (Table 4). The regression equation overall was statistically significant, as indicated by the F-statistic.

Table 4. Fama-French 3 Factor + Leverage factor Model on a Full Sample Basis

$ER_{im} = a_i + b_i MRP + s_i SMB + h_i HML + l_i HLMLL + e_i$							
Panel A: Italy							
P/F	a_i	b_i	s_i	h_i	l_i	R^2 adj.	DW
(1)	-0.0045 (-1.18)	0.9534 (17.36)***	1.4114 (1.70)*	-0.6337 (-0.44)	-1.5065 (-1.38)**	0.76	1.79
(2)	-0.0035 (-1.10)	0.9843 (21.19)***	2.3098 (3.29)***	2.3158 (1.90)*	-0.4728 (-0.51)	0.82	1.92
(3)	-0.0023 (-0.74)	0.9929 (22.16)***	2.2804 (3.36)***	0.6590 (0.56)	2.3679 (2.66)***	0.84	1.94
(4)	-0.0042 (-1.53)	0.9481 (18.50)***	2.1956 (2.83)***	0.6751 (0.50)	4.0265 (3.96)***	0.79	2.14
ALL	-0.0036 (-1.16)	0.9697 (21.32)***	2.0493 (2.97)***	0.7540 (0.63)	1.1037 (1.22)	0.82	1.95
Panel B: Greece							
(1)	-0.0092 (-2.15)***	1.0613 (11.29)***	6.0739 (7.06)***	3.1347 (1.43)	-3.6084 (-2.19)***	0.82	1.87
(2)	-0.0087 (-1.93)*	1.1265 (14.62)***	6.2590 (6.08)***	3.1814 (1.66)	-2.7145 (-1.77)*	0.84	1.96
(3)	-0.0123 (-2.2)**	1.1439 (14.16)***	5.4919 (4.68)***	5.5023 (2.49)***	1.1701 (0.50)	0.80	1.90
(4)	-0.0105 (-1.82)*	1.1442 (13.63)***	5.8351 (4.68)***	4.2123 (1.90)*	0.5050 (0.20)	0.81	2.10
ALL	-0.0102 (-2.11)	1.1190 (14.15)***	5.9150 (5.68)***	4.0077 (1.99)**	-1.1619 (-0.61)	0.83	1.95
Panel C: Portugal							
(1)	-0.0101 (-1.88)	0.8294 (9.24)***	0.1683 (0.26)	2.77157 (2.59)**	-2.92668 (-4.70)***	0.52	2.40
(2)	-0.0051 (-1.46)	0.8506 (14.52)***	0.11152 (0.26)	-0.6280 (-0.90)	-1.6739 (-4.12)***	0.73	2.44
(3)	-0.0015 (-0.40)	0.8699 (13.13)***	-0.4116 (-0.86)	1.2544 (1.59)	1.15338 (2.51)***	0.73	2.07
(4)	-0.014 (-2.46)***	0.7176 (7.58)***	0.4953 (0.72)	1,.5047 (1.33)	2.7057 (4.12)***	0.49	2.16
ALL	-0.0077 (-2.36)***	0.8169 (15.01***	0.0909 (0.23)	1.2256 (1.89)	-0.18536 (-0.49)	0.73	2.12
Panel D: Spain							
(1)	-0.0094 (-3.25)***	0.72643 (15.34)***	2.5969 (3.09)***	3.7523 (3.32)***	-2.3493 (-3.75)***	0.7	2.07
(2)	-0.0064 (-1.79)**	0.85154 (14.67)***	1.60383 (1.56)	5.7438 (4.15)***	-4.12413 (-5.37)***	0.68	1.89
(3)	-0.00953 (-2.6)**	0.73865 (12.43)***	1.12907 (1.07)	7.79599 (5.5)***	1.63058 (2.08)**	0.73	2.04
(4)	-0.0046 (-1.37)	0.93036 (16.79)***	4.0086 (4.08)***	0.5963 (0.45)	1.0777 (1.47)	0.77	2.23
ALL	-0.0075 (-2.53)**	0.81175 (16.79)***	2.3346 (2.72)***	4.4721 (3.88)***	-0.9413 (-1.47)	0.76	2.03

The alpha intercept was negative at all leverage deciles and on the full sample level (insignificant in most Italian, Spanish and Portuguese deciles but significant almost in all cases in Greece). The coefficients of the market risk premium and the size factor are positive and statistically significant in almost all deciles in Italy, Greece and Spain. However, in Portugal we detect an unexpected observation: size is a statistically and economically insignificant risk factor.

The HML factor showed a positive (except Italian L1 decile and in most cases, statistical significant in Greece and Spain but insignificant in Italy and Portugal) relationship with the levered portfolios, which is validated also at the all stocks level. So, the value effect seems to be almost negligible for Italian and Portuguese investors.

The direction of the relationship between leverage and returns is round the same with this spotted in the previous model in Italy, Portugal and Spain. On the contrary in Greece we observe a change in the sign and in the direction of the significance at the leverage coefficient. So, it becomes negative and significant in the first leverage deciles (from positive and significant in the high leverage deciles presented in the previous model). Furthermore, we evidenced an even higher coefficient of determination, which means that the explanatory power of the model increased as we included the additional risk factors.

5.1.4. Five Factor Model

The final model involved the regression of the excess returns of the levered portfolios against the four factors of the model proposed by Carhart (1997) plus the leverage factor. The empirical results indicate (Table 5) that the overall regression is statistically significant, revealing that the risk factors used in the model explain the return of the sample stocks.

The above results once again verified the significant role of MRP and SMB factors in explaining stock returns. The coefficients of the market risk premium and SMB, are statistically significant in most of the cases and remain stable in terms of sign and magnitude as in the previous regression models for Greece, Italy and Spain alike.

From the above tables, it can be shown that the value effect, which is significant in most cases in Greece and Spain, in Italy and Portugal is insignificant, almost in all cases. Furthermore, in Greece and Spain momentum is a significant risk factor (almost in all deciles), which is related positive with stock returns, whereas in Italy and Portugal turns to be negative (and insignificant in all deciles in Italy). So, Greek as well as Italian and Spanish investors do take under consideration the market risk premium and the size effect in discriminating between levered companies. In Portugal, although market risk premium is a factor of great importance, like in the above pair countries, size is not (statistically and economically) a significant investors-guide variable. Besides, the value effect is important in Greece and Spain, whereas it's almost negligible in Italy and Portugal. In conclusion, a lucrative momentum strategy is traced only in Greek and Spanish market.

The leverage mimicking factor HLMLL is negative in the first two (low leverage) quartiles, while it changes sign and becomes positive in the remaining two quartiles of high levered firms, in all countries, revealing that the relationship between leverage and returns is negative for the low levered firms and positive for the high levered ones. However, the statistical and economical significance is placed in the low debt quadrants in Greece (in which we spot significant, negative and big in magnitude leverage coefficient) and in high debt portfolios in Italy (in which we isolate very significant, positive and big in magnitude leverage coefficient).

Table 5. Carhart Four Factor + Leverage Factor Model on a Full Sample Basis

$ER_{im} = a_i + b_i\,MRP + s_i\,SMB + h_i\,HML + w_i\,WML + l_i\,HLMLL + e_i$								
Panel A: Italy								
P/F	a_i	b_i	s_i	h_i	w_i	l_i	R^2 adj.	DW
(1)	-0.0043 (-1.23)	0.903 (11.89)***	1.032 (1.20)	-0.776 (-0.43)	-2.343 (-1.47)	-1.161 (-1.07)	0.75	1.81
(2)	-0.0035 (-1.08)	0.974 (17.42)***	2.232 (3)***	2.286 (1.87)*	-0.481 (-0.32)	-0.402 (-0.42)	0.81	1.92
(3)	-0.002 (-0.69)	0.951 (17.79)***	1.959 (2.75)***	0.538 (0.46)	-1.984 (-1.42)	2.660 (2.93)***	0.83	1.95
(4)	-0.0041 (-1.14)	0.9127 (11.19)***	1.924 (2.63)***	0.573 (0.40)	-1.67 (-1.05)	4.274*** (3.94)	0.78	2.12
ALL	-0.003 (-1.11)	0.935 (17.18)***	1.786 (2.47)**	0.655 (0.55)	-1.621 (-1.14)	1.343 (1.45)	0.82	1.94
Panel B: Greece								
(1)	-0.008 (-2.07)**	1.049 (11.17)***	5.868 (6.70)***	3.699 (1.66)	0.107 (5.21)***	-2.082 (-2.08)**	0.82	1.78
(2)	-0.008 (-1.82)*	1.109 (14.92)***	5.967 (5.71)***	3.982 (2.14)**	0.152 (7.84)***	-2.431 (-1.663)*	0.86	1.80
(3)	-0.011 (-2.11)**	1.124 (14.29)***	5.158 (4.32)***	6.417 (2.95)***	0.174 (5.73)***	1.494 (0.67)	0.81	1.76
(4)	-0.009 (-1.73)*	1.124 (13.85)***	5.50 (4.33)***	5.129 (2.36)**	0.175 (5.33)***	0.829 (0.35)	0.83	1.91
ALL	-0.009 (-2.10)**	1.102 (14.29)***	5.623 (5.29)***	4.807 (2.42)**	0.153 (6.17)***	-0.879 (-0.48)	0.85	1.80

Table 5. (Continued)

Panel C: Portugal								
(1)	-0.00816 (-1.72)	0.78493 (8.00)***	0.62372 (0.99)	1.63212 (1.47)	-3.8150 (-3.61)***	-2.8079 (-5.36)***	0.58	2.15
(2)	-0.0044 (-1.35)	0.8347 (14.42)***	0.2745 (0.79)	-1.03583 (-1.52)	-1.3655 (-2)***	-1.6314 (-2.73)***	0.74	2.40
(3)	-0.0009 (-0.24)	0.856 (12.90)***	-0.2686 (-0.55)	0.8966 (1.1)	-1.1978 (-1.59)	1.190676 (2.60)***	0.74	2.09
(4)	-0.0133 (-2.33)**	0.7012 (7.37)	0.6638 (0.95)	1.008 (0.92)	-1.4113 (-1.31)	2.7497 (4.19)***	0.49	2.18
ALL	-0.0067 (-2.49)**	0.79419 (13.53)***	0.3233 (0.90)	0.644 (0.90)	-1.9474 (-2.90)***	1.343 (1.45)	0.76	2.16
Panel D: Spain								
(1)	-0.009 (-3.2)***	0.7453 (14.89)***	2.7412 (3.23)***	3.7973 (3.37)***	1.0433 (1.15)	-2.266 (-3.6)***	0.70	2.1
(2)	-0.006 (-1.73)	0.8928 (14.76)***	1.9183 (1.87)	5.8418 (4.28)***	2.2738 (2.08)**	-3.9424 (-5.18)***	0.69	1.9
(3)	-0.0092 (-2.56)**	0.7795 (12.57)***	1.4405 (1.37)	7.8930 (5.65)***	2.2523 (2.01)**	1.8105 (2.32)**	0.74	2.1
(4)	-0.0046 (-1.35)	0.93137 (15.81)***	4.0163 (4.02)***	0.5986 (0.45)	0.0556 (0.05)	1.082 (1.46)	0.77	2.2
ALL	-0.0073 (-2.48)**	0.8372 (16.47)***	2.5291 (2.94)***	4.5327 (3.96)***	1.4062 (1.53)	-0.8289 (-1.3)	0.76	2.07

The table reports the results of the Carhart plus the leverage factor model regression. ER_{im} is the realized monthly return in excess of the risk free rate of the 4 levered and the all stocks portfolios, calculated from April 1st of the year following the announcement of the leverage ratios. MRP is the realized monthly return of the market and leverage risk premium. SMB_m is the realized monthly return on a portfolio that is long on small sized stocks and short on high sized stocks. HML_m is the realized monthly return on a portfolio that is long on high BE/ME stocks and short on low BE/ME stocks. HML_m is the realized monthly return on a portfolio that is long on high BE/ME stocks and short on low BE/ME stocks. $HLMLL_m$ is the realized monthly return on a portfolio that is long on winner stocks and short on loser stocks. Total number of observations are 120 for Greece and 108 for Italy and Portugal respectively. *, ** and *** denote statistical significance at the 10%, 5% and 1% level, respectively and t-statistics are in parentheses.

In Portugal and Spain the abovementioned relationship is significant, almost in all cases. The high levered firms earn considerable superior returns in Italy and Portugal. For instance, a 1% increase in leverage-at the L4 quartile- is associated with a 4,27 % increase in returns in Italy and a 2.75% in Portugal, respectively. On the contrary, in Spanish at L2 quartile, a 1% increase in debt yields to a 3.9% reduction in returns.

A delicate hint, about a non monotonic relation between book leverage and risk-free excess returns, is given. This is in line with Garlapi et al. (2011) who isolate in a simple equity valuation model the amplifying effect of leverage on the book-to-market effect and empirically show a hump-shaped relationship between default probabilities and expected returns and a momentum profits concentration among high credit-risk firms with significant expected shareholder recovery upon financial distress. They consider that the presence of potential shareholder recovery upon financial distress alters the risk structure of equity (non-linear dependence of equity beta) and causes the expected return to be hump-shaped in default probabilities. This non-monotonic relationship between risk and default probability in turn leads to hump-shaped value premia with respect to default probability and predicts a concentration of momentum profits among firms with poor credit quality.

The negative coefficient (found at the Low Levered quartiles) has been spotted by several researchers and they have named it "distress risk puzzle". George et al. 2010 argued that the negative relation between leverage and returns is not a market mispricing. They suggest that equity risk is increasing in leverage relies on the frictionless markets assumption that makes investment and financing decisions separable.

It is possible that market friction leads low leverage firms to have greater exposure to systematic risk, which dominates the amplification effect of leverage on equity risk. In this case, expected returns to low leverage firms will indeed be exposed to greater systematic risk than high leverage firms. Working on this base they empirically proved that the "puzzle" can be explained by a rational model, albeit one with market frictions.

Caskey et al. (2011), having confirmed the "anomalous" finding of Penman et al. (2007), attribute the negative relation to market inefficiency. They argue that the market does not seem to fully understand the information contained in excess leverage about future fundamentals (especially investments) and under-levered firms earn superior risk adjust returns. We find that in the Italian, Portuguese and Spanish market, the information contained in leverage is integrated in stock prices and investors of high levered firms earn superior returns.

5.2. Industry Level

5.2.1. One Factor Model

The empirical results of the one factor model (Table 6) involving the leverage risk factor, display a positive (but insignificant in most cases) relationship between stock returns and leverage, almost in all industries, for all countries. Nevertheless, the very low coefficient of determination indicates that leverage cannot explain by itself the cross-section of industry stock returns.

Table 6. One Factor Model on an Industry Basis

$ER_{im} = a_i + l_i\ HLMLL_m + e_i$				
Industry	a_i	l_i	R^2 adj.	DW
Panel A: Italy				
Basic Materials	-0.0341 (-4.22)***	4.1714 (1.68)*	0.020	1.44
Consumer Goods	-0.0386 (-6.11)***	3.0545 (1.57)	0.013	1.37
Consumer Services	-0.0448 (-5.61)***	1.1677 (0.47)	-0.007	1.55
Health Care	-0.02617 (-4.21)***	6.2845 (3.16)***	0.082	1.39
Industrials	-0.03170 (-5.32)***	2.3902 (1.31)	0.0065	1.27
Oil and Gas	-0.0275 (-4.82)***	2.2203 (1.27)	0.0055	1.73
Technology	-0.0473 (-5.19)***	-1.3037 (-0.47)	-0.0073	1.73
Telecoms	-0.0490 (-4.57)***	-0.1406 (-0.04)	-0.0094	1.87
Utilities	-0.0332 (-6.10)***	2.2557 (1.34)	0.0075	1.66
Panel B: Greece				
Basic Materials	-0.014147 (-1.32)	3.76757 (1.16)	0.011	1.67
Consumer Goods	-0.01862 (-1.55)	4.5596 (1.22)	0.013	1.97
Consumer Services	-0.01346 (-1.05)	2.3493 (0.81)	-0.003	1.58
Health Care	-0.01255 (-1.96)	4.25111 (1.43)	0.0087	1.61
Industrials	-0.0171 (-1.51)	2.1449 (0.84)	-0.0025	1.92
Oil and Gas	-0.0046 (-0.49)	-0.72735 (-0.34)	-0.0075	2.19
Technology	-0.0229 (-1.83)	3.9742 (1.40)	0.0081	1.75
Telecoms	-0.0099 (-0.77)	3.0596 (1.07)	0.0012	1.85

$ER_{im} = a_i + l_i\ HLMLL_m + e_i$				
Industry	a_i	l_i	R^2 adj.	DW
Utilities	-0.0052 (-0.61)	0.0163 (0.09)	-0.0106	1.68
Panel C: Portugal				
Basic Materials	-0.030232 (-5.01)***	1.647924 (2.25)**	0.04	1.5
Consumer Goods	-0.034737 (-5.52)***	-0.031037 (-0.04)	-0.009	2.1
Consumer Services	-0.030055 (-3.8)***	0.178201 (0.19)	-0.009	1.7
Industrials	-0.037826 (-4.85)***	3.561080 (3.76)***	0.11	1.5
Oil and Gas	-0.019903 (-1.01)***	4.877997 (1.61)	0.04	1.9
Technology	-0.037536 (-4.55)***	1.210286 (1.3)	0.004	1.7
Telecoms	-0.035562 (-4.49)***	1.907004 (2)**	0.03	1.4
Utilities	-0.032468 (-5.2)***	2.337049 (3.08)***	0.07	1.4
Panel D: Spain				
Basic Materials	-0.018075 (-2.80)***	7.089698 (5.66)***	0.22	1.56
Consumer Goods	-0.025621 (-5.87)***	2.793758 (3.29)***	0.08	1.46
Consumer Services	-0.027109 (-3.63)***	3.952593 (2.72)***	0.05	1.43
Health Care	-0.024582 (-3.65)***	-0.107947 (-0.08)	-0.009	1.59
Industrials	-0.018716 (-3.53)	2.350606 (2.28)***	0.03	1.06
Oil and Gas	-0.025008 (-3.40)***	3.926802 (2.75)***	0.05	1.67
Technology	-0.027702 (-3.08)***	5.818068 (3.32)***	0.08	1.7
Telecoms	-0.036368 (-2.97)***	8.767692 (3.69)***	0.11	1.65
Utilities	-0.019446 (-3.73)***	2.825538 (2.79)***	0.05	1.40

The table reports the results of the one factor model regression on an industry basis. ER_{im} is the realized monthly return in excess of the risk free rate of each industry portfolio, calculated from April 1st of the year following the announcement of the leverage ratios. HLMLLm is the realized monthly return on a portfolio that is long on high leveraged stocks and short on low levered stocks.

Total number of observations are are 120 for Greece and 108 for Italy and Portugal respectively. *, ** and *** denote statistical significance at the 10%, 5% and 1% level, respectively and t-statistics are in parentheses.

Table 7. Carhart and Leverage Five Factors Model on an Industry Basis

$ER_{im} = a_i + b_i MRP + s_i SMB + h_i HML + w_i WML + l_i HLMLL + e_i$								
Industry	a_i	b_i	s_i	h_i	w_i	l_i	R^2 adj.	DW
Panel A: Italy								
Basic Materials	-0.003 (-0.05)	1.094 (6.55)***	4.167 (3.54)***	6.057 (2.42)**	3.467 (1.09)	2.366 (1.28)	0.57	1.98
Consumer Goods	-0.0065 (-1.95)*	0.929 (16.09)***	1.996 (2.6)**	2.504 (1.98)*	-0.647 (-0.43)	1.993 (2.03)**	0.79	2.06
Consumer Services	-0.002 (-0.76)	1.023 (11.95)***	0.702 (0.85)	-1.994 (-1.16)	-6.764 (-3.956)***	1.244 (1.12)	0.82	1.98
Health Care	-0.0034 (-0.62)	0.692 (7,35)***	0.078 (0.06)	2.958 (1.44)	-0.581 (-0.23)	4.811 (3)***	0.47	1.87
Industrials	-0.002 (-0.66)	0.887 (14.95)***	2.344 (2.97)***	2.331 (1.79)	1.133 (0.73)	1.261 (1.25)	0.75	1.74
Oil and Gas	-0.003 (-0.87)	0.751 (9.83)***	0.5781 (0.57)	0.472 (0.28)	2.218 (1.11)	0.803 (0.62)	0.54	2.25
Technology	-0.002 (-0.37)	1.091 (14.19)***	1.514 (1.04)	-3.759 (-1.17)	-6.346 (-2.59)**	-0.802 (-0.50)	0.71	2.08
Telecoms	-0.0008 (-0.11)	1.152 (9.19)***	-0.86 (-0,5)	-4.275 (-0.89)	-8.813 (-2.89)***	-0.115 (-0.05)	0.61	1.91
Utilities	-0.006 (-1.94)*	0.741 (12.19)***	2.907 (3.59)***	0.439 (0.33)	0.251 (0.16)	2.027 (1.96)	0.68	2.10
Panel B: Greece								
Basic Materials	-0.009 (-1.85)	1.048 (12.29)***	4.135 (3.57)***	6.290 (3.26)***	0.191 (7.98)***	0.528 (0.30)	0.80	2..21
Consumer Goods	-0.0155 (-2.08)**	1.0271 (13.11)***	6.7739 (4.95)***	5.9619 (1.86)*	0.1419 (4.27)***	-0.5761 (-0.20)	0.71	2.33
Consumer Services	-0.008 (-1.18)	1.1432 (9.20)***	5.4824 (4.01)***	5.6594 (1.66)	0.224 (7.40)***	-2.0422 (-0.83)	0.69	1.84
Health Care	-0.0065 (-0.84)	1.2311 (11,86)***	4.6218 (2.24)**	5.7111 (2.02)**	0.1719 (5.59)***	0.4116 (0.15)	0.68	1.85

$ER_{im} = a_i + b_i MRP + s_i SMB + h_i HML + w_i WML + l_i HLMLL + e_i$								
Industry	a_i	b_i	s_i	h_i	w_i	l_i	R^2 adj.	DW
Industrials	-0.009 (-1.37)	1.160 (11.97)***	4.144 (2.96)***	1.8139 (0.62)	0.1095 (4.46)***	-1.7751 (-0.86)	0.68	2.14
Oil and Gas	0.002 (0.37)	0.80585 (8.33)***	-1.6829 (-1.37)	0.059 (0.26)	-0.00831 (-0.10)	-0.313 (-0.16)	0.37	2.5
Technology	-0.0159 (-2.06)**	1.1708 (11.9)***	4.6534 (3.72)***	3.6956 (1.56)	0.1861 (2.24)**	-0.0977 (-0.05)	0.64	2.11
Telecoms	0.0036 (0.27)	0.9998 (4.44)***	0.1788 (0,06)	-6.8706 (-1.49)	0.0113 (0.23)	1.0242 (0.21)	0.30	1.53
Utilities	0.001 (0.20)	0.8269 (12.19)***	0.2642 (0.19)	3.429 (1.58)	0.55288 (0.67)	0.68752 (0.40)	0.66	1.55
Panel C: Portugal								
Basic Materials	-0.0053 (-1.01)	0.7273 (8.25)***	0.3280 (0.50)	-0.4376 (-0.40)	-2.129 (-2.14)***	0.0769 (0.12)	0.50	2
Consumer Goods	-0.0073 (-1.34)	0.7578 (8.32)***	3.2655 (4.89)***	1.7515 (1.56)	-2.6735 (-2.6)***	0.6045 (0.96)	0.48	2.4
Consumer Services	-0.0082 (-0.97)	0.6646 (4.7)***	0.5980 (0.58)	3.455 (1.98)***	-1.8025 (-1.13)	0.2871 (0.29)	0.21	2.09
Industrials	-0.0087 (-1.19)	0.8850 (7.27)***	-0.0308 (-0.03)	0.639 (0.47)	-1.7186 (-1.25)	1.8172 (2.17)***	0.47	2.12
Oil and Gas	0.0357 (1.86)*	1.3760 (5.30)***	1.5020 (0.89)	0.0489 (0.014)	4.1847 (0.98)	-0.9638 (-0.35)	0.44	2.18
Technology	-0.0021 (-0.32)	0.9161 (8.22)***	1.5070 (1.85)*	-5.008 (-3.65)***	-5.7381 (-4.56)***	-1.6883 (-2.20)***	0.56	2.23
Telecoms	-0.0010 (-0.21)	1.0895 (12.77)***	-0.1454 (-0.23)	-1.4041 (-1.34)	-2.5917 (-2.69)***	-1.0658 (-1.81)*	0.73	2.09
Utilities	-0.0053 (-1.02)	0.8044 (9.28)***	0.5143 (0.81)	-1.2653 (-1.19)	-1.4965 (-1.53)	0.3432 (0.58)	0.57	2.07
Panel D: Spain								
Basic Materials	-0.0134 (-2.9)***	0.7716 (9.8)***	-0.4193 (-0.31)	15.577 (8.77)***	3.1136 (2.19)**	0.2182 (0.22)	0.69	2.08

Table 7. (Continued)

$ER_{im} = a_i + b_i\,MRP + s_i\,SMB + h_i\,HML + w_i\,WML + l_i\,HLMLL + e_i$								
Industry	a_i	b_i	s_i	h_i	w_i	l_i	R^2 adj.	DW
Consumer Goods	-0.0143 (-4.26)***	0.6070 (10.47)***	3.7896 (3.86)***	2.2499 (1.7)*	0.5944 (0.56)	-0.3508 (-0.48)	0.57	1.97
Consumer Services	-0.0033 (-0.71)	1.0979 (13.75)***	0.6446 (0.47)	3.2310 (1.8)*	-2.6140 (-1.8)*	-1.8073 (-1.8)*	0.71	1.87
Health Care	-0.0056 (-1.04)	0.9050 (9.7)***	7.2420 (4.58)***	0.2280 (0.11)	1.0854 (0.64)	-3.9722 (-3.39)***	0.48	2.07
Industrials	-0.0026 (-0.81)	0.8737 (15.39)***	3.1514 (3.28)***	3.6365 (2.8)***	3.3192 (3.24)***	-1.7432 (-2.44)***	0.71	1.88
Oil and Gas	-0.0084 (-1.4)	0.9155 (9.02)***	-3.4668 (-2.01)**	6.6457 (2.9)***	3.3370 (1.8)*	-0.8237 (-0.64)	0.52	2.19
Technology	-0.0028 (-0.37)	1.0731 (8.08)***	9.5619 (4.25)***	-2.3986 (-0.8)	-0.9299 (0.39)	1.5502 (0.93)	0.47	2.22
Telecoms	-0.0023 (-0.22)	1.1609 (6.13)***	11.2894 (3.52)***	-9.9022 (-2.32)**	-6.6509 (-1.95)*	5.1747 (2.17)**	0.43	1.8
Utilities	-0.0048 (-1.2)	0.7408 (10.92)***	0.3731 (0.32)	2.9772 (1.95)*	1.8290 (1.49)	-0.6640 (-0.78)	0.57	2.08

The table reports the results of the Fama and French plus the leverage factor model regression on an industry level. ER_{im} is the realized monthly return in excess of the risk free rate of each of the industry portfolios, calculated from April 1st of the year following the announcement of the leverage ratios. MRP is the realized monthly return of the market and leverage risk premium. SMB_m is the realized monthly return on a portfolio that is long on small sized stocks and short on high sized stocks. HML_m is the realized monthly return on a portfolio that is long on high BE/ME stocks and short on low BE/ME stocks. HML_m is the realized monthly return on a portfolio that is long on high BE/ME stocks and short on low BE/ME stocks. $HLMLL_m$ is the realized monthly return on a portfolio that is long on winner stocks and short on loser stocks. Total number of observations are 120 for Greece and 108 for Italy and Portugal respectively. *, ** and *** denote statistical significance at the 10%, 5% and 1% level, respectively and t-statistics are in parentheses.

5.2.2. Five Factors Model

The results of the final five factor model at industry level reveal that the above paradigm can explain a large proportion of returns volatility, as indicated by adjusted R^2 of the regression model in all countries, which is quite high. The alpha coefficient is negative but insignificant for the most industries. The coefficient of the market risk premium is positive and statistically significant for all industries in all investigated countries (Table 7). The SMB, is also positive, almost for all industries, in the four countries but statistically significant only for some industries. The HML coefficient is positive but not always significant for the majority of industries in all countries. Only in Spanish Telecommunication sector we detect a statistical and economical significant negative value effect. Andritzky et al. (2003), included Technology and Telecommunications in a group of young or risky industries which are anticipated to have lower debt levels and great investment opportunities. The momentum factor exhibited a mixed sign across the industries in Italy and Spain. In Portugal, past period's price performance is also negative, almost in all industries and very significant in four of them whereas in Greece is positive almost in all cases and very significant in six industries. The empirical results for the leverage factor in the investigated countries reveal an insignificant relation between leverage and returns for most industries. Italian and Spanish Health Care, Italian Basic Materials and Consumer Goods, Portuguese and Spanish Industrials, Portuguese Technology, and finally Portuguese and Spanish Telecommunication sectors are the only industries with statistical significant coefficients.

CONCLUSIONS, POLICY IMPLICATIONS AND SUGGESTIONS FOR FURTHER RESEARCH

The present paper aimed to investigate the relation between leverage and stock returns, both at a full sample level and an industry level in a Southern European Frame. Regression analysis was employed in a Greek, Italian, Portuguese and Spanish database to address the controversy in the results of the earlier empirical studies. It was shown that the market risk premium keeps the scepters of significance among the traditional idiosyncratic risk factors. The size risk factor has a positive and statistically significant relationship with stock returns similarly in Greece, Italy and Spain. Unexpectedly, in Portugal, size is not a significant risk factor. The momentum and value risk factors have an insignificant relation with equity returns (negative the first but positive the second) in most cases in Italy. In Portugal the aforementioned variables follow the same sign pattern with the difference that momentum effect is very significant at the low leverage quartiles, as well as at the full sample. On the contrary, in Greece and Spain, both, value and momentum effects on returns are positive and significant. The leverage risk factor presents also a strong - positive (statistically significant in Italy, Portugal and Spain) relationship with stock returns, at the last leverage quartiles (L3 and L4) and a negative (statistically and economical significant in Greece, Portugal and Spain) relationship with stock returns, at the first leverage quartiles (L1 and L2) in all investigated countries. Our results overall are in line with the findings from the literature (Arditti, 1967; Hall et al., 1967; Fama and French, 1992; Kortweg, 2004; Dimitrov and Jain, 2008; George and Hwang, 2010; Penman, 2007; Sivaprasad and Muradoglu, 2007, 2010).

The industry level analysis results are approximately the same as those from the full sample level. The market risk premium and size factor had a positive and statistically significant relationship with stock returns. For the leverage factor, the results reveal a positive but insignificant relation with excess returns for most industries.

Our results indicate that in the Southern European Region, leverage is a risk that is priced, although in a different way, among the quad of the investigated countries. We find that in the Italian, Portuguese and Spanish market, the information contained in leverage is integrated in stock prices and investors of high levered firms earn considerable superior returns, whereas in Greece, investors turn a blind eye to the higher risk of the high levered firms as they may translate the debt raise as a managerial confidence sign, a "quasi" investment opportunity or even a strategic tool improving the bargain power of firms against take over demands or other stakeholders (like workforce) claims. Or, the above fact can be simply attributed to Greek market inefficiency, as investors don't fully understand the implicit risk they take on.

In order to further investigate and validate the relationship between leverage and stock returns we should extent the sampling period and expand the research to other European countries. Furthermore, one could consider integrating additional macro and micro variables into the research model. Finally, one could work on the quasi-concept of investigating the explanatory power of leverage on the human capital's cost based on some recent results which reveal a significant impact of leverage on employees' payment.

REFERENCES

Alves, P., Ferreira, M., 2011. Capital structure and law around the world. *Journal of Multinational Financial Management, 21(3),* pp.119-150.

Antoniou, A., Guney, Y., Paudyal, K., 2008. The determinants of capital structure: Capital market oriented versus bank oriented institutions. *Journal of Finance and Quantitative Analysis,* 43(1), pp. 59-82.

Andritzky, R. J., 2003. Leverage, industries, and countries. Evidence from seven countries. *University of St. Gallen, Working paper.*

Arditti, F. D., 1967. Risk and return on equity. *Journal of Finance*, 22(1), pp.19-36.

Bancel, F., Mittoo, U., 2004. Cross Country Determinants of Capital Structure Choice: A Survey of European Firms, *Financial Management,* 33(4) pp.5-26.

Banz,R W 1981. The relationship between return and market value of common stocks. *Journal of Financial Economics 9(1) pp. 3-18.*

Ball R 1978, Anomalies in Relationship Between Securities' Yields and Yields Surrogates. *Journal of Financial Economics 6 pp.103-126.*

Bhandari, L. C., 1988. Debt/Equity ratio and expected common stock returns: Empirical evidence. *Journal of Finance*, XLIII, pp.507-528.

Brounen, D., Jong, A., Koedijk, K., 2006. Capital structure policies in Europe: Survey evidence. *Journal of Banking and Finance,* 30(5), pp.1409-1442.

Carhart, M. M., 1997. On persistence in mutual fund performance. *Journal of Finance,* 52(1), pp.87-82.

Caskey J. (2009). Information in Equity Markets with Ambiguity Averse Investors. *Journal of Financial Studies 22(9) pp.3595-3627.*

Caskey J. Hughes J. and Liu J. (2011). Leverage, Execs Leverage, and Future Returns. *Review of Accounting Studies, forthcoming.*

Cochrane, J. H., 2005. Asset pricing, Second Edition. Princeton.

Chan K C and Chen N F 1991. Structural and return characteristics of small and large firms. *Journal of Finance 46 pp.1467-1481.*

Dimitrov, V., Jain, P. C., (2008). The value relevance of changes in financial leverage. *Journal of Accounting and Finance, 191-222.*

Drobetz, W. and Pensa, P., 2007. Capital structure and stock returns: The European evidence. *University of Hamburg,* Working paper, http://ssrn.com/abstract=957302.

Fama, E. F., French, K., 1992. The cross-section in expected stock returns. *Journal of Finance,* 47, pp.427-466.

Fama, E. F., French, K. R., 1996. Multifactor explanations of asset pricing anomalies. *Journal of Finance,* 11(1), pp.55-83.

Fama, E. F., French, K. R., 1999. The corporate cost of capital and the return on corporate investment. *Journal of Finance,* (6), pp.1939-1967.

Fama, E. F., French, K., 2002. Testing tradeoff and pecking order predictions about dividends and debt. *The Review of Financial Studies,* 15(1), pp.1-33.

Fama, E. F., French, K., 2006. The Value Premium and the CAMP. *Journal of Finance, 61* pp.2163-2185.

Garlappi, L., Yan, H., 2011. Financial distress and the cross section of equity returns. *Journal of Finance,*66(3), p.p.789-822.

George, T., Hwang, C., 2006. Leverage, Financial Distress and the Cross Section of Stock Returns. *http://ssrn.com/abstract=890838.*

George, T., Hwang, C., 2010. A resolution of the distress risk and leverage puzzles in the cross section of stock returns. *Journal of Financial Economics,* 96, pp.56-79.

Gomes, J., Schmid, L., 2010. Levered returns. *Journal of Finance,* 65(2), p.p.467-494.

Hall M and Weiss l 1967. Firm size and Profitability. *The Review of Economics and Statistics, 49(3) pp 319-331.*

Hamada, R. S., 1969. Portfolio analysis, market equilibrium and corporation finance. *Journal of Finance,* 24, pp.13-31.

Hanhard, A., and Ansotegui, C., 2008. Do the Fama and French Factors Proxy for State Variables that Predict Macroeconomic Growth in the Eurozone?. *Social Science Securiry Research Network, http://www.ssrn.com.*

Jarque, C. M. and Bera, A. K., 1980. Efficient tests for normality, homoscedasticity and serial independence of regression residuals. *Economics Letters*, 6(3), pp.255-259.

Jegadeesh, N., and Titman, S., 1993. Returns to buying winners and selling losers: Implications for stock market efficiency. *Journal of Finance*, 48(1), pp.65-91.

Jong, A., Kabir, R., Nguyen, T. T., 2008. Capital structure around the world: The roles of firm-and country-specific determinants. *Journal of Banking and Finance,* 32(9), pp.1954-1969.

Korteweg, A., 2004. Financial leverage and expected stock returns: Evidence from pure exchange offers. *University of Chicago, Working paper,* http://ssrn.com/abstract=597922.

Lakonishok, J., Shleifer, A., Vishny, R. W., 1994. Contrarian investment, extrapolation and risk. *Journal of Finance,* 49, pp.1541-1578.

Liew, J., and Vassalou, M., 2000. Can book-to-market, size and momentum be risk factors that predict economic growth?. *Journal of Financial Economics*, 57(2), pp.221-245.

Masulis, R. W., 1983. The impact of capital structure change on firm value: Some estimates. *The Journal of Finance,* 38(1), pp.107-126.

Matsa, David, (2010). Capital Structure as a Strategic Variable: Evidence from Collective Bargain. *Journal of Finance, 65(3),*p.p. 1197-1232.

Modigliani, F., Miller, M. H., 1958. The cost of capital, corporation finance and the theory of investment. *American Economic Review,* 48(3), pp.261-297.

Modigliani, F., Miller, M. H., 1963. Corporate income taxes and the cost of capital: A correction. *American Economic Review,* 53(3), pp.433-443.

Mura Roberto and Marchica M., (2010). Financial Flexibility, Investment Ability and Firm Value: Evidence from Firms with Space Capacity. *Financial Management, 39(4),* p.p.1339-1365.

Muradoglu, G., Sivaprasad, S., 2009. Leverage and common risk factors in stock returns. City University of London, Cass Business School, Research Paper. http://ssrn.com/ abstract=1101504.

Nissim, D., Penman, S. H., 2003. Financial statement analysis of leverage and how it informs about profitability and price-to-book ratios. *Review of Accounting Studies,* 8, pp.531-560.

Oztekin, O., 2009. Capital structure decisions around the world. Which factors are reliably important. *University of Kansas, Working paper,* http://ssrn.com/abstract=1464471.

Penman, S. H., Richardson, S. A., Tuna, I., 2007. The book-to-price effect in stock returns: Accounting for Leverage. *Journal of Accounting Research,* 2(45), pp.427-467.

Psillaki, M., Daskalakis N., 2009. Are the determinants of capital structure country of firm specific? *Small Business Economics,* 33, pp.319-333.

Rajan, R., Zingales, L., 1995. What do we know about capital structure? Some evidence from international data. *Journal of Finance,* 50, pp.1421-1460.

Rouwenhorst, K.G., 1998. International momentum strategies. *Journal of Finance*, 53(1), pp.267-284.

Schwartz, E., 1959. Theory of the capital structure of the firm. *Journal of Finance,* 14(1), pp.18-39.

Sivaprasad, S., Muradoglu, G., 2007. Capital Stracture and Expected Stock Returns. Working paper, http://ssrn.com/abstract=1031198.

Sivaprasad, S., Muradoglu, G., 2010. Using leverage as a risk factor in explaining the cross section of stock returns. Working paper, http://ssrn.com/abstract=1101504.

In: Computational Data Analysis Techniques ISBN: 978-1-63463-957-6
Editors: M. Doumpos, C. Zopounidis and Ch. Gaganis

Chapter 8

DETERMINING FACTORS IN DECISION TO INVEST IN THE STOCK MARKET FOR A SMALL INVESTOR: APPLICATION FORGOTTEN EFFECTS THEORY

Abdelhamid Hammi* and Anna M. Gil-Lafuente
University of Barcelona,
Department of Organization and Business Economics, Barcelona, Spain

ABSTRACT

In investment approaches, the decision maker must choose the best option based on future experience historical data, expert recommendations, macroeconomic and microeconomic factors, which are usually not precise, and the way levels of uncertainty behave. In this study we examined the key factors that influence the decision at investing in stock market for a small investor under the prism of fuzzy logic. Based on this scenario, we have considered how an investor would analyze the different scenarios to form a prediction. In order to achieve this, we have presented the forgotten effects model to determine the degree of influence of each variable. Therefore, the proceedings will be useful for small investors as expectations of their future performance, as well as an indicator of the potential risk of unexpected variation.

Keywords: Small investor, stock market, expert advice, the forgotten effects theory

1. INTRODUCTION

Among all the alternatives to invest a certain capital, perhaps one of the clearest and most studied in the present conditions of uncertainty is the issue of the securities portfolio. The prediction of price movements of the stocks and stock indexes has been a topic of great interest in the financial area. Various studies show that stock returns are predictable to some degree. For example , Lo & MacKinlay (1988 , 2007) , using data from developed stock

* Author for correspondence: aroba1981@gmail.com

markets recorded a positive serial correlation between the weekly returns ; De Bondt and Thaler (1985), Fama and French (1993) , Poterba & Summers (1987) and Chopra , Lakonishok and Ritter (1992) found a negative serial correlation in returns of individual assets and portfolios over several intervals of three to ten years. Predicting the movements of future stock prices from time series analysis of stock prices has led analysts to focus on the psychology of the investor and the latter's reply to the movements of stock prices. It is shown in Smithson (1987)'s and also Smithson and Oden (1999)'s studies. The first study suggests that thinking and decision making can be modeled using fuzzy logic techniques. The second study shows how the expectations of the economic agents according to the criteria fuzzy patterns yields allow obtaining similar statistical properties to those observed. The idea lies in the price at which an investor is willing to buy or sell, depending on his expectations: if he expects a future in the asset price, he will buy it. If on the other hand, he expects a drop in the share price, he will then sell. This behavior appears to be trivial; it is very complex as it responds to the expectations and attitudes of the human behavior.

In real life, banks, saving banks, brokers, dealers, independent advisors ... flood the market with recommendations; they recommend us what to do with a particular action as of their sources of information and analysis. But, are these recommendations useful? Are they accured? Some studies suggest that experts' opinions have economic value. For example, Kim, Lin, and Slovin (1997)'s study, or Barber et al. (2001)'s study suggest that financial institutions are worthy, at least at short term. In other recent studies this issue is also seen, for example, Narasimhan (2004), and Woolridge (2004), who find different results depending on the kind of company which elaborates the recommendations.

There are different theories, methods and approaches for the analysis and calculations or estimations of the factors that help the decision making:

1. One of the early approaches was the financial evaluation and prediction of the critical financial. It pretends to establish a theoretical value of the financial assets from the macro variables and real variables of the economy, industry, company ... To calculate or estimate the real value we work whether with concrete or contemporary data at a rate determined by the discounting of the forecast future cash flow, associated with the asset valued. In this approach we find common indicators such as PER (Price Earnings Ratio) or ROA (Return on Operating Assets). Even though there are many advocates of this approach, we also found some critics like Malkiel (1980).
2. Another technique is known as charting or technical analysis, defended by authors such as Murphy (1999), although the first studies of this technique are much earlier and date back to the early work of Charles H. Dow, who worked at the Wall Street Journal. This approach tries to establish the evolution of asset prices analyzed through the study of the graphs of asset prices and statistics. Neither this approach is particularly saved from harsh critics (Malkiel and Cragg (2003), and others).
3. Other alternative approaches to the problem could be the alternative theory which separates investors involved in the trade market between Noise and Smart money, where the early investors are described as irrational or random, and the other ones who follow a logical investment decision and end up gaining more than the average. In this line we can mention the work of Campbell and Kyle (1993).

From our part, in this paper, we will consider an alternative to financial forecasting to help us with the problem of the small investor decision. We also look for the alternative to not be biased by assumptions about mathematical and / or statistical, which is the application of the Forgotten Effects. The decision to invest in the stock market can be performed as recommended by the experts in the field, which are often made on the basis of variables and factors that determine the tendency of these markets at any given time. Therefore, it is a sequential nature model to enter the causal relationships in the study of the stock market, being a useful tool to be used in the targeting process.

Our goal is to predict the behavior of the stock market through a logical system of data processing. We will study how to treat this information from the point of view of fuzzy mathematics applying the theory of Forgotten Effects, provided to find out if this information can be the basis for the investment decision in the stock market. We also pretend to know the factors which influence more than others at the decision making time by the small investor. Specifically how a small investor can take advantage of the implicit knowledge in the information received and which is the key factor to get a good future estimation of the stock movement, being useful or having economic value for his decision to invest in the market.

This work is structured using a sequential analysis from the role of the factors influencing the stock market to the decision of investing in the stock market. The second section will describe the model that we will implement, and the third section will show how we select the variables that will be studied. In the fourth section we will apply the model of the Forgotten Effects, and in the fifth section the results will be analyzed. We end up this study by commenting the results obtained as the conclusion section.

2. Variable Selection

As an illustrative example, at this stage of our work we have proceeded to select the data and the variables we considered important to help the small investor to make investment decisions in the stock market. These data will be equally studied, and subsequently be part of the model.

As an analysis tool to investigate the approach of this paper, we propose the analysis of the cause and effect relation, taking into account the Forgotten Effects Model developed by Kaufmann and Gil Aluja (1988), which allows choosing alternatives with a fuzzy logical approach that offer a specific risk which the small investor is willing whether to take on or not, and define alternative actions to address changes that may show during the process.

A rational investor faced with a set of investment decisions, will look for maximizing his profitability or generated value and minimize the associated risk or eventually, to minimize the risk to a profitability or desired generated value. When deciding, he faces a typical problem of how to divide a sum of money between different investment options in stock market.

The problem of selecting the portfolio (effect) arises because the cost or present value of it depends on many factors (causes) beyond the control of the investor. In other words, a decision problem under uncertainty is configured.

In this sense, as an illustrative example, we have proceeded to establish two sets of elements: those which represent factors from the economic, political and financial environment and act as causes, and those who respond to the characteristics of the small investor's portfolio, which will act as effects.

We will then be able to identify the main causes and effects which are guiding the small investor at the decision making time. These variables can be reduced or extended depending on the case studied.

We have selected the following causes and effects which can help the investor at the decision time in our example.

Causes:

- *International Summit*: when the G-20 countries, for example, discuss financial markets and the global economy to review the progress made in addressing the financial crisis, to promote a common understanding of its causes, and to avoid repeating the same problem, agreeing on a number of principles to reform the regulatory and institutional regimes of the global financial sectors. These decisions will impact on the financial market developments.
- *Elections*: The effect of a change of government and its economic and financial ideology is relevant.
- *Political and economic stability*: It is decisive factor, although there have occasionally been sharp falls in markets with healthy economies. A high economic stability is normally associated to an economic growth with a controlled inflation, and with a job creation and deficit also under control. In this kind of scenario, which reduces the number of basic uncertainties, companies will have opportunities to generate wealth and the actions will have a good performance.
- *Cost of risk*: the market may be well assessed or not, based on market expectations.
- *The correlation between international markets*: The correlation between the various exchanges is a very important variable for the stock price. Year after year this correlation tends to increase due to the globalization of the world's economy, in such way that an investor can not only look at what is happening in his environment, but has to be very attentive to developments in other markets too.
- *Reports on economic situation*: the investor invests because he expects to take in return profitability in line with his expectations and economic analysis.
- *The taxation of investment in shares*: net profitability influences over the one which the investor gets.
- *Corporative results*: information about a company's health, its trajectory and strength, etc. And over all, it is a detailed analysis about how the issues are managed and how they could evolve in a posterior state (sum of profits and losses).
- *The Interest Rate:* The interest rate level will decide the investor in a large part. If interest rates are too low, it will not be interested to be invested assets whose return may be too poor. Therefore there will be a flow of funds from fixed income assets to equities. This low profitability will cause the higher risk aversion decrease in stock market investment. The opposite occurs with high interest rates.
- *The dividend policy of listed companies:* an increase in profits, which agrees with expectations of a better future performance by the managers of the companies, will lead to an increase in shared out dividends, with the purpose of transmitting signals to the market which advertise better earnings expectations. Where profits shrink and

managers anticipate a worse future, then the dividend reduction makes the market part of less favorable expectations.

Effects:

- *Profitability:* The purchase of a stock investor can bring profitability through three channels: Gains, Dividends and Rights of preferred subscription.
- *Market price:* The forces of supply and demand direct the stock prices. The demand is governed by the desire of investors to buy or sell a stock.
- *Earnings per share:* it is a meter used in the analysis of balance to measure profitability per share for a period of time. It is calculated by dividing the profit of the company of the period of time between the numbers of shares on which it is constituted.
- *Volatility*: it is the measure of the frequency and intensity of the changes in the price of an asset or a defined type such as the standard deviation of the change in a specific temporal horizon.
- *Quotes:* official appraisal made from its value (usually daily), based on pre-established criteria which relies on purchase orders and sales of that title. It can also be regulated by the State.
- *Purchase Diversification:* Diversification is based on prudence. Diversifying consists in accepting lower returns in exchange for a lower risk.
- *Dividend per share*: It is a piece of information used by the stock investor as dividend policy sometimes means a significant portion of the income of the shareholder.
- *Stop- Loss:* these are orders to buy or sell exchange-traded securities conditioned by a certain price reach. These orders are increasingly used in financial markets, as they allow taking more investment risk with safety.
- *Cash flows:* The amount of money that exists in the market is a factor to consider. The inflow of money always makes the bag go up or, at least, not fall, as money translates into purchases.

In the following table we summarize the variables in our study:

Table 1. Cause and effect

	Cause (C)	Effect (E)
1	International Summit	Profitability
2	Elections	Market price
3	Political and economic stability	Earnings per share
4	Cost of risk	Volatility
5	The correlation between international markets	Quotes
6	Reports on economic situation	Purchase Diversification
7	The taxation of investment in shares	Dividend per share
8	The Interest Rate	Stop-Loss
9	The dividend policy of listed companies	Cash flow

3. Application of the Model of the Effects Forgotten[1]

From the table above we define the set $\widetilde{C}$ (inversion determinant) as the set of causes of effects on the portfolio of the investor (set $\widetilde{E}$) According to the mathematical model of the Forgotten Effects to evaluate the influence of different factors over the results of the investment portfolio, applying direct fuzzy implication relation. Below are the incidence matrices of the first order $\widetilde{M}$ (matrix nº 1), the causes $\widetilde{A}$ (matrix nº 2) and the effects $\widetilde{B}$ (matrix nº 3):

Table 3. Estimated Incidents between causes and effects $\left[\widetilde{M}\right]$

↱	E_1	E_2	E_3	E_4	E_5	E_6	E_7	E_8	E_9
C_1	0,7	0,6	0,5	0,7	0,9	0,8	0,7	0,7	0,6
C_2	0,1	0,9	0,4	0,8	0,7	0,7	0,7	0,6	0,7
C_3	0,7	0,6	0,2	0,3	0,9	0,7	0,6	0,8	0,6
C_4	0,9	1	0,4	1	0,9	0,9	0,8	1	0,7
C_5	0,6	0,7	0,6	0,9	0,9	0,9	0,9	0,8	0,9
C_6	0,1	0,8	0,6	0,7	0,8	0,8	0,9	0,7	0,8
C_7	0,1	0,8	0,9	0,8	0,9	0	1	0,8	0,7
C_8	0,8	0,8	0,8	0,7	0,7	0,7	0,8	0,7	0,8
C_9	0,3	0,6	0,9	0,8	0,6	0,3	0,7	0,9	0,8

This way, the matrix above ultimately reflects the degree of incidence of some factors on the investment portfolio of the small investor. This incidence is measured between 0 and 1 so that the closer to 1, the greater is the impact of factors affecting investment in the stock market on the portfolio of the investor and, instead, the closer 0, the lower the incidence.

As mentioned in section 2, then there are incidence relations represented by matrices (self-advocacy: cause-cause) and (self-advocacy: effect-effect), defined from AXA Cartesian products and BxB representing accuracy or strength of relationship between cause incidence i-th, and j-th, and effects between the i-th and j-th, respectively, which modify the relationship of direct involvement through relations which are expressed as:

Table 4. Incidents between different causes $\left[\widetilde{A}\right]$

↱	C_1	C_2	C_3	C_4	C_5	C_6	C_7	C_8	C_9
C_1	1	0,8	0,9	0,2	0,9	0,5	0,7	0,7	0,4
C_2	0,8	1	1	0,5	0,9	0,8	1	0,9	0,6
C_3	0,8	0,8	1	0,5	0,8	0,6	0,4	0,1	0,6
C_4	0,9	0,7	0,7	1	0,9	0,9	0,5	0,5	0,1
C_5	0,8	0,9	0,9	0,8	1	0,8	0,9	0,7	0,3

[1] Applying calculation was performed using the software Fuzzylog

↱	C_1	C_2	C_3	C_4	C_5	C_6	C_7	C_8	C_9
C_6	0,7	0,8	0,7	0,8	1	1	0,4	0,2	0,5
C_7	0,7	0,6	0,5	0,6	0,7	0,6	1	0,9	0,4
C_8	0,7	0,8	0,7	0,9	0,7	0,1	0,8	1	0,7
C_9	0	0,1	0,1	0,5	0	0,4	0,7	0,7	1

Table 5. Incidents between the different effects $\left[\tilde{B}\right]$

↱	E_1	E_2	E_3	E_4	E_5	E_6	E_7	E_8	E_9
E_1	1	0,2	0,7	0	0,8	0,8	0,1	0,7	0,7
E_2	0,7	1	0,7	0,3	0,2	0,2	0,4	0,5	0,7
E_3	0,7	0,7	1	0	0,6	0,6	0,2	0,5	0,3
E_4	0,6	0,5	0,3	1	0,1	0,1	0,7	0,6	0,6
E_5	0,5	0	0,8	0	1	0,5	0,2	0,7	0,4
E_6	0,6	0,5	0,5	0,2	0,5	1	0,3	0,5	0,6
E_7	0,6	0,7	0,5	0,7	0,5	0,5	1	0,8	0,8
E_8	0,8	0,3	0,8	0,9	0,5	0,4	0,6	1	0,7
E_9	0,9	0,4	0,8	0,4	0,4	0,6	0,6	0,7	1

Once the matrices are built must, we must proceed to the establishment of direct and indirect incident; in other words, incidents in which, in turn, typically involve some of the brought causes or effects. To do so, we proceed to the max-min composition of the three matrices:

Table 6. Max-Min convolution between the matrices $\left[\tilde{A}\right]\circ\left[\tilde{M}\right]$

↱	E_1	E_2	E_3	E_4	E_5	E_6	E_7	E_8	E_9
C_1	0,7	0,8	0,7	0,9	0,9	0,9	0,9	0,8	0,9
C_2	0,8	0,9	0,9	0,9	0,9	0,9	1	0,8	0,9
C_3	0,7	0,8	0,6	0,8	0,9	0,8	0,8	0,8	0,8
C_4	0,9	1	0,6	1	0,9	0,9	0,9	1	0,9
C_5	0,8	0,9	0,9	0,9	0,9	0,9	0,9	0,8	0,9
C_6	0,8	0,8	0,6	0,9	0,9	0,9	0,9	0,8	0,9
C_7	0,8	0,8	0,9	0,8	0,9	0,7	1	0,8	0,8
C_8	0,9	0,9	0,8	0,9	0,9	0,9	0,8	0,9	0,8
C_9	0,7	0,7	0,9	0,8	0,7	0,7	0,7	0,9	0,8

Table 7. Max-Min convolution between the matrices $\left[\tilde{M}\right]^* = \left[\tilde{A}\right]\circ\left[\tilde{M}\right]\circ\left[\tilde{B}\right]$

↱	E_1	E_2	E_3	E_4	E_5	E_6	E_7	E_8	E_9
C_1	0,9	0,8	0,8	0,9	0,9	0,9	0,9	0,8	0,9
C_2	0,9	0,9	0,9	0,9	0,9	0,9	1	0,8	0,9
C_3	0,8	0,8	0,8	0,8	0,9	0,8	0,8	0,8	0,8

Table 7. (Continued)

	E_1	E_2	E_3	E_4	E_5	E_6	E_7	E_8	E_9
C_4	0,9	1	0,8	1	0,9	0,9	0,9	1	0,9
C_5	0,9	0,9	0,9	0,9	0,9	0,9	0,9	0,8	0,9
C_6	0,9	0,8	0,8	0,9	0,9	0,9	0,9	0,8	0,9
C_7	0,8	0,8	0,9	0,8	0,9	0,8	1	0,8	0,8
C_8	0,9	0,9	0,8	0,9	0,9	0,9	0,8	0,9	0,8
C_9	0,8	0,7	0,9	0,9	0,7	0,7	0,7	0,9	0,8

Table 8. Effects forgotten $[\tilde{O}] = [\tilde{\mathrm{M}}]^* - [\tilde{M}]$

	E_1	E_2	E_3	E_4	E_5	E_6	E_7	E_8	E_9
C_1	0,2	0,2	0,3	0,2	0	0,1	0,2	0,1	0,3
C_2	**0,8**	0	0,5	0,1	0,2	0,2	0,3	0,2	0,2
C_3	0,1	0,2	0,6	0,5	0	0,1	0,2	0	0,2
C_4	0	0	0,4	0	0	0	0,1	0	0,2
C_5	0,3	0,2	0,3	0	0	0	0	0	0
C_6	**0,8**	0	0,2	0,2	0,1	0,1	0	0,1	0,1
C_7	0,7	0	0	0	0	**0,8**	0	0	0,1
C_8	0,1	0,1	0	0,2	0,2	0,2	0	0,2	0
C_9	0,5	0,1	0	0,1	0,1	0,4	0	0	0

ANALYSIS OF RESULTS

In general, an investor sentiment regarding the Exchange may take three forms: bullish, bearish or neutral. So we can say that, as prices rise, more and more investors become the creed bullish. While the more and lower the bag, more investors are choosing to be bearish. Which are the factors affecting the market movement?

To clarify the issues we will analyze the highlighted values listed on the matrix, which correspond to effects that were overlapped to carry out the matrix ´´M´´ from direct incidences. In this case, the intermediate incidences will be found with greater values than or equal to 0.7, those being the most striking ones.

For example, the cause of the elections on the profitability effect:

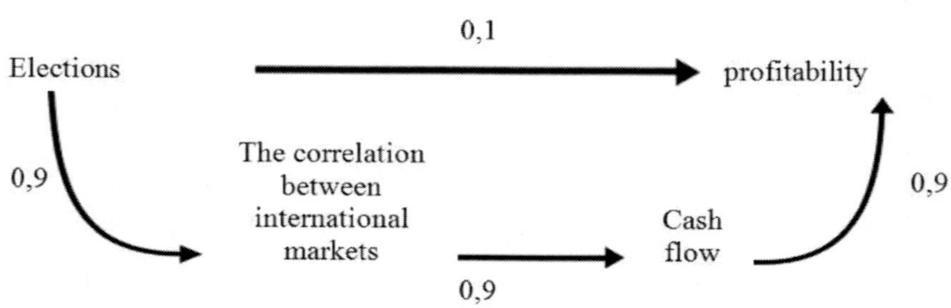

In this case the indirect effect of elections on profitability is greater than that posed as a direct effect (0.1) in the original matrix. We found two items that apparently are not related shown in the initial matrix, which analytically collects incidents detected by the consulted experts. The presence of two elements which act as a bridge and make up a causal link, which appears negligible a priori, earn up to 90 % of indirect incidence by the existence of two interposed elements (the correlation between international markets and cash flow) effects that enhance and build on causation. The result can be interpreted as the following: the return that an investor can reap has an indirect relationship with the reaction of the international markets; therefore, the investor must know the amount of money he has to invest. In this case, the investor tries to avoid large losses that may arise, for example, from foreign investors' speculations.

Another example: the cause of the economic report on the profitability effect:

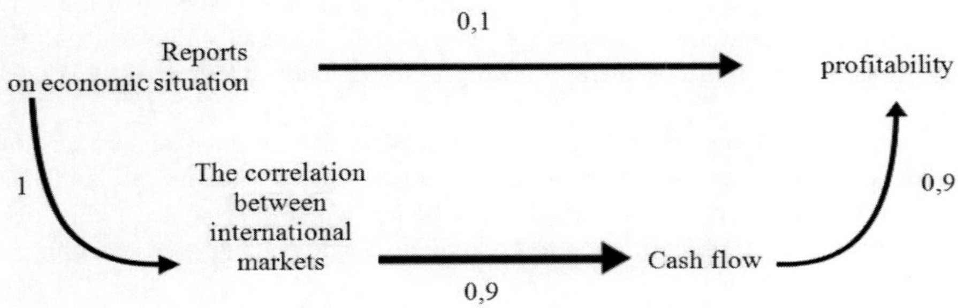

As for the impact of economic reports due on the profitability effect, there are two interposed key relationships: the correlation between international markets and cash flows. Although an estimate of 10% in the incidence reports on economic and profitability was initially provided, this ratio really increased to 90%, since the two elements enhance and gather brought effects on causation. This result can be interpreted as the investors' need to relate the information they own together with the international market taking into account the amount of money they can invest to rationalize their choice and have a good definition of the risk.

We also find two cases in the cause of the taxation of investment in shares on the diversification purchase:

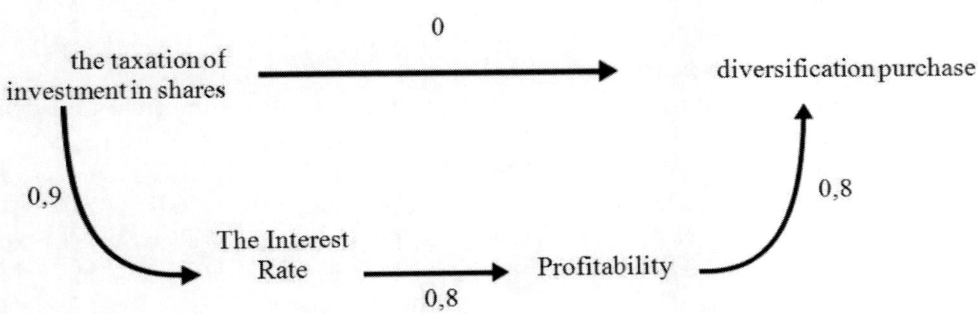

In this case, before an initial incidence which was originally established as 0 in the incidence of taxation on investment and diversification of purchase, this ratio really increased to 80% by the presence of two elements: the interest rates and the profitability, which have been Forgotten Effects.

CONCLUSION

In this work we have proceeded to the application of the theory of forgotten effects for the decision making under uncertainty in the financial sector by the small investor in the stock market. While classic formulated models have provided good solutions in times of stability, they have required a thorough review of their approaches in times of global changes, such as the one we are living in. It is in this order of facts that it has become necessary to use tools for the treatment of uncertainty. The use of the technique based on the Theory of the Forgotten Effects has allowed to the small investor designing more accurately his own policies and investment strategies in the stock market, having a deeper understanding of the factors that affect his decision.

To conclude, it is possible involving other variables for decision makings which allow the investor the conscious and appropriate management of conflicting goals. Thus, the applicability of the forgotten effects method would be less expensive and accessible to a small investor. We believe in our contribution to be a great support for future researching lines in this field.

REFERENCES

Barber, B. Reuven, L.; Maureen, M.; and Brett T. (2001). Can investors profit from the Prophets? Consensus Analyst Recommendations and Stock Return, *Journal of Finance*, 56, 531-563.

Campbell, J. Y and Kyle, A. S. (1993). Smart Money, Noise Trading and Stock Price Behaviour. *Review of Economic Studies*, 60, 1, 1-34.

De Bondt, W. F. M. and Thaler, R. (1985). Does the Stock Market Overreact? *The Journal of Financ*,. 40, 3, 793-805.

Chopra, N.; Lakonishok, J. and Ritter, J. (1992). Measuring Abnormal Performance: Do Stocks Overreact?. the Journal of Finance, 49, 5, 1541-1578.

Fama E.F. and French, K. R. (1993). Common risk factors in the returns on stocks and bonds. *Journal of Financial Economics*, 33, 33-56.

Kaufmann, A. and Gil Aluja, J. (1988). Models for forgotten effects research. Milladoiro, Santiago de Compostela.

Kim, S. T.; J-C. Lin and Slovin, M. B. (1997). Marked Structure, Informed Trading, and Analysts Recommendations. Journal of Finance and Quantitative Analysis, 32, 507-524.

Lo & MacKinlay (1988). Stock Market Prices Do Not Follow Random Walks: Evidence from a Simple Specification Test. The review of financial Studies, 1, 41-66.

Lo & MacKinlay (2007). The Taiwan stock market does follow a random walk. Economics Bulletin, 7, 3, 1-8.

Malkiel, B. G and Cragg, J. (1980). Expectations and the valuation of Share. National bureau of Economic Research, Working paper, 471.

Malkiel, B. G. (2003). The Efficient Market Hypothesis and Its Critics. Journal of Economic Perspectives, 17, 1, 59-82.

Murphy, J. J. (1999). Technical analysis of financial markets. New York Institute of Finance.

Narasimhan, J. (2004). Analyzing the Analysts: When do Recommendations add value? *Journal of Finance*, 59, 3, 1083-1124.

Poterba, J.M and Summers, H. (1987). Mean reversion in stock prices: evidence and implications *National Bureau of Economic Research.*

Smithson, M. (1987). Fuzzy Set Analysis for the Behavioral and Social Sciences. *New York: Springer Verlag,* p. 327.

Smithson, M. and Verkuilen, J. (2006). Fuzzy Set Theory: Applications in the Social Sciences *Quantitative Applications in the Social Sciences Series*. Belmont, CA: Sage, 97.

Smithson, M. & Oden, G. C. (1999). Fuzzy set theory and applications in psychology: In D. Dubois & H. Prade (Eds.) International Handbook of Fuzzy Sets and Possibility Theory´´ *Applications. Amsterdam*: Kluwer, 5, 557-585.

Woolridge, J. R. (2004). Performance of Stocks Recommended by Brokerages. *Journal of Investing,* 13, 1, 23-34.

In: Computational Data Analysis Techniques
Editors: M. Doumpos, C. Zopounidis and Ch. Gaganis
ISBN: 978-1-63463-957-6

Chapter 9

PORTFOLIO DIVERSIFICATION: PRINCIPAL COMPONENT ANALYSIS AND PICHAT ALGORITHM, FOR THE CONTEMPORARY ECONOMIC SITUATION

***Xavier Colominas Garcia*[1] *and Juan G. Rusinque Campos*[2]**
Business and Economics Faculty, University of Barcelona, Barcelona, Spain

ABSTRACT

The actual economic situation has shown us the importance of diversification of the inversions we make as companies but also as single investors. This has been one of the points supervisors demanded while got involved in the recovery of some countries. In this article our objective is to obtain a reduced share portfolio that adjust the best to the initial portfolio we have, so we can have a pretty diversified portfolio without investing in all the shares.

For that, we obtain the proportions of the shares that are going to compose our reduced portfolio using a principal components analysis (using EViews software) and we compared with other portfolios made by using the Pichat method (both based on the correlation matrix) which offers a more generalized analysis with the possibility of including non-complete information to our samples.

Keywords: Pichat algorithm, principal component analysis, diversification, portfolio, shares

1. INTRODUCTION

Many studies have been done within the principal component analysis for investor's decision making in the financial field. For example, a general explanation in its application on financial data analysis was made by Alexander, C. (2001).

[1] E-mail: xavi.colominas@gmail.com
[2] E-mail: juanrus89@gmail.com

Joel R. Barber and Mark L. Copper (1996) applied principal component analysis to secure investors from interest rates using immunization.

Gary Chamberlain and Michael Rothschild (1984) made a study of the implications of arbitrage in the markets, using the principal component analysis as the only empirical tool.

Also, Lessard, D.R. (1973) applied PCAs into portfolio diversification for a group of Latin American countries.

Joel Hasbrouck and Duane J. Seppi (2001) use principal components and canonical correlation analyses in order to analyze the 30 Dow stocks returns.

Gil-Lafuente, Gil-Aluja and De Paula (2013) used the Pichat Algorithm in order to determine an algorithm able to reduce the number of elements in a power set when applying a grouping model in portfolio management. We will focus on Pichat algorithm developed by Pichat. E (1969).

So now we present a model to diversify portfolios in the considered world indexes, which prove the utility that principal component analysis offers in the investing areas comparing it with the Pichat algorithm.

This work is structured as follows: Section 2 presents the used data and the periods we make in order to find reliable conclusions. In section 3 we apply the principal component analysis model and in section 4 the Pichat algorithm. Finally in section 5 we take some conclusions.

2. Data

Weekly values from the http://finance.yahoo.com, from the following index have been used:

1. CAC-40(CAC)
2. DAX-30(DAX)
3. Dow Jones Industrial Average-30 (DJIA)
4. FTSE-100 (FTSE-100)
5. IBEX-35 (IBEX)
6. NASDAQ-100 (NASDAQ)
7. NIKKEI-225 (NIKKEI)
8. Standard & Poor's-500 (S&P)

From the 3rd January 2000 to the 31 of December 2012.

Omitting the observations from 26 December 2011 to the end, principal components are characterized to represent a high percent of the fluctuations from the full shares portfolio. From the initial series we have, we take its differences to obtain each index daily income which is transformed into a stationary variable.

To obtain more adequate values for our analysis, we use the logarithm differentiation. Having analyzed the data only until 26 December 2011, allows us to use the remaining values (the whole 2012) to compare and evaluate our final portfolio.

As we said, this principal components analysis is based on the correlation matrix that we obtain using the EViews software for data analysis, introducing the involved series for afterwards drawing its correlations.

The correlation matrix obtained is as follows:

In the table above, it's visible that the returns from every index are highly and positively correlated, being the lowest correlation the one between the NASDAQ and the NIKKEI with a value of 0.466346 which is something more than irrelevant.

Table 1. Correlation matrix

	DCAC	DDAX	DDJIA	DFTSE	DIBEX	DNASDAQ	DNIKKEI	DSP
DCAC	1.000000							
DDAX	0.916291	1.000000						
DDJIA	0.800609	0.799599	1.000000					
DFTSE	0.902844	0.856321	0.805220	1.000000				
DIBEX	0.858038	0.822364	0.719920	0.791065	1.000000			
DNASDAQ	0.664237	0.685122	0.709201	0.622492	0.574729	1.000000		
DNIKKEI	0.599481	0.596991	0.537057	0.587566	0.539168	0.466346	1.000000	
DSP	0.831329	0.824507	0.957516	0.829502	0.738497	0.817802	0.558801	1.000000

3. Principal Component Analysis

The PCA produces the same amount of auto values as index we want to test, and from those auto values it is possible to observe the amount they explain from the total sample. Then, from the three or four most significant auto values (that usually represent an enough part of the sample) we obtain the auto vectors which show one value for every index we have. Those values of the auto vectors from the chosen auto values will be the amount taken into account for the portfolio composition process.

The auto values related to that matrix are represented in the following table:

Table 2. Auto values

Eigenvalues: (Sum = 8, Average = 1)

Number	Value	Difference	Proportion	Cumulative Value	Cumulative Proportion
1	6.159246	5.544734	0.7699	6.159246	0.7699
2	0.614512	0.091448	0.0768	6.773759	0.8467
3	0.523064	0.238630	0.0654	7.296823	0.9121
4	0.284434	0.088604	0.0356	7.581257	0.9477
5	0.195831	0.064591	0.0245	7.777087	0.9721
6	0.131240	0.064193	0.0164	7.908327	0.9885
7	0.067046	0.042420	0.0084	7.975374	0.9969
8	0.024626	---	0.0031	8.000000	1.0000

In this table we can notice that the first auto value (6.159246) is representing a 0.7699 of the total variability. For this work, the three principal components will be considered as they can explain a 0.9121 of the sample's variation. Moreover, the auto vectors generated matrix is as follows:

So when this matrix is put under study, one can easily understand the first component to be a general index level according to the fact that all its auto vectors have a similar weight.

In the second component we can spot EE.UU. and Japan as being more relevant than the other four European index (CAC, DAX, FTSE e IBEX).

Finally, the third principal component also exhibits a clear evidence of geographical distinction, as the four European indexes are negative values unlike the rest that are positive.

So now, we are treating the linear combination obtained as portfolios, for being afterwards followed up through the whole subsample we did ignored in the first section.

As said, the three first principal components will be taken into account but also only its two indexes with the more representative values in each component will be considered. So at least we are going to have a total of six indexes distributed in three sub portfolios.

Table 3. Auto vectors matrix

Eigenvectors (loadings):

Variable	PC 1	PC 2	PC 3	PC 4	PC 5	PC 6	PC 7	PC 8
DCAC	0.380516	0.090087	-0.276026	0.123411	-0.253208	-0.055957	-0.828232	0.049590
DDAX	0.376121	0.055218	-0.195723	0.178814	-0.291034	-0.730155	0.405940	-0.050871
DDJIA	0.366536	-0.249782	0.084690	-0.600597	0.287837	-0.164990	-0.019209	0.570026
DFTSE	0.370370	0.082809	-0.248640	-0.199368	-0.507718	0.607381	0.350640	0.069005
DIBEX	0.349522	0.148790	-0.429230	0.361211	0.691508	0.201835	0.148536	-0.000950
DNASDAQ	0.317844	-0.463192	0.530489	0.571090	-0.083840	0.162616	0.030924	0.206001
DNIKKEI	0.274392	0.772784	0.566423	-0.043226	0.068757	0.006348	-0.006579	-0.000610
DSP	0.379129	-0.292756	0.173253	-0.306341	0.143588	0.019687	-0.053527	-0.789192

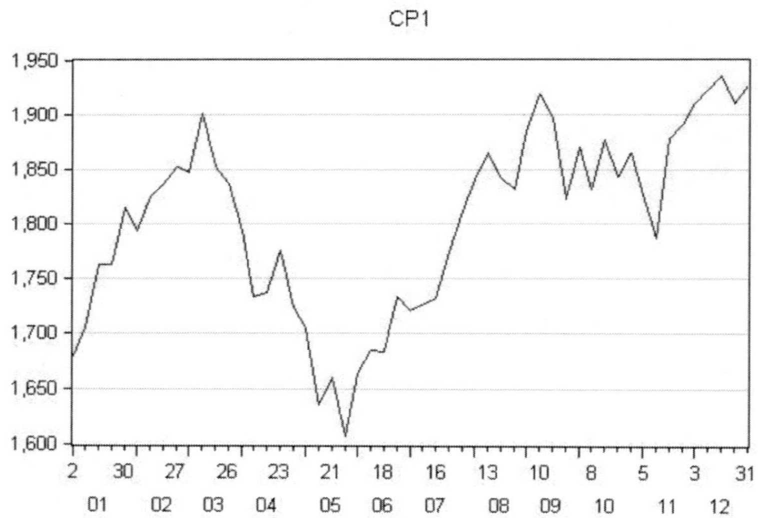

Figure 1. CP1 portfolio evolution.

For the first sub portfolio, corresponding to the first principal component, we are going to include the CAC and S&P index as they have values of 0.380516 and 0.379129 respectively. Thereupon, the first sub portfolio will result from doing:

$$CP1 = 0.380516 * CAC + 0.379129 * S\&P$$

We are following the same method in the way to obtain the second and third sub portfolios, which are finally represented as:

$$CP2 = 0.772784 * NIKKEI + 0.148790 * IBEX$$
$$CP3 = 0.530489 * NASDAQ + 0.084690 * DJIA$$

In the third component, we had bigger values of the auto values, but we left them out because they represented index already captured in the other two sub portfolios and in this article we are seeking for diversification.

Now we can observe the three sub portfolios evolution during the sample period.

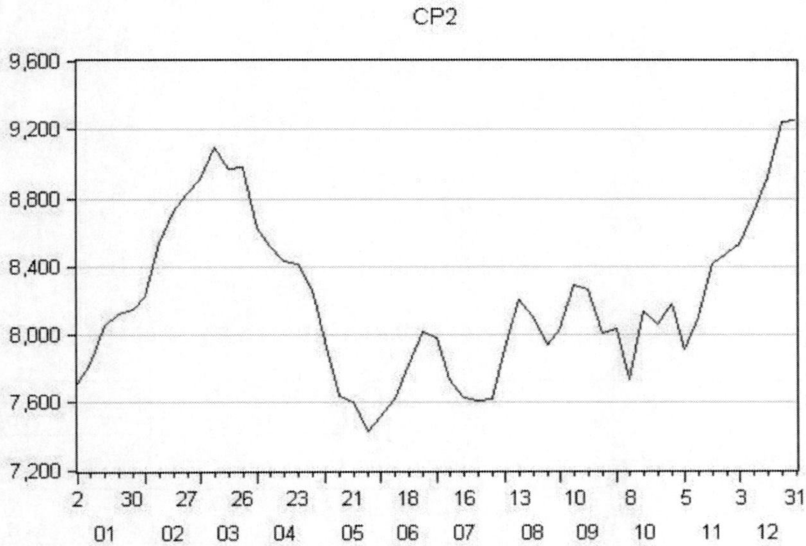

Figure 2. CP2 portfolio evolution.

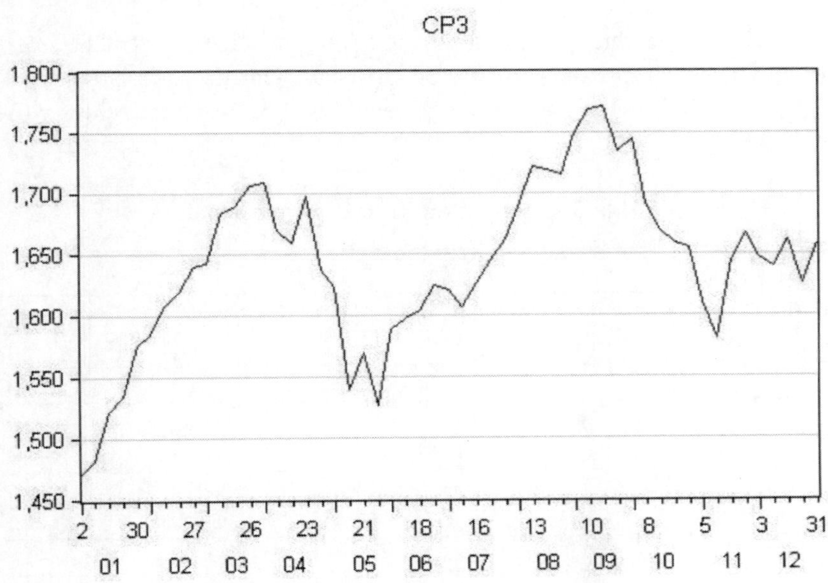

Figure 3. CP3 portfolio evolution.

4. PICHAT ALGORITHM

Using the correlation matrix we are going to introduce the Pichat algorithm to see the possible groupings of the different international market indexes. First, we will change the name of them:

- P1: CAC
- P2: DAX
- P3: DJIA
- P4: FTSE
- P5: IBEX
- P6: NASDAQ
- P7: NIKKEI
- P8: S&P

Now, we have the following correlation matrix:

Table 4. Correlation Matrix

	P1	P2	P3	P4	P5	P6	P7	P8
P1	1	0,92	0,8	0,9	0,86	0,66	0,6	0,83
P2		1	0,8	0,86	0,82	0,69	0,6	0,82
P3			1	0,81	0,72	0,71	0,54	0,96
P4				1	0,79	0,62	0,59	0,83
P5					1	0,57	0,54	0,74
P6						1	0,47	0,82
P7							1	0,56
P8								1

And we will assume three minimum correlation thresholds ($\alpha \geq 0{,}85, \alpha \geq 0{,}80, \alpha \geq 0{,}75$) to see the groupings of the indexes. So, we start with the correlation threshold $\alpha \geq 0{,}80$. All the correlations that are above this threshold will be 1 and the others will be 0. We have the next table:

Table 5. Correlation Matrix with α ≥0.80

	α≥0,80							
	P1	P2	P3	P4	P5	P6	P7	P8
P1	1	1	1	1	1			1
P2		1		1	1			1
P3			1	1				1
P4				1				1
P5					1			
P6						1		1
P7							1	
P8								1

For each row we have:

- $\boldsymbol{P_1 = 1 \dotplus 67}$
- $\boldsymbol{P_2 = 2 \dotplus 367}$
- $\boldsymbol{P_3 = 3 \dotplus 567}$
- $\boldsymbol{P_4 = 4 \dotplus 567}$
- $\boldsymbol{P_5 = 5 \dotplus 678}$
- $\boldsymbol{P_6 = 6 \dotplus 7}$
- $\boldsymbol{P_7 = 7 \dotplus 8}$
- $\boldsymbol{P_8 = 1}$

Doing the multiplication, it results:

$$
\begin{aligned}
S = (1 \dotplus 67)(2 \dotplus 367)(3 \dotplus 567)(4 \dotplus 567)(5 \dotplus 678)(6 \dotplus 7)(7 \dotplus 8) = \\
&= (12 \dotplus \cancel{1367} \dotplus 267 \dotplus 367)(3 \dotplus 567)(4 \dotplus 567)(5 \dotplus 678)(6 \dotplus 7)(7 \dotplus 8) = \\
&= (123 \dotplus \cancel{12567} \dotplus \cancel{2367} \dotplus 2567 \dotplus 367 \dotplus \cancel{3567})(4 \dotplus 567)(5 \dotplus 678)(6 \dotplus 7)(7 \dotplus 8) = \\
&= (1234 \dotplus \cancel{123567} \dotplus \cancel{24567} \dotplus 2567 \dotplus 3467 \dotplus 3567)(5 \dotplus 678)(6 \dotplus 7)(7 \dotplus 8) = \\
&= (12345 \dotplus \cancel{1234678} \dotplus 2567 \dotplus \cancel{25678} \dotplus 34567 \dotplus 34678 \dotplus 3567 \dotplus \cancel{35678})(6 \dotplus 7)(7 \dotplus 8) = \\
&= (123456 \dotplus 123457 \dotplus 2567 \dotplus \cancel{2567} \dotplus 34567 \dotplus \cancel{34567} \dotplus 34678 \dotplus \cancel{34678} \dotplus 3567 \dotplus \cancel{3567})(7 \dotplus 8) = \\
&= (\cancel{1234567} \dotplus 1234568 \dotplus 123457 \dotplus \cancel{1234578} \dotplus 2567 \dotplus \cancel{25678} \dotplus \cancel{34567} \dotplus \cancel{345678} \dotplus 34678 \dotplus \cancel{34678} \dotplus 3567 \dotplus \cancel{35678}) \\
&= 1234568 \dotplus 123457 \dotplus 2567 \dotplus 34678 \dotplus 3567
\end{aligned}
$$

We obtain the complementary for each element

$$S' = 7 \dotplus 68 \dotplus 1348 \dotplus 125 \dotplus 1248$$

Finally we have the possible groupings based on the correlations:

- Group 1: P7 = NIKKEI
- Group 2: P6P8 = NASDAQ, S&P
- Group 3: P1P3P4P8 = CAC, DJIA, FTSE, S&P
- Group 4: P1P2P5 = CAC, DAX, IBEX
- Group 5: P1P2P4P8 = CAC, DAX, FTSE, S&P

So we finally have five groups where the investor should choose one index from each grouping in order to have a diversified portfolio.

This means that the investor can select any index from the group 3 because they have a high correlation and that implies that they have a similar risk (i.e., any of the index of this group will have a similar behavior).

We see that CAC and S&P are present in many groups, so it would be reasonable to pick one of each from the aggrupation we prefer, but only once each one, without repeating an index in a same portfolio.

We can also see the possible results if we increase or decrease the threshold of correlation. Now we will do the analysis with a higher level of correlation ($\alpha \geq 0{,}85$) and with a lower level of correlation. For reasons of space we won't show all the process of the Pichat algorithm.

When we assume the higher correlation threshold, we obtain five possible groupings for the indexes:

- Group 1: P7 = NIKKEI
- Group 2: P6P8 = NASDAQ, S&P
- Group 3: P3P8 = DJIA, S&P
- Group 4: P1P6 = CAC, NASDAQ
- Group 5: P1P2P4 = CAC, DAX, FTSE

We see that the groups 3, 4 and 5 have been reduced, the group 1 and 2 have not changed. It is an analysis more accurate because the threshold increased. It implies that the investor requires a higher correlation to create the portfolio. In this case the decision of the investor will be easier because of the elements in each group. Only NASDAQ, CAC and S&P appear in two groups. The IBEX is the only index that doesn't appear in any of the groups. It is possibly due to group 5 that includes the most important indexes in the European region that are highly correlated.

If we assume a lower correlation threshold, it results the possible groupings based on the correlations:

- Group 1: P7 = NIKKEI
- Group 2: P6P8 = NASDAQ, S&P
- Group 3: P1P2P4P5 = CAC, DAX, FTSE, IBEX
- Group 4: P1P2P3P4P8 = CAC, DAX, DJIA, FTSE, S&P

It concludes that we have four groups and the investor shall choose one index for each group to create the portfolio.

We have fewer groups because of the lower threshold and the group 4 includes five indexes that have a similar high correlation. Now IBEX appears in the group of the indexes of the European region (group 3). Then, the investor has fewer groups but has more possibilities within the groups 3 and 4.

In all of the cases that we studied, we have two groups with the same elements for each analysis. One of them is the group with the element NIKKEI that is the index with the lowest correlation.

It is because its highest correlation is 0.5994 with CAC and 0.5969 with DAX. These values do not exceed any of the thresholds. In the other hand we have the group with the elements NASDAQ and S&P. It is possibly due to the index NASDAQ which has a correlation level of 0.8178 with S&P and the rest of its correlations with the other indexes are lower than 0.71.

CONCLUSION

The results from this analysis give us interesting information while showing similar returns for the portfolios done with the PCA and an equipoised portfolio with the entire index we are analyzing. This means that with a smaller amount of shares, we could reply the benefits of the global portfolio without necessary buying shares from all of them.

Significant differences between countries are found during the analysis but also in the profit obtained in the sample observed.

We have seen that with the Pichat algorithm, we could reach portfolios with the same index composition that the ones made by the PCA, but the Pichat ones, would have to be an equipoised portfolio from the entire index selected, while we are not having values for each of them.

An investor could try to invest more in the index that are in more than one group, such as CAC or S&P, but we have no empirical evidence that it should be a better option.

REFERENCES

Alexander, C. (2001), "Principal Component Analysis of Volatility Smiles and Skews" *ISMA Centre Discussion Papers in Finance* 2000-06 University of Reading, UK.

Barber, J. R. and Cooper, M. L. (1996), "Immunization Using Principal Component Analysis", *The Journal of Portfolio Management* 23(1), 99-105.

Gil-Lafuente, A. M., Gil-Aluja, J. and De Paula, L. B. (2013), "Determining the composition of a portfolio management from a groupings model", *International Journal of Uncertainty Fuzziness and Knowledge-based systems* 21 (4), 561-578.

Hasbrouck, J. and Seppi, D. J. (2001), "Common factors in prices, order flows and liquidity", *Journal of Financial Economics* 59, 383-411.

Lessard, D.R. (1973), "International portfolio diversification: A multivariate analysis for a group of Latin American countries", *The Journal of Finance* 28(3), 619-633.

Rothschild, M. and Chamberlain, G. (1984), "Arbitrage, Factor Structure, and Mean-Variance Analysis on Large Asset Markets", NBER Working Papers 0996, *National Bureau of Economic Research*, Inc.

In: Computational Data Analysis Techniques
Editors: M. Doumpos, C. Zopounidis and Ch. Gaganis
ISBN: 978-1-63463-957-6

Chapter 10

A COMPARATIVE EMPIRICAL STUDY FOR THE DIFFERENT APPROACHES OF THE OPERATIONAL LEASES CAPITALIZATION

***D. Henraat*[1], *G. Georgakopoulos*[2], *P. Kalantonis*[3] *and M. Rodosthenous*[4]**
[1,2]University of Amsterdam
[3,4]Technological Education Institute of Piraeus

ABSTRACT

Ever since the 1960's there has been debate about the impact of disclosure versus recognition of operating leases. The topic was interesting for preparers of financial statements, users of financial statements, as well as for regulators. Much research has been conducted to assess the impact of capitalization of operating leases. The number of studies increased along as the leasing industry developed with great speed in the twentieth century. Because the IASB , in cooperation with the FASB, drafted a new standard on lease accounting to replace the current standard, it became even more important to understand the impact of capitalization of operating leases on financial ratios. The results of these studies, however, could not come to a general agreement. This disagreement could be caused by the differences between the constructive capitalization methods which were used in the different studies. In this study we compare two of the most widely used methods in order to assess which method has more explanatory power over the other.

LIST OF DEFINITIONS

Variables	**Definitions**
PVOLt	Present Value at balance sheet date of the future lease payment
CFLeasePaymentst+1	Future lease payments in the following period

i	Implicit interest rate
RL	Remaining life to expiry
AFi,RL	Annuity factor for interest rate i and remaining life to expiry RL
Stdev	Standard deviation of daily stock returns around fiscal year-end (-125 trading days, +125 trading days).
D/A	Debt to Asset Ratio (Total interest-bearing debt / Total asets).
D/A F8	D/A, adjusted for off-balance operating leases based on the factor method, using a fixed number of 8-times rent.
D/A F6	D/A, adjusted for off-balance operating leases based on the factor method, using a fixed number of 6-times rent.
D/A DCF	D/A, adjusted for off-balance operating leases based on the DCF method.
ΔD/A F8	D/A F8 minus D/A ; The change from unadjusted D/A to adjusted D/A using the factor method with a fixed number of 8-times rent.
ΔD/A F6	D/A F6 minus D/A ; The change from unadjusted D/A to adjusted D/A using the factor method with a fixed number of 6-times rent.
ΔD/A DCF	D/A DCF minus D/A ; The change from unadjusted D/A to adjusted D/A using the DCF method.

INTRODUCTION

In March 2009 the International Accounting Standards Board (IASB) and the U.S. Financial Accounting Standards Board (FASB) issued a Discussion paper proposing a new model that will significantly change lease accounting for lessees. This proposal eliminates the current distinction between accounting for operating leases (which are accounted for off-balance) and finance leases (which are accounted for on-balance), as defined in IAS17. This means that all leases will be accounted for on-balance, including existing operating leases which are now accounted for off-balance. The comment period for this Discussion Paper ended on July 17, 2009 and some 300 comments were received. Then the boards evaluated the feedback and issued an Exposure Draft on August 17, 2010. The comment period for this Exposure Draft ended on December 15, 2010. The intention was to issue the new standard in June 2011, but in May 2011 the IASB decided to postpone the issue to the fourth quarter of 2011. The final standard will probably be taken into use in 2015, with comparing figures of 2014.

According to the current standard (IAS 17) leases are classified either as an operating lease or as a finance lease. This classification is based on the extent to which risks and rewards incidental to ownership of a leased asset lie with the lessor or the lessee. A lease is classified as a finance lease if it transfers substantially all the risks and rewards incidental to ownership. A lease is classified as an operating lease if it does not transfer substantially all the risks and rewards incidental to ownership. This so called "Risk and Reward approach" does not recognize assets and liabilities in the way defined in the IASB's Conceptual Framework. Therefore a new approach is needed, which could recognize and measure assets and liabilities in consistence with the Framework.

This new "Assets and Liability approach" determines that all leases will be capitalized on the balance sheet using the present value of the minimum lease payments. The transfer of "substantially all the risks and rewards incidental to ownership" is no longer the determinant in this conceptual basis. The new determinant in this conceptual basis is the recognition of the "right to use" assets. Since operating leases are such an important source of finance for many companies the adoption of a new standard in accounting for leases will have a significant impact on these companies (Goodacre, 2001) Operating leases. In 1999 operating leases in the United Kingdom amounted to £71 billion, equal to 50% of long-term debt financing and 28% of net fixed assets (Goodacre, 2001). In 2005 the SEC staff report in the United States estimated the total outstanding lease payments to be $1.25 trillion. Compustat data showed that in 2004 39.7% of total fixed claims was accounted for by operating lease liabilities, against 58.8% by long-term debt (Ge, 2006).

The current accounting standard does not require companies to disclose operating lease contracts on the balance sheet, mere as footnotes, despite the fact that these companies heavily rely on operating lease as a source of financing. This resulted in companies constructing their lease contracts in such a way that they could be classified as operating leases. This behaviour can be considered to cause a distortion of the company's financial picture which investor's use to make their investment decisions (Ge et al., 2008). Therefore, it became questionable whether or not it is appropriate to report operating leases off-balance Gallery and Imhoff, 1998). Because of this question much research has been done to assess the impact of capitalizing operating leases on financial ratios (Imhoff et al., 1991; Ely, 1995; Gallery and Imhoff, 1998; Beattie et al., 2000; Ge et al., 2008)

In these studies different methods were used to capitalize the operating leases. These methods can be divided into two types. One type is the factor method, which uses a fixed number to multiply a companies' next year operating lease commitment to compute the value of all future lease payments for all companies (Imhoff et al., 1993; Bennet et al., 2003). The other type is a constructive capitalization method, based on the present value of all future lease payments (Imhoff et al., 1991; Beattie et al., 1998). This type discounts all future lease commitments. Imhoff et al. (1991) were the first to develop a capitalization method for off-balance operating lease obligations based on the present value. Their constructive capitalization (DCF) method is a method of estimating the amounts of operating lease assets or debt that would have been reported on balance if leases had been treated as financial leases from their inception (Imhoff et al., 1991). More specifically, the constructive capitalization (DCF) method is the present value of the scheduled minimum future cash flows disclosed in the financial statement footnotes and based on the economic logic of discounted future cash flow (Ge et al., 2008). This method of Imhoff et al. is the most used in practice.

The oldest methods to estimate the amount of unrecorded debt as a multiple of the current period's rent expense, are the factor methods (Ge et al., 2008). These methods are still also widely used by analysts to capitalize operating leases, despite that they are considered to be simple (rules-of-thumb) methods. Under the factor methods, off-balance operating lease obligations are calculated by multiplying a company's next-year lease rent with a fixed multiple. The most frequent used fixed numbers are 6- or 8- times rent.

During the last five decades much research has been conducted to assess the potential impact of lease capitalization on financial ratios (Imhoff et al., 1991; Ely, 1995; Gallery and Imhoff, 1998; Beattie et al., 2000; Ge et al., 2008). Also, researchers wanted to understand whether or not users of financial reports use the financial information about operating leases, disclosed in footnotes, when assessing a firm's equity risk. Or that the users would benefit from capitalizing operating leases (Ge et al., 2008).

The results of these studies are rather conflicting. One explanation for these conflicting results could be the different settings in which the studies were conducted. It appears that studies carried out in different countries give different results. At the same time, also studies carried out in the same country (i.e. the US) gave different results. These studies could not come to a general agreement. Another explanation for the conflicting results could be the differences between the capitalization methods used. The main purpose of our this research is to shed some more light on this topic to narrow the gap left by these studies.

This paper is developed as follows: First we explain the incentives of firms to choose leasing over other debt alternatives in acquiring capital and we state the current and proposed approaches of IFRS for the accounting treatment of operating leases. We go on with the literature review for the impact of the lease capitalization to the financial ratios of forms which also contains a short description of the two capitalization methods. The research goals and research question are presented next. The sampling method and the model description are included in following section. Finally our findings and the conclusion close this paper.

Incentives to Choose Leasing Over Other Debt Alternatives

The incentives for companies to choose leasing over other debt alternatives in acquiring capital can be divided into four categories (Lückerath-Rovers, 2007): (1) Risk-sharing reasons, (2) Tax-savings reasons, (3) Borrowing-related reasons and (4) Other financial /transactional reasons.

Risk-Sharing Reasons

Because technology is developing rapidly, companies need to have their equipment upgraded after relatively short periods of time. Operating leases could provide companies with the flexibility to do so, by reducing the risk of obsolescence (Thomson, 2003; Lückerath-Rovers, 2007). The one who the risk is shared with, the lessor, might be able to both purchase the assets at lower costs, by buying large samples (Thomson, 2003), and dispose the assets at the end of the lease, by selling it at bargain prices.

Tax-Saving Reasons

Under a lease contract the lessor has the legal ownership and the right to claim capital tax allowances (Thomson, 2003). By engaging in an operational lease contract the possible tax advantage would be transferred from the lessee to the lessor. Who, in turn, might share this tax benefit with the lessee by giving a discount on the lease rentals.

Borrowing-Related Reasons

This category comprises three reasons. The first and most important reason is the extension of the debt capacity. The company's debt capacity is its ability to borrow funds to a certain extent as from which the corporate value of the company will not increase any further. This debt capacity is often limited because of debt covenants or rules imposed by investors (Lückerath-Rovers, 2007, see also an example in Appendix 10.1). The suggestion is that lease contracts use less or even no debt capacity at all, providing companies the opportunity to extend their debt capacity. Investors might ignore the off-balance operating lease obligations because they are not recognized on the balance sheet.

The second reason is that from the lessee no (additional) collateral is needed, which reduces the effort required and the risk incurred in the agreement. After all the lessor provides all the funds and keeps the ownership over the leased assets.

The third reason refers to the restrictive covenants which are used to mitigate conflicts of interest between debt holders and shareholders by restricting risky investments. Risky investments create possible upside for investors, while possible downsides will be shared with the debtors. Leasing contracts contain less of these restrictive covenants (Lückerath-Rovers, 2007). Because leasing is a high priority claim, leasing reduces under-investment by limiting the risk (Thomson, 2003).

Other Financial/Transactional Reasons

This category contains four reasons. Sometimes companies choose to have the benefits of having different kinds of services, maintenance and insurance directly attached to the lease agreement. The best known example is the car lease industry, where large companies choose to lease their cars rather than purchasing the cars themselves. Even if they have access to sufficient funds and if they are in the position to purchase at a discount because of buying large quantities.

Another reason is that companies improve their financial ratios by leasing in-stead of borrowing funds, because of the off-balance sheet character of operating leases. This improvement of the financial ratios gives an incentive to managers to choose operating lease over other debt alternatives, because management compensation most of the times is based on these financial ratios (Lückerath-Rovers, 2007). So, the third reason is the own interest of management.

The last reason is that leasing might be cheaper than borrowing (Rauh and Sufi, 2010; Sharpe and Nguyen, 1995; Eisfeldt and Rampini, 2009). Where lease and secured debt have one major similarity, they both represent future payments which the lessee or borrower has to pay to use the asset, there is also a major difference, which is the treatment in case of bankruptcy of the lessee or borrower. In such a case it is less costly for the lessor to repossess leased assets than it is for lenders to repossess pledged assets.

THE CURRENT APPROACH (IAS17)

A finance lease (or capital lease) is a lease that, in economic substance, transfers substantially all the risks and rewards inherent in the leased property to the lessee. Because of this characteristic, this approach is referred to as the "Risk and Reward approach". This classification is made at the inception of the lease (IAS 17.4).

IAS 17.10 states that a lease has to be classified as a finance lease by the lessee if one of the following criteria apply at the inception of the lease:

- The lease transfers ownership of the asset to the lessee at the end of the lease term:
- The lessee has the option to purchase the asset at a "bargain price";
- The lease term is for the major part of the economic life of the asset, even if title is not transferred;
- At the inception of the lease, the present value of the minimum lease payments amounts to at least substantially all of the fair value of the leased assets;
- The leased asset is of such a specialized nature that only the lessee can use it without making major modifications.

THE PROPOSED APPROACH

Users of financial reports trust the information in these reports to be reliable. To provide the market with reliable information about a firm's assets and liabilities, that's one of the objectives of financial reporting. The conceptual basis of the current standard is to distinguish the economic ownership of the leased asset to classify leases either as finance lease or operating lease. This is not compliant with the IASB's Conceptual Framework, because it does not recognize assets and liabilities according to the definition in the Framework.

Moreover, the current standard encourages firms to construct their lease contracts to be categorized as operating leases. Which can be considered to make the financial reporting less reliable. Because users of financial reports might ignore the off-balance disclosure of operating leases and thus understate the true degree of leverage of a firm (Rampini and Viswanathan, 2010b). The new approach is to overcome this weakness of the current approach. The new approach considers all leases to have assets and liabilities (for both lessee and lessor). According to the new standard all leases should be accounted for by valuing these assets and liabilities and present them on the balance sheet. Because of this characteristic, this approach is called the "Asset and Liability approach". This new approach shows many similarities with the arguments raised by researchers in the 1960's and 1970's, before FAS13 was issued. Nelson (1963) already argued that recognizing operating leases on the balance sheet is value relevant for investors.

The Impact of the Proposed Approach

In 2009 PriceWaterhouseCoopers and the Rotterdam School of Management (PWC and RSM, 2009) conducted a research to assess the impact of the proposed approach. Their sample consisted of the financial statements of 2008 of more than 3,000 companies in 54 countries worldwide. Based on the disclosure in the financial statements regarding operating leases, they concluded that for these companies the interest bearing debt will increase with an average of 58%.

This is even a cautious estimation, since the actual impact will depend on the specific details in the final standard. The results of this study show that of 24% of these companies the interest bearing debt will increase by over 25%.

This research also showed that the impact of the proposed approach on financial ratios per industry is significantly different. Figure 1 shows that the leverage within the Retail and Trade industry will suffer the highest impact, followed by the Other Services and Transportation and Warehousing industry.

	Average increase in interest bearing debt	% companies with over 25% increase	Average increase in leverage (percentage points)	Average increase in EBITDA
Retail and Trade	213	71	64	55
Other Services	51	35	34	25
Transportation and Warehousing	95	38	31	44
Telecom	23	21	20	16
Professional Services	158	52	19	27
Amusement	25	18	19	13
Accommodation	101	41	18	30
Wholesale Trade	34	28	17	21
All companies	58	24	13	18
Manufacturing	50	21	9	13
Construction	68	20	8	14
Oil, Gas and Mining	30	16	7	10
Financial services	27	11	6	15
Utilities	3	3	2	6

Source: Proposed lease accounting: Research of impact on companies – PriceWaterhouseCoopers and Erasmus School of Management, 2009, p.2.

Figure 1. The average impact per industry.

The impact is not only differentiated per industry, but also per individual company within an industry. This difference in impact per company depends on the size and country of residence. Comparing the impact across countries, we see that the leverage of companies in the Netherlands will be influenced the most with an average increase of 27% (see figure 2).

The leverage in The United Kingdom, Italy and France will increase by 20%.

LITERATURE REVIEW

Factor Method

This is the oldest method to estimate the amount of unrecorded debt, by multiplying the current period's lease expense (Ge et al., 2008). This method is still used by analysts to capitalize operating leases, despite that this method is considered to be a simple method. This method estimates the off-balance operating lease obligations by multiplying a firm's next-year lease expenses with a fixed multiple. The most frequently used fixed numbers are the 6- and 8- times rent. The 8- times rent is the oldest method still in use and dates back to the early 1930's (Ge et al., 2008). The 6-times rent is of later date and is used (for example) by Morgan Stanley for the airline industry (Ely, 1995). The fixed number used, implies a borrowing rate and a number of lease periods.[4] The multiple applied, increases along with the economic life of the leased assets.

	Average increase in interest bearing debt	% Companies with more than 25% increase	Average increase in leverage (percentage points)	Average increase in EBITDA 2008
Netherlands	111	35	27	27
United Kingdom	110	42	20	24
Italy	42	18	20	30
France	27	36	20	31
Sweden	68	33	17	21
Germany	84	33	16	18
United States	34	19	15	15
All companies	58	24	13	18
Switzerland	100	34	12	28
Singapore	48	28	8	20
Hong Kong	75	19	7	18
China	41	18	5	13
Japan	187	19	2	30

Source: Proposed lease accounting: Research of impact on companies – PriceWaterhouseCoopers and Erasmus School of Management, 2009, p.3.

Figure 2. The average impact per country.

CONSTRUCTIVE CAPITALIZATION METHOD (DCF)

The constructive capitalization method (DCF) is a method of estimating the amounts of operating lease assets or debt that would have been reported on balance if operating leases had been treated as financial leases from their inception (Imhoff et al., 1991). More specifically, the constructive capitalization method (DCF) is the present value of the scheduled minimum future cash flows disclosed in the financial statement footnotes and based on the economic logic of discounted future cash flow (Ge et al., 2008). In theory, this method is considered to be superior to the factor method. The time value of money is captured more accurate by the constructive capitalization method (DCF). This method is based on a set of assumptions, which have to be carried out when using this method. These assumptions are the remaining life to expiry and the implicit interest rate.

Remaining Life to Expiration

A firm's lease portfolio often consist of a variety of assets groups, that all have a different economic lifetime. For example, buildings have an average economic lifetime of 50 years,while computers often have an economic life of 3 years. This makes it complicated to use a unified remaining lifetime for a firm's lease portfolio. Imhoff et al. (1991) made the assumption that the remaining life of leased assets is 15 years, which presents a decreasing future lease payment after year 5.

In 1997 Imhoff et al. suggested that this assumption of one uniform approach of the economic life of a lease portfolio is somewhat short sighted, because often a lease portfolio can be divided into two categories: "Land and Buildings" and "Other". Which have totally different characteristics. This was also the main objective of Beattie et al. (1998). In their paper they distinct "Land and Buildings" with a remaining lifetime of 25 years after year 5 and "Other" with a remaining lifetime of 10 years after year 5. By doing so they took into account whether a company was more engaged in long-term or short-term leases. To reduce the complexity of the model, in this study a remaining lifetime of 15 years for all leased assets will be used. This will also allow easy comparison of the results with a larger number of studies.

Implicit Interest Rate

Every lease has its own implicit interest rate and the constructive capitalization should be made based on this implicit interest rate which should be the most accurate discount rate (Lückerath-Rovers, 2007;). However, disclosure of implicit interest rates by firms is not required. So, both users of financial statements and researchers have to assume an interest rate in order to discount the future lease payments.

Imhoff et al. (1991) choose to use an interest rate of 10%. This was assumed to be similar to the average historical interest rate for secured long-term debt at that time. Ely (1995) also uses an interest rate of 10%. She argues that this percentage is representative of the interest rates of the long-term debts (mortgages) of the companies in her sample.

However, Lückerath-Rovers (2007) argues that this interest rate is no longer appropriate, due to the lower interest rates since the 1990's. Alternatively, one should use an interest rate equal to the interest rate of a firm's similar debt. IAS17 and RJ29 also recommend this approach. On the other hand, this rate is often not disclosed and thus not available to the users of financial statements. Because of this reason we used a fixed interest rate of 10% in this research.

Lease Capitalization and Financial Ratios

The earliest study examining the impact of lease capitalization on financial ratios was of Nelson (1963). Nelson argued that not recognizing operating leases on the balance sheet caused financial ratios to be unreliable. Capitalization of operating leases, which recognizes a lease as a means of financing, resulted in more reliable financial ratios. Nelson argued that disclosure of the operating leasing obligations was value relevant.

In 1993 Imhoff et al. examined the relationship between equity risk, measured in the volatility of stock prices, and the Debt/Equity ratio. They recognized two types of industry, one that uses operating lease more intensively (the airline industry) and one that does not (the grocery industry). According to Beattie et al. (2000) the use of two types of industries provides nature control for cross-sectional differences. Imhoff et al. (1993) used two methodologies in their research: (1) the constructive capitalization method (DCF); to constructively capitalize operating leases, they used estimates of average total life, remaining life and interest rates of the operating lease agreements and (2) the factor method; they multiplied the annual lease expense or rent by a factor which reflected the average life of leased assets. For this study they used data from US listed firms during the period of 1984 to 1989. One of the findings of this study was that the factor method provides more explanatory power than the constructive capitalization (DCF) method.

In 2008 Ge et al. examined the relationship between stock prices and the adjustments made in the off-balance sheet operating leases. They also used two methods to estimate these adjustments: the constructive capitalization method (DCF) and the factor method. They used data from US firms, for the years 2000 to 2006. Their data sample was divided in two samples, one sample consisted of Compustat firms and one sample was covered by Moody's Financial Metrics. They found that for the Compustat sample the stock prices were more closely related to the adjustments made by the factor method. While on the other hand the stock prices of the Moody's firms were more closely associated with the adjustments based on the constructive capitalization method (DCF).

Ely (1995a) also used both the factor method and the constructive capitalization method (DCF) to adjust for off-balance operating leases. In this study she also used a US sample. She, however, found no significant difference in explanatory powers of the factor method and the constructive capitalization method (DCF).

Gallery and Imhoff (1998) examined the impact of capitalizing operating leases in Australia. They used a data sample for the years 1987 to 1992. Despite using the same methods to capitalize operating leases as Imhoff et al. did in 1993, their findings were different. Gallery and Imhoff (1998), opposite to Imhoff et al. (1993), could not find any significant relationship between disclosure of operating leases and stock prices. So, they found that neither method to capitalize operating leases has any explanatory power.

Beattie et al. (2000) examined the impact of capitalizing operating leases in the UK. They used a random sample of 300 listed UK firms for the years 1981 to 1994. In this study no strong evidence was found suggesting that "the factor method of estimating operating leases liability reflects actual behaviour more accurately than a process of constructive capitalization".

Research Question

Much studies examined the potential economic consequences of the proposed changes to lease accounting (Füllbier et al., 2008; Bennet et al., 2003; Beattie et al., 1998). To assess the magnitude of the capitalization of leases they examined the effect on several key accounting ratios. These ratios were mostly debt-equity, return on assets, return on equity, profit margin, asset turnover, earnings per share and equity-assets. In addition most studies also examined whether or not the capitalization of operating leases is value relevant for investors (Nelson, 1963; Gallery and Imhoff, 1998; Ge, 2006). However, the results of previous academic research are rather conflicting.

In 1993 Imhoff et al. examined the relationship between equity risk, measured in the volatility of stock prices, and the Debt/Equity ratio. They recognized two types of industry, one that uses operating lease more intensively and one that does not, the airline industry and the grocery industry. According to Beattie et al. (2000) the use of two types of industries provides nature control for cross-sectional differences.

The evidence found in previous studies with regard to the processing of lease accounting information by users of financial statements is rather conflicting. Some studies (Beattie et al., 2006; Breton and Taffler, 1995) find that users of financial statements do not take into account off-balance lease obligations, which are merely disclosed in the footnotes, in their assessment of equity risk. These studies provided evidence from the UK. This was also the result from a study in Australia (Gallery and Imhoff, 1998). However, other studies in the UK (Finnerty et al., 1980) and US (Imhoff et al., 1993) suggest that the users of financial statements do take into account the off-balance lease obligations when assessing a firm's equity risk.

The conflicting results can be explained by several factors. The research was done within different industries and in different countries. However, the disagreement in their results is also about which capitalization method has a higher explanatory power. In this paper we will assess which capitalization method has a higher explanatory power.

RESEARCH METHODOLOGY

Sampling

To avoid the influence of the context in which the research is done, data from several countries will be examined. This will strengthen the validity of the results. The countries which have been chosen are the United States (US), the United Kingdom (UK) and the Netherlands. One reason for choosing these countries is the availability of data. Another reason is the use of different accounting systems in these countries. In 2005 reporting under IFRS became mandatory for European firms. Using data as from the year 2005 will give a more comparable picture between the different countries. However, in the US IFRS is not the accounting standard used, there they use USGAAP.

To avoid the bias towards large firms, the data set contains data of Large-Cap, Mid-Cap and Small-Cap stock indices. The data concern a period of 5 years (2005-2009) and are derived from Compustat databases. The financial statement information for US companies was obtained from the North America database, the financial statement information for UK and NL companies was obtained from the Global database. For the US companies also off-balance sheet items could be retrieved from the Compustat database. For the NL and UK companies the off-balance sheet items had to be retrieved manually from the publicly available annual reports on the internet. The daily stock returns were available at the Compustat Global Security Daily database.

The Model

In order to assess which method of capitalization has more explanatory power, the following regression model will be used.

$Stdev_i = \beta_0 + \beta_1 \Delta D/A\ F8 + \beta_2 \Delta D/A\ F6 + \beta_3 \Delta D/A\ DCF + \beta_4 Country + \beta_6 CapSize + e_i$

Stdev; the dependent variable, Stdev, is the standard deviation of the daily stock price of each frim 125 days prior and after the fiscal year-end of the firm. This is in line with Imhoff et al. (1991).
ΔD/A F8; D/A F8 – D/A, where D/A_F8 includes an adjustment based on the factor method, using a fixed number of 8-times rent.
ΔD/A F6; D/A F6 – D/A, where D/A_F6 includes an adjustment based on the factor method, using a fixed number of 6-times rent.
ΔD/A DCF; D/A DCF – D/A, where D/A_DCF includes an adjustment based on the DCF method.
Country; Dummy variable with three categories: US, UK and NL.
CapSize; Dummy variable with three categories: LargeCap, MidCap and SmallCap.

The answer to the research question could be revealed by comparing the coefficient of the D/A ratio adjusted by using the factor method and the coefficient of the D/A ratio adjusted by the DCF method.

The method with the higher coefficient will have more explanatory power to the users of financial statements, when they intend to capitalize off-balance sheet information regarding operating leases. The assets were available in the Compustat database under code AT, which represents total assets and liabilities at a company at the point of time requested for.

Total debt was calculated as debt in current liabilities plus long term debt. Formulated in Compustat codes: Total debt = DLC + DLTT. The code DLC contains the sum of short-term notes payable and long-term debt due within one year. The code DLTT represents long-term debt due in more than a year. For the US companies the off-balance sheet information regarding lease obligations was obtained using Compustat codes MRC1, MRC2, MRC3, MRC4, MRC4 and MRCTA. The codes MRC1 – MRC5 represent the minimum rental commitments of all existing noncancelable operating leases in the first, second, third, fourth and fifth year from the balance sheet date. These are amounts payable in the respective periods, these amounts are not cumulative. The code MRCTA shows the cumulative total amount of all future rental commitments after the fifth year from the balance sheet date. For the NL and UK companies this information was collected manually.

The Market Capitalization was calculated as follows: Common shares outstanding X Price of a common share. In Compustat codes: PRCCD X CSHO for US companies and PRCCD X CSHOI for NL and UK companies.

In Compustat daily closing prices of shares are available under the code PRCCD. The number of common/ordinary shares outstanding at year-end are represented by code CSHO. This code was not available in the Global Database, there the number of outstanding shares at fiscal year-end are found under code CSHOI.

RESULTS

The data set was divided into two samples. One sample contained financial data of 50 Dutch (NL) companies and 49 companies in the United Kingdom (UK). For all companies data was collected for 5 continuous years (2005-2009), resulting in 495 (company-years) observations. The second sample contained data of 5 continuous years of 4.422 companies in the United States (US), resulting in 22.110 (company-years) observations. These samples were analysed separately because of the different accounting systems used in the respective countries.

Findings – Univariate Analysis

Tables 1 and 2 show an overall usage of 94,95% in the sample from the UK and The Netherlands against an overall usage of 74,51% in the sample from the US. In this thesis the question what causes this difference remains unanswered.

Table 1. Usage of Operating Leases in the UK and NL (in percentages)

Size		# Companies using Operating Leases	# Companies not using Operating Leases	Total
Small	Number	58	4	62
	Percentage	93,55%	6,45%	
Medium	Number	11	1	12
	Percentage	91,67%	8,33%	
Large	Number	25	0	25
	Percentage	100,00%	0,00%	
Total	Number	94	5	99
	Percentage	94,95%	5,05%	

Table 2. Usage of Operating Leases in the US (in percentages)

Size		# Companies using Operating Leases	# Companies not using Operating Leases	Total
Small	Number	2.673	1.019	3.692
	Percentage	72,40%	27,60%	
Medium	Number	292	55	347
	Percentage	84,15%	15,85%	
Large	Number	330	53	383
	Percentage	86,16%	13,84%	
Total	Number	3.295	1.127	4.422
	Percentage	74,51%	25,49%	

Tables 3 and 4 present the descriptive statistics off the variables used in the regression, as well as other relevant variables. These statistics were calculated by doing an univariate analysis and after filtering the data set from outliers. Data which deviated +3 or -3 standard deviations from the mean were considered to be outliers.

Tables 3 and 4 show that in both samples the present value of future operating lease obligations (PVOL) is higher when calculated using a factor method (PVOL F6 and PVOL F8) rather than the constructive capitalization method (PVOL DCF). Also, the mean of the adjusted D/A ratio is higher when a factor method is used for calculation. Both these observations indicate that the factor methods are being overstated when it comes to adjusting for off-balance obligations with regard to operating leases. This is in line with previous findings of Imhoff et al. (1993), Beattie et al. (1998) and Ge et al. (2008).

Table 3. Descriptive Statistics UK and NL

Variables used in the Regression Model				
	Minimum	**Maximum**	**Mean**	**St. Deviation**
St. Dev. Stock Return	0,0071	9,6034	1,4362	1,6384
ΔD/A DCF	0,0000	0,5918	0,0500	0,0898
ΔD/A F6	0,0000	0,6576	0,0715	0,1069
ΔD/A F8	0,0000	0,7186	0,0882	0,1221
Other relevant variables				
	Minimum	**Maximum**	**Mean**	**St. Deviation**
D/A DCF	0,0000	0,9327	0,2872	0,1610
D/A F6	0,0000	0,9360	0,3088	0,1586
D/A F8	0,0000	0,9402	0,3256	0,1634
PVOL DCF	0,0000	3.972,8110	259,7384	571,5363
PVOL F6	0,0000	5.022,0000	342,4476	665,6678
PVOL F8	0,0000	6.696,0000	456,5968	887,5571

Table 4. Descriptive Statistics US

Variables used in the Regression Model				
	Minimum	**Maximum**	**Mean**	**St. Deviation**
St. Dev. Stock Return	0,0000	4,7994	1,5644	1,2476
ΔD/A DCF	0,0000	0,7342	0,0368	0,0679
ΔD/A F6	0,0000	0,9403	0,0642	0,0948
ΔD/A F8	0,0000	0,9545	0,0769	0,1113
Other relevant variables				
	Minimum	**Maximum**	**Mean**	**St. Deviation**
D/A DCF	0,0000	0,9981	0,2612	0,2108
D/A F6	0,0000	0,9982	0,2864	0,2114
D/A F8	0,0000	0,9982	0,3012	0,2145
PVOL DCF	0,0000	17.832,0210	128,8384	650,6939
PVOL F6	0,0000	25.080,0000	208,4285	936,9366
PVOL F8	0,0000	33.440,0000	277,9047	1.249,2488

Findings – Bivariate Analysis

Tables 5 and 6 show the Pearson correlations between the continuous variables used in the regression model. Interesting to observe is the high correlation coefficient (0,9987 and 0,9987) between the adjustment of off-balance operating lease obligations using the factor method 6-times rent (ΔD/A F6) and the adjustment using the factor method 8-times rent (ΔD/A F8). This indicates the possibility of multicollinearity between these two independent variables. An additional test on this possible multicollinearity is also done in the multivariate regression, since this is only a simple pair wise correlation analysis. Also, in this test no control variables are taken applied.

Findings – Regression Analysis

The multicollinearity mentioned in the previous paragraph (7.2) between both variables regarding factor methods is confirmed by running the regression. In the regression both variables show very large standard errors in both samples. This means that the correlation between these two variables has a negative influence on the regression. Therefore, to mitigate this influence, the independent variable ΔD/A F6 is removed from the regression. The variable ΔD/A F6 was selected for removal from the regression because the variable ΔD/A F8 was used more often in previous studies.

Table 5. Pearson correlations between the variables of the regression for NL and UK sample

	St. Dev. Stock Return	ΔD/A DCF	ΔD/A F6	ΔD/A F8
St. Dev. Stock Return				
ΔD/A DCF	-0,1883			
ΔD/A F6	-0,1388	0,9405		
ΔD/A F8	-0,1384	0,9319	0,9987	

Table 6. Pearson correlations between the variables of the regression for US sample

	St. Dev. Stock Return	ΔD/A DCF	ΔD/A F6	ΔD/A F8
St. Dev. Stock Return				
ΔD/A DCF	-0,0531			
ΔD/A F6	-0,1130	0,9205		
ΔD/A F8	-0,1127	0,9127	0,9983	

The regression model turns out to be significant, although the explanatory power is low (Adjusted R2 = 27,72% for UK and NL and Adjusted R2 = 10,66% for US). This means that the independent variables which were used in this model, ΔD/A DCF and ΔD/A F8, can explain respective 27,72% and 10,66% of the changes that occur in the dependent variable (= the volatility in stock returns). To control for Country and Capsize, these were added to the regression model as dummy variables.

The results also show that the adjustments calculated with the DCF method for the UK and NL sample are positively related to the volatility in stock returns, but not significantly. On the other hand the results reveal that the adjustments made under the factor method 8-times rent is significantly negative related to the changes in the stock returns.

This could mean that users of financial statements are very much aware of the dangers of overstating the off-balance operating lease commitments by using the factor method. Thus, this could reflect an increasing sophistication over time of users of financial statements, which was also suggested by Beattie et al. in 2000.

Table 7. Summary of regression results

UK and NL Sample		*Coëfficients*	*T- stat*
Multiple R	0,53369		
R Square	0,28483		
Adjusted R Square	0,27717		
Standard Error	1,39300		
Observations	473		
Intercept		0,61743	4,07125
ΔD/A DCF		0,68617	0,32137
ΔD/A F8		-1,57651	-1,00894

US Sample		*Coëfficients*	*T- stat*
Multiple R	0,32683		
R Square	0,10682		
Adjusted R Square	0,10662		
Standard Error	1,17920		
Observations	18.140		
Intercept		2,59648	76,68896
ΔD/A DCF		4,61770	14,60312
ΔD/A F8		-3,64927	-18,88027

Confirmation for this idea comes from the results for the US sample. There we find both a significant and positive relation between the DCF method and the volatility in stock returns, as well as a significant and negative relation between the factor method and the volatility of stock returns. This is in line with what one could expect, since the DCF method is a more accurate, theoretically even superior method than the factor method. A summary of the regression results can be found in table 7.

CONCLUSION

Ever since the 1960's there has been much debate about the recognition and disclosure of off-balance commitments regarding operating leases. Lots of studies examined the necessity and the impact of capitalizing operating lease commitments. In order to measure this impact, several methods of capitalizing were developed.

The first capitalization method (DCF method) based on the present value of the future lease payments was developed in 1991 by Imhoff et al., which is now the most used method in practice. Other, widely used, methods are the factor methods. These methods estimate the amount of unrecorded debt as a multiple (6-times or 8-times) of the lease payment of the current period. However, the results from all the studies to assess the impact throughout the years were rather conflicting. In 1993 Imhoff et al. concluded that the factor method provides more explanatory power than the DCF method. Later in 1995 Ely found that both methods hold equal explanatory power, while in 1998 Gallery and Imhoff suggested that neither method had significant explanatory power. Ge et al. (2008) found the DCF method more significant using a sample from Moody's, while the factor method was more significant using a Compustat sample. These studies were done in the US, US, Australia and the UK respectively.

In this study the two samples were from the Compustat database. One sample of US based companies reporting under US GAAP and one sample of UK and NL based companies, reporting under IFRS. Interesting to find was that the present value of the future lease payments calculated under the factor method have the tendency to be overstated, consistent with the findings of Imhoff et al. (1993), Beattie et al. (1998) and Ge et al. (2008).

Moreover, we find that users of financial statements seem to be well aware of the possibility to overstate the future lease payments using the factor method. Both in the UK and NL sample and the US sample, the DCF method is positively related to the volatility of the stock returns and the factor method has a significant negative relation with the volatility of the stock returns. Limitations of this research are the small number of countries involved as well as the short period of time. This particular time period was chosen, because in 2005 it became mandatory for listed European firms to adopt IFRS. Also, the sample of UK and NL firms was rather small compared to the US sample.

An interesting subject for future research ould be the difference in the usage of operating lease between the US (overall usage: 74, 51%) on the one hand and the UK and The Netherlands (overall usage: 94,95%) on the other hand, which we found in this study. It would also be interesting to see whether or not the findings hold when a sample of more than two countries would be examined.

REFERENCES

Beattie, V., K. Edwards and A. Goodacre (1998), "The impact of constructive operating lease capitalization on key accounting ratios", *Accounting and business research*, autumn, 233-254.

Beattie, V., A. Goodacre and S. Thompson (2000), "Recognition versus disclosure: an investigation of the impact on equity risk using UK operating lease disclosures", *Journal of Business Finance and Accounting*, 27 (9and10), 1185-1224.

Beattie, V., A. Goodacre and S. Thompson (2006), "International lease accounting reform and economic consequences: the view of UK users and preparers", *International journal of accounting*, 41, 75-103.

Bennet, B. and M. Bradbury (2003), "Capitalizing non-cancelable operating leases", *Journal of International Financial Management and Accounting*, 14, 101-114.

Breton, G. and R. Taffler (1995), "Creative accounting and investment analyst response", *Accounting and business research*, 25, 81-92.

Eisfeldt, A. and A. Rampini (2009), "Leasing, ability to reposess, and debt capacity", *Review of Financial Studies*, 22, 1621-1657.

El-Gazar, S. (1993), "Stock market effects of the closeness to debt covenant restrictions resulting from capitalization of leases", *Accounting review*, 68, 258-272.

Ely, K. (1995), "Operating lease accounting and the market's assessment of equity risk", *Journal of accounting research*, Autumn, 397-415.

Finnerty, J., R. Fitzsimmons and W. Thomas (1980), "Lease capitalization and systematic risk", *Accounting review*, 55, 631-639.

Fuelbier, R.U., J.L. Silva and M.H. Pferdehirt (2008), "Impact of lease capitalization on financial ratios of listed German companies", Electronic copy available at: http//ssrn.com/abstract=1280187.

Gallery, G. and Q.Q. Imhoff Jr. (1998), "Disclosure versus recognition: some evidence from the Australian capital market regarding off-balance sheet leasing", paper presented at the University of Melbourne, Research Seminar Series.

Ge, W.(2006), "Off-balance-sheet activities, earnings persistence and stock prices: Evidence from operating leases", University of Washington.

Ge, W., G. Imhoff and L.F. Lee (2008), "Is recognition for operating leases necessary?", Working paper, University of Washington and University of Michigan.

Goodacre, A. (2001), "The potential impact of enforced lease capitalization in the UK retail sector", University of Stirling, Department of Accounting, Finance and Law, Discussion Paper No. 01/01, Electronic copy available at SSRN: http://ssrn.com/abstract=279030 or doi:10.2139/ssrn.279030.

Imhoff, E. A., R.C. Lipe Jr and D.W. Wright (1991), "Operating leases: impact of constructive capitalization", *Accounting Horizons*, 5(1), March, 51-63.

Imhoff, E.A., R.C. Lipe Jr and D.W. Wright (1993), "The effects of recognition versus disclosure on shareholder risk and executive compensation", *Journal of Accounting,* Auditing and Finance, Vol. 8, No. 4 (Fall), 335-368.

Jesswein, K.R. (2008), "Methodological issues in analyzing financial statements in the presence of operating leases", *Proceedings of the Academy of Accounting and Financial Studies*, Volume 13, Number 1, 27-32.

Lückerath-Rovers, M. (2007), "Operating-Lease disclosure: an empirical investigation", Doctoral Thesis, Erasmus Universtity Rotterdam.

Moody's Investor Services (1999), "Off-balance sheet leases: capitalization and rating implications; Out of sight but not out of mind, rating methodology report".

Nelson, A.T. (1963), "Capitalizing leases: the effect on financial ratios", *Journal of accountancy*, 41, 49-58.

Noland, T. (2006), "Leasing agreements and their impact on financial ratios of small companies", *Academy of accounting and financial studies journal*, 10(2), 1-15.

Pricewaterhousecooper and the Rotterdam School of Management, The Netherlands (2009), "Proposed Lease Accounting: Research of Impact on Companies".

Rampini, A. and S. Viswanathan (2010b), "Collateral, risk management, and the distribution of debt capacity", *Journal of Finance*, 65, 6, 2293-2322.

Rauh, J.D. and A. Sufi (2010), "Explaining corporate capital structure: product markets, leases, and asset similarity", Electronic copy available at: http://ssrn.com/abstract=1592463

Sharpe, S. and H. Nguyen (1995), "Capital market imperfections and the incentives to lease", *Journal of Financial Economics*, 39 (2), 271-294.

Thomson, S.J. (2003), "The role of leasing in the UK corporate financing decisions, accounting treatment and market impact", PhD-Thesis, University of Stirling.

In: Computational Data Analysis Techniques
ISBN: 978-1-63463-957-6
Editors: M. Doumpos, C. Zopounidis and Ch. Gaganis

Chapter 11

CHARACTERIZATION AND GROUPING OF THE COLOMBIA REGIONS FOR DEVELOPMENT OF CLUSTERS: AN APPLICATION OF THE PICHAT ALGORITHM

Fabio R. Blanco Mesa * ***and Anna M. Gil-Lafuente***

Department of Business Administration,
University of Barcelona, Barcelona, Spain

ABSTRACT

The present paper has main aim to establish of similarity relationship between each Colombia Regions to development of Clusters. The methodology used is based in Pichat Algorithm, which are be able to establish closer sub-relations of each of characteristic analysed. Results have shown three different structures of groups of regions based with (GRDP) characteristics: *Divergent Regions, Big Group and Convergent Regions.* We have been concluded that theses grouping could help in policy-makers to development fostering regional cooperation, entrepreneurship, and productivity growth. Likewise, These results can be also to treat with a second technic to establish direct relationship between each of regions studied.

Keywords: Regional Development, Clusters, Colombia, Decision Making and Fuzzy Logic

1. INTRODUCTION

In the last decades economic liberalization and globalization have been simplified of the barrier trades causing economics are more dependent on each other and a higher degree of uncertainty. Based on the above, the nation have been considering about competitiveness and promoting an economic policy as key factor to boost regional development into global

* Corresponding author: Tel +34634514053 e-mail: fblancme7@alumnes.ub.edu

economic context. Hence, competitiveness is subject to ability to develop competitive advantage, which will be a key success factor to regional and business development. Competitive advantage could be developed from differentiation, which is advisable to build from cooperation between governments, companies and academics boosting entrepreneurship to develop clusters.

Colombia as emerging economic has been shown a sustained economy growth in last years highlighting productive regions as Bogotá D.C., Cundinamarca, Barranquilla, Bucaramanga, Medellin and Cali. However, Colombia still needs in areas of improvement in regional and social development, especially in regions are located far from the economic centres. In this sense, the aim main of this paper is to establish similarity relationships between regions of Colombia through application of Pichat Algorithm, which allows identifying groupings with homogeneous characteristics. This application can contribute to design of policy and decision-making to develop of cluster. The paper is structured in four steps: firstly, theoretical framework that emphasizes the importance of the region and the creation of cluster; secondly, it is explained methodology of the study, variables and the model used; Thirdly, it is shown results and its analysis; finally, it is presented conclusions and implications.

2. Theoretical Framework

Economic liberalization and globalization have been simplified of the barrier trades causing economics are more dependent on each other, which leads to generate a higher uncertainty and dynamic into global market. In this global context, the nations have been focused its efforts in pursuit of competitiveness through encouraging of policy economic as key factor to develop of nation, regions and towns, which allows promoting initiatives to regional development within global economic context (Cumbers and MacKinnon, 2004; Moncayo, 2003; M. Porter, 2000; M. Porter, 2009). In this sense, the creation of clusters have prominent role in the development of competitiveness highlighting the importance of location in the development of competitive and comparative advantage to promote business agglomeration and to encourage economic growth (Delgado, Porter, and Stern, 2010; Ferreira and Estevao, 2012; Fujita and Thisse, 1996; Furman, Porter, and Stern, 2002; Helmsing, 2001; Krugman, 1991; M. Porter, 1998; M. Porter, 2000; M. Porter, 2003; M. Porter, 2009; Silva, 2005). In Latin American economies such initiatives have been promoted from a structural change with a shift in focus of public policies with greater coherence, articulation and coordination between infrastructure policies, service provision and sectorial policies emphasizing the importance of regions and the promotion of SMEs in the productive sectors (OECD and CEPAL, 2012)

In Colombia competitiveness initiatives started in the 90s with an Analysis of Competitiveness, inn the period 1994-1998 was created National Competitiveness Council, then in the period 1998-2002 was raised Exporter Strategic Plan, in the following period 2002-2010 was launched in the domestic agenda, However, these initiatives did not take into account the region as critical determinant for competitiveness (Ramírez, 2013). Currently, Government is formulating policies to encourage the competitiveness into regions, to promote entrepreneurship and to correct coordination failures vertical and horizontal, in order to develop a New Structural Economics taking into account market signals for resource allocation (Informe de Competitividad, 2012-2013). This initiative tries to create the necessary conditions that transform towns and regions in locations for productive economic development.

Likewise, for development the new structural economics the territory and location are essential to create competitive and comparative advantages, which can aid development of local supply chains that encourage the formation of small and medium enterprises in production clusters organized (Silva, 2005), aiding to improve the utilization of endogenous available resources (Muñoz, 2002). A correct location creates closer networks of suppliers, buyers and other Organizations, improving innovation and efficient of sector, which in turn have influence directly in productivity local growth (M. Porter, 2000; M. E. Porter, 2009). Clusters aid mobility, reduce the costs of communication and transportation, link closer buyers and suppliers; encourage the creation of new businesses, attract qualified human talent at lower cost and generate higher mobility and accumulation of knowledge in a industrial sector (Cumbers and MacKinnon, 2004; Delgado et al., 2010; Ferreira and Estevao, 2012; Helmsing, 2001; Nolan, Morrison, Kumar, Galloway, and Cordes, 2011; M. Porter, 2003). Thus, selection of the territory in which to develop these agglomerations should analyse possible relationships between regions or nearby towns considering market signals, and endogenous, geographic and ethnographic characteristics of the region (Fujita and Thisse, 1996; Furman et al., 2002; Moncayo, 2003). In order, this allows promote its own strengths and develop its opportunities of economic growth, basing on promoting and sustaining national and local economic conditions that drive the emergence of new clusters.

3. Methodology

The data have been taken of National Administrative Department of Statistics (DANE) of the Regional accounts related at Gross Regional Domestic Product (GRDP). It has applied a mathematical algorithm that allows groups of regions by the establishment of relations of similarity between each of the branches of economic activity in the regions. This process has two steps: firstly, it calculates the differences between the characteristics using the Hamming Distance and secondly, the groups are formed using the Pichat algorithm. Next we define each of the two mathematical processes: Hamming distance (Hamming, 1950) is useful for calculating the differences between two elements, two groups or two groups fuzzy technique. For two groups $X = \{x_1, \dots, x_n\}$ and $Y = \{y_1, \dots, y_n\}$, the weighting of hamming distance is defined as: the weight of the Hamming distance of a dimension n is an assignment is an assignment $WHD: R^n X R^n \rightarrow R$ having a weight associated with vector W of dimension n with $\sum_{j=1}^{n} w_j = 1$ and $w_j \in [0, 1]$, such as:

$$WHD(\langle x_1, y_1 \rangle, \dots, \langle x_n, y_n \rangle) = \left(\sum_{i=1}^{n} w_i \, |a_i - b_i|\right) \tag{1}$$

where x_i and y_i are arguing groups X and Y respectively

Pichat algorithm (Pichat, 1970) is a technique that gets sub-transitive graphs expressed in maximum similarity relations, which form groups of similar characteristics. These characteristics are called maximum similarity sub-relation, which are not disjunctive obtaining as a result a fuzzy graph likeness. When this property is became a requirement the fuzzy graph likeness is transformed in a fuzzy graph of similarities through transitive closure.

If it is started of a reflexive and symmetric fuzzy graph (the relation of likeness) $\tilde{G}$ should obtain G such that complies,

$$\tilde{G} = \cup \left(\tilde{G} \circ \tilde{G}\right) \cup \left(\tilde{G} \circ \tilde{G} \circ \tilde{G}\right) \cup \ldots \quad (2)$$

Until it reaches a term equal to the union of the above. Graph $\tilde{G}$ is the transitive closure de $\tilde{G}$ and has the properties of reflexivity, symmetry and transitivity. When obtained maximum similarity sub-relation of graph $\tilde{G}$ are disjunctive (Gil Aluja, 1996; Gil Lafuente, 2001).

3.1. Variables of Study

Table 1. Regions of Colombia

COD.	Regions	COD.	Regions
A1	Amazonas	A18	Huila
A2	Antioquia	A19	La Guajira
A3	Arauca	A20	Magdalena
A4	Atlántico	A21	Meta
A5	Bogotá D. C.	A22	Nariño
A6	Bolívar	A23	Norte Santander
A7	Boyacá	A24	Putumayo
A8	Caldas	A25	Quindío
A9	Caquetá	A26	Risaralda
A10	Casanare	A27	San Andrés y Prov
A11	Cauca	A28	Santander
A12	Cesar	A29	Sucre
A13	Chocó	A30	Tolima
A14	Córdoba	A31	Valle
A15	Cundinamarca	A32	Vaupés
A16	Guainía	A33	Vichada
A17	Guaviare		

Table 2. Gross Regional Domestic Product/ Branches of Economic Activity

COD.	Gross Regional Domestic Product Branches of Economic Activity
C1	Cultivation of coffee (1)
C2	Cultivation of Other Agricultural Products (2)
C3	Animal Husbandry and hunting including veterinary activities (3)
C4	Forestry, logging and related activities (4)

C5	Fishing, fish production hatcheries in fish farms and fishing related activities (5)
C6	Extraction of Coal, coal lignified and peat (6)
C7	Extraction of crude petroleum and natural gas; services for oil and gas extraction, excluding surveying; extraction of uranium and thorium (7)
COD.	Gross Regional Domestic Product Branches of Economic Activity
C8	Mining of metal ores (8)
C9	Extraction of non-metallic minerals (9)
C10	Total Manufacturing Industry (10-37)
C11	Production, transmission and distribution of electricity (38)
C12	Manufacture of gas, distribution of gaseous fuels through mains; supply of steam and hot water (39)
C13	Collection, purification and distribution of water (40)
C14	Construction of complete buildings and parts of buildings, design of buildings (41)
C15	Construction of civil engineering works (42)
C16	Commerce (43)
C17	Maintenance and repair of motor vehicles, repair of personal and household goods (44)
C18	Hotels, restaurants, bars and similar (45)
C19	Land transport (46)
C20	Water transport (47)
C21	Transportation by air (48)
C22	Supporting and auxiliary transport activities, activities of travel agencies (49)
C23	Post and telecommunications (50)
C24	Financial Intermediation (51)
C25	Real estate activities and rental housing (52)
C26	Activities of business services, other financial and real estate (53)
C27	Public administration and defense, compulsory social security (54)
C28	Education Market (55)
C29	Education non market (56)
C30	Social and health services market (57)
C31	Elimination of waste and wastewater, sanitation and similar activities (58)
C32	Activities of membership organizations nec, recreation and cultural and sports activities, other service activities mark (59)
C33	Activities of membership organizations nec, recreation and cultural and sports activities, other service activities not market (60)
C34	Private households with employed persons (61)
C35	Duties and Taxes

Source: DANE - National Administrative Department of Statistics. Regional Accounts-Colombia. 2011pr.

4. Results

Table 3. Matrix of Similarities [Š]

A1	1	0,97	0,95	0,97	0,97	0,97	0,97	0,97	0,98	0,95	0,97	0,96	0,97	0,97	0,97	0,99	0,99	0,96	0,96	0,97	0,95	0,98	0,97	0,96	0,97	0,97	0,98	0,96	0,98	0,97	0,97	0,99	0,98
A2		1	0,96	0,99	0,99	0,99	0,98	0,99	0,97	0,96	0,98	0,97	0,96	0,98	0,99	0,97	0,97	0,98	0,96	0,98	0,96	0,98	0,99	0,96	0,99	0,99	0,97	0,99	0,98	0,98	0,99	0,97	0,98
A3			1	0,96	0,96	0,96	0,97	0,96	0,96	0,99	0,96	0,96	0,96	0,96	0,96	0,96	0,96	0,97	0,96	0,96	0,99	0,96	0,96	0,99	0,96	0,96	0,96	0,96	0,96	0,97	0,96	0,95	0,96
A4				1	0,99	0,99	0,98	0,99	0,97	0,96	0,98	0,97	0,96	0,98	0,99	0,97	0,97	0,98	0,96	0,98	0,96	0,98	0,99	0,96	0,98	0,99	0,97	0,98	0,98	0,98	0,99	0,97	0,97
A5					1	0,98	0,98	0,98	0,97	0,96	0,98	0,97	0,96	0,97	0,98	0,97	0,97	0,97	0,96	0,98	0,96	0,98	0,98	0,96	0,98	0,99	0,97	0,98	0,98	0,98	0,99	0,97	0,97
A6						1	0,98	0,99	0,98	0,96	0,99	0,97	0,97	0,98	0,99	0,97	0,97	0,98	0,97	0,98	0,96	0,98	0,98	0,97	0,98	0,99	0,97	0,99	0,98	0,98	0,99	0,97	0,98
A7							1	0,98	0,98	0,97	0,98	0,97	0,96	0,98	0,99	0,97	0,97	0,98	0,97	0,99	0,97	0,98	0,99	0,97	0,98	0,98	0,97	0,98	0,98	0,99	0,98	0,96	0,98
A8								1	0,98	0,96	0,99	0,97	0,97	0,98	0,99	0,97	0,97	0,98	0,96	0,99	0,96	0,98	0,99	0,96	0,99	0,99	0,97	0,98	0,98	0,99	0,99	0,97	0,98
A9									1	0,96	0,98	0,97	0,97	0,99	0,98	0,98	0,99	0,98	0,96	0,99	0,96	0,99	0,98	0,97	0,98	0,98	0,97	0,98	0,99	0,98	0,97	0,98	0,99
A10										1	0,96	0,96	0,95	0,96	0,96	0,96	0,96	0,97	0,96	0,96	1	0,96	0,96	0,99	0,96	0,96	0,95	0,96	0,96	0,97	0,96	0,95	0,96
A11											1	0,97	0,97	0,98	0,99	0,97	0,98	0,98	0,96	0,99	0,96	0,98	0,98	0,97	0,98	0,99	0,97	0,98	0,99	0,98	0,99	0,97	0,98
A12												1	0,96	0,97	0,97	0,96	0,96	0,97	0,99	0,97	0,96	0,97	0,97	0,96	0,97	0,97	0,96	0,97	0,97	0,97	0,97	0,96	0,97
A13													1	0,97	0,96	0,97	0,97	0,96	0,96	0,97	0,96	0,97	0,97	0,96	0,97	0,97	0,96	0,96	0,97	0,97	0,96	0,97	0,97
A14														1	0,98	0,97	0,98	0,98	0,96	0,99	0,96	0,98	0,98	0,96	0,98	0,98	0,97	0,97	0,99	0,98	0,98	0,97	0,98
A15															1	0,97	0,97	0,98	0,96	0,99	0,96	0,98	0,98	0,96	0,99	0,99	0,97	0,99	0,98	0,98	0,99	0,97	0,97
A16																1	0,99	0,97	0,96	0,98	0,96	0,98	0,98	0,96	0,98	0,97	0,97	0,97	0,98	0,97	0,97	0,99	0,98
A17																	1	0,97	0,96	0,98	0,96	0,98	0,98	0,97	0,98	0,97	0,98	0,97	0,98	0,97	0,97	0,99	0,99
A18																		1	0,96	0,98	0,97	0,98	0,98	0,97	0,98	0,98	0,97	0,98	0,98	0,99	0,98	0,97	0,98
A19																			1	0,96	0,96	0,96	0,97	0,96	0,96	0,96	0,96	0,96	0,96	0,97	0,96	0,96	0,96
A20																				1	0,96	0,99	0,99	0,97	0,99	0,99	0,97	0,98	0,99	0,99	0,98	0,97	0,98
A21																					1	0,96	0,96	0,99	0,96	0,96	0,96	0,97	0,96	0,97	0,96	0,95	0,96
A22																						1	0,99	0,97	0,99	0.98	0.98	0.98	0,99	0,99	0.98	0,97	0.98
A23																							1	0,97	0,99	0,99	0,97	0,98	0,99	0,99	0,98	0,97	0,98
A24																								1	0,96	0,96	0,96	0,97	0,97	0,97	0,96	0,96	0,97
A25																									1	0,99	0,97	0,98	0,99	0,99	0,98	0,97	0,98
A26																										1	0,97	0,98	0,98	0,99	0,99	0,97	0,98
A27																											1	0,97	0,98	0,97	0,97	0,97	0,97
A28																												1	0,98	0,98	0,99	0,96	0,98
A29																													1	0,98	0,98	0,98	0,98
A30																														1	0,98	0,97	0,98
A31																															1	0,97	0,97
A32																																1	0,98
A33																																	1

Source: Own Elaboration.

Table 4. Maximum Sub-relation of Similarities with a level of requirement of 96%

A0	Colombia	1	2	3	4	5	6	7	8	9	10	11
A1	Amazonas									■	■	■
A2	Antioquia					■	■	■	■	■	■	■
A3	Arauca	■	■	■	■							
A4	Atlántico						■	■	■	■	■	■
A5	Bogotá D. C.										■	■
A6	Bolívar	■	■	■	■	■	■	■	■	■	■	■
A7	Boyacá	■	■	■	■	■	■	■	■	■	■	■
A8	Caldas					■	■	■	■	■	■	■
A9	Caquetá				■		■	■	■	■	■	■
A10	Casanare			■								
A11	Cauca				■		■	■	■	■	■	■
A12	Cesar									■		
A13	Chocó						■	■	■	■		
A14	Córdoba				■		■	■	■	■	■	■
A15	Cundinamarca	■	■	■	■	■	■	■	■	■	■	■
A16	Guainía						■	■	■	■	■	■
A17	Guaviare				■		■	■	■	■	■	■

A18	Huila
A19	La Guajira
A20	Magdalena
A21	Meta
A22	Nariño
A23	Norte de Santander
A24	Putumayo
A25	Quindío
A26	Risaralda
A27	San Andrés y Providencia
A28	Santander
A29	Sucre
A30	Tolima
A31	Valle
A32	Vaupés
A33	Vichada

Source: Own Elaboration

5. Analysis of Results

As a result of the similarity matrix $\tilde{S}$ is obtained a sub-matrix relationship, which represents a given number of groupings regarding minimum level of requirement. Based on this sub-matrix is set different groups up between each of the regions by its macroeconomic criteria.

This work is carried out from 30 different levels of requirement, which are within the range of 99% and 70%. We have obtained a total of 30 sub-matrices, one of which gets representative results with a significant level of requirement of 96%. This sub-matrix is analysed from its homogeneous similarities between regions.

The sub-matrix is noted that the regions are grouped into 11 groups of homogeneous activities. It also is noted that groups 1 to 4 grouped fewer regions and groups of 5 to 11 take into account almost all regions. Based on this observation states that, greater agglomeration of regions in a group can be a greater diversity of economic activities of each of them, and less agglomeration of regions in a group may be a more homogeneous activity economic, which can be a particular activity or (almost) exclusively in the region.

Based on the above, the regions could be describing based on three particularities. The first suggests that each region belongs to at least one group is called *Divergent Region*. The second that each region belongs to all or almost all groups is called *Convergent Region*. The third that group has almost all regions grouped is called *Great Group*.

Divergent Region: These are present in one or two groups that make up the sub-grouping matrix. These regions have a unique homogeneous similarity that only allows them to belong to that specific group and diverged from the other groups by not sharing heterogeneous economic activities. The regions of Cesar and Casanare belong to a single group, and regions of Meta and Bogotá D.C. belong to two groups. Of these four regions has been observed:

Cesar Bogota and are located in the side of higher agglomeration of the sub-matrix, however, Meta and Casanare are located in the side of less agglomeration. It is also noted that while Bogotá D.C. and Cesar are divergent from each other, Meta and Casanare are converging in the same group (group 3).

Convergent Regions: these regions are present in all or almost all the groups that make up the sub-matrix of grouping. This is given because the number of activities is more diverse and is accommodated the converging intensity of activity of each group. The regions belonging to all groups are the following: Bolivar, Boyacá, Guainía, Santander and Vichada. The regions belonging to 10 of the 11 groups are the following: Huila, Tolima and Putumayo. These groups have in common that they do not converge in-group 2. Regions belonging to 9 groups los11 are the following: Nariño, Norte de Santander, Quindío, Sucre. These groups have in common that they do not converge in groups 2 and 3.

Great Group: Within this sub-matrix regions are groups that a level of requirement of 96% share significant similarities homogeneous, due, they are formed by heterogeneous significant activities, i.e., that each region shares generality (similarity), which is configured by various elements (characteristics). These elements are present in each of the regions but at a different level of intensity, hence, it lies in its heterogeneity. In addition, these groups show a tendency of agglomeration from group 5 to group 11. This can occur because the amount of heterogeneous activities and the intensity level of each activity of each of these regions are similar.

Conclusion and Future Considerations

We have analysed the similarity relations in the branches of economic activity between different regions of Colombia. The application is based on macroeconomic data GRDP each department. We have been used methodology Pichat algorithm and the similarity measure used in making business decisions such as the Hamming Distance to establish the sub-maximal similarity relations. It has highlighted the similarities between many of the regions in terms of production, whose characteristics would aid in the formulation and development of policies for growth and productivity of regions, promoting cooperation and collaboration among these. Likewise, it is also seen that there are regions that have mild convergence with other, this phenomenon can be given either for the uniqueness of their regional economy or the concentration of economic activities heterogeneous, which are only develop in the economic centres of the country.

In this sense, we have been distinguished in three types of clusters from different regions with common characteristics: Divergent Region, Convergent Region and Great Group. The distinction of these three groups could aid managers and agencies responsible for decision making and planning territorial and growth strategies. In the same way, the data obtained can be used for a second methodological process and determine which are common characteristics and direct relationships between regions.

The application has been made from statistical data, however, this model is able to group a large number of features and economic and social indicators simultaneously, and whose results could contribute to policy design and decision making for the development of productive sectors. Finally, the application of this mathematical algorithm could allow analysis of factors related to regional development.

REFERENCES

Cumbers, A., and MacKinnon, D. (2004), Introduction: Clusters in urban and regional development, *Urban Studies*, 41(5-6), 959-969.

Delgado, M., Porter, M. E., and Stern, S. (2010), Clusters and entrepreneurship, *Journal of Economic Geography*, 10(4), 495-518.

Ferreira, J., and Estevao, C. (2012), Do the cluster locations really matter to regional performance? evidence from the tourism industry, *Transformations in Business and Economics*, 11(3), 72-89.

Fujita, M., and Thisse, J. (1996), Economics of agglomeration, *Journal of the Japanese and International Economies*, 10(4), 339-378.

Furman, J., Porter, M., and Stern, S. (2002), The determinants of national innovative capacity, *Research Policy*, 31(6), 899-933.

Gil Aluja, J. (1996). Lances and misadventures of the new paradigm of decision theory. In *Proceedings of the III Congress of SIGEF*, Volume I.

Gil Lafuente, A. M. (2001). *New strategies for the financial analysis at the company*. Ariel, Barcelona.

Hamming, R. W. (1950), Error-detecting and error-correcting codes, *Bell Systems Technical Journal,* 29, 147-160.

Helmsing, A. (2001), Externalities, learning and governance: New perspectives on local economic development, *Development and Change*, 32(2), 277-308.

Krugman, P. (1991), Increasing returns and economic-geography, *Journal of Political Economy*, 99(3), 483-499.

Moncayo, E. (2003). New theories and conceptual approaches on regional development: towards a new paradigm? *Journal of Institutional Economics*, 5(8), 32-65.

Nolan, C., Morrison, E., Kumar, I., Galloway, H., and Cordes, S. (2011), Linking industry and occupation clusters in regional economic development, *Economic Development Quarterly*, 25(1), 26-35.

Muñoz, O. (2002). Public management and its importance in the process of planning and management of local development in Colombian municipalities. *Trends Journal*, 3(2). Consulted in http://revistas.udenar.edu.co/index.php/rtend/article/view/741

OCDE, and CEPAL. (2012), *CEPAL - economic prospects for Latin America 2013. SME policies for structural change*, Retrieved 11/20/2012, from http://www.eclac.org/cgi-bin/getProd.asp?xml=/publicaciones/xml/4/48374/ P48374.xml&xsl=/tpl/p9f.xsl&base=/tpl/top -bottom.xsl

Pichat, E. (1970), Contribution to non-numerical algorithms of ordered sets, *Faculty of Science of Grenoble*.

Porter, M. (1998), Clusters and the new economics of competition, *Harvard Business Review*, 76(6), 77-+.

Porter, M. (2000), Location, competition, and economic development: Local clusters in a global economy, *Economic Development Quarterly*, 14(1), 15-34.

Porter, M. (2003), The economic performance of regions, *Regional Studies*, 37(6-7), 549-578.

Porter, M. E. (2009). *To be competitive*. Deusto (ed.), Barcelona.

Private Competitiveness Council: National Competitiveness Report 2012-2013. Retrieved 2/14/2013, 2013, http://www.compite.com.co/site/wp-content/uploads/2012/11/INC-2012-2013.pdf

Ramírez, J. (2013), *Regional competitiveness in Colombia: conceptual framework, findings and recommendations of the center for strategy and competitiveness*. Retrieved 2/14/2013, 2013, http://cec.uniandes.edu.co/index.php/observatorio/articulos

In: Computational Data Analysis Techniques ISBN: 978-1-63463-957-6
Editors: M. Doumpos, C. Zopounidis and Ch. Gaganis

Chapter 12

ALGORITHMS FOR THE EVALUATION AND SELECTION OF ADAPTATION STRATEGIES TO CLIMATE CHANGE

Anna M. Gil-Lafuente and Jaime Alexander López Guauque*
University of Barcelona, Barcelona, Spain

ABSTRACT

The impacts of climate change have become a growing question for the various players in the field. Adapting to such impacts is seen as an uncertain and complex phenomenon the more one gets involved in each of the key processes. Therefore, the degree of involvement or impact will have a larger or lesser effect, on an uncertain scale, in a given a period of time, and under homogenous conditions. Several elements of success in the decision-making are analyzed and discussed. Such elements, with different weightings, are implicit in the decision-making processes. From the forgotten effects theory, we can establish the accumulated effects of first and second generation in order to determine multiplier or enhancer effects - where our efforts will be focused. This will allow a longer scope for decisions to be made and strategies to be formulated as well as for the valuation of various groups and scales in which adaptations will be evaluated.

Keywords: Climate change, adaptation, forgotten effects theory, decision making

1. INTRODUCTION

We are in a time of great change in all areas. A time, in which man is leaving his footprint, causing irreversible climate changes worldwide, according to scientific sources. Climate change is responsible for the increase in the frequency and severity of extreme weather events in all aspects of nature.

* Corresponding author: Tel. +34.662.40.59.85, Email: jalopez_2004@hotmail.com

Consequently, the economic losses caused by natural disasters could increase significantly in the coming years. This will have considerable negative effects on the various socio-economic actors worldwide. On the one hand, an increased risk of extreme weather requires a reassessment of the expected changes in the damage and the inclusion of an appropriate projection of climate change in risk management. Furthermore, the establishment and quantification of the added value can be generated in the formulation of globalized economic strategies and social solutions.

Disaster-related losses have been significant in the last decade, which poses significant challenges to the insurance industry worldwide. For example, in the last two decades (1991-2010) the United States experienced the second most damaging hurricane season in a century quantified in terms of damage normalized by inflation and wealth. In the decade 1926-1935, there was more damaged with higher costs due to hurricanes (Pielke et al., 2008). Referring to the climate in Europe, there have been substantial losses. Floods in Germany during the year 2002 caused losses of about €9.2 billion (Munich Re 2006). England has experienced two major floods in the summer of 2007, caused by extreme rainfall. Overall economic losses amounted to about four billion dollars, a catastrophic event, of which three million were secured. The magnitude of the economic losses suffered highlights the vulnerability of modern societies to changes in climate.

According to projections of the Intergovernmental Panel on Climate Change - IPCC (2007), it is noted that there may be an increase in the frequency and severity of extreme weather events such as rain (extreme), tropical cyclones and heat waves in some regions. The effects of climate change on small extreme weather events such as lightning and hail, remain uncertain (IPCC 2007). The global warming potential of increasing vulnerability to extreme weather events is especially relevant to the insurance industry (Vellinga et al., 2001). The insurance industry is the largest industry in the world in terms of revenue and insurers bear a large part of climate risks, such as damage caused by floods and storms (Mills 2007).

Insurers argue that the settings of premiums and coverage levels are enough to adapt to changes in the patterns of loss. In fact, the flexible nature of the industry that is characterized by mostly short term contracts, allow fairly quick adjustment of premiums, ensuring their resilience against climate change. However, the lack of interest can be problematic, meaning greater exposure and insufficient loss and considerable decrease in the incorporation of premiums and risk management practices. The premium adjustments based on the experiences of previous claims may insufficiently reflect changes in the paradigm of the calculations of the probability of occurrence of extreme weather events due to its low loss situation.

The relevance of climate risks for the insurance sector is evident by observing past trends in insured economic losses and other natural disaster types. Data from past events relating to natural catastrophe losses collected by Munich Re (2006), indicate the increase in global trends losses are already observable. The main factor behind this increase in losses has been social change. Continued economic growth, economic development and population growth, especially in vulnerable regions (e.g., coastal areas), combined with rapid extreme climate change, makes it possible to increase, acceleration and magnification rate and the size of the damage. The influence of climate change on trends in catastrophe losses is likely to be exacerbated by a large change in extreme climates, therefore, expected occurrence due to a change in average climatic conditions (Dlugolecki 2006). The best strategy for insurers seems to incorporate not only the expected changes in the likelihood of extreme weather conditions in the exposure assessment, pricing and management of risk, but perform a rethinking of models, ushering in capable tools, the treatment of uncertainty, getting hybrid based algorithms which involve stochastic data and subjective information. Projected changes in the likelihood of extreme weather events can be obtained from regional climate models, in which Royal Dutch Meteorological Institute (KNMI) has developed climate scenarios for the Netherlands (Van den Hurk et al., 2006-01). There is a clear need for adaptation measures to reduce risk exposure given the historical emissions of greenhouse gases and its consequent effect on radioactive forcing in the future (Pielke et al., 2008). Furthermore, the evolution of society such as increased economic development in vulnerable areas such as coastal areas require the completion of risk reduction policies in order to guarantee the insurability of climate risks. Along with traditional measures commonly used to limit the risks, such as increased premiums and limited coverage, the insurance industry could play an important role in stimulating and promoting climate change mitigation and adaptation (Mills 2007).

Climate change projections for the various countries mainly indicate an increased risk of extreme weather events (Van den Hurk et al., 2006-01). However, the consequences of climate change for insurers not only are negative. For example, the probability of frost may decrease in the future which could reduce claims on certain crop insurance policies. Climate change and things, we can introduce new profitable business opportunities. Demand for insurance products today can increase and market new insurance contracts, non-existent so far, due to the changes that lie ahead as the economic losses due to climate change will increase the risks (Botzen, Bouwer and van den Bergh 2010). However, the problem with the insurability of risks due to weather can hinder the development of markets, primarily because of the inherent correlation of these risks associated with the likelihood and impact of extreme weather events [9]. Various associations worldwide have raised promising solutions to meet demand and compensate for weather-related damages that are not currently covered by private insurance, such as the risk of drought, floods, among others.

This paper will review several elements of success in the decision-making. Such elements are implicit in the decision-making processes.

The formulation of strategies in such uncertain scenarios greatly hinders the application of numerical methods. We propose the use of techniques arising from the theory of fuzzy subsets (Zadeh 1965). We know of the implementation of these theories in many scientific fields by various authors and applications to various fields of knowledge (Canós and Liern 2008; Chen et al., 2009; Gil-Lafuente 2005; Gil-Lafuente and Merigo 2010; Kaufmann 1975; Kaufmann and Gil Aluja 1986; Li and Ho 2009; Lin et al., 2009; Merigo and Gil-Lafuente 2008; Merigo and Gil-Lafuente 2009; Merigo and Gil-Lafuente 2010; Merigo et al., 2010)

Given the forgotten effects theory (FET), developed by teachers Kaufmann and Gil Aluja (1988), which allows a fuzzy logic approach, identifying the contribution of the causal relationships between adaptation strategies to climate change (variables), on the one hand, and between the guiding principles and indirect relationships with each of the actors on the other, provides important information in the decision making process for the design and improvement of the adaptive strategies and management of natural risks, both to countries and companies.

This paper aims to highlight the direct relationships between the guiding principles. The importance of each guiding principle depends on the context they are applied to, in particular regarding the stages in the adaptation process, the level of decision-making or the specific regional conditions. Also, indirect relations for each of the adaptation strategies, in response to climate change outlined variables.

The work is divided after the introduction - a section which summarizes the general characteristics that identify the basics of adaptation on climate change and decision-making under uncertainty. The following section discusses the forgotten effects. The next section outlines the methodological approach of the forgotten effects theory. The next section presents, in summary, the results of the model. Finally, the conclusions are presented highlighting the values of the model proposed and implemented, showing how it contributes to the improvement of adaptive strategies management.

2. Adaptation on Climate Change

At the 2010 climate conference in Cancun, Mexico, parties to the United Nations Framework Convention on Climate Change (UNFCCC) affirmed that adaptation must be placed on a par with climate change mitigation. In practice, adaptation is climate-resilient development and natural resources management. In recent years, adaptation has emerged as a top priority on the international development agenda (GEF - http://www.thegef.org).

The question of evaluating and defining success of climate change adaptation activities has been widely discussed throughout the international evaluation community. Adaptation presents a range of uncertainties that makes evaluation particularly challenging. Despite, the uncertainties that plague climate change adaptation efforts, successful action is possible.

Evaluating climate change is made particularly difficult due to the uncertainty surrounding not only the climate change science, but also the overall scenario in which climate change adaptation activities are implemented. Climate change activities are presented by a multitude of potentially shifting baselines. Adaptation activities are constantly threatened by potential changes in economic, social, and other environmental conditions. The adaptation is still in its early stages however, it provides dimensions for assessing the likelihood of success of adaptation activities.

As we have seen, a large body of work is not totally directed at adaptation to specific climate change impacts but also focused on addressing the root causes of vulnerability. That we find many adaptation efforts in this middle ground of the continuum reflects the main challenge of climate change: learning to live with new sources of uncertainty. Given the relatively high uncertainty associated with the effects of climate change in many places, adaptation efforts can not universally focus on the planning of a new climate expected. Instead, actors reduce vulnerability to an uncertain climate for selected integrated strategies that can be assigned to a number of potential future climate change, and reducing vulnerability to climatic sources of damage.

Over time, as understanding improves climate risks, adaptation experience grows, and the effects of climate change are felt more strongly in more places, impacts oriented approaches, especially climate risk management approaches appear to reach be more widely implemented. However, the effectiveness of climate risk management depends largely on the ability to reduce the uncertainties surrounding climate impacts to a level at which the risk management tools can be applied reliably.

In some sectors and locations, this reduction of uncertainty will happen relatively quickly, while others may occur only in recent decades, or not at all. It is essential, therefore, that certainty about climate risk becoming a prerequisite for action on adaptation. Many of the places and the most vulnerable communities will not be able to address climate risks in the normal sense of risk management, for them, the task of adapting the core in place to strengthen the ability to cope with uncertainty.

However, the availability of good climate risk information does not necessarily mean that adaptation decisions easier or better.

3. Forgotten Effects Theory

In all natural sequential processes, it is usual to ignore voluntarily or involuntarily some stage. Each result has forgotten side effects ranging repercussions throughout the web of incidence in a kind of combinatorial process. The incidence is a highly subjective concept, usually difficult to measure, but the analysis improves reasoned action and decision-making. Always and at all moments, mistakes and oversights have been made as a result of forgetfulness or neglect. When the sequences of incidents, inferences or consequences appear, they are usually not treated properly. Often only two or three steps of reasoning are treated. In order to improve the investigation of forgotten effects or oversights computers and adequate mathematical models are used.

These models are usually the graphs with binary values in the arcs or vertices; these graphs can be valued by numbers in [0;1] or by intervals of confidence of [0;1]. Semantic judgments to unify and have a single evaluation criterion of the truth of the incident are used (Kaufmann and Gil-Aluja 1988). The Boolean theory, the theory of fuzzy subsets or the "expertons" are used. The importance of the effects of the second, third, etc. generation is appreciable in all areas of decision making such as political, economic, business, medicine, biology, etc. (Kaufmann and Gil-Aluja 1993). Qualitative incidence matrices are used to investigate different mechanisms of cause/ effect that it is not yet possible to find out with the help of intuition or experience; it is possible to create new mechanisms between different sectors in order to transform certain situations (Gil-Lafuente 2001).

The idea of the effects of the second generation in the socio-economic and ecological fields has been developed by Jean Fourastié. There are the effects that have not been considered during decision making process. These "forgotten effects" become obvious later. It is convenient to detect them in advance and take necessary measures a priori. Using this concept Fourastié developed a method that allows obtain forgotten effects during the decision making process.

Recently, other authors that have dedicated their research works to the theme of the forgotten effects: Kaufmann and Gil-Aluja (1988, 1995); Gil-Lafuente and Barcellos (2010).

4. Methodology

The objective of this study is to obtain the causal relationships between the strategies and principles of climate change adaptation; rated these as success factors. This study shows the different views of the experts relating to the adaptation policies and the actions that influence its basic principles. Creating the cause-effect relations between the principles and strategies, it was obtained not only an overview of the adaptation response measures, with a more nuanced and broader approaches, but also the "forgotten effects" that were significant for the analysis but have not been taken into account.

Each of the variables proposed in this research have been carefully derived. Other studies have been made available to select variables (Prutsch et al., 2010).

The guiding principles[1] of climate change (subset A), which are causes for this case, are the following:

C1 Initiate adaptation, ensure commitment and management
C2 Build knowledge and awareness
C3 Identify and cooperate with relevant stakeholders
C4 Work with uncertainties
C5 Explore potential climate change impacts and vulnerabilities and identify priority concerns
C6 Explore a wide spectrum of adaptation options
C7 Prioritise adaptation options
C8 Modify existing policies, structures and processes
C9 Avoid mal adaptation
C10 Monitor and evaluate systematically

The adaptation strategies[2] (McGray et al., 2007) of climate change (subset B), which are effects for this case, are the following:

Table 1. Adaptation strategies

Strategy	Description	Number of cases
E1- Changing natural resource management practices	Emphasizes new or different natural resource management practices (e.g., for managing water, land, protected areas, fisheries) as adaptation strategies.	57
E2 -Building institutions	Creates new or strengthens existing institutions (e.g., establishing committees, identifying mechanisms for sharing information across institutional boundaries, training staff responsible for policy development).	43
E3 -Launching planning processes	Sets in motion a specific process for adaptation planning (e.g., developing a disaster preparedness plan, convening stakeholders around vulnerability assessment findings).	35
E4-Raising awareness	Raises stakeholder awareness of climate change, specific climate impacts, adaptation strategies, or the environment in general.	33
E5 -Promoting technology change	Promotes implementation or development of a technology new to the location (e.g., irrigation technology, communications technology).	31

[1] Source: (Prutsch, A. et al. 2010) The following ten guiding principles are strongly interlinked and should be understood in an integrated way. The importance of each guiding principle depends on the context they are applied to, in particular regarding the stages in the adaptation process, the level of decision-making or the specific regional conditions.

[2] Adaptation strategies employed in the 135 cases examined.

Strategy	Description	Number of cases
E6 -Establishing monitoring /early warning systems	Emphasizes the importance of creating, implementing, and/or maintaining monitoring and/or early warning systems.	25
E7 -Changing agricultural practices	Focuses on new or different agricultural practices as adaptation strategies.	23
E8 -Empowering people	Emphasizes literacy, gender empowerment, or the creation of income generation opportunities as a basis for adaptation.	22
E9- Promoting policy change	Promotes establishing a new policy or adjusting an existing policy.	14
E10 -Improving infrastructure	Focuses on creating or improving built infrastructure (e.g., roads, sea walls, irrigation systems).	13
E11- Providing insurance mechanisms	Creates, modifies, or plans an insurance scheme.	4
E12- Other strategies	Consists of three instances of relief work and one focused on eradication of climate-related diseases.	4

Source: Adapted from McGray, Hammil and Bradley (2007).

The analysis of the relations between each cause and effect gives a 10x12 rectangular matrix $\underset{\sim}{M}$ where the cells show the direct impact of each principle on each strategy. The valuations are made using an endecadario system {0;0,1;...0,7;..;1}. The results are the following:

Table 2. Matrix $\underset{\sim}{M}$

$[\underset{\sim}{M}]$	E_1	E_2	E_3	E_4	E_5	E_6	E_7	E_8	E_9	E_{10}	E_{11}	E_{12}
C_1	0,7	0,6	0,8	0,6	0,2	0,8	0,6	0,7	0,6	0	0,7	0,6
C_2	0	0,4	0,5	0,4	0,7	0	0,4	0,9	0,6	0,1	0,3	0,8
C_3	0,8	0,5	0,7	0,8	0,7	0,8	0,2	0,8	0,6	0,1	0,2	0,8
C_4	0,9	0,3	0,8	0	0,1	0,6	0,1	0	0,1	0,1	0	0,2
C_5	0,8	0,2	0,8	0,2	0,5	0,9	0,5	0,7	0,5	0,2	0,3	0,8
C_6	0,7	0,8	0,7	0,5	0,6	0,8	0,4	0,8	0,7	0,7	0,4	0,8
C_7	0,6	0	0,8	0,4	0,6	0,9	0,4	0,6	0,4	0,7	0,1	0,7
C_8	0,8	0,7	0,9	0,4	0,8	0,4	0,5	0,6	0,9	0,9	0	0,3
C_9	0,8	0,5	0	0,6	0,4	0,5	0,7	0	0,6	0,4	0	0,3
C_{10}	0,5	0,7	0,7	0,4	0	0,5	0,7	0,1	0,2	0,2	0	0,6

Let's determine the effect that a cause produces on itself and through another relation effect/ cause, so that in all effects will be accumulated a result of a direct cause and a result produced through an indirect way.

A square matrix $\underset{\sim}{A}$ is made where the "causes" are placed as the rows and columns. The causes represent the principles that have to been done to participate in adaptation process. The valuation is made in [0;1].

A new square matrix $\underset{\sim}{B}$ is made by means of fuzzy cause-effect relations where both rows and columns represent “effects” taken from the matrix $\underset{\sim}{M}$.

Basing on the fuzzy matrixes of incidence such as $\underset{\sim}{M}$, $\underset{\sim}{A}$ and $\underset{\sim}{B}$ and in order to get accumulated effects of the 1 and 2 generation a new fuzzy matrix of incidence $\underset{\sim}{M}^* = \underset{\sim}{A} \circ \underset{\sim}{M} \circ \underset{\sim}{B}$ is obtained by maximin convolution between $\underset{\sim}{M}$, $\underset{\sim}{A}$ and $\underset{\sim}{B}$. The results are the following:

Table 3. Matrix of incidence $\underset{\sim}{M}^* = \underset{\sim}{A} \circ \underset{\sim}{M} \circ \underset{\sim}{B}$

$\underset{\sim}{M}$ *	E_1	E_2	E_3	E_4	E_5	E_6	E_7	E_8	E_9	E_{10}	E_{11}	E_{12}
C_1	0,7	0,7	0,8	0,7	0,8	0,8	0,7	0,7	0,7	0,8	0,7	0,7
C_2	0,8	0,7	0,7	0,8	0,7	0,8	0,7	**0,9**	0,7	0,7	0,8	0,8
C_3	0,8	0,7	0,8	0,8	0,8	0,8	0,7	0,8	0,7	0,8	0,8	0,8
C_4	**0,9**	0,7	0,8	0,7	0,7	0,7	0,6	0,7	0,7	0,8	0,7	0,7
C_5	0,8	0,8	0,8	0,8	0,8	**0,9**	0,6	0,8	0,8	0,8	0,8	0,8
C_6	0,8	0,8	0,8	0,8	0,8	**0,9**	0,7	**0,9**	0,8	0,8	0,8	0,8
C_7	0,8	0,7	0,8	0,8	0,8	**0,9**	0,7	0,8	0,7	0,8	0,8	0,8
C_8	0,8	0,8	**0,9**	0,8	0,8	0,8	0,7	0,8	**0,9**	**0,9**	0,8	0,8
C_9	0,8	0,7	0,7	0,7	0,7	0,7	0,7	0,7	0,7	0,7	0,7	0,7
C_{10}	0,8	0,7	0,8	0,8	0,8	0,8	0,7	0,7	0,7	0,8	0,8	0,8

To find the effects of the 2 generation let’s separate from accumulated effects of $\underset{\sim}{M}^*$ the direct effects given in $\underset{\sim}{M}$. In this case a simple algebraic difference $\underset{\sim}{M}^* - \underset{\sim}{M}$ is made.

Table 4. Results Matrix of difference $\underset{\sim}{M}^* - \underset{\sim}{M}$

	E_1	E_2	E_3	E_4	E_5	E_6	E_7	E_8	E_9	E_{10}	E_{11}	E_{12}
C_1	0	0,1	0	0,1	0,6	0	0,1	0	0,1	**0,8**	0	0,1
C_2	**0,8**	0,3	0,2	0,4	0	**0,8**	0,3	0	0,1	0,6	0,5	0
C_3	0	0,2	0,1	0	0,1	0	0,5	0	0,1	0,7	0,6	0
C_4	0	0,4	0	0,7	0,6	0,1	0,5	0,7	0,6	0,7	0,7	0,5
C_5	0	0,6	0	0,6	0,3	0	0,1	0,1	0,3	0,6	0,5	0
C_6	0,1	0	0,1	0,3	0,2	0,1	0,3	0,1	0,1	0,1	0,4	0
C_7	0,2	0,7	0	0,4	0,2	0	0,3	0,2	0,3	0,1	0,7	0,1
C_8	0	0,1	0	0,4	0	0,4	0,2	0,2	0	0	**0,8**	0,5
C_9	0	0,2	0,7	0,1	0,3	0,2	0	0,7	0,1	0,3	0,7	0,4
C_{10}	0,3	0	0,1	0,4	**0,8**	0,3	0	0,6	0,5	0,6	**0,8**	0,2

These cells are the following: (1;10) the effect of “Initiate adaptation, ensure commitment and management” on “Improving infrastructure” with 0,8; (2;1) the effect of “Build knowledge and awareness” on “Changing natural resource management practices” with 0,8; (2;6) the effect of “Build knowledge and awareness” on “Establishing monitoring/early warning systems” with 0,8; (8;11) the effect of “Modify existing policies, structures and processes” on “Providing insurance mechanisms” with 0,8; (10;5) the effect of “Monitor and evaluate systematically"on "Promoting technology change" with 0,8; (10;11) the effect of "Monitor and evaluate systematically" on "Providing insurance mechanisms" with 0,8.

These causal relations have not been taken into account, it is the case for the cells with 0,8 level or have been considered too weak, the case of the cells with 0,7 level.

The results of the maximum accumulated incidence or the optimal way of incidence of the cause a_i to the effect $b_{j,}$.

The results are the following: C1-C1-E3-E10, C2-C2-E8-E1, C2-C2-E12-E6, C8-C6-E12-E11, C10-C5-E6-E5, C10-C5-E12-E11.

5. Analysis

The matrix includes the cumulative effects of first and second generation and shows indeed that all variables without exception have a cross effect of, at least, an 80% multiplier effect. That is, it is generally observed that the variables corresponding to the principles have a direct impact through some element brought about by specific variables to climate change adaptation.

The direct implication of these considerations caused the need for decisional models that take into account the entire battery of variables involved in the study but apparently the incidence relation is not appreciated in advance.

This means that prospective studies will be necessary to consider these elements primarily, though apparently not reflect direct effects if they cause very high levels and implications.

The incidences of first generation are very clear on the guiding principles that correspond to the process of adaptation, and the incidences hidden variables override conceptualization of adaptation.

In the case of strategies, we present a direct impact on short-term strategies, this means more tactics that obey monitoring activities and early warning systems, together with those that affect or have higher risks regarding people. The incidences of hidden strategies are primarily those involving technology and infrastructure and risk of damage.

Conclusion

The methodology proposed in this study for recovering forgotten effects in the field of adaptation of climate change policies, such as the valuation of actions aimed at its integration within a global legality and socio-political framework, has obtained a wide interest.

We have shown a useful tool for the analysis and evaluation of policies and strategies in various fields, here tested in the field of climate change, specifically in adaptation strategies.

This model specifies the incidents that produce multiplier effects important for decision-makers in the decision-making of high uncertainty. The necessity of a precise analysis of the exterior position of a cooperating country and the preferences in the policies aimed at its incorporation into a common market is one of the most complex and unavoidable targets.

This model specifies the actions/causes that should be performed and that would result in a higher accumulated incidence to the aspects that are proper for each country in its foreign economic policy.

We emphasize the E6 strategy "Establishing monitoring/early warning systems" and the C8 principle "Modify existing policies, structures and processes", multiplier elements, finding a 90% multiplier effect and tapping in its class.

The policies need to be directed under the set of regulatory principles. This is of great importance for the evaluation of management activities.

Adaptation should be seen as a process involving scarce resources and political skills.

Adaptive elements that are used in strategies obey those involved in the definition, i.e., selection, planning, priorities, and not in the implementation of solutions.

The principles of adaptation support a sustainable development in decision making under any context, providing a solid basis for identifying adaptation priorities and promoting the creation of institutions.

In times of crisis in which the limitations of resources and capacities are high, it is necessary to focus efforts on those strategies and decisions, the positive effects are higher and achieve more reach.

Adaptation measures to climate change should be marked in inclusive and sustainable policies, integrating the transition to a sustainable economy in collective decision processes.

Large cities are a reference to undertake adaptation measures to climate change, exploiting comparative advantages they have, and the potential for innovation, both as victims and as responsible for the climate change.

References

Botzen, W.J.W; L. Bouwer and J.C.J.M. van den Bergh (2010), "Climate change and increased risk for the insurance sector: a global perspective and an assessment for the Netherlands", *Springer link,* 577-598, http://www.icrea.cat.

Canós, L. and V. Liern (2008), "Soft computing-based aggregation methods for human resource management", *European Journal of Operational Research,* 189: 669-681.

Chen, H.J., SY. Huang and CS. Lin (2009), "Alternative diagnosis of corporate bankruptcy: neuro fuzzy approach", *Expert Systems with Applications*, 36: 7710-7720.

Dlugolecki, A.F. (2006), "Thoughts about the impact of climate change on insurance claims", in: Höppe P, Pielke RA Jr (eds) Workshop on climate change and disaster losses. *Hohenkammer*, Germany.

Global Environment Facility – GEF. Strategic Priority on Adaptation. (Varios) http://www.thegef.org

Gil Lafuente, A.M. and L. Barcellos (2010), "An application of the methodology of the forgotten affects: the factors that contribute to sustainable growth of the company", *Cuadernos del CIMBAGE*, 12: 23-52.

Gil Lafuente, A.M. (2001), *New strategies for financial analysis in uncertainty*, Barcelona: Ariel.

Gil-Lafuente, A.M (2005), *Fuzzy logic in financial analysis,* Berlin: Springer.

Gil-Lafuente, A.M. and JM. Merigo (2010), "Computational intelligence in business and economics", *World Scientific*, Singapore.

IPCC(2007): Climate change 2007: the physical science basis, in: Solomon S, Qin D, Manning M, Chen Z, Marquis M, Averyt KB, Tignor M, Miller HL (eds) *Contribution of*

Working Group I to the Fourth Assessment Report of the Intergovernmental Panel on Climate Change, Cambridge: Cambridge University Press.

Kaufmann, A. and J. Gil Aluja (1986), *Introduction to fuzzy subsets theory in business management*, Santiago de Compostela: Ed. Milladoiro.

Kaufmann, A. and J. Gil Aluja (1995), *Neural graphs for economics and business management,* Madrid: Pirámide.

Kaufmann, A. and J. Gil Aluja (1993), *Special techniques for experts management*, Santiago de Compostela: Ed. Milladoiro.

Kaufmann, A. and J. Gil Aluja (1988*), Models for the forgotten effects research*, Vigo: Ed. Milladoiro.

Kunreuter, H.C. and Michel-Kerjan, EO. (2006), *Climate change, insurability of large-scale disasters and the emerging liability challenge.* Paper prepared for the University of Pennsylvania Law Conference on Climate Change, 16, 17 November 2006, Philadelphia, PA, USA. Available at: www.climateandinsurance.org/news/ClimateChange PaperforPennLawReview.pdf

Li, S.T. and HF. Ho (2009), "Predicting financial activity with evolutionary fuzzy case based reasoning", *Expert Systems with Applications*, 36: 411-422.

Lim, Bo and E. Sapanger-Siegried (2004), *"Adaptation policy frameworks for climate change: Developing strategies, policies and measures",* Cambridge University Press. USA.

Lin, H.C.; FC. Lin, TY. Hsiao Lin and YC. Lin (2009), "Fuzzy set theory in managerial contract analysis", *Expert Systems with Applications*, 36: 4535-4540.

McGray, H.; A. Hammil and R. Bradley (2007*), "Weathering the Storm: Options for Framing Adaptation and Development",* World Resources Institute. Washington DC http://www.gsdrc.org/go/display&type=Document&id=3912

Merigo, J.M. and AM. Gil-Lafuente (2010), "New decision making techniques and their application in the selection of financial products", *Information Sciences*, 180: 2085-2094.

Merigo, J.M. and AM. Gil-Lafuente (2008), "The generalized adequacy coefficient and its application in strategic decision making", *Fuzzy Economic Review*, 13: 17-36.

Merigo, J.M. and AM. Gil-Lafuente (2009), "The induced generalized OWA operator", *Information Sciences*, 179: 729-741.

Merigo, J.M.; AM. Gil-Lafuente and L. Barcellos (2010), "Uncertain induced generalized aggregation operators and its application in the theory of expertons", *Fuzzy Economic Review,* 15: 25-42.

Mills, E. (2007), "From risk to opportunity: insurer responses to climate change", *Ceres Report*, November.

Munich Re (2006), "Topics geo annual review natural catastrophes 2005". *Munich Reinsurance Group*, Munich.

Pielke, R.A; J. Gratz; CW. Landsea; D. Collins; MA. Suanders and R. Musulin (2008), "Normalized hurricane damage in the United States: 1900–2005", *Nat Hazards* Rev 9(1): 29–42.

Prutsch, A.; T. Grothmann, I. Schauser, S. Otto and S. McCallum (2010), *Guiding principles for adaptation to climate change in Europe.* November. (ETC/ACC): http://acm.eionet.europa.eu/docs/ETCACC_TP_2010_6_guiding_principles_cc_adaptation.pdf

Swiss Re (2005, 2006, 2010, 2011), Natural catastrophes and man-made disasters 2005: high earthquake casualties, new dimension in windstorm losses, *Sigma Report* 1, 2, Swiss Re Reinsurance Company, Zurich.

Van den Hurk, B.; Tank, AK.; Lenderink, G.; van Ulden, A.; van Oldenborgh, GJ.; Katsman, C.; van den Brink, H.; Keller, F.; Bessembinder, J.; Burgers, G.; Komen, G.; Hazeleger, W. and S. Drijfhout, (2006-001), "KNMI climate change scenarios 2006 for the Netherlands", *KNMI scientific report*, WR.

Vellinga, P.; Mills, E.; Berz, G.; Bouwer, LM.; Huq, S.; Kozak, LA.; Palutikof, J.; Schanzenbacher, B. and G. Soler (2001), "Insurance and other financial services", Chap. 8, in: McCarthy JJ, Canziani OF, Leary NA, Dokken DJ. White KS (eds): *Climate change 2001: Impacts, adaptation, and vulnerability*, Cambridge: Cambridge University Press, 417–450.

Weitzman, M.L. (2007), "The Stern Review of the Economics of Climate Change", *Journal of Economic Literature*, 45(3): 703-724.

Zadeh, L.A. (1965), "Fuzzy sets", *Inform and Control* 8: 338–353.

In: Computational Data Analysis Techniques ISBN: 978-1-63463-957-6
Editors: M. Doumpos, C. Zopounidis and Ch. Gaganis

Chapter 13

INNOVATION AND MANUFACTURING EXPORTS: THE CASE OF GREEK FIRMS

***Christos Lemonakis*[1], *Vassakis Konstantinos*[2] *and Fotini Voulgaris*[2]**
[1]Technological Educational Institute of Crete,
Department of Finance and Insurance
[2]MSc, UoPortsmouth

ABSTRACT

Innovation is considered as the major key for growth and competitiveness for firms worldwide. Nowadays, because of the eruption of the financial crisis firms turn their interest to export activities, since domestic demand is been decreasing. In that context, this paper explores the relationship between innovation and export performance on a firm oriented level. The main research question formulated is: what is the relation between innovation and export activity? To answer this, quantitative and qualitative data taken from 100 Greek exporting manufacturing small and medium sized enterprises (SMEs). The econometric analysis made suggests that manufacturing firms with high export performance are less likely to innovate. The findings indicate that innovation does not affect positively export activity of Greek manufacturing exporting SMEs.

Keywords: Innovation; Manufacturing sector; Export performance; SMEs; logit regression model

1. INTRODUCTION

Innovation is “derived from the Latin word ‘innovare’ meaning to take something new” (Tidd et al., 2001) and Porter (1990) with regard to that newness argues that companies can achieve competitive advantage through innovation. Innovation both as process and as outcome has been determined in many ways by researchers (Garcia and Calantone, 2002). According to “Oslo Manual”, OECD (1997) the concept of innovation is defined as a new or significantly improved product (good or service) introduced to the market and rely on the results of new technological developments, new combinations of existing technology or the utilization of the knowledge acquired by the firm during its operation. However, in empirical studies there is distinction between product and process innovation. Thus, product innovation is the introduction on the market of "a product whose technological characteristics or intended uses differ significantly from those of previously produced products or an existing product with significantly enhanced or upgraded performance" and process innovation is defined as "the adoption of technologically new or significantly improved production methods"(OECD, 2005a, p.32).

Innovation is considered as the major key for the survival, growth and development of the small and medium-sized enterprises (Acs and Audretsch, 1990). Thus, SMEs in order to sustain their competitive advantage must continuously exploit new opportunities, as their capacity to develop new products and to innovate "are in the very core of value creation" (Hurmelinna-Laukkanen et al., 2008). Manufacturing SMEs more specifically must continuously improve their manufacturing processes in order to achieve long-term sustainability (Lagace and Bourgault, 2003). In addition, there is strong evidence to support the significance of innovation in the manufacturing sector. Manufacturing SMEs are capable to maintain their position in the market through product innovation (Wright et al., 2005). Furthermore, through a process innovation scheme they can improve their competitiveness by reducing production costs and increasing the flexibility of their productive mechanism (Lefebvre et al., 1991). Several empirical studies are focused on the relationship between innovation and exporting activity (Bernand and Jensen 2004; Dhanaraj & Beamish, 2003; Ozcelik & Taymaz, 2004).

In the recent years, firms turn their interest to exports as the domestic demand for their goods or services has been decreased. Therefore, many studies have focused on the determinants of firm's export activity. More specifically literature is focused on innovation and productivity, as the major determinants of promoting the firm's export performance (Wagner, 2007). In addition, innovation seems to play a significant role to the firm's decision to export and for the amount of total exports. Innovation is the key factor in reducing the consequences of the current financial crisis in EU regions (European Commission, 2009).

2. Innovation Activity in the Greek Context

Greece requires in general a more integrated and directed policy of innovative efforts in order to develop its capabilities. Therefore, Kitsos et al. (2005) based on a survey on Greek enterprises concludes that the most significant factors that may affect frequency of innovation and its rate of spread are: finance, technical applicability, efficiency, size, structure, Research and Development (R&D) activities and others. On a macro level, as Greek economic growth is significantly connected with education, business development and education, Hatzikian and Bouris (2007) are focused on the analysis of the factors that influence the innovation processes in Greece compared with other members of European Union. They used linear and exponential models to estimate the statistical relationship between R&D expenditures and GDP per capita. They concluded that R&D is a driver of county's growth (GNP). The role of R&D in the explanation on innovation outcomes of the firms is significant and thus investments in R&D are one of the most significant mechanisms in the determination of the level of innovation in an industry or sector. In the last decade Greece presents low levels of

R&D expenditures as percentage of national GDP. That level is under 1% of the national GDP and remains stable mainly because of very low R&D expenditures in the private sector. According to Innovation Union Scoreboard (2011), Greece is one of the moderate innovators as its innovative performance is below that of EU27 average. For the period 2007-2013, the majority of the actions for encouraging the capacity of research and development at national as well as regional level are dependent on funding from European Union programs. The national innovation system seems to grow faster than the European average, but the private sector is not that strong with regard to R&D expenditures. Therefore, it is obvious that enterprises do not show high demand for research-based knowledge. Moreover, the unwillingness of financial institutions to finance innovative activities and risky investments are some of the determinants that prevent resources for R&D.

In Greece the last decade and mostly after the eruption of the financial crisis, the need for development of entrepreneurial activity and strengthening of competitiveness is emphasized. In the improvement of economic climate, value creation is appropriate and R&D orientation can play a significant role in that. Therefore, research institutions and clusters focus on innovative products and services through R&D, but also in their business exploitation.

The Greek research institutions and clusters are very appreciable choices for public as well as private institutions, since they have well-qualified personnel, good material and technical infrastructure and collaborations with universities, institutions and research centres' abroad. Moreover, clusters between research groups and technology companies are designed to promote the liaison between information and knowledge. Their activity enhances entrepreneurship, supports domestic industries and helps local and national economy as a whole. One more effort in enhancing innovation in Greece has been made in 2012 with the establishment of Fund Portfolio, which is called "Innovation Fund". Its aim is to encourage innovative firms especially high-tech with venture capital funding through increasing capital shares.

3. LITERATURE REVIEW

In general, firms' R&D is considered to be indicator of innovation (Nassimbeni, 2001). R&D is also defined as the key of overcoming financial crisis as well as transformation of money to knowledge (Yetis, 2009). R&D has received the most attention from researchers as a determinant of innovation. However, the relationship between R&D and innovative activities in small and medium enterprises (SMEs) requires more specification. As of that, Raymond and St-Pierre (2010) in their research made an effort to make clear the impact of R&D upon innovation in SMEs. In order to achieve that, they distinguish process R&D form product R&D and process innovation from product innovation. Additionally, they used data from 205 manufacturing SMEs from Canada and they concluded that the impact of R&D in product innovation is achieved through the mediation of process innovation. Oerlemans et al. (1998) indicated an instant positive connection between R&D expenditures and innovation. Keizer et al. (2002) examined the determinants that enhance innovative efforts of SMEs and data used was based on Dutch SMEs. The dependent variable was innovation and 14 independent variables also were used. From these independent variables only three appeared to be significantly related with innovative efforts: usage of innovation subsidies, linkages with innovation centres' and R&D investments as percentage of firms' turnover.

Becker and Egger (2007) indicate that firms that focused on product innovation in general target to enter a specific market. Thus, as the domestic market is limited in that stage, the firm moves to enter in export market in order to exploit its market power (Hirsch and Bijaoui, 1985). Pla-Barber & Alegre (2007) highlight the role of innovation in international markets with the argument that a single market can cover the innovation needs of the firm and thus, the firm tries to export. Moreover, Teece (1996) argues that innovative firms have incentives to expand their activities in other markets, as they can earn more from investments returns or exploit their innovations and improve its economic performance (Love & Mansury, 2009). Firms through innovation can be differentiated and obtain international competitive advantage (Filipescu, Rialp, & Rialp, 2009; Lopez & Garcia, 2005).

In that sense, DiPietro and Anoruo (2006) with the adoption of cross-country regression analysis found that innovation is positively connected with country's exporting volumes. Additionally, Iacovone and Javorcik (2008) and Kugler and Verhoogen (2008) indicate that exports from firms are highly priced. Therefore, products that are being exported are better in terms of quality. Moreover, Halkos and Kitsos (2011) in an analysis on Greek firms examine the factors that determine the innovation activities. With the adoption of logistic regression (logit model) they concluded that exporting firms and firms that have an increase of more than ten per cent in their turnover, have higher odds on implementing innovation activities.

Most of the studies that analyzed relationship between innovation and export activity, found a positive relation. Greenhalgh (1990), Buxton et al. (1991) and Grenhalgh et al. (1994) search for the relationship between innovation and trade performance in UK and found some evidence of positive role for innovation in trading. Rodriguez et al. (2005) analyzed the impact of technological resources on Spanish manufacturing firms' export intensity. They concluded that R&D investments, innovations and patents influence positively the exports of Spanish enterprises. Kumar and Siddharthan (1994) examine the link between R&D expenditure and exports for 640 Indian firms grouped according to industry for the period 1988-1990.

They found that although India in high technology sectors does not have competitive advantage, innovation induces positively the other sectors. Willmore (1992) examine the determinants of exports and imports through the role of multinationals in Brazil's trade. He found that R&D expenditure has not significant role in exports. However, R&D efforts help in the increase of domestic inputs and the decrease of the imports. Hirsch and Bijaoiu (1985) examine the link between R&D expenditure and export behaviour for Israel. They tested the significance of innovation benefits for 111 Israeli firms, all of which are classified as innovators as they bound R&D expenditure and they found that innovating firms had better export performance. Girma et al. (2009) considered the relationship between innovative capacity and exports for Irish and British firms and he found that the previous exporting experience of Irish firms enhances their innovative capability. Pla-Barber & Alegre (2007) in their empirical study utilizing a sample of 121 French firms of the biotechnology industry found significant and positive relationship between innovation and export intensity.

In addition, in empirical studies there is also analysis of the relationship between firm size and export performance. Thus, the elements that lead on enterprises' export success attract the interest of researchers.

In the majority of these studies, firm size appears as a significant variable that affects export intensity. Furthermore, Papadogonas et al. (2007) examined the factors that impact export performance of Greek manufacturing firms by using cross-sectional data and a tobit regression model. They found that larger firms have higher propensity to export.

4. MODEL APPROACH AND VARIABLES SELECTION

In many empirical researches the models used have continuous dependent variables, but there are many cases that dependent variables are categorical. In these cases, logistic regression theory can be used. That framework is based on proportions and probabilities, which are different from continuous variables in several ways. The main difference is that continuous variables can take any value, instead of proportions and probabilities delimited by zero or one. The simplest way to deal with binary dependent variables is the linear probability model because of the assumption that the probability of an event happening (P_i) is linearly correlated with a set of explanatory variables ($X_{1i}, X_{2i},\ldots X_{ki}$), which can be qualitative or dummies or both. More specifically, the model has the form:

$$Pi= p\ (y_i=1) = \beta_0+\beta_1 X_{1i}+\ldots+\beta_{ki} X_{ki} +\varepsilon_i$$

With the estimation of above model we take the binary output variable Y, where we model the conditional probability Pr(Y=1|X=x) as a function of X, for each observation i, with the use of k input variables.

Table 1. Variables selection

	Symbol	Variable	Description
Dependent Variable	*INN*	Innovation (Dummy/Qualitative)	*Innovation (process or product). It takes values 1 for innovation or 0 for no innovation existence. Response is taken from the questionnaire survey.*
Explanatory Variables	*EXP*	Exports (Dummy/Qualitative)	*Dummy Variable that denotes export activity as percentage (%) of total sales. It takes the 0 for 0%-10% of total sales, value 1 for 10%-25% of total sales, and 2 for greater than 25% of total sales. Response is taken from the questionnaire survey.*
	R&D	R&D expenditures (Dummy/Qualitative)	*R&D expenditures of the firm, as percentage (%) of total sales, in period 2008-2010. Response is taken from the questionnaire survey.*
	SIZE	Size (Quantitative)	*Total assets of the firm in logarithm during the period 2008-2010.*
	OPEXP	Operational costs (Quantitative)	*Supplies and the operational costs of the firm.*
	ALIQ	Acid Liquidity (Quantitative)	*Acid Liquidity (or quick liquidity) of the firm during the period 2008-2010. It is calculated by dividing all current assets with the exception of inventory by current liabilities.*
	WC	Working Capital (Quantitative)	*Working Capital of the firm during the period 2008-2010. Equals to the amount of current assets minus the amount of current liabilities as of specific sample year.*

A binary choice model is used (Haas and Hansen, 2005) with a dummy dependent variable, Innovation, in order to control for possible selection bias arising from the exclusion of non-innovative firms in the analysis. That model is designed to the choice of two discrete alternatives and essentially describe the probability of y_i=1. Proportions and probabilities differ from continuous variables in several ways.

The sample consists of 100 exporting manufacturing firms of Metal Products & Structures for the time period 2008 to 2010. The regression β's (coefficients) of the proposed logistic model quantifies the relationship between depended variable and independent variables involving the odds ratio.

Thus, the logit form of the fitted model used in this paper can be represented as:

$$\text{Logit}\,[\Pr(Yi=1)] = \beta_0+\beta_1 EXP+\beta_2 R\&D+\beta_3 SIZE+\beta_4 WC+\beta 5ALIQ+\beta_6\, OPEXP+\varepsilon_t$$

where Y is the depended variable that denotes innovation (INN) in product or process and it takes values 1 for innovation and 0 for non-innovation existence. The β's are the linear coefficients that should be estimated and ε_t is the error term. The independent (explanatory) variables used in the model are presented in Table 1 above. Selected variables were based on theory and the aforementioned literature review.

Additionally, in order to collect the necessary data for the variables of innovation (INN) and exports (EXP), a survey in the sample firms was made with the use of questionnaire. The questionnaire made is based on the Community Innovation Survey (CIS) framework (Tether, 2002; Miotti and Sachwald, 2003; Laursen and Salter, 2006; Monreal- Perez et al., 2011), whilst the source of the survey is provided by "Oslo Manual", a joint publication of Eurostat and OECD. The survey made with the use of an online questionnaire via Google Docs as well as with telephone communication with firms' managers in order to improve the accuracy of the data taken. All the financial ratios used as explanatory variables obtained from ICAP SA database (the largest Business Information, Services and Consulting firm in Greece).

In this paper, innovation is used as dependent variable and export performance is used as an explanatory variable in order to examine its relationship with exporting activity following the empirical studies of Keizer et al. (2002), Silva & Leitao (2007) and Halkos & Kitsos (2011).

In innovation's literature, exports variable (EXP) is often used as determinant of innovation activities (Lefebvre et al., 1998; Alonso & Donoso, 1998; Harris & Li, 2009; Monreal- Perez et al., 2011; De Marchi, 2012). In this paper, exports variable is a dummy that takes values accordingly to the export activity of the firm as percentage of total sales similarly with previous research: Rodriguez et al. (2005), Nassimbeni (2001) and Harris & Li (2009).

R&D expenditures (R&D) is used in logit model following the empirical studies of Keizer et al. (2002), Harris & Li (2009), Monreal- Perez et al. (2011) and De Marchi (2012). In innovation's literature a debate between innovation and firm size do exists and therefore size of firm is often used as explanatory variable in the examination of innovation (Willmore, 1992; Lefebvre et al., 1998; Nassimbeni, 2001; Rodriguez et al., 2005). Firm's size (SIZE) is used also in the proposed model and measured by the log of total assets similarly to Sahayam et al. (2012) research. The rest of the explanatory variables used in the model are financial ratios of the sample firms.

5. EMPIRICAL RESULTS

Information criteria and McFadden were taken into account in order to achieve accurate and correct results. The results are presented in the Table 2 below. From the results, it is shown that five statistically significant variables do exist. More specifically, two are statistically significant at 1% level of significant and three at 5% level of significance. Moreover, McFadden R^2 remains at 67.19%.

Table 2. Empirical results

Dependent Variable: INN			
Method: ML - Binary Logit (Quadratic hill climbing)			
Variables	Coefficients	St. Error	*McFadden R^2*
C	1.286.958 (0.0227)	5.647659	0.671938
EXP	-0.926923 (0.0020) **	0.300555	*Information Criteria*
R&D	0.0000253 (0.0000) **	5.38E-06	AIC
SIZE	-0.902054 (0.0202) *	0.388256	0.376523
WC	0.000223 (0.0218) *	0.0000974	SBC
ALIQ	-0.763809 (0.0487) *	0.387399	0.463368
OPEXP	3.83E-06 (0.5006)	5.69E-06	

Prob. is in parentheses.
*: statistical significant at 5% level of significance.
**: statistical significant at 1% level of significance.

The estimated coefficient of exports (EXP), since it has negative value, shows that the innovation is negatively related with exports. Consequently, manufacturing firms that present high export performance will have lower probability to innovate in contradiction to findings of other empirical studies abroad. Numerous empirical studies examined and analyzed the relationship of innovation and export performance found that positive correlation exists. More specifically, the empirical studies in which it was concluded that positive correlation are among others: Alvarez & Robertson (2004), Pla-Barber & Alegre (2007), Monreal- Perez (2011).

The estimated coefficient of R&D expenditures (R&D) shows that there is a positive relationship between R&D investments and innovation. In that sense, manufacturing firms that invest more in R&D activities have higher probability to innovate (i.e.: Alvarez & Robertson (2004), Pla-Barber & Alegre (2007), Monreal- Perez (2011)). In addition, other empirical studies with the usage of R&D expenditures as indicator of innovation concluded also in the positive relationship between innovation and exports, i.e.: Oerlemans et al. (1998), Rodriguez et al. (2005) and DiPietro & Anoruo (2006).

In addition, the estimated coefficient of size (SIZE) displays a negative relation between firm's size and innovation. Size shows that a manufacturing firm with smaller size (lower total assets) has greater potential to innovate.

Table 3. Descriptive Statistics

	INN	OPEXP	R&D	SIZE	WC	ALIQ
Mean	0.80	0.97	927211.30	16.24	24382.98	1.1039
Median	1	1	383605	16.0054	5112.00	0.8900
St. Dev	0.4006	0.9010	1519546	1.5449	57575.49	0.7643
Skewness	-1.50	0.0588	3.2228	0.2101	4.8210	1.6377
Kurtosis	3.25	1.2384	15.9444	3.2523	31.1521	6.2962
Jarque-Bera	113.2813	38.9595	2605.13	2.9934	11032.04	269.0309
Prob.	0.0000	0.0000	0.0000	0.2238	0.0000	0.0000

Thereafter, the estimated coefficient of working capital (WC) shows a positive relationship between working capital and innovation. Manufacturing firms with higher working capital will have higher probability to present innovative activity. The estimated coefficient of acid liquidity (ALIQ) shows a negative relationship between acid liquidity and innovation. Therefore, manufacturing firms that present innovative activity will present lower acid liquidity.

Additionally, another factor that is used as determinant of innovation in previous research as well as in this study is firm's R&D expenditures. In innovation's literature, R&D is considered to be indicator of innovation. In the model used here R&D expenditures' variable (R&D) is significant and positively related to innovation, which shows that firms with higher R&D expenditures present a higher probability to innovate. Similar to our results, Oerlemans et al. (1998) indicated an instant positive relationship between R&D expenditures and innovation. Keizer et al. (2002) investigated the factors that enhance innovative efforts of SMEs using regression based methodology and data from Dutch SMEs. He concluded that R&D investments (as percentage of firm's turnover) is significantly and positively related to innovative efforts of SMEs. Kleinknecht et al. (1989) and Kleinknecht & Alfred (1991) concluded that R&D comprises only attempts for the establishment of innovative activities.

Similar research to ours also finds negative relationship between innovation and export performance. In that context, Silva and Leitao (2007) conclude that enterprises with high exporting activity present low intense in innovation. Sriram et al. (1989) also find that there is a negative relation between innovation and exports, while Reid (1986) conclude that there is a little correlation between export intensity and innovation. A possible explanation for this is that Greek SMEs are small firms and they do not have enough resources to use for innovation activity. Furthermore, the products of those firms are either characterized by other competitive advantages, or are products where innovation is not a critical determinant of competitiveness.

As R&D intensity is considered an indicator of innovation, there are several empirical studies that show negative relation between R&D intensity and export activity. Willmore (1992) examined the determinants of exports and imports using data for a cross-section of Brazilian enterprises. He concluded that R&D expenditures do not influence significantly exports. In a micro level empirical study that carried out by Lefebvre et al. (1998) using data from Canadian enterprises and by Bechetti and Rossi (2000) using data from Italian enterprises, they both concluded that R&D intensity does not induce exports. As of that we see that our findings agree with findings abroad.

Furthermore, another determinant of innovation is the firm's size. In our paper firm's size (SIZE) is measured by the log of total assets similarly to Sahayam et al. (2012). We find that firm's size is significant determinant of innovation and that is negatively correlated with innovation, which means that smaller manufacturing firms present a higher probability to innovate. In addition, Simonen & McCann (2008) in their empirical study concluded that small enterprises are more innovative than larger ones.

Also, Working Capital (WC), measured as the amount of current assets minus the amount of current liabilities as of specific year, comes to have a positive and significant effect on innovation, indicating that innovative firms must have enough liquidity for their everyday operations.

CONCLUSION AND FURTHER RESEARCH

Innovation plays a significant role in small and medium enterprises, especially in the manufacturing sector. Enterprises through innovation have the ability to gain competitive advantages against their rivals. Thus, SMEs in order to improve their competitiveness, must continuously exploit new opportunities for innovation.

On the other hand, acid liquidity, measured as cash and accounts receivables over short term liabilities, is found to be negatively correlated, indicating that innovative firms are careful in the use of their liquid assets, preferably investing their funds in innovation activities.

The recent financial crisis, make firms turn their interest to exports as the domestic demand for their goods or services has been decreased. In this context, this paper constitutes an attempt to provide new evidence on the relationship between innovation and Greek manufacturing export activity. Emphasis is given on the manufacturing sector, since the most R&D is funded and performed mainly in that sector. In addition, manufacturing sector is one of the most significant sectors for the Greek economy because of its important participation in national GDP and its contribution to the development of the real economy.

A survey in a representative sample of 100 Greek manufacturing exporting enterprises was performed to investigate innovation use in Greek exporting enterprises. The survey carried out with the use of questionnaire was based on the Community Innovation Survey (CIS) framework. The bulk of the empirical studies that examined and analyzed the relationship of innovation and export performance concluded that there is a positive correlation. Unlike what was expected, our results indicate that manufacturing SMEs with higher export performance present a lower ability to innovate. However, we found a positive relation between innovation and R&D expenditures as it was expected. Therefore, the Greek manufacturing exporting SMEs with higher R&D investments present higher capability to acquire innovative activity. Moreover, negative relationship between innovation and size exists. Thus, a Greek manufacturing exporting firm with smaller size is more likely to innovate. Furthermore, it is observed a negative relationship between acid liquidity and innovation. Therefore, manufacturing firms that present innovative activity will present lower acid liquidity.

R&D investments sustain significantly the Greek manufacturing exporting SMEs in increasing their innovative activities. Also, size shows that small manufacturing firms have an increased capability to innovate in terms of product or process orientation. In recent years, because of financial crisis, firms face significant reductions in the domestic demand for their products. Therefore, they turn to exporting activities in order to offset the substantial decrease in their sales volumes.

To be competitive in both the domestic and foreign markets, SMEs must open the floor for innovative activities. Due to the lack of funds for R&D, SMEs should cooperate with various organizations and research institutions on R&D development of new products or production techniques, making innovative methods in promoting their products, packaging, etc. A very good option is also the clustering of SMEs on R&D activities.

Governmental agencies and managers should support research and innovative activities for SMEs through funding and regulations on cooperating with universities and research institutions. Since Greek manufacturing exporting SMEs innovation does not enhance export performance, more research needs to be placed on factors that do enhance their exporting activity, such as SMEs specific product orientation and competitive advantage, the use of externalities and better allocation of internal or external resources.

REFERENCES

Acs, Z.J., & Audretsch, D.B. (1990). Innovation and Small Firms. *MIT Press,* Cambridge, Massachusetts.

Alonso, J. A., & Donoso, V. (1998). Competir en el exterior. La empresa espanola y los mercados internacionales. Madrid: ICEX.

Alvarez, R., & Robertson, R. (2004).Exposure to foreign markets and plant-level innovation: Evidence from Chile and Mexico. *The Journal of International Trade & Economic Development,* 13 (1), 57–87.

Becker, S.O., & Egger, P.H. (2007).Endogenous product versus process innovation and a firm's propensity to export (CESifo Working Paper 1906).

Buxton, T., & Mayes, D., Murfin, A. (1991). UK trade performance and R&D. *Econ. Innovation New Technol,* 1, 243–256.

De Marchi, V. (2012). Environmental innovation and R&D cooperation: Empirical evidence from Spanish manufacturing firms, *Research Policy 41,* 614– 623

Dhanaraj, C., & Beamish, P. (2003). A resource-based approach to the study of export performance. *Journal of Small Business Management, 41, 242–261.*

DiPietro, W.R., & Anoruo E. (2006). Creativity, innovation and export performance. Journal of Policy Modeling, 28, 133-139.

European Commission, (2009). Regional Innovation Scoreboard—RIS. Enterprise & Industry Magazine, *Inno Europe Paper no.14 European Communities.*

Filipescu,A., Rialp,A., & Rialp,J.(2009). Internationalisation and technological innovation: Empirical evidence on their mutual relationship. *Advances in International Marketing*, 20, 125–154.

Garcia, R., Calantone, R. (2002). A critical look at technological innovation typology and innovativeness terminology: a literature review. *Journal of Product Innovation Management,* 19, 110–132.

Girma, S., Gorg, H., Hanley, A. (2009). R&D and exporting: a comparison of British and Irish firms. *Review of World Economics,* 144(4*),* 750–773.

Greenhalgh, C., Taylor, P., & Wilson, R.(1994).Innovation and export volumes and prices, a disaggregated study. *Oxford Economic Papers* 46, 102–134.

Haas, M., & Hansen, M.(2005). When using knowledge can hurt performance: the value of organizational capabilities in a management consulting company. *Strategic Management Journal,* 26, 1–24.

Halkos, G., & Kitsos, C. (2011). A qualitative analysis of Greek innovation activities. *Journal of Applied Economic Sciences,* 6, 1(15).

Harris, R., & Li, Q.C. (2009). Exporting, R&D, and absorptive capacity in UK establishments. *Oxford Economic Papers*, 61(1), 74–103.

Hirsch, S., Bijaoui, I.(1985). R&D intensity and export performance: a micro view. *Weltwirtschaftliches Archiv*, 121, 138–251.

Hurmelinna-Laukkanen, P., Sainio, L.-M., Jauhiainen, T., (2008). Appropriability regime for radical and incremental innovations. *R&D Management* ,38 (3), 278–289.

Iacovone, L., & Javorcik, B. (2008). Shipping Good Tequila Out: Investment, Domestic Unit Value and Entry of Multi-Product Plants into Export Markets. Mimeo, University of Sussex.

Keizer, J.A., Dijkstra, L., & Halman J.I.M. (2002). Explaining innovative efforts of SMEs. An explanatory survey among SMEs in the mechanical and electrical engineering sector in The Netherlands. *Technovation*, 22, 1-13.

Kitsos, C.,Korres, G. M.,& Hatzikian, Y. C. (2005). Innovation activities in Greece: A statistical and empirical approach. *Greek Statistical Institute: Practical of 18th Panhellenic Conference of Statistics,* 459-465.

Kleinknecht, Alfred & Bart Verspagen, (1989). "R&D and Market Structure: The Impact of Measurement and Aggregation Problems," *Small Business Economics*, 1(4), 297-302.

Kleinknecht, & Alfred. (1991). Firm Size and Innovation: Reply to Scheirer. *Small Business Economics*, 3(2), 157-158.

Kugler, M., & Verhoogen, E.(2008). The Quality-Complementarity Hypothesis: Theory and Evidence from Colombia (NBER Working Paper No. 14418).

Lagace, D., & Bourgault, M. (2003). Linking manufacturing improvement programs to the competitive priorities of Canadian SMEs. *Technovation,*23, 705–715.

Laursen, K., & Salter, A. (2006). Open for innovation: the role of openness in explaining innovation performance among UK manufacturing firms. Strategic *Management Journal,* 27, 131–150.

Lefebvre, E., Lefebvre, L. A., & Bourgault, M. (1998). R&D-related capabilities as determinants of export performance. *Small Business Economics,* 10, 365–377.

Lefebvre, L.-A., Lefebvre, E., Colin, D., (1991). Process innovation, productivity, and competitiveness in smaller manufacturing firms. *Canadian Journal of Administrative Sciences,* 8 (1), 19–28.

Lopez, J., & Garcia, R.M. (2005).Technology and export behaviour: A resource-based view approach. *International Business Review,* 14(5), *539–557.*

Love, J.H., & Mansury, M.A. (2009). Exporting and productivity in business services: Evidence from the United States. *International Business Review,* 18, 630–642.

Miotti, L., & Sachwald, F. (2003). Co-operative R&D: why and with whom? An integrated framework of analysis. *Research Policy,* 32, 1481–1499.

Monreal- Perez, J., et al. (2011). A longitudinal study of the relationship between export activity and innovation in the Spanish firm: The moderating role of productivity. *International Business Review.*

Nassimbeni, G. (2001). Technology, innovation capacity, and the export attitude of small manufacturing firms: a logit tobit / model. *Research Policy*, 30, 245–262.

OECD.(1997). *Oslo Manual: The Measurement of Scientific and Technological Activities*, OECD-EUROSTAT, Paris.

OECD.(2002). Frascati Manual: Proposed Standard Practice for Surveys on Research and Experimental Development. *OECD Publications Service*, p. 30

OECD. (2005a). *Oslo Manual: Guidelines for Collecting and Interpreting Innovation Data*, Third ed. OECD, Paris.

Oerlemans, L.A.G., Meeus, M.T.H., & Boekema, F.W.M.(1998). Do networks matter for innovation: the usefulness of the economic network approach in analyzing innovation, *Journal of Economic and Social Geography*, 89 (3), 298–309.

Ozcelik, E., & Taymaz, E. (2004). Does innovativeness matter for international competitiveness in developing countries? The case of Turkish manufacturing industries. *Research Policy*, 33, 409–425.

Papadogonas, T., Voulgaris, F. & Agiomirgianakis, G. (2007). Determinants of export behavior in the Greek manufacturing sector. *Operational Research: An Intemational Journal*. Vol.7, No 1, pp.121-135.

Pla-Barber, J., & Alegre, J. (2007). Analyzing the link between export intensity, innovation and firm size in a science-based industry. *International Business Review*, 16, 275–293.

Porter, M. (1990). *The Competitive Advantage of Nations*. Macmillan, London.

Raymond, L., & St-Pierre, J. (2010). Strategic Capabilities for the Internationalization of Manufacturing SMEs: A Configurational Approach. Entrepreneurial Practice Review, Vol. 1 (2).

Reid, S.D. (1986). Is Technology Linked With Export Performance in Small Firms? In: Hubner, H. (ed.): The Art and Science of Innovation Management. *Elesevier Science*, Amsterdam, pp. 273–283.

Rodriguez, L.R. & Rodriguez, L.R. (2005). Technological Resources and Export Intensity: A Microview. *International Business & Economics Research Journal*, Vol. 4 (11).

Sahaym, A. et al. (2012). The influence of managerial discretion, innovation and uncertainty on export intensity: A real options perspective, *International Business Review.*

Silva, M.J., & Leitao, J. (2007). What determines the entrepreneurial innovative capability of Portuguese industrial firms? , Munich Personal RePEc Archive Paper, no.5216.

Simonen, J., & McCann, P. (2008). Innovation, R&D cooperation and labor recruitment: evidence from Finland. *Small Business Economics,* 31, 181–194.

Sriram, V., Neelankavil, S., & Moore, R..(1989). Export policy and strategic implications for small-to-medium sized firms. *Journal of Global Marketing* ,3(2), 43–60.

Teece, D.J. (1996). Firm organization, industrial structure and technological innovation. *Journal of Economic behavior and Organization*, 31, 192–224.

Tether, B.S., & Tajar, A. (2008). Beyond industry–university links: sourcing knowledge for innovation from consultants, private research organisations and the public science-base. *Research Policy,* 37, 1079–1095.

Tidd, J., Bessant, J. & Pavitt, K. (2001). *Managing Innovation: Integrating Technological, Market and Organisational Change*. Wiley, Chichester.

Wagner, J. (2007).Exports and productivity: A survey of the evidence from firm-level data. *The World Economy*, 30(1), 60–82.

Willmore, L., (1992). Transnationals and foreign trade: evidence from Brazil. J. *Dev. Studies,* 28(2), 314–335.

Wright, R.E., Palmer, J.C., & Perkins, D. (2005). Types of product innovations and small business performance in hostile and benign environments. *Journal of Small Business Strategy,* 15 (2), 33–44.

Yetis, N . (2009). Design R&D Innovation. *Journal of the Framework*, 17(52), 28-34.

In: Computational Data Analysis Techniques ISBN: 978-1-63463-957-6
Editors: M. Doumpos, C. Zopounidis and Ch. Gaganis

Chapter 14

ANALYSIS OF THE ENTREPRENEURIAL CONDITIONS WITH THE USE OF THE THEORY OF FORGOTTEN EFFECTS

***Ana Maria Gil–Lafuente*[1]*, Anna Klimova*[*2] *and Sefa Boria Reverter*[3]**
University of Barcelona, Barcelona, Spain

ABSTRACT

Sustainable development of any economic system is impossible without taking into account the changes that take place in the small and medium-sized enterprise (SME) sector. A well-balanced development of this sector is an indicator of a success of the economic reforms that promote a competitive market environment. In this paper we have considered the SME sector of two countries such as Spain and Russia. The aim of our study was to familiarize the entrepreneurs who want to create a small or medium-sized enterprise in Spain or Russia with the principal features that each of the two economies represents taking into account the current context of mobility between two countries. The Theory of forgotten effects has been used. The directors of different companies have been interviewed in order to obtain their opinions and create an input data. The results of this analysis create an additional basis that any entrepreneur can consult obtaining an adequate solution for his investments.

Keywords: Globalization, SME Sector Development, Theory of Forgotten Effects, Decision Making

1. INTRODUCTION

Sustainable development of any economic system is impossible without taking into account the changes that take place in the SME sector. A well-balanced development of this

[*] Corresponding author: Tel.: +34.93.402.19.62 Fax: +34.93.201.80.47. Email addresses: amgil@ub.edu (Ana Maria Gil-Lafuente), aklimova@ub.edu (Anna Klimova), jboriar@ub.edu (Sefa Boria Reverter). [1,2,3] Tel.: +34.93.402.19.62 Fax: +34.93.201.80.47

sector is an indicator of a success of the economic reforms that promote a competitive market environment.

In this paper we have considered the SME sector of two countries such as Spain and Russia. In Spain, a small business is a result of a long evolutionary process based on the spontaneous entrepreneurial initiative of people. In Russia, however, entrepreneurship has been developed with an approval of authorities. The period of small business creation in today's Russia is short.

Although the historical development of the two countries was different the SME sector represents a vital importance for the economic competitiveness for each of them. This fact becomes more evident in times of globalization and current economic crisis.

The aim of our study was to familiarize the entrepreneurs who want to create a small or medium-sized enterprise in Spain or Russia with the principal features that each of the two economies represents taking into account the current context of mobility between two countries. The mathematical technique proposed in this study is a sure way to avoid losing or leaving without consideration the information that has been initially considered in the analysis and that is useful for decision making. The Theory of forgotten effects has been used. The directors of different companies have been interviewed in order to obtain their opinions and create an input data. The results of this analysis create an additional basis that any entrepreneur can consult obtaining an adequate solution for his investments.

The structure of the paper is the following. In section 2, we describe the changes produced in the world economy due to the process of globalization as well as the current economic crisis. In section 3 and 4, some historical facts of the SME's development and the actual state of this sector in Spain and Russia are described. Section 5 covers theoretical aspects of the Theory of forgotten effects. In the last section we develop the empirical case and represent the final results and conclusions.

2. Globalization and the World Economic Crisis

Globalization is an historical process that initially referred to the commercial interchange between different international economies.

The process of globalization has started, due to some authors, in the decade of the 60s when the companies in search of new markets extended their scope of actions beyond national borders passing from being producers in their countries of origin to establishing their manufacturing plants in the foreign countries (Fletcher, 2001; Johanson & Vahlne, 1977).

In the 70s globalization has expanded its field of influence. Several industrial and developing countries have moved toward financial liberalization (Demirgüç-Kunt & Detragiache, 2001; Stiglitz, 2000, 2004).

From the decade of the 80s the linkages between different international economies have tightened resulting in a participation of foreign shareholders in the local companies. This phenomenon has increased due to the transnational corporate mergers and corporate investment that took place in the 90s of the last century (Caves, 1982; Johanson & Vahlne, 1993).

Nowadays globalization has an impact on nearly every aspect of our daily life (Al-Rodhan, 2006; Bordo et al., 1999; Crafts, 2000; IMF, 2000; Orlova, 2010; Stiglitz, 2000, 2004; World Bank, 1999, 2005, 2008, 2012).

In this paper we have paid special attention to the effects the globalization has made on the entrepreneurial conditions of the two countries such as Spain and Russia. We have analysed a new entrepreneurial situation that an entrepreneur may face with in setting up a new business.

There are some factors that influence the performance of the domestic small and medium-sized businesses. The increased multinational corporations' (MNCs) presence, for example, implies more intense product market competition that may cause the local firms will reduce the price markups leading to the reduction of their profits (Caves, 1982; Gorg & Greenway, 2004; Informe España, 2012; Saggi, 2002). From the other hand the linkages between MNCs and domestic firms create businesses opportunities and enhance their technological know-how and productivity (Javorcik, 2004).

From the other point of view, some typical characteristics of the companies such as organization size, simple structure or independent ownership can also perform as advantages or disadvantages. Small size provides a basis for specialization, often successful with niche strategies, but it results in limited financial and manpower resources, limited funds to finance investments and initial operating losses for new activates, etc. (Informe España, 1994, 2012; Izryadnova et al., 2009; Recklies, 2001).

Another subject that it is necessary to mention is the current economic and financial crisis. It has destabilized the usual performance of almost all economic sectors (Informe España, 1994, 2012; Zhavoronkov, 2009). The devastating effect of this phenomenon has influenced significantly the way the SMEs perform on the market (Camisón & De Lucio, 2010; Informe España, 1994, 2012; Kalinin, 2011; Zhavoronkov, 2009).

Nowadays the economic turbulence and the situation of uncertainty occur in the market constantly. This is characterized not only by the constantly changing environment which affects the way the companies develop their activity but also by the fact of the permanent technological revolution that makes everything become obsolete in short time (Informe España, 1994, 2012; Zhavoronkov, 2009).

3. The Paper of Entrepreneurship and SMEs in Spain

Nowadays the small and medium-sized company is the most important engine of a progress for any advanced capitalist society (Informe España, 1994, 2012; Izryadnova et al., 2009; Valdaliso, 1997).

SMEs are the key actors of a social and economic order contributing decisively to the economic growth, technological progress and job creation. In case of Spain, this potential has been multiplied due to the internalization, modernization and renewal that the national SME has developed over the past decades (Camisón & De Lucio, 2010; García Tabuenca et al., 2004; Informe España, 1994, 2012).

Throughout the nineteenth and twentieth century's the SMEs have predominated in almost all manufacturing and trade sectors of Spain creating almost all national productive structure of the country (Camisón, 2013; Comín & Aceña, 1996).

Some studies show that the national business register was already wide and varied during the Restoration period. In the first third of the twentieth century, the business landscape was represented not only by the ten largest corporations and some railway and mining companies, among others, but also by the companies of food industry and construction that was a major industry since the beginning of the cities' extension (Gómez Mendoza, 1986; Tafunell, 1992).

There were also services companies represented by the distribution, retail and hospitality industry. Small businesses dominated almost entirely in the sectors such as agriculture, flour, textiles and footwear. From the beginning of the twentieth century a smallholder commercial agriculture and export have expanded resulting in highly dynamic companies of Mediterranean areas (Barciela, 1996; Bernal, 1994; Palafox, 1996).

In the 50s and 60s a highly integrated and large-scale industry was imposed in all countries, including Spain (Informe España, 1994).

The economic crisis that started later due to increasing prices of oil has changed this situation profoundly. The stiffness of the large companies obstructed their adaptation to the new conditions causing severe economic and social problems. SMEs, however, have proved major capacity of flexibility in the new economic environment (Informe España, 1994).

During the "golden age" of the economic growth that lasted in Spain from 1999 to 2008, the enterprises with different sizes have grown significantly in volume and rates. In 2008, the Spanish business reached its zenith, estimated at 3.422.239 companies. According to Eurostat yearbook 2008, the SMEs represented 78% of the total number of enterprises that was higher than in EU, in average. The cyclic economic changes that began in 2008 have stopped this positive tendency. In absolute terms, the biggest decline has occurred in micro-enterprises sector. Critical situation has also formed in SMEs sector where there have been lost 49.895 and 6.466 companies, respectively, representing 29% and 22,4% of their total number in 2008 (Informe España, 2012).

4. Development and the Current State of the Small and Medium Business in Russia

The process of small business creation in Russia has begun in the second half of the 1980s through leasing relationships, self-employment and cooperatives. The process has passed through several stages (Kalinin, 2011; Rovenskii, 1996; Rybina, 2001).

In the first phase (1985-1992) it developed mainly in the form of cooperatives the main activity of which was small wholesale, retail trade and services. A large number of cooperatives at the big state enterprises and in the sphere of science was created. In 1987 a new law on "State-owned enterprises" introduced new methods of payment stimulating the development of new forms of leasing relationships. The law on "Self-employment" has removed restrictions on occupancy in popular arts, crafts and domestic services. The spontaneous creation of new companies has begun.

The second phase (1992-1994) is characterized by the expansion of the business sector. The price liberalization and massive privatization of the state-owned assets has led to a significant increase in the number of small businesses.

The third o modern stage of the SME sector development started in 1995. During this period the growth of the small sector has been significantly reduced. There were two main reasons. The first one was the lack of the effective institutional spheres. The second one consisted in orientation of Russian economy to the exploitation of the natural resources where the small business was not demanded by the primary production sector. This fact has led to a strong specialization of the small businesses guaranteeing the survival of many existing businesses and population in general (Shirabon, 2007).

The end of the 90s was characterized by the negative changes produced in the world situation that have led to a withdrawal of the capital from Russian financial markets. The Russian debt crisis of 1998 has become a new stage for the development of the SME sector creating opportunities in entering the market and niches of employment left by the big companies.

The period 2001-2008 was not characterized by a large-scale development of the SMEs as expected initially. There were two main reasons such as an increase of the economic barriers that blocked market entry and a failure in the attempt to reduce administrative restrictions.

Nowadays the development of the small and medium-sized business is highly controversial. The declarative government policy characterized by the separate and non-systemic measures slows down significantly the development of this sector (Esina & Vorotyntseva, 2001; Kalinin, 2011; Rostejnadzor: Nash region, 2009). Economic chaos and legal confusion have led to a situation where legitimate entrepreneurs have found themselves in an extremely difficult position (Ablyaev, 2008).

5. The Theory of Forgotten Effects

Mistakes and oversights have been made always as a result of human forgetfulness or neglect. Even with the help of the most advanced equipment for data processing and techniques designed for memory improvement the risk of forgetfulness won't disappear totally (Kaufmann & Gil Aluja, 1988).

When the sequences of incidents, inferences or consequences take place they are usually not treated properly. In order to improve the investigation relating to forgotten effects or oversights computers and adequate mathematical models are used.

These models are usually the graphs with binary values in the arcs or vertices; these graphs can be valued by numbers in [0;1] or intervals of confidence in [0;1]. The Boolean theory, the theory of fuzzy subsets or "expertons" are used.

The importance of the effects of the second, third, etc. generation is appreciable in all areas of decision making such as politics, economy and medicine, etc. (Kaufmann & Gil Aluja, 1988). The idea of the effects of the second generation in the socio-economic and ecologic fields has been developed by Jean Fourastié. Qualitative incidence matrices are used to investigate different mechanisms of cause-effect that it is not yet possible to find out with the help of intuition or experience (Gil Lafuente, 2001).

The following authors have dedicated their recent research works to the Theory of forgotten effects: A. Kaufmann, J. Gil Aluja, A. M. Gil Lafuente, among others (Gil Lafuente & Barcellos, 2010; Gil Lafuente & Klimova, 2013; Kaufmann & Gil Aluja, 1988).

6. Empirical Study

The objective of this study is to do a novel use of the "forgotten effects" method for the evaluation of the situation of entrepreneurship of two countries such as Spain and Russia.

This study demonstrates the differences these countries have in this area taking into account globalization and current economic crisis. We have used different opinions of the experts in relation to the concept such as "entrepreneurship" as well as the actions that affect its representative characteristics. Creating the cause-effect relationships between properties and actions we have obtained not only an overview of the existing conditions for entrepreneurship for each country but also the forgotten effects that are significant in the analysis but that have not been taken into account.

Entrepreneurial conditions are characterized by the following properties (subset *B*), which represent "effects" for our study:

A1. Growing interest in starting up new business
A2. Less competition on the market
A3. Higher interest credit rates
A4. Material supplies at cheaper prices
A5. Distrust of the investors
A6. Cheaper labor for hire
A7. Fewer customers in service and product sales sectors
A8. More affordable renting
A9. Uncertainty of politics for the local entrepreneurial activity
A10. Confidence of customers and markets in SMEs

The actions affecting the entrepreneurial activity (subset *A*) that represent "causes" are the following:

A1. Current financial and economic crisis
A2. Favorable taxation for SMEs
A3. State/ local legislation for SME development and better functioning
A4. Support programs and subsidies for SMEs
A5. Easy access to financing
A6. Easy access to business information (about a product, market, competition,...)
A7. Favorable legislation on SME workers' rights
A8. Absence of a positive image of the national entrepreneur
A9. Previous evaluation and risk tolerance
A10. Work in partnership with a faithful and secure partner
A11. Increasing number of motivated workers
A12. Programs and funding support provided by the partner countries (EU, USA, Japan, etc.)

The analysis of the relationships between each cause and effect gives a 12x10 rectangular matrix $\underset{\sim}{M}$ where the cells show the direct impact of each action on each property (cause-effect). The valuations are made using an endecadario system {0;0,1;...;0,9;1} assigning a number in [0;1] to each cell. A group of Spanish and Russian experts were interviewed in order to obtain the opinions with respect to the relationships.

The results are the following:

Let's determine an effect that a cause produces on itself and through another relationship such as effect-cause, so that the result of a direct cause as well as the result produced through an indirect way (side effect) will be accumulated in the total effect.

A square matrix $\underset{\sim}{A}$ is established where the "causes" are placed as the rows and columns. The causes represent the actions affecting the entrepreneurial activity whether positively or negatively. The experts are asked to give opinions about the incidence of each cause on the others. The valuation is made in [0;1].

$\underset{\sim}{M}$	B1	B2	B3	B4	B5	B6	B7	B8	B9	B10
A1	0,3	0,6	0,8	0,6	0,8	0,8	0,7	0,7	0,7	0,3
A2	0,8	0,2	0,6	0,2	0,3	0,2	0,2	0,1	0,2	0,5
A3	0,7	0,2	0,6	0,2	0,2	0,3	0,3	0,4	0,3	0,8
A4	0,8	0,1	0,7	0,2	0,2	0,2	0,2	0,5	0,2	0,7
A5	0,9	0,1	0,7	0,3	0,2	0,3	0,2	0,6	0,3	0,8
A6	0,7	0,5	0,4	0,1	0,1	0,1	0,3	0,4	0,1	0,7
A7	0,7	0,4	0,3	0	0,1	0,2	0,1	0,1	0,3	0,5
A8	0,7	0,5	0,3	0	0,8	0,1	0,7	0,1	0,3	0
A9	0,6	0,4	0,5	0,2	0,3	0,1	0,2	0,5	0,2	0,7
A10	0,7	0,3	0,4	0,3	0,2	0,1	0,1	0,4	0,2	0,7
A11	0,6	0,4	0,2	0	0,2	0,2	0	0	0,1	0,6
A12	0,3	0,3	0,4	0,1	0,1	0,2	0,1	0,4	0,1	0,6

Figure 1. $\underset{\sim}{M}$ for Spain.

$\underset{\sim}{M}$	B1	B2	B3	B4	B5	B6	B7	B8	B9	B10
A1	0,6	0,4	0,4	0,3	0,5	0,5	0,6	0,5	0,5	0,3
A2	0,6	0,4	0,3	0,2	0,4	0,3	0,2	0,1	0,3	0,2
A3	0,5	0,4	0,4	0,1	0,4	0,3	0,3	0,2	0,3	0,5
A4	0,6	0,3	0,5	0,1	0,5	0,2	0,2	0,3	0,2	0,6
A5	0,7	0,4	0,7	0,2	0,4	0,6	0,3	0,4	0,3	0,5
A6	0,5	0,3	0,4	0,1	0,2	0,2	0,3	0,2	0,1	0,4
A7	0,6	0,4	0,3	0	0,1	0,3	0,1	0	0,3	0,4
A8	0,3	0,7	0,8	0,2	0,8	0,3	0,7	0	0,5	0
A9	0,5	0,6	0,4	0,2	0,3	0,2	0,2	0,2	0,4	0,3
A10	0,6	0,5	0,4	0,2	0,3	0,1	0,1	0,2	0,4	0,4
A11	0,4	0,5	0,2	0	0,2	0,2	0	0	0,2	0,3
A12	0,5	0,5	0,6	0	0,4	0,3	0,1	0,3	0,3	0,5

Figure 2. $\underset{\sim}{M}$ for Russia.

$\underset{\sim}{A}$	A1	A2	A3	A4	A5	A6	A7	A8	A9	A10	A11	A12
A1	1	0,7	0,6	0,7	0,4	0,5	0,4	0,7	0,7	0,7	0,7	0,6
A2	0,4	1	0,7	0,7	0,7	0,3	0,5	0,1	0,6	0,3	0,4	0,5
A3	0,6	0,6	1	0,8	0,6	0,4	0,6	0,1	0,6	0,4	0,6	0,6
A4	0,6	0,5	0,8	1	0,8	0,3	0,6	0,1	0,6	0,3	0,6	0,4
A5	0,5	0,4	0,7	0,8	1	0,2	0,3	0,1	0,7	0,3	0,7	0,6
A6	0,4	0,1	0,7	0,7	0,6	1	0,2	0,1	0,5	0,2	0,4	0,3
A7	0,6	0,4	0,6	0,4	0,3	0,2	1	0,1	0,3	0,2	0,8	0,4
A8	0,1	0,1	0,2	0,2	0,2	0,1	0	1	0,1	0,1	0,2	0,1
A9	0,5	0,4	0,5	0,6	0,6	0,3	0,4	0	1	0,1	0,5	0,3
A10	0,4	0,4	0,3	0,4	0,6	0,2	0,5	0	0,4	1	0,6	0,2
A11	0,3	0	0,5	0,3	0,5	0,1	0,4	0,1	0,2	0,1	1	0,2
A12	0,6	0,4	0,7	0,6	0,7	0,2	0,6	0,1	0,6	0,1	0,7	1

Figure 3. $\underset{\sim}{A}$ for Spain.

$\underset{\sim}{A}$	A1	A2	A3	A4	A5	A6	A7	A8	A9	A10	A11	A12
A1	1	0,4	0,6	0,5	0,2	0,4	0,3	0,6	0,5	0,6	0,6	0,3
A2	0,4	1	0,7	0,6	0,5	0,3	0,3	0,1	0,6	0,3	0,3	0,4
A3	0,6	0,6	1	0,6	0,5	0,4	0,5	0,1	0,6	0,4	0,5	0,4
A4	0,5	0,4	0,6	1	0,6	0,3	0,4	0,1	0,6	0,3	0,5	0,3
A5	0,5	0,4	0,6	0,6	1	0,2	0,4	0,1	0,5	0,3	0,6	0,4
A6	0,3	0,1	0,5	0,4	0,3	1	0,2	0,1	0,4	0,2	0,2	0,3
A7	0,3	0,2	0,4	0,2	0,1	0,2	1	0,1	0,3	0,2	0,6	0,4
A8	0,1	0	0,2	0,2	0	0,1	0	1	0,1	0,1	0,2	0,1
A9	0,3	0,2	0,3	0,4	0,4	0,3	0,3	0	1	0,1	0,4	0,3
A10	0,3	0,2	0,3	0,3	0,3	0,2	0,3	0	0,3	1	0,4	0,2
A11	0,2	0	0,2	0,2	0,2	0,1	0,2	0,1	0,2	0,1	1	0,2
A12	0,4	0,3	0,5	0,5	0,5	0,2	0,4	0,1	0,4	0,2	0,5	1

Figure 4. $\underset{\sim}{A}$ for Russia.

A new square matrix $\underset{\sim}{B}$ is made by means of fuzzy cause-effect relationship where both rows and columns represent "effects" taken from the matrix $\underset{\sim}{M}$. The experts are interviewed to give their opinions about the impact of each effect on the others.

$\underset{\sim}{B}$	B1	B2	B3	B4	B5	B6	B7	B8	B9	B10
B1	1	0,2	0,5	0,4	0,2	0,2	0,2	0,2	0,2	0,7
B2	0,8	1	0,3	0,6	0,6	0,8	0,2	0,7	0,3	0,2
B3	0,4	0,6	1	0,3	0,8	0,7	0,1	0,6	0,4	0,2
B4	0,7	0,4	0,2	1	0,2	0,5	0,1	0,3	0,2	0,6
B5	0,2	0,7	0,8	0,4	1	0,7	0,3	0,6	0,3	0,2
B6	0,7	0,5	0,2	0	0,4	1	0,1	0,2	0,1	0,2
B7	0,4	0,2	0,3	0,7	0,6	0,7	1	0,6	0,2	0,1
B8	0,4	0,3	0,2	0,2	0,2	0,6	0,1	1	0,1	0,1
B9	0,3	0,6	0,6	0,4	0,5	0,6	0,2	0,6	1	0,1
B10	0,8	0,2	0,5	0,5	0	0,3	0,1	0,3	0,1	1

Figure 5. $\underset{\sim}{B}$ for Spain.

$\underset{\sim}{A}$	B1	B2	B3	B4	B5	B6	B7	B8	B9	B10
B1	1	0,2	0,2	0,3	0,2	0,3	0,2	0,2	0,3	0,5
B2	0,6	1	0,3	0,5	0,4	0,8	0,3	0,6	0,4	0,2
B3	0,2	0,6	1	0,2	0,6	0,5	0,1	0,6	0,5	0,2
B4	0,6	0,4	0,2	1	0,2	0,4	0,1	0,3	0,2	0,4
B5	0,4	0,7	0,6	0,3	1	0,7	0,3	0,4	0,5	0,2
B6	0,6	0,5	0,2	0	0,4	1	0,1	0,2	0,3	0,2
B7	0,3	0,3	0,3	0,4	0,6	0,5	1	0,6	0,3	0,1
B8	0,4	0,3	0,4	0,1	0,2	0,4	0,1	1	0,1	0,1
B9	0,2	0,6	0,8	0,3	0,8	0,8	0,2	0,5	1	0,1
B10	0,6	0,3	0,3	0,3	0,1	0,4	0,1	0,3	0,1	1

Figure 6. $\underset{\sim}{B}$ for Russia.

Basing on the fuzzy matrixes of incidence such as $\underset{\sim}{M}$, $\underset{\sim}{A}$ and $\underset{\sim}{B}$ and, in order to get accumulated effects of the 1 and 2 generations a new fuzzy matrix of incidence such as $\underset{\sim}{M}^* = \underset{\sim}{A} \circ \underset{\sim}{M} \circ \underset{\sim}{B}$ is obtained by means of maximin convolution between $\underset{\sim}{M}$, $\underset{\sim}{A}$ and $\underset{\sim}{B}$. The results are the following:

$\underset{\sim}{M}^*$	B1	B2	B3	B4	B5	B6	B7	B8	B9	B10
A1	0,7	0,7	0,8	0,7	0,8	0,8	0,7	0,7	0,7	0,7
A2	0,8	0,6	0,7	0,5	0,7	0,7	0,4	0,6	0,4	0,7
A3	0,8	0,6	0,7	0,6	0,7	0,7	0,6	0,6	0,6	0,8
A4	0,8	0,6	0,7	0,6	0,7	0,7	0,6	0,6	0,6	0,8
A5	0,9	0,6	0,7	0,5	0,7	0,7	0,5	0,6	0,5	0,8
A6	0,7	0,6	0,7	0,5	0,7	0,7	0,4	0,6	0,4	0,7
A7	0,7	0,6	0,6	0,6	0,6	0,6	0,6	0,6	0,6	0,7
A8	0,7	0,7	0,8	0,7	0,8	0,7	0,7	0,6	0,3	0,7
A9	0,7	0,6	0,6	0,5	0,6	0,6	0,5	0,6	0,5	0,7
A10	0,7	0,6	0,6	0,5	0,6	0,6	0,4	0,6	0,4	0,7
A11	0,6	0,5	0,5	0,5	0,5	0,5	0,3	0,5	0,4	0,6
A12	0,7	0,6	0,7	0,6	0,7	0,7	0,6	0,6	0,6	0,7

Figure 7. $\underset{\sim}{M}^*$ for Spain.

In order to find the effects of the 2 generation it is necessary to separate the direct effects given by means of $\underset{\sim}{M}$ from the accumulated effects of $\underset{\sim}{M}^*$. In this case a simple algebraic difference $\underset{\sim}{M}^* - \underset{\sim}{M}$ is made. The matrix $\underset{\sim}{M}^* - \underset{\sim}{M}$ shown in the figures 9 and 10 represents the effects of the second generation. It can be seen some cells where the figures are close to unit. For Spain these cells are the following: (8;4) the effect of "Absence of a positive image of the national entrepreneur" on "Material supplies at cheaper prices" with 0,7; (8;10) the effect of "Absence of a positive image of the national entrepreneur" on "Confidence of customers and markets in SMEs" with 0,7; (8;6) the effect of "Absence of a positive image of the national entrepreneur" on "Cheaper labor for hire" with 0,6; (12;5) the effect of "Programs and funding support provided by the partner countries (EU, USA, Japan, China, etc.)" on "Distrust of the investors" with 0,6; (6;5) the effect of "Easy access to business information (about a product, market, competition, etc.)" on "Distrust of the investors" with 0,6; (6;6) the effect of "Easy access to business information (about a product, market, competition, etc.)" on "Cheaper labor for hire" with 0,6.

$\underset{\sim}{M}^*$	**B1**	**B2**	**B3**	**B4**	**B5**	**B6**	**B7**	**B8**	**B9**	**B10**
A1	0,6	0,6	0,6	0,5	0,6	0,6	0,6	0,6	0,5	0,5
A2	0,6	0,6	0,5	0,5	0,5	0,6	0,4	0,6	0,5	0,6
A3	0,6	0,6	0,5	0,5	0,6	0,6	0,6	0,6	0,5	0,6
A4	0,6	0,6	0,6	0,5	0,6	0,6	0,5	0,6	0,5	0,6
A5	0,7	0,6	0,7	0,5	0,6	0,6	0,5	0,6	0,5	0,6
A6	0,5	0,4	0,4	0,4	0,4	0,4	0,3	0,4	0,4	0,5
A7	0,6	0,5	0,4	0,5	0,4	0,5	0,3	0,5	0,4	0,5
A8	0,6	0,7	0,8	0,5	0,8	0,7	0,7	0,6	0,5	0,3
A9	0,6	0,6	0,4	0,5	0,4	0,6	0,3	0,6	0,4	0,5
A10	0,6	0,5	0,4	0,5	0,4	0,5	0,3	0,5	0,4	0,5
A11	0,5	0,5	0,3	0,5	0,4	0,5	0,3	0,5	0,4	0,4
A12	0,5	0,6	0,6	0,5	0,6	0,5	0,4	0,6	0,5	0,5

Figure 8. $\underset{\sim}{M}^*$ for Russia.

	B1	**B2**	**B3**	**B4**	**B5**	**B6**	**B7**	**B8**	**B9**	**B10**
A1	0,4	0,1	0	0,1	0	0	0	0	0	0,4
A2	0	0,4	0,1	0,3	0,4	0,5	0,2	0,5	0,2	0,2
A3	0,1	0,4	0,1	0,4	0,5	0,4	0,3	0,2	0,3	0
A4	0	0,5	0	0,4	0,5	0,5	0,4	0,1	0,4	0,1
A5	0	0,5	0	0,2	0,5	0,4	0,3	0	0,2	0
A6	0	0,1	0,3	0,4	0,6	0,6	0,1	0,2	0,3	0
A7	0	0,2	0,3	0,6	0,5	0,4	0,5	0,5	0,3	0,2
A8	0	0,2	0,5	0,7	0	0,6	0	0,5	0	0,7
A9	0,1	0,2	0,1	0,3	0,3	0,5	0,3	0,1	0,3	0
A10	0	0,3	0,2	0,2	0,4	0,5	0,3	0,2	0,2	0
A11	0	0,1	0,3	0,5	0,3	0,3	0,3	0,5	0,3	0
A12	0,4	0,3	0,3	0,5	0,6	0,5	0,5	0,2	0,5	0,1

Figure 9. $\underset{\sim}{M}^* - \underset{\sim}{M}$ for Spain.

For Russia these cells are the following: (8;8) the effect of "Absence of a positive image of the national entrepreneur" on "More affordable renting" with 0,6; (7;4) the effect of "Favorable legislation on SME workers' rights" on "Material supplies at cheaper prices" with 0,5; (7;8) the effects of "Favorable legislation on SME workers' rights" on "More affordable renting" with 0,5; (11;4) the effects of "Increasing number of motivated workers" on "Material supplies at cheaper prices" with 0,5; (11;8) the effects of "Increasing number of motivated workers" on "More affordable renting" with 0,5; (12;4) the effect of "Programs and funding support provided by the partner countries" on "Material supplies at cheaper prices" with 0,5. These relationships of cause have not been taken into account, that is the case of cells with 0,7 level or, these relationships have been considered as "too weak", that is the case of cells with 0,6 level. The proposed technique allows recovering the effects forgotten initially in the analysis. In order to find a maximum cumulative incidence, that is to say, an optimal way of incidence of the cause a_i on the effect b_j it is necessary to do a series of steps using the max-min convolution. The process will begin from the element a_i checking incidence of a_i on itself and of a_i on $b_1, b_2, \ldots, b_n$ and of each b_n (n = 1,2,...,10) on b_n.

	B1	**B2**	**B3**	**B4**	**B5**	**B6**	**B7**	**B8**	**B9**	**B10**
A1	0	0,2	0,2	0,2	0,1	0,1	0	0,1	0	0,2
A2	0	0,2	0,2	0,3	0,1	0,3	0,2	0,5	0,2	0,4
A3	0,1	0,2	0,1	0,4	0,2	0,3	0,3	0,4	0,2	0,1
A4	0	0,3	0,1	0,4	0,1	0,4	0,3	0,3	0,3	0
A5	0	0,2	0	0,3	0,2	0	0,2	0,2	0,2	0,1
A6	0	0,1	0	0,3	0,2	0,2	0	0,2	0,3	0,1
A7	0	0,1	0,1	0,5	0,3	0,2	0,2	0,5	0,1	0,1
A8	0,3	0	0	0,3	0	0,4	0	0,6	0	0,3
A9	0,1	0	0	0,3	0,1	0,4	0,1	0,4	0	0,2
A10	0	0	0	0,3	0,1	0,4	0,2	0,3	0	0,1
A11	0,1	0	0,1	0,5	0,2	0,3	0,3	0,5	0,2	0,1
A12	0	0,1	0	0,5	0,2	0,2	0,3	0,3	0,2	0

Figure 10. $\underset{\sim}{M}^{*} - \underset{\sim}{M}$ for Russia.

The results of the maximum accumulative incidence for Spain are the following: A8-A8-B7-B4; A8-A8-B1-B10; A8-A8-B5(B7)-B6; A12-A12-B3-B5; A6-A6-B3-B5; A6-A6-B3-B6.

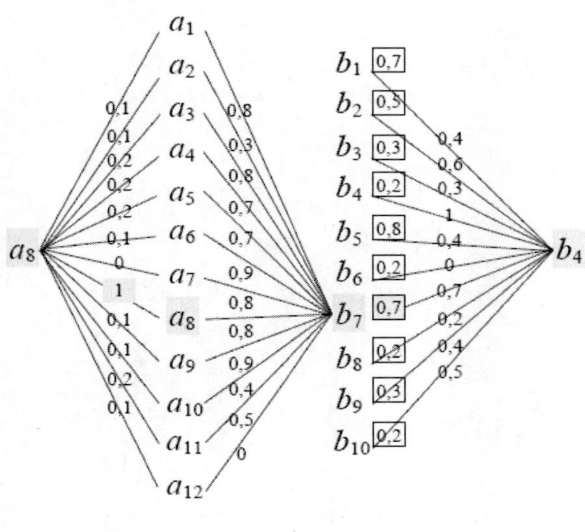

Figure 11. A8-A8-B7-B4.

The figures 11 and 12 represent the way that it is possible to follow to get from the cause 8 (Absence of a positive image of the national entrepreneur) to the effect 4 (Material supplies at cheaper prices) and, from the cause 8 (Absence of a positive image of the national entrepreneur) to the effect 10 (Confidence of customers and markets in SMEs) which relationships had been forgotten or ignored by the consulted experts by assigning them a valuation of 0. The results for the rest of the cases are mentioned above.

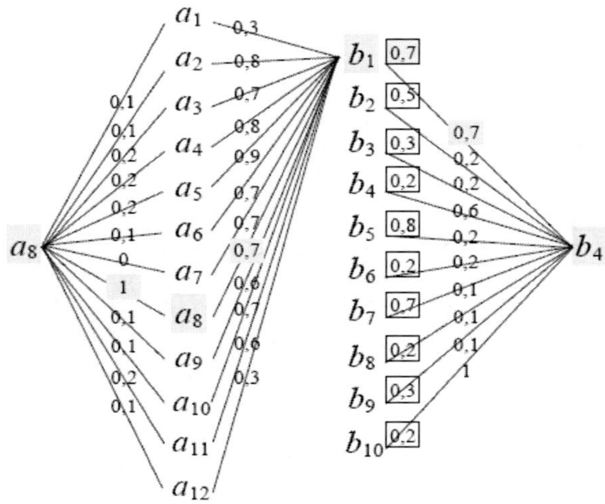

Figure 12. A8-A8-B1-B10.

The results of the maximum accumulative incidence for Russia are the following: A8-A8-B2(B3,B7)-B8; A7-A7-B2-B4; A7-A7-B2-B8; A11-A11-B2-B4; A11-A11-B2-B8; A12-A12-B2-B4.

The figures 13 and 14 represent the ways it is possible to follow to get from the cause 8 (Absence of a positive image of the national entrepreneur) to the effect 8 (More affordable renting) which relationship had been forgotten or ignored by the consulted experts by assigning it a valuation of 0. The results for the rest of the cases are mentioned above.

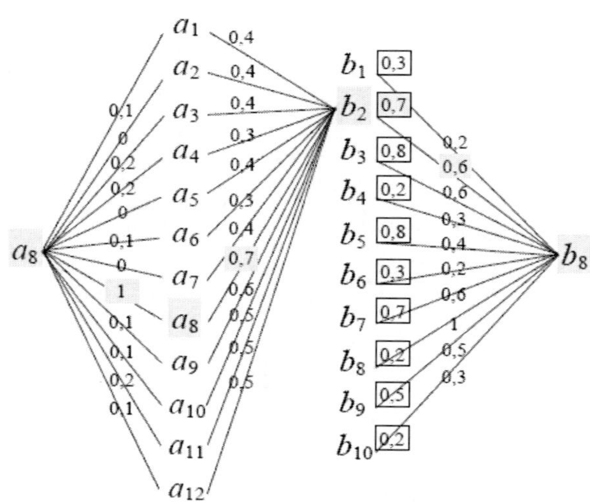

Figure 13. A8-A8-B2-B8.

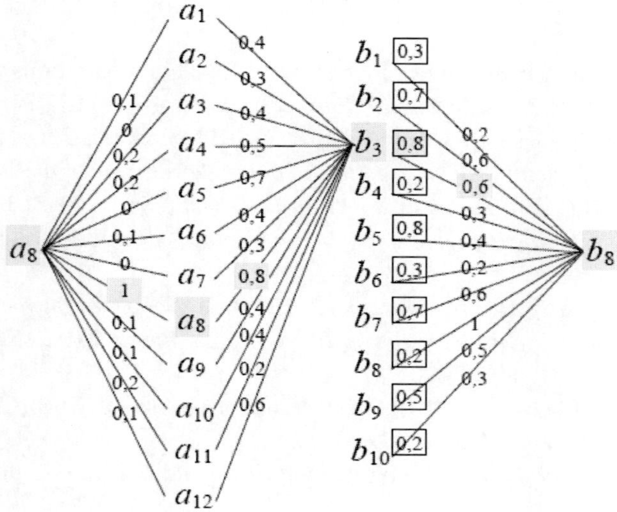

Figure 14. A8-A8-B3-B8.

CONCLUSION

In this paper we have used the technique based on the Theory of forgotten effects that allows recovering the relationships of causes and effects forgotten or omitted initially but which are important in the decision making. This method has been used for the analysis of the current economic and financial situation in the SME sector. International globalization and the current economic crises have changed significantly the conditions of the enterprises' performance at the local markets as well as at the world markets. Nowadays each entrepreneur has to take into account new conditions at the moment of setting up a business abroad. In this context we considered the technique based on the Theory of forgotten effects as one of the most adequate for the evaluation of the possible market opportunities and threats without omitting initial data.

The paper consists of some parts where we describe briefly: structural changes produced in the world economy due to globalization and the current economic crisis; new conditions the small and medium-sized enterprises have to take into account to perform at the global market; the role the SME sector plays in the economy of two countries such as Spain and Russia; theoretical aspects of the mathematical method based on the forgotten effects theory; empirical study and conclusions.

The obtained results prove the accuracy we have had in choosing the method for analysis. We have detected the relationships that have been omitted by the experts but which are significant in the decision making. As a future proposal we suggest to continue to develop the empirical part using an input data basis wider than it have been proposed initially. The results could provide a complete panorama on the current conditions of the SME sector that exist in both countries and could serve as an action guide for any entrepreneur who wants to set up a new business abroad.

REFERENCES

Ablyaev, S. (2008), The mechanism of functioning of financial institutions in lending to small and medium-sized enterprises, *Russian Entrepreneurship*, 7(1/114), 34-39.

Al-Rodhan N.R.F. (2006), The pillars of globalization, Ed. Slatkine, Genève.

Barciela, C. (1996), *Agricultural enterprises and the development of Spanish agriculture during the twentieth century*, in Comín y Martín Aceña (eds.), 203-218.

Bernal, A.M. (1994), *The agricultural company in Spain* (XIX and XX century), in Núñez y Segreto (eds.), 141-164.

Bordo, M.D., Eichengreen, B. and Irwin, D.A. (1999), *Is globalization today really different than globalization a hundred years ago?* Working Paper 7195, National Bureau of Economic Research, Cambridge.

Camisón, C. and De Lucio, J. (2010), The competitiveness of Spanish SMEs faces the challenge of globalization, *Industrial economy*, 375.

Caves, R.E. (1982), *Multinational enterprise and economic analysis*, Cambridge University Press, Cambridge.

Camisón, C. (2013), *SMEs and the exit of the crisis*, http://www.informe-espana.es/participa/blogs/posts/700/las-pymes-y-la-salida-de-la-crisis

Comín, F. and Aceña P.M. (1996), *Historical features of companies' development in Spain: an overview*, University of Alcalá and Public Enterprise Foundation.

Crafts, N. (2000), *Globalization and Growth in the Twentieth Century*, IMF Working Paper, WP/00/44, Washington.

Demirgüç-Kunt, A. and Detragiache, E. (2001), Financial liberalization and financial fragility, in G. Caprio, P. Honohan, and J. E. Stiglitz, (eds.), *Financial Liberalization: How far, How fast?*, Cambridge University Press. Cambridge, 96-122.

Esina, Y. and Vorotyntseva, S. (2001), Features of the legal framework creation of the state support of small business in Russia, *Russian Entrepreneurship*, 1(1/175), 16-22.

Fletcher, R. (2001), A holistic approach to internationalisation, *International Business Review*, 10(1), 25-49.

García Tabuenca, A., Moreno, J. and Martí, F. (2004), Entrepreneurs and entrepreneurship in Spain in the twenty-first century: report on entrepreneurship. *Businesses and entrepreneurs in Spain: Causes, attitudes, opportunities and threats,* Madrid, Marcial Pons, Rafael del Pino Foundation.

Gil Lafuente, A.M. (2001), *New strategies for financial analysis in uncertainty*, Ariel, Barcelona.

Gil Lafuente, A.M. and Barcellos, L. (2010), *An application of the methodology of the forgotten affects: the factors that contribute to sustainable growth of the company*, Cuadernos de CIMBAGE, 12, 23-52.

Gil Lafuente, A.M., Klimova, A. and Kondratenko, Y. P. (2013), *From the repeated errors in the occurrence of crisis to the sustainable social welfare*, Proceedings of the International Conference on Automatic Control. Mykolayiv, Ukraine, September 25-27, 2013.

Gómez Mendoza, A. (1986), The residual construction industry: Madrid 1820-1935, *Money and Credit*, 53-85.

Gorg, H. and Greenway, D. (2004), Much ado about nothing? Do domestic firms really benefit from foreign direct investment? *The World Bank Research Observer*, 19(2), 171-197.

IMF (2000), *Globalization: Threat or opportunity*? http://www.imf.org/external/np/exr/ib/2000/esl/041200s.htm#P129_14009

IMF (2000), *Progress in strengthening the architecture of the international monetary system, fuente*: http://www.imf.org/external/np/exr/facts/arcguide.htm

Izryadnova, O., Fomina, E. and Kazantsev, D. (2009), Small business in Russia: current situation and problems, *Economic and political situation in Russia* 07'2009, 58-69, www.iet.ru

Javorcik, B.S. (2004), Does foreign direct investment increase the productivity of domestic firms?, *American Economic Review*, 94 (3), 605-627.

Johanson, J. and Vahlne, J. (1977), The Internationalization process of the firm - a model of knowledge development and increasing foreign market commitments, *Journal of International Business Studies*, 8(1), 23-32.

Johanson, J. and Vahlne, J.-E. (1993), Management of internationalisation, in Z. L. Zambou and A. M. Pettigrew (eds), *Perspectives on strategic change*, Kluwer Academic Publishers, Boston, 43-78.

Kalinin, A.V. (2011), Key trends and characteristics of small and medium business in Russia, *Russian Entrepreneurship*, 1(2/176), 30-35.

Kaufmann, A. and Gil Aluja, J. (1988), *Models for forgotten effects research*, Milladoiro, Santiago de Compostela.

Orlova, M. (2010), Contradictions of the globalization process, *Entrepreneurship*, 4, 95-98.

Palafox, J. (1996), Export expansion, growth, industrial diversification and industrialization, in J. Azagra, E. Maateu y J. Vidal (eds.), *From traditional society to the modern economy*, Alicante, Diputación Provincial, 321-345.

Recklies, D. (2001), Impact of globalization on small and medium-sized enterprises (SMEs), *The Manager* (Electronic Journal), http://www.themanager.org/strategy/global.htm#[2]

Report: Spain (1994), *Fundación Encuentro*, isbn: 84-89019-01-0.

Rostechnadzor (Federal Environmental, Industrial and Nuclear Supervision Service): Our region (2009), *The impact of the crisis in the Russian economy on small businesses*, 4, http://www.energopress.ru/allmaterials/1302/ http://bishelp.ru/ekonomika/detail.php?ID=78156

Rovenskii, Y. (1996), The evolution of small business in Russia, *Socio-political magazine*, 2.

Rybina, M. (2001), *Main stages of small business creation in the conditions of modern radical market reforms in Russia*, 2, http://www.cfin.ru/press/management/2001-2/ribina.shtml

Saggi, K. (2002), Trade, foreign direct investment and international technology transfer: a survey, *World Bank Research Observer*, 17(2), 191-235.

Shirabon, N. (2007), State support of small business in Russia, *Economics and Management*, 2, 129-132.

Stiglitz, J.E. (2000), Capital market liberalization, economic growth and instability, *World Development*, 28(6), 1075-86.

Stiglitz, J.E. (2004), Capital-market liberalization, globalization, and the IMF, *Oxford Review of Economic Policy*, 20(1), 57-71.

Tafunell, X. (1992), Construction in Barcelona, 1860-1935: Continuity and change, in García Delgado (ed.), *Cities in the modernization of Spain*, 3-20.

Valdaliso, J.M. (1997), The history of business sector in Spain. Origins, development and controversies in a new discipline. *Latin America in economic history*, 7, 103-132

World Bank (1999;2005;2008;2012), *Global economic prospects*, Washington, DC, World Bank.

Zhavoronkov, S. (2009), Political and economic results of July 2009, *Economic and political situation in Russia* 07'2009, 4-8, www.iet.ru

In: Computational Data Analysis Techniques
Editors: M. Doumpos, C. Zopounidis and Ch. Gaganis
ISBN: 978-1-63463-957-6

Chapter 15

THE EFFICIENCY OF GREEK CONSTRUCTION COMPANIES: A DEA AND DEA-PROBABILISTIC NEURAL NETWORK APPROACH

Eirini Lazaridou[1]*, Efstratios Livanis[2#] and Ioannis Lazaridis[2‡]
[1]Aristotle University, Greece
[2]University of Macedonia, Greece

ABSTRACT

The Construction Sector is very important for the development and growth of national economy. The development of these companies is a sign of growth and prosperity. The purpose of this paper is to evaluate the profitability and efficiency of Construction Companies through the consideration of DEA (Data Envelopment Analysis) method during the period of 2004-2011. These years are very critical because they refer to the period before and after the Greece's entry into the financial crisis. Moreover, we extend our analysis using a DEA – PNN approach in order to classify Greek Construction Companies as efficient or inefficient. Therefore, this analysis and its results are very important for the viability and future of construction companies, especially under the current climate of uncertainty.

Keywords: DEA, neural networks, efficiency, construction sector, Greece
JEL: G39, C45, O16

1. INTRODUCTION

In recent years, given the international financial crisis, it is observed that the construction industry is badly suffering, dragging down dozens of companies such as the building

* PhD Student, rinolaz@hotmail.com
# Lecturer, slivanis@uom.gr
‡ Professor, +302310891697, lazarid@uom.gr

materials industries, which have also entered into deep crisis. With this situation prevailing in the construction industry, we felt it appropriate to study its effectiveness for the five years 2007-2011, when crisis strongly appeared in Greece. We tried to verify the theoretical framework of the examination using non-parametric models, and more specifically the DEA model.

2. LITERATURE REVIEW

This paper, describes a series of studies by which we tried initially to identify the indicators and methods that should be used to assess efficiency.

Libby (1975), used the Factor Analysis Method in order to select five of the fourteen financial ratios. He chooses these five indicators because only them have such a good predictive power in random samples, as showed by the Chi-square test results as well as the F-test results. This model had achieved predictive power 74%, a percentage which renders the model quite effective. Still, Mason and Harris (1979) based on studies on construction companies in Britain, concluded that six are the financial ratios which can be used as indicators to assess efficiency. The ROA, the ROI index, the capital movement, the financial leverage, the average time of payment obligations and the trend of accounts receivable can be included to assess efficiency. On this basis, they constructed a model in order to predict crisis in the construction industry using the discriminant analysis. By using this model, it appears that the ratios of ROA and ROI are the most significant ratios.

Kangari and Elgharid, (1992) used financial ratios to assess effectiveness in construction companies in the U.S.A. The financial indicators were divided into three categories that included six financial ratios. These indicators were used in order to separate the business into five groups, according to their performance, through the method of regression.

Langford et al. (Langford, Iyagba and Komba, 1993) made an analysis through the use of ratios and discriminant analysis to find out if the construction companies in the United Kingdom tended to bankruptcy. Six indicators were used again, to predict the financial crisis of business. The financial indicators proposed by Mason and Harris in 1979 were used in discriminant analysis and brought answers to questions of efficiency.

Kimberly Cleason, Lynette Knowles Mathur and IkeMathur (2000), studied initially the effect of national culture and further the relationship between capital structure and performance in the company. This study found, through the method of regression, that capital structure varies depending on the cultural classification of the retailer. The results showed that the conflicts of businesses due to overleveraged vendors resulted to a negative relationship between capital structure and performance.

Cheah et al. (Cheah, Garvin and Millen, 2004) presented an empirical study of factors that contributed to the success and failure of 24 major international construction companies headquartered in the U.S., Europe and Spain. They used the foundation of analysis to show the effectiveness which results from financial ratios, including the index of ROA and ROE.

McCabe and Tran Ramani (2005) applied the DEA model using the concept of scoring criteria, as selection criterion for construction companies, in order to find the efficient frontier for these companies. In their turn, Chung Yee Yan and Charles Y. J. Cheah (2006), worked on the effectiveness of large international construction companies in areas of North America, Europe and East Asia through the fundamental and sceening methods. Through this method, they concluded to the fact that firm size and profitability are two sizes independent of each other. Ocal, Oral, Erdis and Vural (2007) deduced to the fact that there are 25 indicators that are important for analyzing the construction sector and can describe its trend.

In 2010, Kim and Nam (2010) tried to analyze the efficiency of construction companies with comprehensive construction capability. Lee, Moon and Kim (Moon and Kim, 2000) analyzed the efficiency of construction companies aiming to help select a contractor company in order to carry on the construction project.

El-Mashaleh deploy DEA in order to measure and compare subcontractors' productivity at the firm-level as well as to evaluate the firm- level performance of construction companies (El-Mashaleh, 2003, El-Mashaleh et al., 2005, El Mashaleh et al., 2007).

Chau and Wang (2003) and Chau et al. (2005), tried to measure the Productivity efficiency in Hong Kong while Sueyoshi and Goto (Sueyoshi and Goto, 2009) and Chiang et al. (Chiang et al., 2006) used the DEA model in order to evaluate the construction industry policies in Japan.

3. The Construction Sector in Greece

The structure of the construction sector is simpler than others equally important sectors of the Greek Economy (Studies and Reasearch Center Commerce and Industry of Athens, 2007). The distinction between wholesale and retail business sales is not obvious. The construction companies are primarily the companies that supply finished products and offer them for sale to the buying public. Moreover, the foreign trade indicators of the industry remain low. The construction companies in the domestic market tend to concentrate their activities. Nevertheless, there are companies that in their future plans include investments in emerging markets. For example, the corporate group of "Michaniki" (Michaniki: A Group of Companies, 2012) plans investments in Bulgaria, Russia and Ukraine (Michaniki: A Group of Companies, 2012), while the company of ''J & P Avax" (J & P AVAX: Interim Financial Statements, 2011) plans to move to Ethiopia. But this fact concerns a small percentage of the overall total.

The year 2007 marks the recovery at both levels of economic growth in businesses and stock returns. Large corporate groups have secured multiple contracts easily unenforceable, compared to those of the Olympic Games period. For 2007-2013, it is planned to apply a new generation of construction projects, amounting to 20 billion euros. This amount also includes the disposal of 10 billion euros for 7 major projects in Greece, which are assigned to large companies in the construction market. The recovery in the sector of the construction market is referred mainly to large construction companies which should have in their disposal the appropriate infrastructure and the required capital to cover construction costs, in order to take over large projects and participate successfully in the competition. Moreover, an important factor in recent years is acquisitions and mergers.

Generally, the construction sector in Greece still tries to recover after the success which was seen in the Olympic Games period in Athens. There are many large construction companies that are able to support the overall improvement of the industry and in relation to the underlying mergers with multinational giants, even in the short term. The industry has the required infrastructure and dynamism and what is lacking is a push which can occur either in the form of new generation construction projects for the period 2007-2013 or in the form of sharpening the competitiveness by making Greek companies more active in major projects. Besides, it should be considered that the form of oligopolistic market, exemplified by the raise in objective values of properties, is keeping prices high.

3.1. The Image of the Sector

The study conducted by the Association of Greek Limited Liability Companies and Personal Techniques (Santorineou, 2011), record appalling conditions for the construction industry. According to data during the period 2004 – 2012, 158 companies closed (Technical Champer of Greece, 2011) and the number of construction companies leapt from 7th up to third place, declining by 22.2%, from 712 to 554 companies (Economists & Accountants Association of Thessaloniki, 2012). Especially a 35.7% decrease is recorded. However, the reducing number did not mean better conditions for the remaining companies.

Indicative of the situation is the average turnover over time, which is significantly reduced. Specifically: The 13.4 million which was the average turnover in 2008 reached 11.8 million euros in 2009, a decrease of 11.3% and 10.1 million euros in 2010 a decrease of 15.3%. This situation marks the systematic reduction of the public investment program, that is to say 5.4% of the GDP in 2000, in contrast with 3.2% in 2011. Specifically, on February 2011 the turnover of the sector declined by 24.3% to 3.9 billion euros, EBITDA reduced by 43.5% to 267.4 million and losses of 148.2, million euros were recorded in contrast with the 36.8 million euros profit in 2009 (Michaniki, 2010).

During the first quarter of 2011 the value of the production index in construction (Association of Greek Contracting Companies, Limited Liability Companies and Personal Engineering, 2011) is receiving the lowest value for the period 2001-2011, that is 54.5 million euros, reduced by 16.9% , compared to 2010, and by 57.6% compared to the value of the third quarter of 2008 (128.47). The prolonged downturn in the sector emerges from the decline of more than 11 consecutive quarters in the price of production index in construction, which is attributed both to the adverse changes in the market field for private projects and to those changes observed in the field of public works.

The deliberate delay of the exploitation of the infrastructure spending program involves not only the public investment and the reduced absorption of funds from the European Union, but also the delay in creation, improvement and maintenance of infrastructure, which in turn ends up to a significant slowdown in labor productivity and growth of the economy.

3.2. The Prospects for Improvement for the Sector

About the future of this sector, we can say that it depends on two factors (Technical Chamber of Greece, 2011): the political system and the development path, something that has not been seen by any political force. Thus, Greece can escape crisis only if an immediate innovative plan is going to be implemented for the improvement of the infrastructure, a plan that will simulate the construction market. Historically, all countries like Greece, faced crisis applying a large infrastructure project, which is even easier now can be used a new production model. Moreover, we observe that the ESPA is lagging behind, although it has been programmed by the European Union to cover 95% of the project's budget by EU funds while the country would have to submit only 5% of the amount as national participation (Economists & Accountants Association of Thessaloniki, 2012).

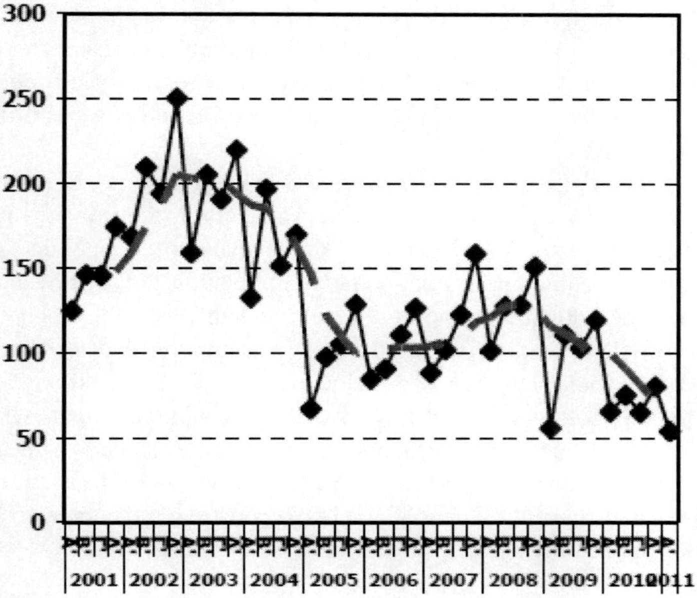

Figure 1. The Quarterly Production Index in Construction Sector & Moving Average of 3 months.

Also, the co-financed projects have stopped and remains unclear what will happen and whether to proceed or not the projects for completion. Also, a significant negative factor is the fact that companies experience both the closure of their companies and the loss of qualified persons that they have profit by in previous years with the Olympic Games projects.

4. The DEA Method

First of all, it is worth mentioning that the selection of indicators and sizes for the evaluation of companies is something which is derived either from the personal assessments of the researcher or from conclusions derived from questionnaires or even directly from other surveys, without any selection process (Chiu and Wang, 2011). Also, it is worth mentioning, that although so far we were using the Factors Analysis, the Discriminate Analysis, the Multi-criteria evaluation and the Regression Analysis method to draw conclusions about the effectiveness, in recent years we use the DEA method.

The DEA method uses a series of inputs and outputs to measure the effectiveness of construction companies and produces the ideal group of weights, using the linear programming while overcoming the problems of the weights of the evaluation index (Pilates, 2000). Moreover, this method combines the inputs and outputs that were chosen and calculates the relative effectiveness of each Decision Management Unit (DMU), identifying the degree of efficiency and inefficiency, making a comparative evaluation between the construction companies which are under study (Chiu and Wang, 2011).

This study makes use of the well-known Charnes-Cooper-Rhodes (CCR) model of DEA to benchmark the performance of the Greek construction companies (Charnes A. et al., 1978). In this model, the objective function is to maximize the efficiency of DMU which is under evaluation and for this purpose it yields efficiency scores that range between 0 and 1.0. The logic of this method is that the efficient companies stand on the efficient frontier and the rest are compared to these. DEA considers a DMU as the entity responsible for converting inputs (i.e. resourches, money, etc.) into outputs (i.e. sales, profits, certain performance measures etc.), (El- Mashaleh et al., 2010).

DEA is based on a concept of efficiency that is widely used in engineering and natural science. The 'added value' which is added due to production is the reason why the concept of engineering efficiency is not immediate applicable to economic production. In microeconomics, the feasible input and output combinations of the available production technology create the production possibility. Also in this analysis, the technological relations create the set of efficient production based on the assumption that all firms that operated efficiently are on the efficient frontier. Consequently, the technological inefficiencies are out of the question. At this point we should specify the inputs and the outputs which we will use in our CCR-model. The inputs and the outputs which were needed to measure efficiency include labor force, machinery, material, etc. These data were hard to acquire in mass so we will try to approach the cost efficiency of Greek construction companies by using data derived from their financial statement. Based on these elements, we aim to evaluate the cost efficiency of the construction sector in Greece.

More specifically, in our paper we define as inputs the Net Fixed Assets (the Capital), the Total Operating Expenses, the Cost of Goods Sold and the Total Equity while as outputs only the measurement of sales. This choice was based on the corresponding selection (Kim and Choi, 2011) of Hing-Yi Chiu, Mei-Wei Wang and Jung-Lo, Sung-Sik Kim, Sun-Young Choi, Ju-Hyung Kim and Jae-Jun Kim studied in related articles (Chiu and Wang, 2011) and Dzeng Ren-Jye and Wu Jih- Shong (Dzeng Ren-Jye et al., 2012). The selection of inputs and outputs must be performed endogenous to the DEA model by incorporating the reward metric (i.e. sales in our example) as an external variable (Edirisinghe N.C.P. et al., 2010). The Total Operating Cost, which is derived from the income statement, includes mainly the cost of goods sold and it also includes fund cost, labor cost and capital cost. The Cost of Goods Sold is a variable which we choose to examine separately in order to determine its exact role on efficiency.

The capital is acquired from the balance sheet and it is the net value of fixed asset which includes: a) land, b) depreciable assets, such as factory, mechanical equipment, transportation equipment, etc., excluding the aforementioned depreciation (Dzeng Ren-Jye et al., 2012). Sales are acquired from income statement and are used as an output factor due to the fact that they represent the operational performance of a construction enterprise. Consequently, they are the most frequently used output in a efficiency analysis.

The factors of: profits of a company including pretax income, the operating cash flow, the net profit during the term and the net income which subtracts expenses from profits and arise from the production activities of an enterprise, represent all the managerial activities although they cannot be used in our method, as they appear negative prices in some cases (Park Jubg-Lo et al., 2011). At this point it is worth noting that some of the measurements, which were considered as outputs for these authors, were not considered as such in our research. The reason is that they presented negative values in the course of the period 2007-2011 and the international literature indicated that the DEA method does not accept negative values (Kerstens, 2009). It is worth noting here that while this method is very useful in assessing the performance of companies, the use of financial ratios as indicators for the DEA method reduces the possibility of assessing the effectiveness due to the relevance of indicators as well as the relevance of financial information. For this reason, some researchers use other theoretical models, such as the SWOT analysis method (Strength, Weakness, Opportunity, Threats) and the CCA (Canonical Correlation Analysis) methods, which are outside the scope of this paper.

The operational cycle for the construction companies must be range between 3 and 5 years or more, in order to proceed from the planning to the manufacture and sale, regardeless the fact that some of the results cannot be used as inputs after many years. For this reason we chose to deal with the short and medium term period and we collected data from 12 construction companies operating in Greece, for the period 2007-2011.

More specifically, we measured the technical and scale efficiency of the Construction Sector in Greece, using the non-parametric approach of DEA, with the help of the program iDEAS (Noulas, 2000). When we refer to the technical efficiency we mean to the production of outputs given the level of inputs. Also, we must have in mind that scale efficiency occurs when the firm produces that output for which the average cost is the least possible while pure technical efficiency refers to the maximum possible reduction in inputs for the firm in order to become technically efficient. In other words, the overall technical efficiency can be seperated into pure technical efficiency and scale efficiency.

Table 1. Overall Technical Efficiency

Overall Technical Efficiency	2007	2008	2009	2010	2011
ATHENA SA	1.0000	1.0000	0.3150	1.0000	1.0000
ATTI-KAT SA	0.9799	1.0000	0.1553	0.4214	0.2164
CRETE CONSTRUCTION SA	1.0000	0.7609	1.0000	0.8168	1.0000
EDRASIS-C PSALLIDAS SA	1.0000	0.8027	0.2482	1.0000	1.0000
EKTER SA	0.9947	0.5526	0.1468	0.7628	0.2665
ELLAKTOR SA	0.9249	0.4208	0.0867	1.0000	0.3177
INTRAKAT SA	0.9909	1.0000	0.3482	1.0000	1.0000
J&P AVAX SA	0.8919	0.9443	0.1406	0.9933	1.0000
MICHANIKI SA	1.0000	1.0000	0.1346	0.6096	0.3237
MOCHLOS SA	1.0000	1.0000	0.1311	0.9869	0.8230
PROODEFTIKI SA	0.9213	0.2947	0.1599	1.0000	1.0000
VIOTER SA	0.9465	0.6238	0.1599	0.5295	0.5673
Mean	0.9708	0.7833	0.2522	0.8434	0.7096

4.1. Empirical Results

First of all, in 2007 the overall technical efficiency ranges from 0.89 to 1, with an average of 0.97, while the minimum price can be seen in 2009 (ELLAKTOR S.A-0,087). In 2009, the average efficiency ratio was 0.25 while in 2010 reached 0.84. Accordingly, the construction companies can produce the same level of output by reducing all inputs by 3% in 2007, by

22% in 2008, by 75% in 2009, by 16% in 2010 and by 29% in 2011. Table 2 presents the pure technical efficiency as a measure of the maximum possible reduction in the inputs of the construction company to become technically efficient. Only 1% reflects pure technical efficiency in 2007, 3% in 2008, 25% in 2009, 11% in 2010, 13% in 2011, on average.

Table 2. Pure Technical Efficiency

Pure Technical Efficiency	**2007**	**2008**	**2009**	**2010**	**2011**
ATHENA SA	1,0000	1,0000	0,6222	1,0000	1,0000
ATTI-KAT SA	1,0000	1,0000	0,1873	0,4763	0,6213
CRETE CONSTRUCTION SA	1,0000	1,0000	1,0000	1,0000	1,0000
EDRASIS-C PSALLIDAS SA	1,0000	0,8794	0,9716	1,0000	1,0000
EKTER SA	1,0000	1,0000	1,0000	1,0000	1,0000
ELLAKTOR SA	1,0000	1,0000	1,0000	1,0000	0,9751
INTRAKAT SA	0,9950	1,0000	0,8211	1,0000	1,0000
J&P AVAX SA	1,0000	1,0000	1,0000	1,0000	1,0000
MICHANIKI SA	1,0000	1,0000	0,1438	0,6146	0,3374
MOCHLOS SA	1,0000	1,0000	0,2687	1,0000	0,8578
PROODEFTIKI SA	0,9525	1,0000	1,0000	1,0000	1,0000
VIOTER SA	0,9604	0,7079	1,0000	0,5304	0,6334
Mean	0,9923	0,9656	0,7512	0,8851	0,8687

Table 3. Scale Efficiency

Scale Efficiency	**2007**	**2008**	**2009**	**2010**	**2011**
ATHENA SA	1.0000	1.0000	0.5062	1.0000	0.5062
ATTI-KAT SA	0.9799	1.0000	0.8293	0.8847	0.9374
CRETE CONSTRUCTION SA	1.0000	0.7609	1.0000	0.8168	1.2243
EDRASIS-C PSALLIDAS SA	1.0000	0.9128	0.2554	1.0000	0.2554
EKTER SA	0.9947	0.5526	0.1468	0.7628	0.1925
ELLAKTOR SA	0.9249	0.4208	0.0867	1.0000	0.0867
INTRAKAT SA	0.9959	1.0000	0.4241	1.0000	0.4241
J&P AVAX SA	0.8919	0.9443	0.1406	0.9933	0.1416
MICHANIKI SA	1.0000	1.0000	0.9364	0.9920	0.9440
MOCHLOS SA	1.0000	1.0000	0.4878	0.9869	0.4943
PROODEFTIKI SA	0.9672	0.2947	0.1599	1.0000	0.1599
VIOTER SA	0.9856	0.8812	0.1599	0.9982	0.1602
Mean	0.9783	0.8139	0.4278	0.9529	0.4605

As we can see in table 3, most of the overall inefficiency reflects scale inefficiency (with an exception of 2010). The degree of scale efficiency may be due to either increasing returns to scale or decreasing returns to scale. In 2007, the construction companies must have tried to produce the same number of sales, with an average cost of production up to 2% lower than the current one. In the same way, the scale inefficiency in 2008 is near 19% while in 2009 is 38% lower than that of the previous year. In 2010, scale efficiency is 95%, which means that construction companies are in a better condition than in 2008 or 2009. In 2011, conditions have changed and scale inefficiency reaches again the low degree of 54%.

Overall, we can see the progress of every kind of efficiency in Figure 2.

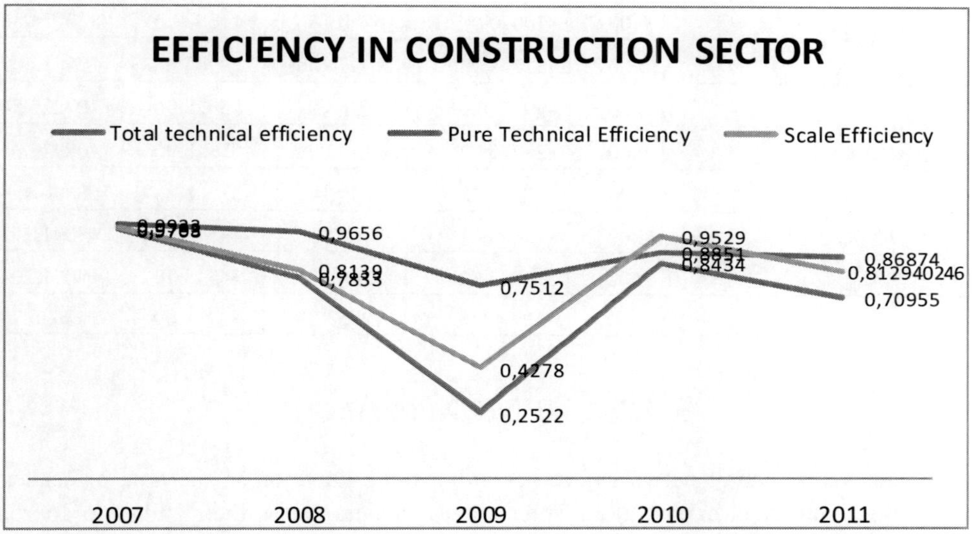

Figure 2. Efficiency in construction sector.

As we can see the worst year in terms of efficiency is the year 2009 while in 2010, the efficiency starts the uptrend course. The certain results of the overall technical efficiency in 2009 can be found at table 4.

In other words, you can see below the required reduction per input[1]. Using the Data Envelopment Analysis (DEA) method with an input-oriented model, we measured the efficiency from the perspective of the possible reduction of expenses (inputs) in order to produce the same level of products (outputs).

In this way, we tried to reduce on average the use of Fixed Assets by 197,996 euros, the Total Operating Expenses by 12,753 euros, the Cost of Sales by 85,911 euros, the Total Equity by 150,627 euros while simultaneously we wanted to achieve the same level of Sales (no change). At this point, we should mentioned that the results at table 4, have been divided by 1000 in order to run the DEA method in our program iDEAS. This means that we we need to multiply the results by 1000 in order to have the real terms.

[1] I1=Fixed Assets, I2=Total Operating Expenses, I3= Cost of Sales, I4=Total Equity, O1= Sales

Table 4. Overall Technicall Inefficiency per Input (CRS)

Overall Technical Inefficiency per Input in 2009 (CRS)	O1	I1	I2	I3	I4
ATHENA SA	0.00	-138104.08	-2807.50	-132712.09	-97728.58
ATTI-KAT SA	0.00	-178486.69	-35135.85	-94141.52	-85279.77
CRETE CONSTRUCTION SA	0.00	0.00	0.00	-28788.82	0.00
EDRASIS-C PSALLIDAS SA	0.00	-103547.63	-40570.79	-8070.63	-14631.35
EKTER SA	0.00	-15718.66	-2785.32	-441.12	-25427.10
ELLAKTOR SA	0.00	-1007074.13	-5760.78	-116629.29	-830524.86
INTRAKAT SA	0.00	-37735.98	-13976.08	-399446.63	-72681.46
J&P AVAX SA	0.00	-597240.95	-24360.97	-85328.96	-407225.54
MICHANIKI SA	0.00	-212735.23	-15462.98	-85328.96	-168949.87
MOCHLOS SA	0.00	-57999.73	-4649.14	-51008.83	-68890.45
PROODEFTIKI SA	0.00	-13653.71	-3764.95	-14518.09	-18091.20
VIOTER SA	0.00	-13653.72	-3764.95	-14518.10	-18091.20
Mean	0.00	-197995.88	-12753.28	-85911.09	-150626.78

5. DEA – PNN Approach

In recent years, neural networks are becoming more common in the area of academic research and commercial exploitation. Their main characteristic is their ability to approach nonlinear relationships without making a priori assumptions regarding the nature of the process that creates the phenomenon under consideration. This is particularly useful in financial applications where there are many hypotheses but little is really known. Among the financial applications of neural networks is their use in predicting the efficiency of operating units determined by DEA.

The combination of DEA and neural networks was first examined by Athanassopoulos & Curram (Athanassopoulos & Curram, 1996) who used simulated and empirical (commercial bank branches) data. Costa and Markellos (Costa and Markellos, 1997) proposed a multi-layer perceptron neural network (MLPs) approach to examine the efficiency of London Underground. More recent applications of DEA-neural network approach related to efficiency were found to literature with Delgado (Delgado, 2005) in the refuse collection services in Spain, with Wu et al. (Wu et al., 2006) for bank branches in Canada, with Liao et al. (Liao et al., 2007) referring to seven East Asian economies at manufacturing level, with Emrouznejad & Shale (Emrouznejad & Shale, 2009) for large data sets, with Özdemir & Temur (Özdemir & Temur, 2009) in the supplier evaluation process, with Farzipoor (Farzipoor, 2009) in robot selection. Aslani et al. (Aslani et al., 2009) proposed a DEA - radial basis function neural network (RBFNN) approach for bank branches in Iran while Mostafa (Mostafa, 2009) used a DEA - probabilistic neural network (PNN) approach to evaluate the efficiency of Arab banks. More recently, Erdem & Kocakoc (Erdem & Kocakoc, 2010) proposed a multi-layer perceptron neural network approach using simulated data while Sreekumar & Mahapatra

(Sreekumar & Mahapatra, 2011) used a DEA - generalized regression neural network (GRNN) approach for the evaluation of Indian business schools.

In this section, using a trial version of Neural Tools (Palisade) we trained the PNN in order to classify each company as efficient or inefficient. The variables which were used to the DEA method are defined as the inputs of PNN. Also, 20% of data (randomly selected) were used for testing. Table 5 presents the results. In the training sample after 190 trials we observe a 87,5% accuracy while in the testing sample the accuracy of the PNN is 66,66%. Moreover, from the classification matrix (table 6 and table 7) we observe that in the training sample inefficient companies were classified as more successful than the efficient ones, while in the testing sample there is no difference between efficient and inefficient companies.

Table 5. Results of DEA-PNN approach

Configuration	**PNN Category Predictor**
Training Sample	
Number of Cases	48
Number of Trials	190
% Bad Predictions	12.5000%
Mean Incorrect Probability	20.1567%
Std. Deviation of Incorrect Prob.	20.9350%
Testing Sample	
Number of Cases	12
% Bad Predictions	33.3333%
Mean Incorrect Probability	39.7847%
Std. Deviation of Incorrect Prob.	39.3421%

Table 6. Classification Matrix (for training cases)

	Efficient	**Inefficient**	**Bad (%)**
Efficient	14	5	26.3158%
Inefficient	1	28	3.4483%

Table 7. Classification Matrix (for testing cases)

	Efficient	**Inefficient**	**Bad (%)**
Efficient	2	1	33.3333%
Inefficient	3	6	33.3333%

Table 8. Variable Impact Analysis

Total_Equity	25.4353%
Fixed_Assets	24.0015%
Total_Operating_Expenses	23.0477%
Sales	20.7405%
Cost_of_Goods_Sold	6.7750%

Finally, we run a sensitivity analysis for the training sample in order to examine the effect of its variable to the prediction of efficiency. As we can observe from table 8 the variable with the greatest impact is *Total Equity* followed by *Fixed Assets* and *Total Operating Expenses*.

CONCLUSION

Trying to study the efficiency of the construction sector in Greece in the period 2007-2011, we used the well-known method of DEA analysis. The oligopolistic sector of construction companies in Greece presents 158 companies that have closed since 2004 and attempts to gain pace after the success which was seen in 2004. Nowadays, the turnover of the sector had declined by 24.3%, EBITDA was reduced by 43.5% and losses recorded up to 148,2 million euros from 36.8 million euros profit in 2009. The industry has the infrastructure and the required. The only thing which is lacking is a push. This can occur either in the form of new generation construction projects, for the period 2007-2013 or in the form of increasing competitiveness and evolving more Greek companies in major projects. Regarding the future of the sector, we can say that it depends on two factors: the political system and the development path of Greece. At the same time, the non-parametric approach of the DEA method testified that the worst year for the overall technical efficiency is the year 2008 (25%) while in 2011 we can see better levels of efficiency by far (71%). In 2007, the overall average technical efficiency was 0.97 while in 2009 the average efficiency ratio was 0.25 and in 2010 reached 0.84. Our research testifies that most of the overall inefficiency reflects scale inefficiency. Moreover, we extend our analysis using a DEA-PNN approach in order to classify each company as efficient or inefficient. The results are promising but it needs further work in this area.

The situation in the sector may be undeniably bleak, given that within three years (2008-2011) 157,000 work positions were lost from the sector. It is significant to agree that the efforts of the Greek financial adjustment can succeed only with the required development in the economy, a basic prerequisite for a long-term debt's reduction. An important perspective could be the public investment in infrastructure, the state funds or the help of the NSRF[2] and other structural funds, which should be directed at medium and small infrastructure projects with direct absorption in order to bring leverage results.

REFERENCES

Aslani G., S. H. Momeni-Masuleh, A. Malek and F. Ghorbani. Bank Efficiency Evaluation Using a Neural Network-DEA Method, *Iranian Journal of Mathematical Sciences and Informatics,* 2009, Vol. 4, No. 2, pp. 33-48.

Association of Greek Contracting Companies, Limited Liability Companies & Personal Engineering Companies., 2011 *The Greek Manufacturing Sector A/2010, Interim Report of Developments*, Issue. 4.

[2] National Strategic Reference Framework: The programming of EU Funds at national level for the period 2007-2013.

Association of Greek Contracting Companies, Limited Liability Companies & Personal Engineering Companies, 2011, *The Greek Manufacturing Sector B/2010, Interim Report of Developments*, Issue. 5.

Athanassopoulos, A.D. and S. P. Curram, A Comparison of Data Envelopment Analysis and Artificial Neural N|etworks as Tools for Assessing the Efficiency of Decision Making Units, *Journal of the Operational Research Society* 47 8, 1996, pp. 1000–1016.

Bao Chiao- Ping, Kun- Cheng Lee and Hisiang-Lin Pu, A study of the input/output variable characteristics in DEA, Journal of the Chinese Institude of Industrial Engineers, 27: 6, pp. 429-437.

Charnes A, Cooper W, Rhodes E. Measuring the Efficiency of Decision Making Units. *Eur J Oper Res* 1978;2(6): 429-44.

Chau K.W. and Y.S. Wang, Factors Affecting the Productive Efficiency of Construction Firms in Hong Kong, *CIM TG 23 International Conference*, Hong Kong, 2003.

Chau K.W., S.W. Poon, Y.S. Wang and L. L. Lu, ''Technological progress and the productive efficiency of construction firms in Hong Kong, J. *Constrct. Res.*, vol.6, no. 2, 2005, pp. 195-207.

Cheah, C., M. Gavrin, & J. Miller,. Empirical Study of Strategic Performance of Global Construction Engineering and Management. *Journal of Construction Engineering and Management*. 130(6), 2004, pp. 808-817.

Cheah, C., M. Garvin, & J. Miller. The Interrelationship Between Culture, Capital Structure, and Performance: Evidence from European Retailers. *Journal of Business Research*., 50, 2000, pp. 185-191.

Chiang Y. H., E.W.L Cheng and B. S. Tang, Examining Repercussions of Consumptions and Inputs Placed on the Construction Sector by Use of I-O Tables and DEA, *Build. Environ.,* Vol. 41n No. 1, 2006, pp. 1-11.

Chiu, H. & M. Wang. An Integrates DEA-based Model to Measuring Financial Performance of Construction Companies. *Wseas Transactions on Business and Economics*. 8 1, 2011, p. 5.

Costa, A. and R.N Markellos, Evaluating Public Transport Efficiency with Neural Network Models, Transportation Research C 5 (5), 1997, pp. 301–312.

Delgado, Francisco J., "Measuring Efficiency with Neural Networks. An Application to the Public Sector." Economics Bulletin, 2005, Vol. 3, No. 15 pp. 1−10.

Dzeng Ren-Jey and Jih-Shong Wu, The Cost Efficiency of Construction Industry in Taiwan, *The Open Construction and Building Technology Journal*, 2012, 6, pp. 8-16.

Edrasis Psallidis SA : PRESS OFFICE: Information for Investors, 2009.

Economists & Accountants Association of Thessaloniki, *The lack of liquidity slows the NSRF,* Naftemporiki, 2012, Avaliable: http://www.solnth.gr (paper in Greek)

El-Mashaleh M. Firm Performance and Information Technology Utilization in the Construction Industry: An Impirical Study. *Ph.D dissertation*. Gainesville, Florida: Unoversity of Florida; 2003.

El- Mashaleh M, Minchin R, O' Brien W. Benchmarking Construction Firm Performance. In: *Proceedings of the 11th joint CIB international symposium,* 13-16 June, Helsinki, Filand; 2005. P. 376-89.

El-Mashaleh M, Minchin R, O' Brien W. Management of Construction Firm Performance Using Benchmarking. *J Manag Eng* 2007; 23(1):10-7.

El- Mashaleh M, Rababeh S, Hyari K., Utilizing Date Envelopment Analysis to Benchmark Safety Performance of Construction Contractors, *International Journal of Project Management* 28, 2010, 1-67.

Emrouznejad A., and E. Shale "A Combined Neural Network and DEA for Measuring Efficiency of Large Scale Datasets", Computers & Industrial Engineering, vol. 56, 2009, pp. 249-254.

Erdem S. and I.D. Kocakoc, A new ANN Training Approach for Efficiency Evaluation, Hacettepe Journal of Mathematics and Statistics Volume 39 (3), 2010, pp. 439 – 447.

Farzipoor Saen, R., The Use of Artificial Neural Networks for Technology Selection in the Presence of Both Continuous and Categorical Data. World Applied Sciences Journal, 6(9), 2009, pp. 1177-1189.

Gleason K., L.K. Mathur, I. Mathur, The Interrelationship between Culture, Capital Structure and Performance: Evidence from European Retailers, *Journal of Business Research,* Vol.50, 2000, pp.185-191.

J & P Avax, A. A Reduction in Net Profits. *Deal News Online*. 2011, Avaliable: http://www.dealnews.gr (paper in Greek).

J & P Avax: Interim Financial Statements for the period 1 January to 3rd June 2011, Avaliable: http://www.jp-avax.gr (paper in Greek).

Kangari, R., F. Faird, . & H. Elgharib,. Financial Performance Analysis for Construction Industry. *Journal of Construction Engineering and Management*. 118(2), 1992, pp. 349-361.

Kerstens K. A Negative Data in DEA: A Simple Proportional Distance Function Approach, *Document de travail du LEM, Ignace Van de Woestyne, Lilie Economie & Management,* 2009, UMR CNRS 8179.

Kim, J., S. Kim., S. Choi,. & J. Kim,. Measuring Relative Efficiency of Korean Construction Company using DEA/ Window''.*World Academy of Science, Engineering and Technology*. 60, 2011, p. 728.

Kim I, Y Nam. The management Efficiency Analysis of Construction Companies .*Korea Real Estate Academy, 2010.*

Kim I, A.Moon. A Correlation Analysis Between the Capability of Construction Firms and Efficiency of Construction Company Using DEA, *Architectural Institude of Korea,* 26 (5), 2010, pp. 124-132.

Klimberg R., K. Lawrence, T. Tanya. Using Data Envelopment Analysis (DEA) to Forecast Bank Performance. *Advances in Business and Management Forecasting*, 6, Emerald Publishing Limited, 2009, pp. 53-61.

Langford, D., Iyagba, R. & Komba, D., Prediction of solvency in construction industry. *Journal of Construction Management and Economics*. 11, 1993, pp. 317-325.

Lazaridis, I. & Papadopoulos, D., *Business Analysis and Determination of Merit (Business, Financial Securities Using the Annual Financial Statements).*, 2010, Thessaloniki, Chapter 9 (book in Greek).

Liao H., B. Wang. and T. Weyman-Jones., "Neural Network Based Models for Efficiency Frontier Analysis: An Application to East Asian Economies' Growth Decomposition," Global Economic Review, vol. 36, no. 4, 2007, pp. 361-384.

Libby, R., Accounting Ratios and thePrediction of Failure: Some Behavioral Evidence. *Journal of Accounting Research*. 13(1), 1975, pp. 150-161.

Lile, P. *Financial Forecasting Methods and Practice Conditions with the Use of Information.* Thesis for the Master Program in Information Systems. 2011, Thessaloniki (thesis in Greek).

Lim Sungmook, A Decisio Three-Based Method for Selection of Input-Output Factors in DEA, *Division of Business Administration*, 2008.

Mason, F. & F. Harris, Prediction Company Failure in the Construction industry. *Proceedings Institution Of Civil Engineers*. 66, 1979, pp. 301-307.

McCabe, B., V. Tran,. & J. Ramani, Construction Prequalification Using Data Envelopment Analysis. *Canadian Journal of Civil Engineering*. 32, 2005, p. 183.

Michaniki: A Group of Companies: Review 2008. " The Machine" has a stake of 21.25% in Russia "Engineering", with 25% in Belarus ‘‘ Mechanics’’ and ‘’Engineering ‘‘ 25% in Egypt. Avaliable: http://www.michaniki.gr, (paper in Greek).

Michaniki, A. In the 256.29 Euros the Requirements of Engineering. *Stock-Imerisia Economic Journal*, August 2011, Avaliable: http://www.xrimatistirio.gr (Posted 8 May, 2010).

Mostafa, M.M., “Modeling the Efficiency of Top Arab Banks: a DEA-Neural Network Approach”, Expert Systems with Applications, Vol. 36, 2009 pp. 309-320.

Narula, S. & Wellington, J., Prediction, Linear Regrassion and the Minimum Sum Of Relate Errors. *Technometrics*, 19(2), 1979, pp. 185-190.

Noulas A. Efficiency Performance of State-Controlled and Private Banks: The Case of the Hellenic Bank sector, *Volume of essays in honor of professor M. Raphael, 2000, Pireus.*

Ocal, M., E. Oral, E. Erdis,. & G. Vural,. Industry Financial Ratios-Application of Factor Analysis in Turkish Construction Industry. *Bulding and Environment*. 42, 2007, pp. 54-66.

Olson, D., & T. A. Zoubi, Using Accounting Ratios to Distinguish Between Islamic and Conventional Banks in the GCC Region., 43(1), 2008, pp. 45-65.

Ozdemir, D., and G. T. Temur, *DEA ANN Approach in Supplier Evaluation System. World Academy of Science, Engineering and Technology,* 2009. *p. 54.*

Park Jung-Lo, Sung Sik KIm, Sun-Young Choi, Ju-Hyung Kim and Jae-Jun Kim, Measuring Relative Efficiency of Korean Construction Company Using DEA/Window, *World Academy of Science, Engineering and Technology 60*, 2011.

Pilateris P. *The Evaluation of Contractors Based on Financial Data Using Data Envelopment Analysis*, 2008, University of Toronto.

Rousanoglou N., Ellaktor: The Loans to Refinance 200 million , *Kathimerini,* 5 April 2012, Avaliable: www.kathimerini.gr, (paper in Greek).

Sanders M., Practitioners Continue to Rely on Judgmental Forecasting Methods Instead of Quantitative Methods, 1994.

Santorinaiou, V. The Shaking the Foundations of the Construction Industry, *Kerdos*, 7 November 2011., page 5. (paper in Greek).

Seiford, L. M., Data Envelopment Analysis: The Evaluation of the State of the Art (1978-1995). *The journal of Productivity*, 9, 2006, pp. 99-137.

Sreekumar S., S.S. Mahapatra, Performance Modeling of Indian Business Schools: A DEA-Neural Network Approach, Benchmarking: An International Journal, Vol. 18 Iss: 2, 2011, pp. 221 – 239.

Studies and Research Center for Commerce and Industry Chamber of Athens, *The Division of Building Construction*. 2007, Athens (paper in Greek).

Sueyoshi T. and M. Goto, DEA-DA for Bankruptcy-Based Performance Assessment: Misclassification Analysis of Japanese Construction Industry, *Eur. J. Oper. Res.*, Vol. 199, 2009, pp. 576-594.

Tsakiri, S. The Manufacturing Sector is Sinking. *To BIMA-economics*, 6 June 2011, page 5, Availiable : http://www.tovima.gr (paper in Greek).

Technical Chamber of Greece: Newsletter August 2011, ISSUE 2638 (work in Greek).

Wu, D., Z. Yang, & L. Liang, Using DEA-Neural Network Approach to Evaluate, Branch Efficiency of a Large Canadian Bank. Expert Systems with Applications, 31, 2006, pp. 108-115.

Yee Yan, C. & C. Cheah, Fundamental Analysis of Profitability of Large Engineering and Construction Firms. *Journal of Management in Engineering*. 130(4), 2006, pp. 203-210.

Ypodomes.com, Maliakos: It Leaves From the Work ATTIKAT Stilida - Backs. *Euro2day*, 13 April 2011, http://www.ypodomes.

In: Computational Data Analysis Techniques
Editors: M. Doumpos, C. Zopounidis and Ch. Gaganis
ISBN: 978-1-63463-957-6

Chapter 16

NEW PRACTICAL TOOLS FOR MINIMIZING HUMAN ERROR IN RESEARCH INTO FORGOTTEN EFFECTS

Salvador Linares Mustarós*[*1], Elvira Cassú Serra[1], Anna M. Gil-Lafuente[2] and Joan C. Ferrer Comalat[1]
[1]Department of Business Administration, University of Girona, Carrer de la Universitat de Girona, Girona, Spain
[2]Department of Business Administration, University of Barcelona, Barcelona, Spain

ABSTRACT

This article aims to present two computer science tools for minimizing human error in solving problems found in research into forgotten effects. The first tool is intended to eliminate calculation errors in using the expertage technique. The second is designed to eliminate errors in calculating the composition of incidences.

To demonstrate the tools, a research problem on forgotten effects is modeled which presents a possible array of causes and effects related to companies in the construction sector. We use the data obtained from the above problem to show the different uses of the software programs: EXPERTONBG, an open access program for calculating expertons, and FUZZYLOG, a freeware program for calculating forgotten incidence matrices and revealing the maximum forgotten incidence relationship.

Keywords: Forgotten effects, computer software, incidence matrices

1. INTRODUCTION

The idea of using fuzzy incidence composition to detect the possible non-obvious influences of a cause on an effect is known in the economic literature as "Forgotten Effects Research". The application of incidence matrices in an economic context was first presented

* Corresponding author: Tel 34 972 41 8760 E-mail:salvador.linares@udg.edu

to the scientific community in 1988 by Professors Arnold Kaufmann and Jaime Gil Aluja in the book published by Milladoiro "Models to research forgotten effects" (Kaufmann and Gil Aluja, 1988). There are a great number of academic papers (Lazzari, 2000; García, 2001; Mallo et al., 2005; Rodriguez et al., 2008; Domech et al., 2008; Gil-Lafuente et al., 2009; Rico, 2010; Gil-Lafuente & Bassa, 2011) and research projects (Lladó et al., 2000; Gil-Lafuente et al., 2011; Gil-Lafuente et al., 2012) in which indirect incidence values are found based on the various models presented by researchers.

Our aim in this article consists in presenting two separate tools that use a rectangular fuzzy matrix model to solve a problem based on searching for forgotten effects, and thereby minimizing human errors committed by negligence or mistake.

To achieve our objective, the chapter has been divided into four sections. The first section presents the terminology used throughout this work, whilst providing an overview of how the method normally functions. The second section presents a solvable-type problem with a forgotten effects model which uses fuzzy rectangular incidence matrixs with elements belonging to the set {0, 0.1, 0.2, 0.3, 0.4, 0.5, 0.6, 0.7, 0.8, 0.9, 1}. In the third section, we present how an experton calculation program, EXPERTONBG, works. Said program was developed at the universities of Barcelona and Girona.

Finally, section four explains how the FUZZYLOG software, a freeware program with licenses for individuals, calculate the "recovery" of forgotten effects.

The chapter ends with conclusions and future considerations, and the bibliography.

2. Project Development

2.1. Presentation of the Normal Method Used to Search for Forgotten Effects Based on Estimates Provided by Experts

Analysis of the concept of fuzzy relationships was first undertaken by Zadeh in the 1971 article "Similarity relations and fuzzy orderings" (Zadeh, 1971), extending ideas conceived a few years previously in the seminal article "Fuzzy logic" (Zadeh, 1965).

In 1988, Arnold Kaufmann and Jaime Gil Aluja established (Kaufmann and Gil, 1988) the "Theory of Forgotten Effects" using models which allow all incidence relations or direct and indirect causalities to be obtained without the possibility of omitting elements that might initially have been fully or partially overlooked.

The following summarizes the general fuzzy rectangular matrix model that will be used to model the specific problem in the following section.

Let A be a set of elements, A = {ai / i=1, 2,..., n}, which we shall call causes, and B a second set of elements, B = {bj / j=1, 2,..., m}, which could possibly be the same set A and we shall call effects.

The resulting set of pairs of elements denoted by the expression v(ai ,bj) shall define what tends to be known as "direct incidence matrix". This matrix shows the cause-effect relationships that occur between the elements of set A (causes) and those set B (effects). Said matrix will be denoted by [$\underline{M}$].

Now let C be a third set of elements, C = {ck / k=1, 2,..., p}, which act as effects of set B (their acting as causes of set A would be treated similarly).

Let [$\underline{N}$] be the incidence matrix that shows the cause-effect relationships occurring between the elements of set B and those of set C.

The mathematical operator that establishes the incidences of A on C is the max-min composition of matrices, represented by [$\underline{M}$]o[$\underline{N}$], whose causal relationship of ai over ck is: (ai ,ck) $= \max_{b_j}\left(\min\left(v(a_i, b_j), v(b_j, c_k)\right)\right)$

Causes-causes will be noted on the incidence matrix for the whole as [$\underline{A}$] and effects-effects as [$\underline{B}$]. The composition [$\underline{M}$ *] =[$\underline{A}$]o [$\underline{M}$]o[$\underline{B}$] between these three types of matrices is designed to obtain a new matrix of incidences from among the elements of set A (causes) and those of set B (effects) to reflect any possible indirect causality relationships that may not be taken into account in strategic decision processes.

To find possible effects which may have been overlooked, the algorithm proposed by Kaufmann and Gil suggests studying the values of the matrix [$\underline{M}$ *] - [$\underline{M}$], as the values obtained thus are maximum values of indirect effects. The fact that values close to one appear in the matrix [$\underline{M}$ *] - [$\underline{M}$] indicates that the initial incidents were not correctly estimated as there are some omissions. Gento, Lazzari and Machado (Gento et al., 2001) point out that when creating a direct incidence matrix, one for causes-causes and another effects-effects, and being aware of possible intermediate incidences thanks to the method of recovering forgotten effects, the construction of a new direct incidence matrix results in greater internal coherence with respect to the basis of the process for recovering intermediate effects, obtaining as a result "few forgotten effects".

Table 1. Version of the classic endecadary scale

null incidence	0
practically null incidence	0.1
almost null incidence	0.2
very weak incidence	0.3
weak incidence	0.4
intermediate incidence	0.5
considerable incidence	0.6
quite incidencia	0.7
strong incidence	0.8
very strong incidence	0.9
absolute incidence	1

Given that in problems involving the selection of certain actions that produce certain benefits on a greater number of actions overlooked incidents can lead to choosing a less efficient set of actions, the aforementioned fact indicates that research into forgotten effects is an essential method for improving the information the decision-maker has to work with.

In studies carried out in the economic sphere, due to ignorance of actual incidence values different values tend to be used for incidences of the same cause on the same effect. These values are provided by a group of experts and aggregated together using special expert management techniques, in order to obtain a single value for each incidence. One of the most common techniques for adding information together in such works is the expertage technique, first proposed by Kaufmann (Kaufmann, 1987) and developed theoretically by the same author and Professor Gil Aluja (Kaufmann & Gil Aluja, 1993). It is also common in most work on forgotten effects for experts' valuation of incidence to be a value belonging to the interval [0,1]. To this end, researchers tend to provide experts with a linguistic table with a numerical scale similar to Table 1, known as linguistic endecadary scales. The model of this scale was presented by Kaufmann and Gil Aluja in the book "Introduction to the Theory of Fuzzy Subsets in Business Management" (Kaufmann & Gil Aluja, 1986).

2.2. Detecting Forgotten Effects that Influence Companies in the Construction Sector

Construction companies, like any other company, pursue a number of diverse objectives in conducting their business activity. That is, the actions of the business owner are not only aimed at obtaining maximum profit, but serving other purposes as well.

This section lists a number of objectives that might represent some of the aims of a construction company. Defining them clearly is key to business success, as if aims are known when developing the business strategy it is possible to be more precise about which variables to emphasized in order to achieve the pursued objectives.

The following eight goals are considered to be some of the most representative.

- b_1 : Increase the value of the company.
- b_2 : Consolidate market reputation.
- b_3 : Foster business expansion.
- b_4 : Increase sales.
- b_5 : Obtain a quality product.
- b_6 : Increase profits.
- b_7 : Ensure permanence on the market.
- b_8 : Improve competitive position.

If the above objectives are to be achieved, construction companies must take into account different socioeconomic factors, which, by their nature, cannot be controlled, such as a drop in the marriage rate. On the other hand, they can also perform controllable actions, such as a real estate marketing campaign.

Listed below are the various actions and factors we consider most representative to take into account when creating items of cause and effect in the incidence matrices.

- a_1 : Innovation.
- a_2 : Conducting real estate marketing.
- a_3 : Declines in the fertility rate.
- a_4 : Decreases in the number of marriages.
- a_5 : The population aging.
- a_6 : Increase in single person households.
- a_7 : The climate.
- a_8 : Costs of labour and construction materials.
- a_9 : Changes in the interest rate.
- a_{10} : Population concentration level.

- a_{11} : Economic cycle.
- a_{12} : Restoration of second-hand homes.
- a_{13} : Increased developable land prices.

The study detailed here involved four construction industry experts assessing the relationships between actions and prior objectives. Altough this number of experts is too small to provide a result that would serve as a sufficient basis for obtaining fully valid valuations, it does meet our aim of demonstrating the practical tools to the reader in a less complex way. The four experts who had no contact with one another, were requested to fill in the qualitative direct incidence matrix [$\underline{M}$] using the semantic endecadary scale in Table 1. The highest incidence values given by each expert can be found in Tables 3, 4, 5 and 6.

Table 3. Expert 1's qualitative direct incidence matrix

	b_1	b_2	b_3	b_4	b_5	b_6	b_7	b_8
a_1	.8	.9	.5	.6	.8	.5	.7	.9
a_2	.9	.9	1	.8	.6	.5	.6	.8
a_3	.1	0	0	.5	0	.5	0	0
a_4	.1	0	0	.5	0	.5	0	0
a_5	.2	0	0	.6	0	.6	.1	0
a_6	.2	0	.5	.8	.5	.8	.2	0
a_7	.1	0	.1	.2	.3	.3	.2	.2
a_8	.6	.6	.8	.6	.6	1	1	1
a_9	.4	.4	.7	.7	0	.7	.5	0
a_{10}	.1	.1	.4	.7	.3	.7	.6	.3
a_{11}	.6	.6	.8	.8	.2	.9	.9	.3
a_{12}	.2	.2	.1	.7	.7	.5	.2	.3
a_{13}	.5	.3	.2	.2	.3	.2	.2	.4

Table 4. Expert 2's qualitative direct incidence matrix

	b_1	b_2	b_3	b_4	b_5	b_6	b_7	b_8
a_1	1	1	1	1	1	1	1	1
a_2	1	1	1	1	.9	1	1	1
a_3	.5	.5	.9	.6	.6	1	.6	.4
a_4	.1	.1	1	1	1	.5	.5	.5
a_5	.4	.3	.4	.3	.3	.2	.3	.3
a_6	.7	.6	.5	.6	.6	.6	.6	.5
a_7	.4	.5	.6	1	.6	.8	1	.6
a_8	.8	.6	.6	.3	.2	1	1	.9
a_9	.8	.6	.4	.9	.5	.5	.6	.9
a_{10}	1	1	1	1	.7	1	1	1
a_{11}	.6	.6	.5	.5	.5	.5	.6	.5
a_{12}	.6	.5	.6	.6	.5	.7	.6	1
a_{13}	.9	.7	.4	.3	.4	.3	.6	.5

Table 5. Expert 3's qualitative direct incidence matrix

	b_1	b_2	b_3	b_4	b_5	b_6	b_7	b_8
a_1	1	1	.9	.8	1	.6	.8	.8
a_2	.7	.8	1	.9	.6	.8	.8	.8
a_3	1	.2	.1	.4	.3	.6	.3	.1
a_4	1	.1	.3	.5	.3	.4	.2	.2
a_5	.3	.3	.3	.9	.3	.6	.7	.3
a_6	.8	.4	.4	.8	.7	1	.7	.5
a_7	.3	.1	.8	.6	.1	.6	.2	.2
a_8	1	.8	.8	.6	.9	1	.9	1
a_9	.9	.6	.8	.9	.7	.9	.7	.9
a_{10}	.3	.2	.2	.7	.6	.8	.7	.4
a_{11}	.8	.8	.8	.8	.5	.8	.7	.7
a_{12}	.3	.3	.7	.6	.7	.5	.7	.6
a_{13}	.5	.6	.2	.2	.5	.3	0	0

Table 6. Expert 4's qualitative direct incidence matrix

	b_1	b_2	b_3	b_4	b_5	b_6	b_7	b_8
a_1	1	.9	.8	.8	.7	.5	1	.9
a_2	.5	1	.8	.9	.5	.7	.6	.7
a_3	0	0	0	.2	0	0	0	0
a_4	0	0	0	0	0	0	0	0
a_5	0	0	.5	.8	.6	.6	.9	0
a_6	.2	.8	1	1	.7	.7	.6	.1
a_7	0	0	.2	.8	.3	.7	0	.2
a_8	.3	.7	.4	.9	.9	.2	.1	.1
a_9	.6	0	.8	.8	.2	.8	.3	.4
a_{10}	.3	.1	.8	1	0	.7	.7	.1
a_{11}	.7	.2	1	.9	.6	.8	.5	.8
a_{12}	.1	.4	.8	.9	1	.9	.7	.3
a_{13}	.4	.2	.1	0	.5	.3	.3	.2

To obtain the aggregated value, calculated as the experton average, we used a frequency table (see Table 7) which listed in each box the number of times experts assigned the same score to each incidence relationship. By calculating the weighted mean for each submatrix, experton values were obtained as the final value of the aggregated data. Where the value was not exactly one decimal, it was rounded up in order not to lose any fraction of maximum incidence. Thus, for example, for the submatrix a_2 over b_1, the added value is calculated as 0.25*0.5+0.25*0.7+0.25*0.9+0.25*1 = 0.775, which is close to 0.8, equivalent to a strong incidence. The final results can be seen in Table 8.

In order to continue with the procedure it was imperative that the same four experts give their views on some new incidences existing between the causes in the matrix and between these and other causes. The responses to our request provided four new matrices, expressing each of the four experts' views on the incidence relationship in terms of maximum value.

Table 7. Aggregated frequencies of direct incidences

		b_1	b_2	b_3	b_4	b_5	b_6	b_7	b_8
	0								
	.1								
	.2								
	.3								
	.4								
a_1	.5			1			2		
	.6				1		1		
	.7					2		1	
	.8	1	1	1	2			1	1
	.9		1	1					2
	1	3	2	1	1	2	1	2	1
	0								
	.1								
	.2								
	.3								
	.4								
a_2	.5	1				1	1		
	.6					2		2	
	.7	1					1		1
	.8		1	1	1		1	1	2
	.9	1	1		2	1			
	1	1	2	3	1		1	1	1
	0	1	2	2		2	1	2	2
	.1	2		1					1
	.2		1		1				
	.3					1		1	
	.4				1				1
a_3	.5	1	1		1		1		
	.6				1	1	1	1	
	.7								
	.8								
	.9			1					
	1						1		
	0	1	2	2	1	2	1	2	2
	.1	3	2						
	.2							1	1
	.3			1		1			
	.4						1		
a_4	.5				2		2	1	1
	.6								
	.7								
	.8								
	.9								

Table 7. (Continued)

		b_1	b_2	b_3	b_4	b_5	b_6	b_7	b_8
	1			1	1	1			
	0	1	2	1		1			2
	.1							1	
	.2	1					1		
	.3	1	2	1	1	2		1	2
	.4	1		1					
a_5	.5			1					
	.6				1	1	3		
	.7							1	
	.8				1				
	.9				1			1	
	1								
		b_1	b_2	b_3	b_4	b_5	b_6	b_7	b_8
	0		1						1
	.1								1
	.2	2						1	
	.3								
	.4		1	1					
a_6	.5			2		1			2
	.6		1		1	1	1	2	
	.7	1				2	1	1	
	.8	1	1		2		1		
	.9								
	1			1	1		1		
	0	1	2					1	
	.1	1	1	1	1	1			
	.2			1				2	3
	.3	1				2	1		
	.4	1							
a_7	.5		1						
	.6			1	1	1	1		1
	.7						1		
	.8			1	1		1		
	.9								
	1				1			1	
	0								
	.1							1	1
	.2					1	1		
	.3	1			1				
	.4			1					
a_8	.5								
	.6	1	2	1	2	1			
	.7		1						

		b_1	b_2	b_3	b_4	b_5	b_6	b_7	b_8
	.8	1	1	2					
	.9				1	2		1	1
	1	1					3	2	2
	0		1			1			1
	.1								
	.2					1			
	.3							1	
	.4	1	1	1					1
a_9	.5					1	1	1	
	.6	1	2					1	
	.7			1	1	1	1	1	
	.8	1		2	1		1		
	.9	1			2		1		2
	1								
	0					1			
	.1	1	2						1
	.2		1	1					
	.3	2				1			1
	.4			1					1
a_{10}	.5								
	.6					1		1	
	.7				2	1	2	2	
	.8			1			1		
	.9								
	1	1	1	1	2		1	1	1

Table 8. Direct incidence matrix

	b_1	b_2	b_3	b_4	b_5	b_6	b_7	b_8
a_1	1	.9	.8	.8	.9	.7	.9	.9
a_2	.8	1	1	.9	.7	.8	.8	.9
a_3	.2	.1	.3	.5	.3	.6	.3	.2
a_4	.1	.5	.4	.5	.4	.4	.3	.3
a_5	.3	.2	.3	.7	.3	.5	.5	.2
a_6	.5	.5	.6	.8	.7	.8	.6	.3
a_7	.2	.2	.5	.4	.4	.6	.4	.3
a_8	.7	.7	.7	.6	.7	.8	.8	.8
a_9	.7	.4	.7	.9	.4	.8	.6	.6
a_{10}	.5	.4	.6	.9	.4	.8	.8	.5
a_{11}	.7	.6	.8	.8	.5	.8	.7	.6
a_{12}	.3	.4	.6	.7	.7	.7	.6	.6
a_{13}	.6	.5	.3	.2	.5	.3	.3	.3

The final matrix of aggregated data is shown in Table 9.

Table 9. Qualitative direct incidence matrix [$\underline{A}$]

	a_1	a_2	a_3	a_4	a_5	a_6	a_7	a_8	a_9	a_{10}	a_{11}	a_{12}	a_{13}
a_1	1	.8	.3	.3	.5	.4	.3	.8	.4	.5	.3	.6	.4
a_2	.6	1	.1	.1	.1	.4	.2	.5	.3	.5	.2	.6	.3
a_3	.3	.3	1	.7	.7	.8	.2	.2	.2	.5	.3	.4	.2
a_4	.3	.3	.9	1	.8	.8	.2	.3	.5	.5	.3	.4	.2
a_5	.4	.5	.6	.4	1	.8	.3	.6	.3	.7	.4	.9	.5
a_6	.4	.5	.3	.3	.2	1	.2	.5	.3	.8	.4	.5	.4
a_7	.4	.4	.3	.2	.5	.3	1	.6	.2	.6	.4	.4	.6
a_8	.7	.4	.2	.3	.2	.3	.2	1	.7	.4	.8	.7	.4
a_9	.3	.4	.5	.7	.1	.4	.2	.8	1	.2	1	.8	.8
a_{10}	.4	.4	.2	.4	.3	.5	.3	.6	.2	1	.4	.8	.8
a_{11}	.7	.6	.5	.7	.3	.6	.2	.9	.9	.5	1	.8	.8
a_{12}	.7	.4	.2	.3	.3	.4	.2	.6	.6	.8	.2	1	.5
a_{13}	.5	.5	.5	.5	.3	.4	.2	.6	.6	.4	.7	.9	1

To continue with the process, one last new matrix was needed which relate the effects with each other and with the other effects. It was thus necessary to again request that the same four experts fill in another matrix to reflect the incidence of group effects (objectives) on one another. The resulting aggregated matrix can be seen in Table 10.

Table 10. Qualitative direct incidence matrix [$\underline{B}$]

	b_1	b_2	b_3	b_4	b_5	b_6	b_7	b_8
b_1	1	1	1	.9	.9	.8	.8	1
b_2	1	1	.9	.9	.8	.8	.9	.9
b_3	.9	.9	1	.8	.5	.9	.9	.9
b_4	.9	.8	.9	1	.6	1	.9	.9
b_5	.7	.9	.7	.8	1	.7	.8	1
b_6	1	.9	.8	.7	.6	1	.9	1
b_7	1	1	.9	.7	.6	.8	1	1
b_8	.9	1	.9	.9	.7	.8	1	1

It was possible to work with these aggregations as if they were actual incidences given by a single expert.

Combining the matrices provides us with [$\underline{M}$ *], as shown in Table 11. A comparison of matrices [$\underline{M}$ *] and [$\underline{M}$] shows the forgotten effects. All we need is the difference between each element in [$\underline{M}$ *] and its corresponding element in [$\underline{M}$]. The resulting matrix can be found in Table 12.

The figures appearing in the forgotten effect matrix demonstrate the need to take into consideration a number of elements that were initially considered to have a zero or near zero incidence on different aspects of the environment, such as the incidence between a_5 and objective b_2. Thus, the most significant oversights should be analysed, in order to demonstrate the need to be aware of not only the incidences that are considered direct, but also those which, although not directly perceivable, have an incidence through the composition of some elements.

Table 11. Incidence matrix $\underline{M}$ *= [$\underline{A}$]o[$\underline{M}$]o[$\underline{B}$]

	b_1	b_2	b_3	b_4	b_5	b_6	b_7	b_8
a_1	1	1	1	.9	.9	.8	.9	1
a_2	1	1	1	.9	.8	.9	.9	.9
a_3	.8	.8	.8	.8	.7	.8	.8	.8
a_4	.8	.8	.8	.8	.7	.8	.8	.8
a_5	.8	.8	.8	.8	.7	.8	.8	.8
a_6	.8	.8	.8	.8	.7	.8	.8	.8
a_7	.6	.6	.6	.6	.6	.6	.6	.6
a_8	.8	.8	.8	.8	.7	.8	.8	.8
a_9	.9	.8	.9	.9	.7	.9	.9	.9
a_{10}	.9	.8	.9	.9	.7	.9	.9	.6
a_{11}	.9	.8	.9	.9	.7	.9	.9	.9
a_{12}	.8	.8	.8	.8	.7	.8	.8	.8
a_{13}	.7	.7	.7	.7	.7	.7	.7	.7

Table 12. Matrix [$\underline{M}$ *] - [$\underline{M}$]

	b_1	b_2	b_3	b_4	b_5	b_6	b_7	b_8
a_1	0	.1	.2	.1	0	.1	0	.1
a_2	.2	0	0	0	.1	.1	.1	0
a_3	.6	.7	.5	.3	.4	.2	.5	.6
a_4	.7	.3	.4	.3	.3	.4	.5	.5
a_5	.5	.6	.5	.1	.4	.3	.3	.6
a_6	.3	.3	.2	0	0	0	.2	.5
a_7	.4	.4	.1	.2	.2	0	.2	.3
a_8	.1	.1	.1	.2	0	0	0	0
a_9	.2	.4	.2	0	.3	.1	.3	.3
a_{10}	.4	.4	.3	0	.3	.1	.1	.1
a_{11}	.2	.2	.1	.1	.2	.1	.2	.3
a_{12}	.5	.4	.2	.1	0	.1	.2	.2
a_{13}	.1	.2	.4	.5	.2	.4	.4	.4

2.3. A Program for the Expertage Technique

To avoid calculation errors when using the expertage technique it is possible to use the software developed by the University of Girona and Barcelona University, which automatically calculates the experton and its mean.

The program can be downloaded from the following address:
http://web2.udg.edu/grmfcee/ExpertonS.html

The open source version can also be downloaded to explore the software further. It has been created in Adobe Flash Professional CS6. The download address is:
http://web2.udg.edu/grmfcee/ExpertonS.fla
http://web2.udg.edu/grmfcee/functionsExpertonS.as

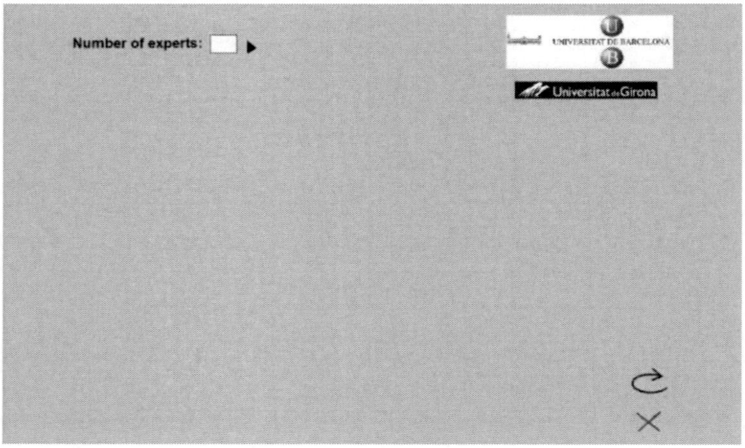

Figure 1. Displays the program start screen.

If, for example, the aim is to calculate the experton for 4 experts, we enter 4 in the text box and click the arrow to the right. Figure 2 shows how the program guides the next step, as 4 new text fields appear for entering the incidence a2 on b1 for each of the four experts along with another continue arrow.

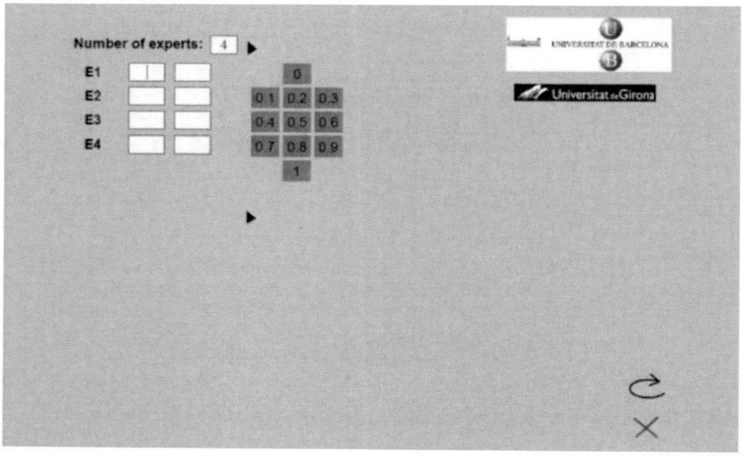

Figure 2. Program guides the next step.

If we enter the values 0.5, 0.7, 0.9 and 1 in these fields and click the continue arrow, the experton and its mean appear, as shown in Figure 3.

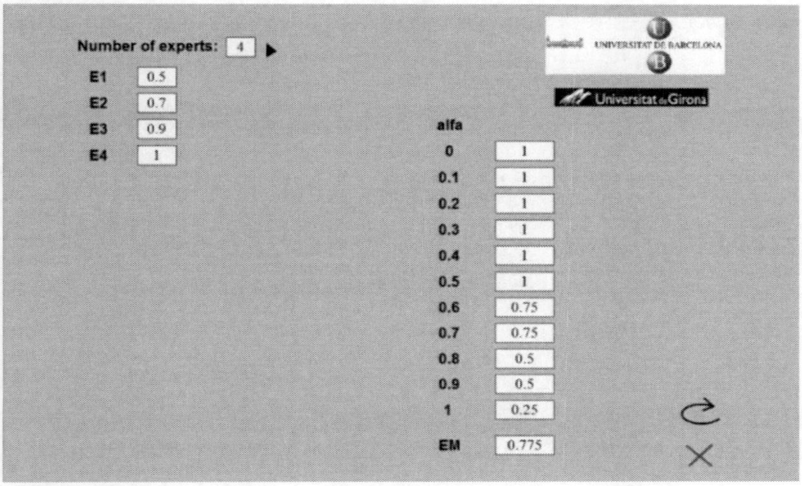

Figure 3. Experton as it appears.

2.4. A Program for Calculating the Compositionof Incidences

In order to avoid miscalculations using the incidence composition technique, it is possible to use a private but free software known as "FUZZYLOG", accessible at the following address: http://www.fuzzyeconomics.com/fuzzylog/

For access, authorization is required from the owner, users requesting a password by mail. Access involves users entering their email address and the password received from the owner in the two text fields located top right, as shown in Figure 4.

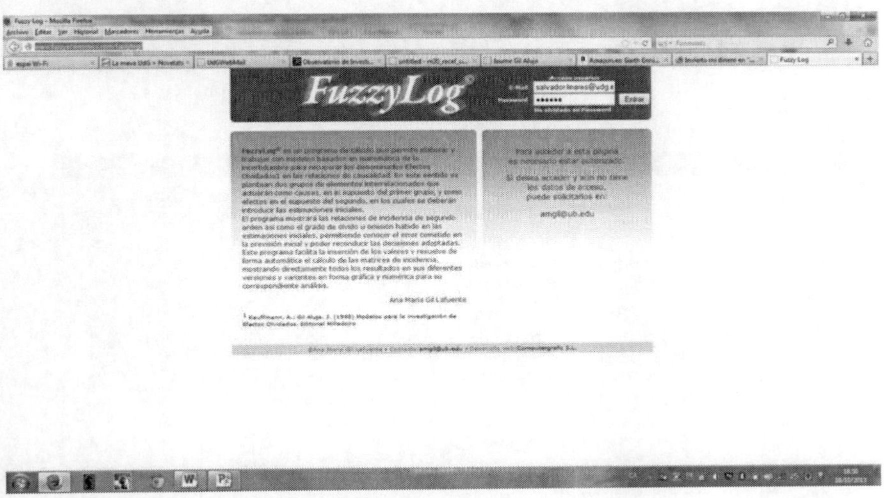

Figure 4. Enter email address and password shown at top right.

Once inside, the user can create new models or retrieve models that have already been entered via the menu shown. The buttons for creating causes and effects are at the bottom of the screen. The "Process" button takes the user to a new screen where the numerical values of the incidence matrices are to be entered. Figure 5 shows how the program presents each incidence.

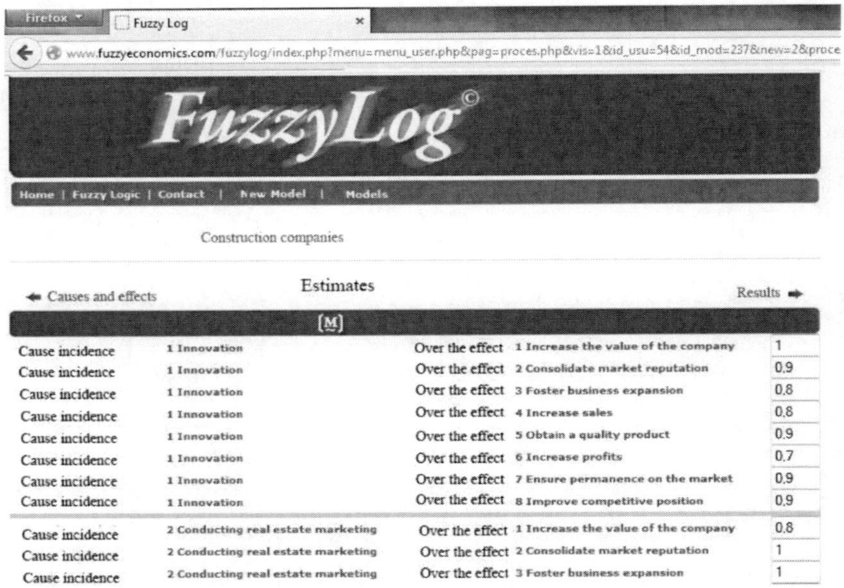

Figure 5. Program presents each incidence.

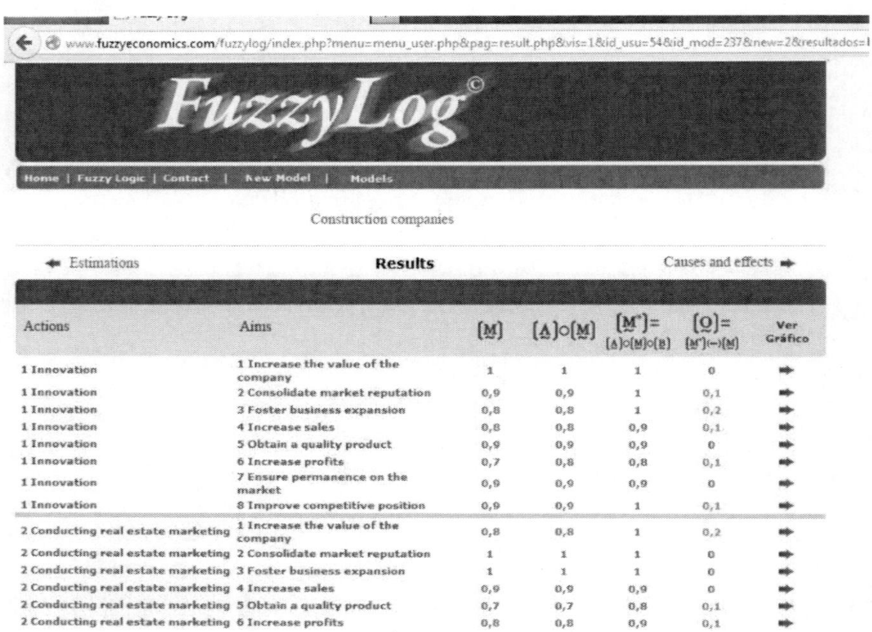

Figure 6. "Result" button display.

After entering all incidences, the "Results" button displays a new screen with the values of the direct matrix, the combined matrix and the forgotten values, as shown in Figure 6.

Finally, Figure 7 shows the screen that is accessed when clicking the green arrows in Figure 6. The new screen displays graphs of incidences that produce forgotten effects.

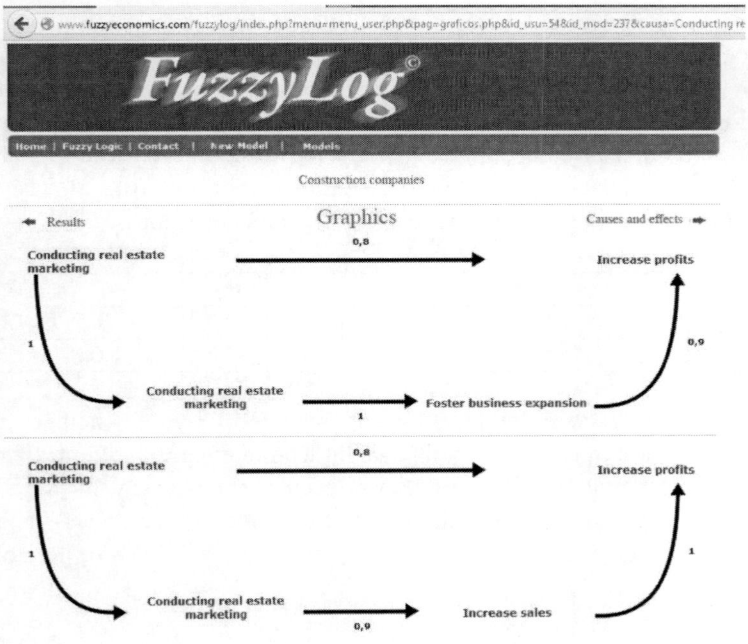

Figure 7. Examples of forgotten effects of a_2 on b_6.

CONCLUSION AND FUTURE CONSIDERATION

Firstly, this article has discussed a new type of research into forgotten effects. Specifically, we have investigated aims and variables pertaining to construction companies. This paves the way for future research on the types of actions undertaken by these companies and their goals. However, this article is based on results obtained using a specific expertage. Different experts may provide new insights into the causes and effects analysed here. Therefore, should further studies be undertaken on this open path, the expertage process would have to be amplified and the results submitted to a subsequent counter-expertage process to award a more "objective" validation to the results obtained here. Secondly, with the aim of ensuring greater reliability in future research into forgotten effects, two tools have been presented which have proven useful in avoiding human error. Although in this study we have not addressed intrinsic errors of the tools or the measurement scale for quantifying incidence relations, we wish to make a brief contribution in this regard for the benefit of future work. To minimize errors inherent in the use of the classic endecadary scale, a scale some authors may consider inappropriate for human thought due to it being a direct classification of more than seven items (Miller, 1956), We suggest the possibility of using a second endecadary scale that may help to determine whether the values experts assign to incidence are correct. The main difference in this scale, presented at the 16th INTERNATIONAL SIGEF CONGRESS (Bonet et al., 2010), with respect to Kaufmann and Gil Aluja's classic scale, is its means of determining subjective inputs. This is achieved via a maximum two-stage process with a ternary selection system after eliminating extreme cases. In the first phase of allocation, there is reflection on the degree of truth inherent in the statement, choosing from the possibilities low (L), medium (M) and high (H), once the possibilities of completely false (N for null) and completely true (T for total) have been rejected. If situated within L, M or H , in a second phase, the question is asked whether comparing with the other reference elements believed to be in the same group, the element being evaluated is within the subgroup low (l), medium (m) or high (h).

The final allocation is obtained from the following table of values:

N	L			M			H			T
	l	m	h	l	m	h	l	m	h	
0	0.1	0.2	0.3	0.4	0.5	0.6	0.7	0.8	0.9	1

Thus, for example, if we aim to associate the possibility of whether incidence that improved water treatment in a certain country might lead to the effect of improving health, we can, in the cases where null (N) and all (T) are rejected, choose as a first step between low (L), medium (M) or high (H). Let us imagine that we have chosen high (H). Then we enter a second phase considering whether this high will be very (h), a little (l) or neither one nor the other (m).

Table 13. Order isomorphism

(S, ≤S)		(T, ≤T)
null incidence	0	N
practically null incidence	0.1	Ll
almost null incidence	0.2	Lm
incidence quite close to null	0.3	Lh
incidence closer to null than full	0.4	Ml
neither null nor full incidence	0.5	Mm
incidence closer to full than null	0.6	Mh
incidence quite close to full	0.7	Hl
almost full incidence	0.8	Hm
practically full incidence	0.9	Hh
full incidence	1	T

Since on the basis of Table 13 we can establish a bijective application h: S → T between the two scales that retains the following order property:

h(u) ≤T h(v) if and only if u ≤S v

it can be concluded that an order isomorphism exists between the two scales.

Although the two-phase scale with ternary classification base can be used to estimate the vagueness of a property or degree of truth of a statement, in some cases replacing the classic scale used to date, with this last idea we open up the possible avenue of investigating whether the subjective valuation of inferences which belong to the set {0, 0.1, 0.2, 0.3, 0.4, 0.5, 0.6, 0.7, 0.8, 0.9, 1} depends on the type of scale used. The order isomorphism between the two endecadary scales is the key to determining the answer to this question. We hope to soon present field experiences that shed more light on this.

REFERENCES

Anselin Ávila, E. and Gil Lafuente, A.M. (2009), Fuzzy logic in the strategic analysis: impact of the external factors over business, *International Journal of Business Innovation and Research*, 5(3), 515-534.

Bonet, J.; Linares, S. and Bertran, X. (2010), Mixed-fuzzy statistical calculation by means of comparison applied to economic variables forecasting, *Proceedings of the XVI International Congress of the SIGEF*, Morelia Michoacán, Mexico.

Domech More, J. and Carvalho Aguia J. (2008), Fuzzy model of influence of social responsibility indicators, *Symposium for Excellence in Management and Technology (SEGeT)*, Rio de Janeiro, Brazil.

Domech More, J. and Mamede Gonzalez Magalhâes, L. (2008), Development of training strategies based on the analysis of an ultrasound procedure using fuzzy methodology. *CIMBAGE Notebooks*, 10, 75-101.

Eugenio Mallo, P.; Antonia Artola, M.; Javier Galante, M.; Enrique Pascual, M.; Morettini, M. and Raúl Busetto, A. (2005), *Application of fuzzy tools to scorecard balance, XXVIII Argentine Congress of academics cost*s. Mendoza, Argentina.

García, P.S.; Lazarri, L.L. and Machado, E.A.M. (2000), A fuzzy approach to define poverty indicators, *CIMBAGE Notebooks*, 3, 11-26.

García, P.S. and Lazarri, L.L. (2000), The quality assessment at the University, *CIMBAGE Notebook*s, 3, 81-97.

García de Fanelli, A.M. (2001), Application of fuzzy methodology to the quality evaluation of graduate programs, *CIMBAGE Notebooks*, 4, 99-132.

Gil Lafuente, A.M.; Vizuete Luciano, E. and Martorell Cunill, O. (2009), *Model for the determination of variables affecting consumption saving financial products.* XV SIGEF International Conference, Lugo, Spain.

Gil Lafuente, A.M. and Luis Bassa, C. (2011), The process of attributes identifying considered by the customers in a CRM strategy, *CIMBAGE Notebooks*, 13, 107-127.

Gil Lafuente, A.M.; Amiguet Molina, L.; Vizuete Luciano, E.; Boria Reverter, S.; Sole Moro, M.L.; Pursals Puig, A.; Imanov, G.; Aliyev, T.; Rzayev Rza, R.; Akbarov Mammad, R. and Yusifzada Arshad, R. (2011 b), *New markets for economic recovery*: Azerbaijan, Publications of the Royal Academy of Economics and Finance, Barcelona.

Gil Lafuente, A.M.; Gil Lafuente, J.; Vizuete Luciano, E.; Amiguet Molina, L.; Boria Reverter, S.; Merigó Lindahl, J.M.; Klimova, A.; Sole Moro, M.L.; (2012), *Exploring new markets: Ukraine,* Publications of the Royal Academy of Economics and Finance, Barcelona.

Gento, A.; Lazzari, L.L. and Machado, E. A. M. (2001), Reflections on the incidence matrices and forgotten effects recovery, *CIMBAGE Notebooks*, 4, 11-27.

Kaufmann, A. (1987), *The experts,* Ed. Hermes, París.

Kaufmann, A. and J. Gil Aluja (1986), *Introduction to fuzzy subsets theory in business management,* Milladoiro, Santiago de Compostela.

Kaufmann, A. and J. Gil Aluja (1988), *Models for the forgotten effects research*, Vigo: Ed. Milladoiro.

Lazzari, L.L. (2000), *Resources allocation in actions to improve the image of an SME*, VI Congress on Small and Medium Enterprises. Buenos Aires, Argentina.

Lladó, M.; Gil Aluja, J.; Rabaseda i Tarrés, J.; Ferrer Comalat, J.C., Gil Lafuente, A.M. and Gil Lafuente, J. (2000), *Establishing the actions of category promotion of Girona FC and their impact on Girona-Costa Brava area*, Publications of the Enterprise Department, Girona.

Rodríguez Rubinos, J.M.; Armando Ramírez Reyes, M. and Díaz Pontones, V. (2008), Forgotten effects in the causal relationships of the actions of the training system in business organizations. *Journal of Quantitative Methods for Economics and Business*, 5, 29-48.

Rico, F.; Marco, A. and Jaime Tinto, A. (2010), Tools based on fuzzy subsets. Procedural proposal to implement expertizaje and recover forgotten effects in the accounting information. *Accounting Actuality FACES*, 13(21), 127-146.

Zadeh, L.A. (1971), Similarity relations and fuzzy orderings, *Information Sciences*, 3(2), 177–200.

Zadeh, L.A. (1965), Fuzzy sets, *Information and Control*, 8, 338–353.

INDEX

A

B

C

D

E

F

G

H

I

J

K

L

M

N

Q

R

S

T

U

V

W

Z